WHO FINANCED HITLER

THE SECRET FUNDING OF HITLER'S RISE TO POWER, 1919–1933

JAMES E. POOL

POCKET BOOKS
New York   London   Toronto   Sydney   Tokyo   Singapore

All insert photos are courtesy of the National Archives.

POCKET BOOKS, a division of Simon & Schuster Inc.
1230 Avenue of the Americas, New York, NY 10020

Copyright © 1978, 1997 by James Pool

All rights reserved, including the right to reproduce
this book or portions thereof in any form whatsoever.
For information address Pocket Books, 1230 Avenue
of the Americas, New York, NY 10020

Library of Congress Cataloging-in-Publication Data

Pool, James, 1948–
    Who financed Hitler : the secret funding of Hitler's rise to power,
        1919–1933 / James Pool.
            p.   cm.
    Originally published: New York : Dial Press, 1978.
    Includes bibliographical references and index.
    ISBN 978-0-671-76083-0
    1. Hitler, Adolf, 1889–1945. 2. Germany—Politics and government—
1918–1933. 3. Industries—Germany. 4. Campaign funds—Germany. 5.
Political parties—Germany. 6. Corporations—Germany—Political activity. 7. Finance. I. Title.
DD247.H5P63   1997
943.086'092—dc21   97-15509
                                                                     CIP

First Pocket Books trade paperback printing October 1997

10 9 8 7 6 5 4 3 2 1

POCKET and colophon are registered trademarks of
Simon & Schuster Inc.

Cover design by Tom McKeveny
Cover photo courtesy of Corbis/Bettmann

Printed in the U.S.A.

To My Parents

Contents

Contents

PREFACE

Adolf Hitler did not come to power easily. He began his political career in 1919 and did not become chancellor until fourteen years later, in 1933. During this time it took a tremendous sum of money to support the Nazi party. Where it came from, who provided it, and why, are the topics of this book.

There have been many books written on the Nazi period, but this most important aspect of Hitler's activity—one of the very keys to his success—has never been dealt with. One reason is that much of the information about financial contributions has only recently come to light, but the primary reason is an understandable reluctance to acknowledge the ease with which money can subvert the democratic process.

History is replete with unsavory tales of political financing, and there is a serious question whether democratic principles can ever ultimately be upheld in an atmosphere of unsupervised and unpublicized political fund-raising. Perhaps the newly created German democracy was more vulnerable than most free societies, yet the story of how Hitler found the necessary money to undermine the Weimer Republic has universal implications. In Germany from 1919 to 1933, political parties were little more than tools for powerful interest groups. Hitler was quick to recognize this and turn his formidable and nefarious talents to the task of fund-raising. His methods were unscrupulous. At first he courted the powerful; then as his party grew in size and strength, he was perfectly willing to use blackmail and bribery to gain his ends. But it must be admitted that he knew the value of money: it could purchase almost all the necessary resources of politics, such as propaganda campaigns, newspaper coverage, full-time staff, etc. In short, Hitler knew that money meant power.

It is even partly true that Hitler was able to sell an evil idea like anti-Semitism simply because he had the support of wealthy contributors. Continuous propaganda will make even the greatest untruth seem believable to some people. There were many anti-Semites in Germany long before Hitler, but they belonged to small splinter parties that were ineffective because of their endless squabbling. Large donations provided Hitler with the needed tools to organize these fringe elements and turn them into a major political force.

Discovering the exact sums of contributions and the identity of contributors is not an easy task. Money moves silently as well as easily. Cash leaves no tracks. Checks can be laundered—passed through intermediaries and false corporations—to obscure the original source of funds. But, despite the difficulties, the search is worthwhile. Following the trail of money gives a rare glimpse behind the scenes of political power.

Hitler was launched on his political career by a wealthy and powerful secret society, none of whose members were big businessmen. Other funds came from the most unexpected sources. Germany's most important Jewish industrialist even gave to the Nazis—to make them dependent on his money in hopes of eventually disrupting them. Hitler got some of his biggest "contributions' by first discovering the corrupt dealings between certain big industrialists and prominent liberal politicians and then blackmailing the industrialists with threats of exposure. Hitler's fund-raising gave birth to many of the techniques of covert funding and dirty tricks that later became the stock-in-trade of most major governments.

One of the most important and unexpected discoveries of this study is the importance of foreign financing in bringing Hitler to power. Hitler received money from Austria, Britain, Czechoslovakia, Finland, France, Italy, Holland, Hungary, Sweden, Switzerland, and the United States. It is true that some money came from Germans living in these countries, but most of it came from prominent foreign citizens. Their motives varied: Henry Ford wanted to spread his anti-Semitic philosophy, Mussolini hoped to encourage German fascism, Grand Duchess Victoria of Russia wanted to support anti-communism, Sir Henri Deterding, the Anglo-Dutch tycoon, aimed to get back his oil interests confiscated by the Communists, etc.

Those who financed Hitler, both Germans and the foreigners, are just as responsible for his coming to power as the active Nazis who spread anti-Semitic propaganda or fought in the streets. Yet, because of their influence and the power of money, few of them were prosecuted at Nuremberg. Many are now exposed here for the first time.

The following introduction, "The World of Hitler's Youth," was written for *Hitler and His Secret Partners*; however, since this period of his life was not covered in *Who Financed Hitler*, it was decided to published it as a part of this book as well.

Introduction
The World of
Hitler's Youth

Although it has been over fifty years since Hitler's death, hardly a day goes by without his name being mentioned in a newspaper, a book, or on television. Yet, biographers and historians still do not understand why he behaved the way he did. How did he captivate the German people? Why did he start World War II? Why did he commit such unspeakable atrocities?

In his youth, it seemed unlikely that Hitler would ever accomplish anything. Indeed it remains one of the great mysteries of history how such a loser without a profession or much of an education was able to take over a great nation. Some light will be shed on this mystery when we learn that he was sponsored by a wealthy, powerful secret society. Later some of the most important industrialists in Germany helped finance him, and high-ranking officers in the army protected him time after time. But why did these powerful well-educated people choose him? In 1939, these same people helped him start a world war and went on to participate with him in some of the worst crimes against humanity in history. What was the real relationship between Hitler and his financiers and partners? Were they his mesmerized followers or was he their puppet?

To understand Hitler it is useful to see the historical background from which he emerged. It is doubtful that he would have been able to acquire the powerful patrons he did at any other time in history. Things that he learned in his youth later helped him get the support of some of the most prominent people in Germany.

Adolph Hitler was born in the small town of Branau on the River Inn, between Germany and Austria, on April 20, 1889. His father, Alois Hitler, was a fifty-two-year-old customs inspector in the Austrian customs service. Both his father and mother came from peasant families that had inhabited the Waldviertel region of Austria for centuries. Socially the family belonged to the lower middle class. Adolf's father earned about double the salary of the average factory worker at the time.

Alois Hitler retired from the customs service about the time his son started school. He received a very generous pension, so money was never a problem; however, the family moved a number of times while Alois looked for a place to settle down. As a result, young Adolf attended a number of different grade schools. He was an average pupil and seemed to be a normal boy who enjoyed playing "cowboys and indians" more than going to school.

Finally, the family moved to Leonding, a suburb of Linz, the provincial capital of Upper Austria, located on the Danube, one of Europe's great rivers. Adolf lived in Linz between the ages of ten and eighteen and always considered it his hometown. Linz, at the turn of the century, was almost an idyllic place for a young boy to grow up. The town was just large enough to have some cultural life, with an opera house, a new cathedral, and a garrison, but none of the social problems of a large city. The countryside around Linz overlooking the Danube was quiet and beautiful. Adolf played outside a lot with the local children in the fields and meadows near his home.

Although some authors have tried to find the seeds of Hitler's later, tyrannical character in his youth, the truth is the Hitlers were a very ordinary family. True, his father had been illegitimate, was much older than his mother, and was said to be a stern disciplinarian, but none of these things were unusual in Austria at the time.

Adolf and his father seemed to get along well enough until, as a teenager, the boy decided he wanted to become an artist. The old man insisted he prepare for career as a civil servant. Partly in rebellion against his father, Adolf began to spend more time with his drawings than his schoolwork, and his grades naturally suffered. He began to hate school and had a low opinion of all his teachers except one, his history teacher, Leopold Poetsch, a fervent pan-German. Poetsch captured the imagination of his young students with heroic tales of the ancient Teutons and German victories.

This was young Adolf's first introduction to politics. His country, the Austro-Hungarian Empire, was a state made up of many diverse nationalities ruled by an Austro-German minority and an Austrian emperor of the Hapsburg dynasty. The empire was really a holdover from earlier centuries when states were based more on dynastic loyalties than national linguistic groups. In order to hold the empire together the Austro-Germans had to make increasing concessions to the Hungarians, Czechs, and other nationalities, as the passions of nationalism were beginning to stir in Eastern Europe. Many Austro-Germans, like Hitler's teacher Leopold Poetsch, wanted to see the old empire break up and Austria join Germany, to the north. Although the whole area around Linz was a hotbed of pan-German nationalism, Hitler's father remained loyal to the Austro-Hungarian Empire and its Hapsburg rulers. There is no indication that there were ever any political arguments between Hitler and his father. Adolf may have been inspired by Leopold Poetsch's classes, but he was not moved enough to become involved in politics. His only obsession was to become an artist.

When Adolf was fourteen, his father died suddenly. The principal obstacle to his becoming an artist was now removed. He continued school for two more years, but his heart was not in it, and at the age of sixteen, he dropped out without graduating. He spent the next two years studying art on his own. He would get up late, walk along the banks of the Danube looking for an isolated spot where he could sit for hours undisturbed sketching the landscape or the ruins of an old castle. At night he would read or attend the opera. Although a loner, he had one close friend who shared his interest in art and music.

Although not handsome, Hitler was always neat and clean and reasonably well dressed. For a time he even carried an ivory-handled cane, which was the custom of young gentlemen of the day. Obviously he was trying to put on airs and probably didn't impress anyone. Physically, he looked somewhat frail. His shoulders were narrow and his chest sunken. He had a pale complexion that was all the more noticeable because of his dark black hair. Because he was thin, he looked taller than his five foot nine inches. When he was seventeen or eighteen, he started to grow a mustache and a small goatee. His eyes were his only attractive physical feature. They were large and light blue. Even when he was an unknown teenager, many people found them hypnotic and compelling.

Adolph's mother was certainly overindulgent, and although she tried to urge her son to get a job, he continued to live at home idling away his time, dreaming about the day when he would become a great artist. According to Hitler, these years in Linz were the happiest of his life.

It was obvious to almost everyone but Adolf himself that without having graduated from high school and without a trade or profession, he was destined for some hard times. However, at this point in his life, about the worst thing that could be said about him was that he was a dreamer and an idler. Although he was sympathetic to the pan-German nationalists, so were most other young men in Linz. There were some Jews who lived in Linz and a few Jewish students attended Hitler's school, but there is little evidence that he was openly anti-Semitic at this time. He probably had some anti-Semitic prejudices typical to Austria of the period, but there is no record indicating that he was ever a member of any anti-Semitic group.

In the spring of 1906, the seventeen-year old Hitler made a brief visit to Vienna. It was the most exciting event in his life. At the turn of the century, Vienna was one of the major capitals of Europe, as splendid as Paris or London. It was a city of cafés and glittering shop windows. Vienna had a reputation for charm and frivolity. Mention of the city produced images of the waltz, the court balls, the opera, and the *Blue Danube*. Naturally court balls and fine shops were beyond Hitler's budget, but many pleasures such as the parks, the public gardens, and the art museums were available to the ordinary people of Vienna. However, it was the great architecture that captivated Hitler. He went in awe from one magnificent building to another.

He returned to Linz full of enthusiasm for Vienna. He finally decided how he would realize his ambition of becoming a great artist. He would go to Vienna and study at the world-famous art academy. Full of high hopes he set out for Vienna again in the fall of 1907 to take the entrance exam for the Academy of Fine Arts. His failure to pass the exam was a severe shock. The director of the academy kindly explained to him that the test indicated his talent lay in the field of architecture rather than painting. Hitler reluctantly acknowledged that this was true, as his best paintings and drawings were always pictures of buildings rather than of people. However, a new problem presented itself: it was very difficult to get into the School of Architecture without having graduated from high school.

While Hitler was brooding about his artistic career, he received an urgent letter from Linz saying that his mother was very ill. He returned home at once to find out that she was dying of breast cancer. With selfless devotion, he nursed her through the last months of her life. Hitler had dearly loved his mother and was devastated by her death. After her burial, he was anxious to get away from the painful memories in Linz, so he returned to Vienna determined somehow to succeed as an artist or an architect.

Hitler suffered from a lack of sense of direction. He wanted to be an artist or architect, but he wasn't sure how to go about it and was too proud to seek advice. So he continued his "studies." He sat in the parks and sketched buildings and palaces; he spent hours at the library reading up on obscure topics; he visited all the major museums regularly. In order to be able to afford the opera he had to skimp on food for a week, but to him the sacrifice was worth it.

When Hitler's money from home ran out, he quickly became desperate. He could no longer afford to pay his rent. He had to pawn his belongings, and his clothes became shabby and worn. Before long, he was in the ranks of the homeless, forced to accept charity just to survive. As he wrote in *Mein Kampf*, his autobiography, these were "years of hardship and suffering during which Hunger was my faithful companion. It never left me for a moment."

He got a job as a laborer on a construction project, but when he refused to join a socialist labor union, some of the other workers who were Marxists beat him up and kicked him off the job. This was his first encounter with socialism (the Social Democratic party) and Marxism. Marxism was repugnant to Hitler because it rejected all his middle-class values and the nationalistic beliefs he had picked up from the pan-Germans while living in Linz. He could not understand how Austro-German workers could reject their own nationality and embrace the idea of international solidarity. One day, while walking through the city, Hitler witnessed a huge Marxist parade. There was a sea of red flags and red banners. Marching workers alternately sang songs and shouted slogans. "For nearly two hours,' said Hitler, "I stood there watching with bated breath the gigantic human dragon slowly winding by. Oppressed with anxiety I finally left and went home."

In an effort to understand more about Marxism and the Social Democratic party, Hitler began to read about politics. Although his initial dislike of the Social Democrats did not change, he soon came to respect their use of propaganda to win over the workers. While reading Social Democratic newspapers, Hitler noticed that many of the party's leaders were Jewish. He considered this a very important discovery.

Precisely when Hitler became an anti-Semite is difficult to say. Thousands of Jews from Eastern Europe were streaming into Vienna every year, seeking an opportunity for a better life. Since most of them were poor, Hitler encountered them daily in the lower-class neighborhood where he lived. In his autobiography, he admitted he found their appearance objectionable; their "strange facial features, the black caftans . . . the black sidelocks" disturbed him. He thought they looked "unclean" and "unheroic."

As an artist, Hitler should have been able to appreciate human diversity and the picturesque traditional dress of Orthodox Jews. However, as a boy, Hitler was taught to admire nationalism, militarism, order, and discipline. The Jews didn't fit into that rigid mold. Hitler conveniently seemed not to notice that many Jews, such as Sigmund Freud and Gustav Mahler, were among Vienna's most creative and brilliant citizens.

Hitler's confrontation with Marxian socialism seems to have been what set him off down the path of anti-Semitism. In other words, he began to hate the Jews because they were the leaders of the Marxian Social Democratic party. He started to read anti-Semitic pamphlets. Some of the worst lunatic fringe anti-Semitism in the world could be found in Vienna at the turn of the century. Hitler read the pamphlets of Lanz von Liebenfels, who wrote of a struggle between blond Aryan heros and dark hairy ape men of inferior races who were trying to seduce blonde women. As an insignia

Liebenfels used the swastika, which he claimed was the sign of racial purity.

It is possible that Hitler was partially converted to anti-Semitism even before he came to Vienna. While still in Linz, he became an ardent admirer of Richard Wagner's operas. When he first read Wagner's writing, however, is not known. But the question is important because Wagner was a fanatical anti-Semite. The composer was also an extreme German nationalist who saw it as his mission to purge German music of all foreign influences, particularly Jewish influence. In a pamphlet he wrote in 1850 entitled *Judiasm in Music* he ridiculed Jewish music. In a more general political attack, Wagner said, "the Jew is the plastic [formative] demon of the decline of mankind."

Even though critics pointed out that Wagner's anti-Semitism was the result of a persecution complex, Hitler considered the composer a credible source, something that could not be said for the gutter pamphlets of Lanz von Liebenfels. If Hitler did not read Wagner's writing while still in Linz, he probably read them during the many hours he spent in the libraries of Vienna. In a revealing comment later in his life, Hitler said, "Whoever wants to understand National Socialism must first know Wagner."

Wagner's stature as a German intellectual meant that many people besides Hitler read his writing. Moreover Wagner was not the only German intellectual who was propagating anti-Semitism and rabid nationalism. Other respected scholars like Paul Lagarde and Julius Langbehn were just as bad. The people who were exposed to this type of thinking were the educated middle and upper classes. Thus many of the people who would finance Hitler in the 1920s and 1930s were reading the same kind of nationalistic literature he read shortly after the turn of the century.

During most of the time he lived in Vienna, Hitler earned his living by painting watercolors that he sold to tourists and merchants, who used them to fill cheap picture frames. He lived in one of the poorest neighborhoods of the city in a cheap men's hostel. He did, however, have a small private cubicle, and the place was reasonably clean.

Hitler still lacked any self-discipline. As soon as he would sell a painting, he would take several days off and either go to the library or sit in a café eating cream puffs and reading newspapers. Although he still took no part in politics he carefully followed the struggle between three of the major new political parties in Vienna; the Pan-German party, the Christian Social party and the Marxian Social Democratic party.

At first Hitler sympathized with the Pan-German party. It was extremely nationalistic and anti-Semitic. He found such ideas acceptable because they were similar to the pan-German nationalism he had been exposed to in Linz as a schoolboy. Growing up on stories of heroic Germanic battles and conquests naturally made him an admirer of nationalism, militarism, and racism. However, Hitler was intelligent enough also to notice the weakness of the Pan-German party. Its members made little attempt to appeal to the workers' economic and social problems, so they remained primarily a middle-class party.

After living in Vienna for a while, Hitler gradually came to respect the Christian Social party and its charismatic leader, Karl Lueger, the mayor of Vienna. Lueger was a dynamic orator who knew how to sway a crowd. The popularity of the Christian Social party was based on its social welfare program and its anti-Semitism. Hitler admired the way Lueger won votes by making economic promises to the working class and the poor. He objected, however, to Lueger's anti-Semitism—because it was not extreme enough. Lueger's anti-Semitism was based on religious prejudice. Like the Pan-Germans, Hitler considered the Jews to be an inferior race and not just to have a different religion. A Jew could always escape religious anti-Semitism, at least theoretically, by converting to Christianity. But there was no escape from racial anti-Semitism because it was a matter determined by birth and ancestry.

The only outward signs that Hitler was interested in politics were occasional arguments he would have with other residents of the men's hostel. Since he did much of his painting in the recreation room of the hostel, he would often discuss politics and paint at the same time. But once the Jews were mentioned in the discussion, he would become very excited, raise his voice, and gesture wildly, paintbrush in hand. It is said that he once became so agitated he knocked over his easel during the argument. However, there is no record of Hitler's ever succeeding in winning anyone over to his point of view. He was regarded as something of a curiosity even among the odd assortment of characters who inhabited the men's hostel.

In the spring of 1913, fed up with his continual failure to accomplish anything, Hitler, who was then twenty-four years old, left Vienna and moved to Munich. He said he decided to move to Germany because he could no longer stand "the conglomeration of races" in Vienna. There was probably another reason he left Vienna. He was fleeing Austrian military service. But whatever his reasons for leaving Austria, he had learned a great deal in Vienna. He later wrote that Vienna was "the hardest, though most thorough school" of his life, where he developed the foundations of a "philosophy . . . and a political view" that remained with him forever.

This statement was certainly true. Hitler always remained more an Austrian than a German. Nationalism and anti-Semitism were more extreme in Austria because the Austro-Germans felt threatened by the rising aspirations of the people they had long dominated. The problem of national hatred was simmering in the Austro-Hungarian Empire years before it erupted in the rest of Europe in 1914. While the old dynastic order held on longer in Austria-Hungary, it was very obvious by 1900 that it was about to collapse. Hence, people like Hitler were already thinking about what kind of government would follow. In contrast no one in Germany thought the Hohenzollern monarchy was about to collapse.

Finally, Hitler's poverty in Vienna led him to experience Marxism and the politics of class warfare with an intensity he would never have encountered if he had lived among the middle class in Germany. In a sense, his life in Vienna gave Hitler a preview of what Europe would be like in 1918 after the end of World War I.

In Munich, Hitler lived a very quiet life. He earned his meager living from selling his paintings, as he had in Vienna. He rented a room above a tailor's shop in the Schwabing district where many artists lived. He had no close friends. The tailor and his family remembered Hitler as a "nice man" who was "very polite" but always kept to himself.

Hitler's solitary life that was seemingly going nowhere was suddenly transformed by world events. In August of 1914, World War I broke out. At last his German nationalism would have an outlet. He gathered with thousands of other patriots in the Odeonplatz in Munich to cheer the declaration of war. He believed Germany would at last have a chance to assert her military might on the battlefield and claim her rightful place as the dominant power in Europe. As much as he had tried to evade service in the Austro-Hungarian army, because he didn't want to serve in the same army as Slavs, he now volunteered for the German Army.

Like most people, Hitler had little knowledge of the real reasons for the war. Most people were so emotionally involved in national pride and honor that they failed to see that the development of great historic and economic forces made war almost inevitable. Behind all the nationalist rhetoric was the industrial rivalry among Germany, Britain, and France. German industrialization had progressed steadily in the latter half of the nineteenth century. By 1871, German industrial production exceeded that of France, and by 1900 it was greater than Britain's. Not only was Germany the greatest industrial power in Europe but its factories were also more modern and efficient than its rivals. Germany's problem was that it did not have access to world markets and raw materials equal to its productive capacity.

A large part of the world's markets and sources of raw materials was dominated by the colonial empires of Britain and France. Germany's leaders had often complained that Germany was being economically encircled and strangled. German industrialists seeking more access to world markets were the financiers of the extreme nationalist parties in the pre-1914 era. Some of the same industrialists who financed the prowar forces prior to 1914 would later help finance Hitler.

A few days after the declaration of war, Hitler was training with the List Regiment and was on his way to the front. The List Regiment went into battle in Flanders and suffered heavy casualties, but Hitler was not even wounded. After a short time as an ordinary infantryman, Hitler became a dispatch runner. His job was to carry messages forward from regimental headquarters to the men in the trenches. It was a dangerous job that required a great deal of courage and initiative. The runners often had to go forward during artillery barrages, running a few hundred yards, taking cover in one shell hole after another, finally crawling on their stomachs through the mud to the forward trenches while enemy bullets whizzed over their heads.

Hitler won the Iron Cross second class in 1914. He was wounded in the leg in 1916. In August of 1918, he won the Iron Cross first class, Germany's highest honor, which was rarely given to enlisted men. The metal was awarded for his single-handedly capturing fifteen French soldiers. It is, however, something of a mystery that in spite of his excellent military record Hitler never rose above the rank of corporal.

This may have been due to several factors. First of all, Hitler's job as a runner was vital and he was good at it. If he had been promoted he would have been replaced by an inexperienced man. There was also the fact that he remained a loner. He didn't fit in. The uneducated working-class soldiers thought he was an aloof bookish intellectual. Yet, he lacked the formal education of middle-class young men who were usually promoted to junior officers. His officers must have thought such a strange fellow didn't seem to have the authority to command men.

Whenever there was a lull in the fighting and Hitler had a free moment, he would find a quiet spot to sit and read. He went to war with a copy of Schopenhauer's *Will to Power* in his knapsack. Besides reading elitist philosophers like Schopenhauer and Nietzsche, he spent a great deal of time reading the political and military news in newspapers. He made a very thorough study of the differences between German and British war propaganda. The British propaganda was far more effective, he concluded. He was open-minded enough to have considerable admiration for the rhetorical skill of British Prime Minister Lloyd George.

In spite of the fact that Hitler recognized the cleverness of enemy propaganda he remained a fervent German nationalist. In the later days of war when Germany was doing poorly, he often argued with the men in his regiment who expressed "defeatist sentiments." He was a patriot to the last.

The war had a decisive effect on Hitler's character. As military service does for many young men, it gave him a sense of discipline and self-confidence. Up to the war, Hitler had so lacked personal self-discipline that in spite of his intelligence he was incapable of accomplishing anything. But the war also had a negative effect on him. The violence and carnage he saw all around him brutalized him. Death and destruction were now commonplace in his world. His regiment had one of the highest casualty rates in the German Army. He watched friends having their bodies blown apart only a few yards away. Of course this is no excuse for the murderous crimes Hitler later committed, because after all, many men who experienced the same brutalities of World War I reacted by later becoming pacifists. But it is an explanation for how he learned to use violence to get what he wanted. Before the war, Hitler's anti-Semitism and fanatical German nationalism were all talk and theory. He never tried to physically assault any Jews or incite a pogrom because he didn't know how. World War I educated him in violence. He now knew how to kill. In later years, when trying to convince his hesitant partners to participate in the Holocaust, he would often refer to the war saying, "If two million of Germany's best youth were slaughtered in the war, we have the right to exterminate subhumans who breed like vermin."

By the end of 1917, the British naval blockade of Germany was beginning to have a decisive effect. During peacetime, Germany imported much of the food consumed by her people. Now, cut off from the rest of the world, there were severe food shortages throughout the country. There was almost no milk and no coffee. The only fresh vegetables available were turnips and potatoes, and bread was made with potato peelings. The revolutionary Marxist underground tried to take advantage of the situation by organizing strikes against the war. On January 28, 1918, there was a general strike throughout Germany. Thousands of munitions workers in Berlin walked off their jobs demanding peace, increased food rations, and worker representation in negotiations with the Allies.

The news of the strike had an effect on the morale of the troops at the front. Many of the soldiers were tired of the war and wanted peace. But others, like Hitler, felt they were being betrayed by the civilian strikes. "What was the army fighting for if the homeland itself no longer wanted victory?" he asked. "For whom were all the immense sacrifices and privations? The soldier is expected to fight for victory and the homeland goes on strike against it!" He called the strike "the greatest villainy of the war."

After the failure of the great Ludendorff offensive in the summer of 1918, there was a serious drop in morale. Discipline began to break down in some places. Desertions increased. Red agitators among the troops encouraged rebellion. There were disorders on troop trains taking men to the front.

On August 8, the Allied troops broke through the German

front line. General Ludendorff said it was "the black day of the German Army." He now realized victory was no longer possible. By September, the military situation had deteriorated so much that the high command told the government to seek an armistice.

While the government tried to open peace negotiations with the Allies, the fighting continued as the Germans gradually pulled back. On the night of October 13, 1918, Hitler's regiment was dug in on a low hill south of Ypres in Belgium. Earlier in the day, the hill had been heavily bombarded by Allied artillery. Germans crouched in their trenches as the exploding shells turned the earth around them into a pock-marked moonscape. Just after sunset, one of the German soldiers shouted the warning: "Gas! Gas!" Hitler and the others hurriedly put on their gas masks. A deadly fog of chlorine gas slowly enveloped the battlefield. The gas attack lasted until midnight. After several hours the gas was able to penetrate the primitive gas masks worn by the German soldiers. By morning, Hitler's eyes felt "like burning coals." Slowly he began to stumble toward the rear carrying with him his last dispatch of the war.

Hitler was soon on board a hospital train, with hundreds of other gas victims, heading eastward back to Germany. He was taken to the military hospital at Pasewalk near Berlin where he was treated for gas poisoning. Responding well to the treatment he regained some vision within a week and could distinguish shapes and outlines. He was, however, depressed because he was afraid he would never be able to see well enough to paint again. He was also uneasy about Germany's military situation. Things were not going well at the front, and there were signs and rumors of antiwar activities at home.

During the latter part of October, the Germany military position was becoming desperate. Rather than face the prospect of defeat, the commanders of the navy decided they wanted to attempt to break the British blockade in one final sea battle. But when the fleet was ordered to sea, the crews of several battleships in the port of Kiel mutinied. The sailors broke into armories and then imprisoned their officers. A sailors' soviet was established, and most of the ships in Kiel harbor ran up the red flag of revolution.

While the Kiel mutiny was taking place, another uprising broke out in Munich, led by a socialist named Kurt Eisner. By the evening of November 7, the revolutionaries were in control of the city. Trucks manned by revolutionaries waving red flags patrolled the streets. The major military posts in Munich were seized when a number of soldiers joined the uprising. Some of Eisner's men set up machine guns at strategic intersections. There was no resistance when the revolutionaries occupied government buildings. The defenders of the old order, including the king of Bavaria, simply faded away without a fight.

Revolution quickly spread throughout Germany. On November 9, the German public learned the kaiser had abdicated and Friedrich Ebert, a moderate Social Democrat, had become chancellor. But Ebert was not radical enough to satisfy many of the revolutionaries; they wanted a Communist government like Soviet Russia. A group of about three thousand mutinous sailors occupied the kaiser's palace and looted everything in sight. When the Ebert government ordered them to leave they refused.

Hitler was in the military hospital at Pasewalk when a truckload of sailors arrived waving red flags and calling for revolution. According to Hitler, the red sailors were led by "a few Jews." He wondered why they were not arrested for treason.

A few days later, an elderly pastor came to the hospital to speak to the wounded men. He told them the news of the kaiser's abdication, that Germany was now a republic, and the government was seeking an armistice with the Allies. As he spoke the pastor began to weep. Hitler was dumbfounded at the sudden realization that Germany had lost the war. "It was impossible for me to listen any longer." Hitler later wrote, "Everything began to go black again before my eyes, stumbling, I groped my way back . . . to my cot and buried my head in the pillows. I had not wept since the day I had stood at my mother's grave."

For days, Hitler was severely depressed. He brooded on all the sacrifices that had been in vain and all the comrades and friends who were lost. He believed the German Army had not been defeated on the field of battle but betrayed, "stabbed in the back" by a gang of Communist traitors led by Jews. His depression turned to rage. He was determined to do something about it and no longer be a passive observer of the political situation. It was the critical turning point of his life. He made up his mind to become a politician.

Like Hitler, most Germans were stunned by their country's sudden defeat. After all, they had defeated Russia, and German troops still occupied enemy soil in France and Belgium. Only the generals of the high command knew how close the German line was to complete collapse. Consequently, in later years most Germans, like Hitler, honestly believed their army had never been defeated but was stabbed in the back by traitors.

By Christmas, Berlin was on the verge of anarchy as fighting erupted between the moderate forces, who supported chancellor Ebert, and the Communists, who called themselves Spartacists, in honor of the slave who led the rebellion against Rome. On January 5, the streets of Berlin were turned into a battlefield when armed Communists seized the railway station and a number of important government buildings. Many of the revolutionaries were supplied with money and weapons by sympathizers at the Soviet embassy. The Russian Communists saw a chance to spread their revolution to Germany.

In desperation, Chancellor Ebert called on the army for help. Units of loyal anti-Communist troops, called Free Corps, were sent to try to retake Berlin. The Communists had set up machine gun nests at the Brandenburg gate and other important intersections. They fought the Free Corps troops from behind barricades in the streets. Heavy fighting continued until January 12, when the Free Corps gradually got the upper hand. A few days later, the Free Corps captured and shot the two most important Communist leaders, Karl Liebknecht and Rosa Luxemburg. Communist uprisings spread to the Ruhr, Leipzig, Hamburg, and Bremen; but they were suppressed everywhere by loyal army troops.

In Munich, on February 22, a nationalist officer assassinated Kurt Eisner, the left-wing socialist leader of the Bavarian government. A month of turmoil followed. Finally the Communists and radicals gained control and proclaimed Bavaria a Soviet Republic. The revolutionary forces in Munich were little more than an undisciplined mob made up of Communist workers, radical intellectuals, and the unemployed. They robbed banks, looted homes, and terrorized the population.

During much of the unrest in Munich, Hitler was serving as a guard at a remote prisoner-of-war camp at Traunstein. He had volunteered for the duty at Traunstein just to get out of Munich because he was so disgusted by the revolutionary atmosphere. But in the spring the prisoner-of-war camp was closed, when the last of the Russian soldiers were sent home. Hitler was forced to return to Munich. Because he had given a speech in the barracks urging his fellow soldiers not to support the revolution, the Communists sent three men to arrest Hitler. When he confronted the three with a rifle, they departed and never returned.

The days of Communist government in Munich were numbered, as anti-Communist Free Corps troops, sent on order of Chancellor Ebert, advanced on the city from several directions. When the troops learned the Communists were shooting hostages, they made preparations to attack the next day.* On May 1 the Free Corps troops moved in on the Communists. There was some heavy fighting, but the undisciplined Reds were no match for trained soldiers. In Moscow, Lenin was hailing the birth of a Soviet Bavaria while Free Corps troops were slaughtering Communists as they

---

*Most of the hostages killed belonged to a right-wing secret society that would later play a decisive role in financing Hitler.

surrendered. Although fighting lasted another two days as the Free Corps cleaned out the last nests of resistance, there was never any doubt about the outcome.

The fact that Germany had almost gone Communist was to play a decisive role in Hitler's rise to power. More than anything else, it explains why many upper-class and upper-middle-class people financed and supported him. The German upper classes were terrified of communism. In spite of the fact that revolutionary uprisings had been suppressed, the threat continued for the next thirteen years. A militant German Communist party, supported by about 20 to 30 percent of the working class, survived the failed uprising of 1919 and kept on agitating for revolution. The Russian Soviets also continued their efforts to stir up working-class unrest in Germany. Against this background were the horror stories that poured out of Soviet Russia about what Lenin's "workers' paradise" was really like—how private property had been confiscated and outlawed; how people were starving and the economy was in ruins, and ultimately how thousands of upper-class men, women, and children including the czar and his family were butchered by Communist fanatics.

The Communist revolution in Germany in 1918 played an important part in the rise of German anti-Semitism. Some of the principal leaders of the revolution, Eisner, Liebknecht and Luxemburg, had been Jewish. This led anti-Semites like Hitler to make the accusation that the Jews were the "secret force" behind communism. In retrospect, such an idea is obviously ridiculous, but the German middle and upper classes were traumatized and seeking answers as to why their society had suddenly collapsed. Such people were vulnerable to conspiracy theories. If it had not been for the Communist uprisings in Germany, Hitler would probably never have found a receptive audience for the anti-Semitic garbage he had learned in Vienna. Moreover he would not have found so many industrialists, aristocrats, and officers willing to contribute to his cause.

PART 1

1

A MYSTERIOUS BEGINNING

In the first week of January 1931 an important dinner party was held at Hermann Goering's residence outside of Berlin. The hostess was Goering's beautiful and charming wife, Carin, a Swedish baroness by birth. Among the guests were Adolf Hitler; Fritz Thyssen, a multimillionaire industrialist who was chairman of the board of Germany's largest firm, the United Steel Works; and Dr. Hjalmar Schacht and his wife.

Dr. Schacht, a prominent banker was generally regarded as Germany's financial wizard. In 1923 he had been appointed special commissioner to stabilize the inflated mark. Shortly after his outstanding success, he became president of the Reichsbank (Germany's national bank). Politically, Schacht was a moderate liberal who had been one the founders of the German Democratic party, but when the Allies continued to force Germany to pay heavy reparations, Schacht resigned his office in disgust. He was, however, still a great power in the financial world and sat on the boards of several important banks and corporations.

Schacht had never met Hitler before, and although he was curious about the man, he was skeptical. "After the many rumors that we had heard about Hitler," wrote Schacht, "and the published criticisms we had read of him, we were pleasantly impressed."[1]

The Nazi leader arrived wearing dark trousers, the brown uniform jacket of the party, a white shirt and a dark tie. "His appearance," said Schacht, "was neither pretentious nor affected."[2]

The meal was rather simple but wholesome: pea soup, pork, potatoes and vegetables, and for dessert Swedish apple tart with vanilla ice cream. After dinner the guests retired to the drawing room. Hitler sat near Carin Goering, who was resting on the couch because of her heart condition. He was in a jovial mood and entertained the ladies with some amusing stories.

A little later Goering, Hitler, Thyssen, Schacht, and some of the other men went into the library for a long discussion. "Our talk quickly turned to political and economic problems," said Schacht. "His [Hitler's] skill in exposition was most striking. Everything he said he stated as incontrovertible truth: nevertheless, his ideas were not unreasonable."[3]

The next day Carin Goering wrote to her mother, Baroness von Fock: "I could tell from Hermann's positively beautific smile that it was a most successful party."[4]

The description of Hitler given by Schacht and most other people who met him personally contrasts very noticeably with the way he is portrayed by present-day biographers. For instance, Alan Bullock has described Hitler's physical appearance as "plebeian through and through."[5]

Although Hitler was known for his ability as a speaker, some authors seem to contend that he was at a total loss with individuals or small groups. "A quiet conversation with him was impossible," said Hermann Rauschning. "Either he was silent or took complete charge of the discussion."[6] Hitler was "unable to argue coolly," Alan Bullock tells us. "His one resort was to shout his opponent down.

The questioning of his assumptions or of his facts rattled him"[7] Above all, he would have found it almost impossible to talk with businessmen, industrialists, or bankers because, as William Shirer reported, "economics . . . bored Hitler and he never bothered to try to learn something about it."[8]

If Hitler behaved in such a fashion, he could hardly have persuaded wealthy, well-educated people to contribute great sums of money to his party. But he had two different sides to his character. The ranting bully of the beer hall could be very charming and persuasive when he wanted to be. It is a dangerous mistake to underestimate the ability and intelligence of an enemy. In fact, to a certain extent, Hitler succeeded because he was dismissed as being more ridiculous than dangerous. The man who shouted crude anti-Semitic slogans in public could, to the amazement of those who met him in private, discuss complex political and economic issues with logic and penetrating insight. He was able to convince his financiers that he was not a rabble-rouser at heart but had to act that way to attract the masses away from the Communists.

In 1919 when his political career began, Hitler's manners were not as polished as they were when Dr. Schacht met him in 1931, nor were his ideas on political or economic policy as fully developed. However, even in 1919 Hitler was not to be underrated. Throughout his youth he had been a keen student of history. In Vienna he had observed and studied the rise of modern mass political movements, especially Marxism, with the thoroughness of a political scientist.[9] He never let his prejudices prevent him from realistically appraising his opponents. Although he was largely self-educated, by the end of the war he was more widely read than most university graduates.[10]

On September 12, 1919, with orders from his commanding officer, Hitler attended a political meeting of a group called the German Workers' party in Munich's Sterneckerbräu beer hall. His mission was to report back on what was said because the Reichswehr (army), wanted to have more exact information about the little group, which seemed to be "well intentioned."[11] Very few people had even heard of the German Workers' party, one of about fifty different political groups and parties that existed in Munich at this turbulent time. The party had been founded nine months earlier by Anton Drexler, a thirty-five-year-old railway locksmith, and its members were mostly his fellow workers from the railway yards. Its program was radical, anti-Semitic, and nationalistic.

Dressed in civilian clothes, Hitler was inconspicuous among the audience of some fifty people. By his own account he went purely as an observer, with no intention of speaking. However, during the discussion period a professor made a speech advocating the separation of Bavaria from Germany and its linking up with Austria to form a new south German state. Detesting the idea of separatism, Hitler stood up on the spur of the moment and made a fiery speech rebutting the arguments of "the professor" and advocating the unity of all Germans. Then he turned and walked out.[12]

Anton Drexler came running down the aisle after him and handed him a pamphlet entitled "My Political Awakening." Although quite pedestrian in style, the pamphlet, written by Drexler himself, expressed some of the very same ideas about a nationalistic workers' party that Hitler had been pondering for a long time. Before Hitler had a chance to consider the little party further, he received a postcard informing him that he had been accepted as a member. He thought it was a curious way of enrolling members and didn't know whether to laugh or be irritated. "I had no intention of joining an existing party," he said, "but wanted to found one of my own."[13] Nevertheless, he attended a committee meeting and two days later made what he called "the most crucial decision of my life" when he signed up as a member.

"This absurd little group with its handful of members," he wrote, "seemed to me to have the advantage that it was not petrified into an 'organization,' but offered the individual an opportunity for truly personal activity."[14] There was another reason Hitler joined, one that he neglected to mention in *Mein Kampf*. Despite this tiny party's weaknesses, it had one outstanding strength. Behind the German Workers' party stood its protector and financial sponsor: the Thule Society, the most powerful secret organization in Germany.*

Outwardly, this mysterious group passed as a literary circle devoted to studying ancient German history and customs. Its name was taken from the mythological land of the north, the ancient Ultima Thule, believed to be the original home of the Germanic race. The Munich branch had been founded during the war by a Baron Rudolf von Sebottendorff, a shadowy individual who enlisted over 250 members from the city and 1,500 throughout Bavaria.[15] The significance of the membership, however, was to be found not in its quantity but in its quality. Among the group's members were lawyers, judges, university professors, police officials, aristocrats, physicians, scientists, as well as rich businessmen.

Only those who could prove their racial purity for at least three generations were admitted to this organization, whose motto was: "Remember that you are a German! Keep your blood pure!"[16] The symbol of the Thule Society was the swastika. Its letterheads and literature displayed the emblem, and large swastika flags decorated its plush meeting rooms and offices. Many of the themes and slogans of the group were later repeated by Hitler almost word for word.

Like many other *völkisch* (racial, nationalist) movements in Germany, the principal objective of the Thule Society was the establishment of a pan-German state of unsurpassed power and grandeur. There were also mystical aspects to the association that involved bardic rituals and occult ceremonies. On the practical political level, the society espoused

---

*Originally, the organization was an offshoot of the Germanen Orden, another powerful secret society whose branches through the country were patterned on Masonic Lodges.

German racial superiority, anti-Semitism, and violent anti-communism.

During World War I, the Thule members were busy fighting "treason' and advocating the most extreme pan-German views. But with the Communist revolutionary uprisings at the end of the war, things became more serious. On November 9, 1918, Sebottendorff spoke before a meeting of the entire membership to issue a call to arms against communism and the Jews.[17] The Thule offices became a center of activities for the counterrevolutionary underground. A secret intelligence network was set up, and caches of arms were assembled. Early in December, Sebottendorff planned to kidnap Eisner, the president of the Bavarian Soviet government, but something went wrong at the last moment and the action was called off.

Operating simultaneously with these covert activities was a more or less open anti-Communist propaganda campaign that involved the distribution of hundreds of thousands of anti-Semitic pamphlets.* The society's propaganda posters were stuck up during the night and leaflets were hurled into crowds from speeding automobiles. A determined effort was made to win over the masses of the population, especially the workers "poisoned with the Jewish ideas of communism and internationalism." Unlike most other conservative nationalists, the Thule Society was aware of the danger presented by the widening gap between the officer class and the workers. It became one of the society's primary objectives to bring the working man back into the nationalist camp.

Thule member Karl Harrer was instructed to form a "Workers Political circle."[18] However, neither Harrer, who was a journalist, nor any of the other upper-middle-class or

---

*It was completely wrong and unfair to blame communism on the Jews. Nevertheless, the anti-Semitic conspiracy theory that the Jews were the "secret force" behind communism was very attractive to some people for psychological reasons. It gave them an excuse to blame all their problems on an "evil" scapegoat while inflating their own egos with the idea they possessed "secret knowledge."

aristocratic members of the society knew anything about the politically minded workers. Given the existing sentiments of the workers and their class hostility, the Thule program would be automatically rejected by the masses if proposed by someone from the privileged class. The circle needed to be directed, nominally at lest, by a manual worker. Harrier decided to back Anton Drexler, who was both a pan-German anti-Semite and a proletarian. In the last years of the war, Drexler had written an article, published in Harrer's newspaper, that urged the workers to rally behind the army.

Shortly after the Communist revolution of November 9, 1918, Drexler and Harrer drew up a general program for a nationalist workers' party. On January 5, 1919, Drexler invited some of his patriotic fellow workers to the first "public meeting," and the German Workers' party was officially founded.[19] Drexler was probably aware that the Thule Society was supporting his efforts, but such a simple man could hardly have understood the extent of the organization's power and influence.

A few days before the liberation of Munich by the Free Corps troops, the Communists raided the hotel headquarters of the Thule Society and took seven members hostage. On May 1, 1919, as the anti-Communist Free Corps units tightened the ring around the city, the hostages were stood up against a wall in the courtyard of the Luitpold High School and shot. Of the seven Thule members killed, four were titled aristocrats, including the beautiful young secretary of the society, Countess Heila von Westarp, and Prince Gustave von Thurn und Taxis, who was related to several European royal families.

Not only Germany but the entire world was shocked by the murders of such respectable people. The London *Times'* headline read, "Shooting of Hostages . . . Munich Savagery"[20] Everyone in Munich was now aware of the Thule Society's existence, and that it had some very important members. Considering Hitler's position as an army agent and his interest in nationalist anti-Semitic politics, it is likely that he was aware of the society's backing this new little movement called the German Workers' party. If Hitler had such information it would explain why he chose this small party from the many other nationalist groups that existed at the time.

Outwardly, it did not seem as if the German Workers' party was supported by anyone with power, influence, or money. In *Mein Kampf* Hitler described with utmost disdain his first impressions of the party: the members assembled in the dimly lit backroom of a beer hall, discussing political ideas they did not understand. They wrote letters to other patriotic movements in Lubeck, Hanover, and elsewhere, and discussed the answers received. The total funds of the party amounted to seven marks and fifty pfennigs.[21] As far as property was concerned, the movement did not even own a rubber stamp. The members were afraid to hold public meetings because they might irritate their opponents, the Social Democrats and Communists.

Hitler urged the party committee to court publicity or else the movement would never become known. But Harrer and the others felt they were not ready to become known. They first wanted jointly to discover "the truth" in order to "get things clear in their own minds." After tedious and exhausting discussions Hitler finally persuaded his comrades to risk a public meeting. Invitations were typed or written out by hand and then dropped into the mailboxes of prospective individuals. Hitler himself walked through the deserted streets of Munich before dawn distributing eighty invitations. But when the long-expected evening arrived, only the seven party committee members turned up; not another soul. The next few meetings were only slightly more successful.

The party finally placed a notice for one of their gatherings in the *Völkischer Beobachter (The Racial Observer)*, an extreme nationalist newspaper owned by the Thule Society.

Hitler claimed that the "poor devils" who were the members of the party paid for this advertisement themselves.[22] The meeting was to be held in a cellar room of the Hofbräuhaus, the most famous beer hall in Munich.* The room would hold about 130 people, a number that seemed enormous to Hitler and his comrades. Hitler had the "unshakable conviction" that if only people would come and listen he could win them over to his cause. The advertisement drew 111, the largest audience the German Workers' party had ever had, and the collection taken at the end of the speech netted 300 marks (about 100 dollars).

It is difficult to determine exactly how much financial assistance the Thule Society gave during this early period, but most likely it was very little. The German Workers' party was only one of the more minor ventures of the Thule Society. The most significant assistance Hitler would get from the Thule Society for the time being was protection from police prosecution thanks to Thule members in the Bavarian government. But as the German Workers' party would begin to grow and develop under Hitler's guidance, able and intelligent Thule sympathizers and members would join it and be of the utmost value to Hitler. Eventually the child of the masses would outgrow its secret society parent. In the meantime, the most important help Hitler received was from his employer, the army.

The seemingly slow, snaillike progress of the German Workers' party was particularly painful to Hitler because he was not engaging in politics merely for his own satisfaction. He was participating with the consent and, in part, by the orders of his superiors at the Army District Headquarters. He was still on the full-time payroll of the Reichswehr as a political agent.[23] The army was looking for a mass political

---

*Many organizations and political parties in Munich held their meetings in beer halls. The owners of the beer halls did not endorse or sympathize with the groups that rented their meeting rooms.

party on which it could rely as a patriotic alternative to communism, but it would not wait forever.

One day an officer who worked with Hitler took him to a meeting of the Iron Fist.[24] There he met the organization's commander, Captain Ernst Roehm, who almost immediately recognized a certain ability in Hitler. In its blunt militarylike way, the Iron Fist was an important patriotic group in Munich in 1919. Roehm and his men, mostly tough young officers and a few loyal troops, would march into a beer hall, and every quarter of an hour they would have the band play a patriotic song. When the tune was blared out, everyone stood up. Those of Marxist sympathies or anyone else who remained seated was soon confronted by a rough figure in military uniform. A silent glance was usually enough, but if the unfortunate individual did not immediately rise to his feet, he just barely lived to regret his error.

Officially the officer "in charge of press and propaganda" for the Bavarian Reichswehr, Roehm had much greater influence than his rank of captain indicated. Unofficially, the generals took his advice on all political matters; he organized new paramilitary Free Corps units, and he directed the clandestine movement of arms to secret hiding places out of the reach of the Allied Control Commission. Under his supervision thousands of rifles, machine guns, and mortars were stockpiled in remote forests and deserted villas. Roehm's activities made him a key figure in the Free Corps, the surreptitious reserve of the reduced legitimate army.

Within a short time after their first meeting, Roehm became so convinced of Hitler's talent as a political agitator that he joined the German Workers' party and began to attend its meetings regularly. He greatly strengthened the little party by recruiting new members from among his troops and the younger officers, men who were all hardened veterans of the trenches, seething with hatred against the Weimar Republic. They supplied the strength and muscle Hitler needed to defend his young party against the Marxists in the streets. Roehm also provided access to the resources and funds of some of the secret paramilitary organizations. "Roehm," said Hitler's close associate Kurt Lüdecke, "was of decisive importance to the (Nazi) Party, finding money, arms and men at the most critical times."[25]

The fact that Captain Roehm treated Hitler as a social equal automatically gave Hitler a certain status among Roehm's fellow officers. But social distinctions were of little importance for Roehm. If a man was a veteran of the trenches and was opposed to communism, that was enough for him. Roehm himself was not exactly a figure of gentlemanly military elegance. He was short bulky man whose face was marked with dueling scars and bullet wounds. In his blunt aggressive manner there was also a hint of brutality. But this was just the kind of man Hitler needed to help him secure the leadership of the German Workers' party away from the cautious, conservative Harrer, who was weary of anything bolder than pedantic backroom discussions.[26]

Hitler, setting his hopes on drawing larger audiences, insisted on renting a bigger hall, and, in hopes of attracting more soldiers, he chose a tavern called Zum Deutschen Reich on Dachauerstrasse, close to the barracks of the List Regiment. The results were disappointing, and expectations were far from being met; only about 140 people came. The party executive committee was discouraged and frightened; Harrer argued that Hitler would ruin the party with such reckless aggressiveness. Finally, Hitler succeeded in convincing Drexler and the others that they were bound to succeed only if they persisted. One of Hitler's obvious strengths was this determination, persistence, and self-confidence even in the face of defeat. The next meeting held at the Zum Deutschen Reich drew slightly more than 200 people. Another meeting attracted 270 listeners, and the fourth was attended by over 400. Hitler was on his way.

Making the rounds of the beer halls and restaurants of Munich, he searched for a headquarters for the party, whose total equipment at that point consisted of a cigar box to hold its funds and a few envelopes for correspondence. He found a dark backroom available in the Sterneckerbräu where the rent was fifty marks a month (about ninety-five cents in U.S. currency). This was regarded as an exorbitant sum by the party committee. As one of the cosigners of the lease, Hitler gave his occupation as "artist," probably to throw off any suspicion of army support.

The new headquarters had only one small window, which faced an alley so narrow that hardly any sunlight entered. "The room," said Hitler, "had more the look of a funeral vault than an office." A table and a few borrowed chairs were obtained, then a telephone was installed, and finally a safe for the party's membership cards and the treasury, which did not have much money in it.

The first party treasurer was a one-armed man named Meir.[27] Being of a humble background with little formal education, his only qualification for the job was his honesty. As the party grew in size and the role of treasurer became more important, Meir was succeeded by a Herr Singer, a lesser official in the Bavarian state government. Hitler later described Singer as "a fine man" whose talents were "exactly what suited us at that time."[28] With inflation eating away the purchasing power of the mark, Singer's regular salary was not sufficient to permit him to make even a small donation to the party, so he took a part-time job in the evenings as a guard at the Bavarian National Museum in order to be a regular monthly contributor.

The collections at all party meetings were directed by Singer, who would stuff the money received into a small tin trunk, which he then lugged home under his arm. A party member who walked home with him one evening remembered watching Singer empty the pile of dirty inflated marks onto his dining room table and start carefully counting and sorting them. There was an unpleasant, damp chill in the unheated room where the "treasurer" worked. Sometimes Singer's wife helped him, but on this occasion it was very late, and she had long since retired to the warmth of the bedroom. As in most Munich homes during that desperately cold winter of 1920, only one room was warmed by a small stove. These were the humble beginnings of the Nazi treasury.

During this early period the only regular contributions Hitler could count on came from a handful of small businessmen in Munich. They were ordinary shopkeepers and a few professional men, so their contributions could not have been large. Being middle-aged or older men, they had been indoctrinated with German nationalism long before Hitler appeared on the scene. There was a strong bond of personal loyalty between Hitler and these men. They considered him their friend as well as their political leader.[29]

A typical example was Oscar Koerner, a man who owned a small toy shop and who was one of the original members of the party. He gave everything he had to the movement and later was even to give his life. (Koerner would be killed in the Nazi putsch, November 9, 1923.)[30] Koerner was always eager and enthusiastic for every new project Hitler had in mind, and on many occasions he would be the first to give a few marks to see that the project was carried out. With his quick, vivacious temperament, Koerner was also one of the activists of the party who frequently defended his beliefs with his fists.

The party's best contributors were invited to attend the Monday evening get-together at an old-fashioned coffeehouse near the Petersplatz. The interior of the café, which had space for about a hundred people, was one long irregular room, with built-in benches and wood-paneled walls. Here every Monday night Hitler would meet informally with his most devoted supporters. Many of them were middle-aged, married couples who had come to have their dinner with Hitler and usually ended up paying for his as well. None of these people were rich; every mark they gave meant a personal sacrifice. Those present on Monday night were usually the first, other than the party officials, to hear Hitler's newest ideas. After dinner Hitler would sit for hours discussing politics in a friendly, conversational manner.

The party's financial subsistence was, however, made possible not just by the donations of the most generous contributors but also by the day-to-day income of the average members. Every member of the party was expected to pay his dues of one mark a month and give whatever his means would permit, but since many of them were unemployed there was very little surplus income. "You have no idea," Hitler later told one of his associates, Gregor Strasser, "what a problem it was in those days to find the money to buy my ticket when I wanted to deliver a speech at Nuremberg."

Even though the dues of impoverished party members and the donations of small shopkeepers may not seem like very much, they were "important" in the early days of the German Workers' party, as Hitler rightly pointed out. By being able to get regular donations out of such people, Hitler demonstrated to the army and other potential big financiers his talent as a fund-raiser. No other political party had such a spirit of dedication and willingness to contribute among its rank-and-file members.[31] The shopkeepers and small businessmen who gave to the German Workers' party were a desperate group.

Unlike the people who supported the traditional German parties and took politics lightly, those who donated to the German Workers' party believed it was a question of life or death. They felt squeezed by Marxist labor on one hand and "monopoly capitalism" on the other. Inflation was rapidly eating away their savings, and the old middle-class virtues of thrift and hard work seemed to be suddenly worthless. These people were Hitler's most sincere supporters. They gave their money without asking for anything in return.

As "true believers," they accepted every point of the Nazi philosophy without question, and it must be remembered that they grew up in a provincial, traditional culture where anti-Semitism was commonplace. They lived through World War I when the most extreme nationalist hatreds were encouraged, and then the bloody excesses of the 1918 Communist revolution made them ripe for someone like Hitler. None of them really understood what the results of their actions would be. They willingly accepted everything Hitler said, and their personal respect for him as the spokesman of their cause was one of the key factors on which he based his strength within the party.

Hitler transformed the German Workers' party from a directionless backroom discussion club into a genuine political force. It is unlikely that at this stage he saw himself as the prospective dictator of Germany, but his imagination was already obsessed with the idea of a "Germanic Revolution" that would sweep away the Communists, Jews, and Social Democrats who had "betrayed" the Fatherland in November of 1918. He proclaimed himself as the drummer of this coming revolution.

Hitler's highest ambition at this time was probably to become the minister of propaganda in a nationalist government headed by some general like Ludendorff. For an ambitious politician like Hitler there were few models who came from a lower-middle-class background and lacking a university education. Since he had never even become an officer during the war, he could not yet seriously consider himself for the role of Napoleon. However, he reasoned that politics had changed since Napoleon's day, when a purely military man could easily suppress the mob. With communism as the enemy, Hitler believed his skill as a propagandist would be more useful in preparing for a nationalist revolution than being trained as a military tactician.

The key to Hitler's political appeal was the idea that nationalism and patriotism must spread beyond the upper middle class. The masses, Hitler insisted, were capable of being as patriotic as anyone else. He was fond of citing how the appeal to patriotism had had an overwhelming effect on the workers at the outbreak of the war in 1914. If a new party wanted to rekindle similar mass patriotism, it would have to convince the workers that they were a valuable part of the national community. The common man, Hitler argued, was in return entitled to social justice, a decent wage, and a secure livelihood.[32] Hitler had a policy; the only difficulty was presenting it to the people.

Traditional nationalist meetings had tended to be dull and academic. Hitler deliberately made his meetings exciting and provocative. He practiced and developed his natural gift for oratory. What he had learned about propaganda in Vienna, during the war, and during the revolution now paid its dividends. Neglecting no technique that might improve his speaking, he spoke at meetings both in the afternoon and evening to see when the emotions of the audience could be more easily aroused. He went to almost every beer hall and public meeting room in Munich to study the acoustics and "atmosphere." Above all, he learned to get the "feeling" of his audience, to tell what they were thinking, and what they wanted.

Perhaps the most compelling and for that very reason the most diabolical thing about Hitler's speeches was their air of sincerity. He was the voice from the trenches, the unknown young war veteran with the Iron Cross who expressed himself so passionately. Although he wore civilian clothes, his stiff bearing, his narrow mustache, and his mannerisms were typical of the noncommissioned officer. Standing stiffly at attention with his chin up, he would begin to speak in a low voice. When he caught the attention of his audience, his voice became deeper and increased in volume. As he relaxed and got the "feel" of his speech, he would begin to use gestures. His right forefinger would point out the evils Germany faced; then a sweeping gesture of the left arm would wipe them away. With variations in pace and style he could keep an audience enraptured for an hour or even two.

Sometimes he used the technique of constructing an imaginary dialogue in which he stated an opponent's case and then completely demolished it with his rebuttal. He planted questioners in the audience to "feed' him and help create the right mood. It was really a kind of dramatic performance. From observation, experience, and instinct, he learned how to arouse and control people's emotions. It is, however, a mistake to think that his arguments made no sense. A progressive logical development was one of the strongest points of a Hitler speech.[33] Toward the conclusion his gestures would become more dramatic and his voice would break with passion as he worked up to the peroration. He finished with a call to arms that had the sting of a lash: "Germany Awake!"[34]

Night after night Hitler spoke to ever-growing crowds in the beer halls of Munich, and his followers multiplied. In light of his success, more important members of the Thule Society began to join the German Workers' party to carry on where Harrer had left off. One of them, Dietrich Eckart, came to exert a tremendously powerful personal influence on Hitler.[35]

Born of well-to-do parents in a little town of northern Bavaria, Eckart had been a failure as a law student because he drank too much and worked too little. Even when he was in his forties in Berlin, he led the life of a poor writer and a vagrant, lodging in flophouses and sleeping on park benches. He blamed the Jews for blocking the success of his works. He had written plays and, like the Marquis de Sade, staged some of them in an insane asylum, using the inmates as actors. His poetry and writing generally had Nordic and mystical themes. Finally he became a success as a writer. His translation of Isben's *Peer Gynt* was considered brilliant and became the standard German version, bringing him a steady income from royalties, and his writings on Norse mythology became widely read, especially in nationalist circles. Before the war, he was for a time the feuilleton editor of the well-known conservative Berlin newspaper the *Lokal-Anzeiger*. By the early twenties he was the editor and publisher of *Auf gut Deutsch (In Plain German)*, a satirical Munich periodical that had a fairly large circulation and was anti-Semitic, pan-German in viewpoint.[36]

To the political philosophy of the Thule Society, Eckart brought the idea that the hour for a great charismatic leader had struck. In 1919, before anyone had ever heard of Adolf Hitler, he composed a bardic verse in which the coming of a national redeemer was prophesied, a leader "familiar and foreign at the same time, a nameless one." In a café he once described in plainer language the man he thought was needed to save Germany:

> We must have a fellow as a leader who won't wince at the rattle of a machine gun. The rabble must be given a damned good fright. An officer wouldn't do; the people don't respect them anymore. Best of all would be a worker, a former soldier who could speak. He needn't be very brainy; politics is the most stupid business in the world and every market-woman in Munich knows as much as the men in Weimar. I'd rather have a stupid vain Jackanapes who can give the Reds a juicy answer and not run away whenever a chair-leg is aimed at him than a dozen learned professors who sit trembling in wet pants.

The final requirement was "He must be a bachelor! Then we'll get the women."[37]

Adolf Hitler met most of Eckart's specifications, and the two soon became close friends. Although usually contemptuous of and hostile to intellectuals, Hitler found in Eckart a kindred spirit with whom he felt at ease. In spite of his social background, university degree, and works published, Eckart was, like Hitler, essentially a rootless revolutionary. The two men made an odd pair, for outwardly Eckart was very different from Hitler. He was a big stout man with an imposing bald head and rather small eyes. Gregarious, with a boisterous humor, he loved to spend his time in cafés and beer halls.

Taking a personal interest in Hitler, Eckart began to groom his young friend for the role of a political leader.[38] Having grown up in a lower-middle-class atmosphere in a provincial town and having been poor most of his adult life, Hitler lacked a certain social style and breeding. He had never been in a formal drawing room nor dined in a first-class restaurant. In order to be able to deal with members of the upper class without their taking a condescending attitude toward him, it would be necessary to polish up his manners, looks, and dress. Eckart gave him his first trench coat and persuaded him to trim his mustache. He began to take Hitler around with him to the better cafés and restaurants of Munich.

Picking up Hitler's check in the cafés and taking him out to dinner in a good restaurant were only some minor services Eckart did for the emerging political leader. He gave Hitler his first introduction to better society and, what is more important, to people who were financial backers of the Thule Society. These were people who would one day render similar services for the Nazi party. Although Eckart was not really a wealthy man himself, he was never short of money and contributed generously to the party treasury.[39] His activities as a party member were also of great value to Hitler. His writing ability and flair for strong, colorful language made him an excellent propagandist. The feverish battle song of the Nazi movement, "Storm! Storm! Storm!," was one of his works.

Another of Hitler's early collaborators who helped provide the funds for the new party was Alfred Rosenberg, a member of the Thule Society. Rosenberg, a Baltic German, came to Munich as a refugee from Reval in 1918. The Russian Revolution had aroused his interests in politics when he was in his midtwenties, and it had turned him into a fanatical anti-Communist and anti-Semite. Although a well-educated man with a doctorate in architecture, Rosenberg was at first unable to find employment in Munich and survived on the charity soup kitchen of the Relief Committee.

One day his interest in anti-Communist politics led him to pay a visit to the office of Dietrich Eckart. The first thing Rosenberg said to Eckart was, "Can you use a fighter against

Jerusalem?" Eckart laughed. "Certainly!"[40] Then he asked whether Rosenberg had ever written anything. Not only had Rosenberg done so, but he had also brought it with him. The article, published under the title "The Russian-Jewish Revolution," ranted about the excesses of the "destructive forces" of Judaism and communism in Russia. This hate-filled poison was perfect for the propaganda series on "the Jewish plan to dominate the world" that Eckart was publishing in his newspaper.

In the autumn of 1919 Rosenberg and Hitler met for the first time in the home of Dietrich Eckart. They discussed how Marxism was undermining the state "the same way that Christianity had corroded the Roman Empire." A few days later Rosenberg attended one of Hitler's speeches: "Here I saw a German frontline soldier," said Rosenberg, "embarking on this struggle in a manner as clear as it was convincing, counting on himself alone with the courage of a free man. It was that which after the first fifteen minutes drew me to Adolf Hitler."[41] Toward the end of 1919 Rosenberg became a member of the German Workers' party. He was assigned the task of researching the role of the Jews in communism.

Speaking Russian fluently and knowing the country well, Rosenberg had no difficulty becoming the party's expert on the East. It was a time of confused fighting on Germany's eastern frontiers, which had not been finally determined by the Treaty of Versailles. Munich was full of White Russians who hoped that the German Free Corps in the Baltic, or possibly a reactionary German government, if one came to power in Berlin, might march into Russia and throw out the Communists. Many of the White Russians had money, and money was one of the essential needs of the struggling German Workers' party. Thus the impoverished refugee Rosenberg became the first contact man between Hitler and the wealthy Russian émigrés.

As the party's expert on the Jewish question, Rosenberg was the first who showed Hitler a booklet entitled *The Proto-*

cols of the Learned Elders of Zion, the most important propaganda literature of the White Russian anti-Semites.[42] The booklet, a complete fake, was said to be the minutes of a secret meeting of Jewish leaders in 1897, the year of the first International Zionist Congress. It told of a terrible plot to undermine European society and overthrow all governments. The principal weapons to be used to accomplish this conspiracy were to be Marxist revolution and international financial manipulations.

Hitler was fascinated with the *Protocols* and immediately recognized its propaganda value. Historian Konrad Heiden, who was then living in Munich, reported: "The little volume was given away and widely distributed: [it] . . . found backers who preferred to remain anonymous."[43]

Throughout the winter of 1919–1920 Hitler remained in the army as an instructor teaching short political courses to soldiers about to be demobilized, but most of his energy was spent working for the German Workers' party. By now he realized that if the party was to grow larger it would have to have an official program. After a number of meetings held in the humble atmosphere of Drexler's kitchen, Hitler and Drexler succeeded in drawing up a twenty-five-point program for the party. Eckart made a few improvements in style, and by February 6, 1920, the program assumed its final form.

Hitler thought the proclamation of the party's new program would be an ideal occasion to give his adherents their first baptism of fire. He needed a large hall and a large audience, preferably one that would include a good percentage of Communists. From his years of studying propaganda tactics he knew that a speech would be remembered more vividly if its advocates put up a fight for its defense. The conservative parties seemed cowardly when they closed down their meetings because of Communist disruptions. Instead, Hitler and his followers planned to stand and fight and in doing so win the admiration of the audience.

After renting the main hall of the Hofbräuhaus for the evening of February 24, Hitler and his comrades put up bright red posters all over Munich advertising the meeting.[44] This irritated the Communists, who claimed red was the color of the workers, so they decided to put an end to such "reactionary tricks." At seven-thirty on the night of the twenty-fourth the hall was filled to capacity with over two thousand people present, many of them Communists determined to break up the meeting.

The first speaker was Dr. Johannes Dingfelder, a conservative nationalist of the traditional school. He said the salvation of the Fatherland depended on work, order, and sacrifice. Sensing that trouble was brewing in the audience, he avoided in his speech any reference to Jews. He concluded with pious abstractions and the customary sort of quotations from Goethe. The chairman of the evening thanked the speaker and then thanked the Communists in the audience for keeping quiet during the speech. Their quiet probably indicated boredom more than tolerance, and in any case they were saving their strength for the next speaker.

The tone of the meeting was no longer polite when Hitler reached the speaker's stand. He attacked the government in Berlin, accusing it of direct responsibility for the mounting inflation that was already eating away hard-earned savings. There was loud applause, because most Bavarians blamed the Berlin government for all their problems. Then Hitler began to denounce the Jews. Almost all Communist leaders were Jews, he said. They were responsible for the 1918 revolution and Germany's defeat. Class hatred served only their interests; they had sold the nation into the slavery of the Versailles Treaty.

An uproar began before he could go any further. The Communists and socialists interrupted him with organized chants and catcalls. However, the Marxists were not the only ones who were organized. Hitler and Roehm had seen to it that "faithful war comrades and other adherents" were strategically grouped throughout the hall. Violent clashes occurred, but within a few minutes order was restored.

Then Hitler took up the subject of the new party program and presented it to the audience point by point. Applause began to drown out the interruptions. By the time Hitler concluded, most of the audience was on his side; he was confident this was a historic moment of victory.

From all outward indications, the program was designed to appeal to the masses and not to the party's financial backers. It was little more than a piece of demagoguery. Combined with an anti-Semitic racist ideology was an attack on the so-called abuses of capitalism.

The program as a whole contained the germ of future National Socialist doctrine. Included were widely accepted platitudes that could ultimately be made the basis of a totalitarian state, for instance: common good takes precedence over the good of the individual. On the matter of foreign policy there were points demanding the abrogation of the Versailles Treaty and the union of all German-speaking people into one Reich.

By incorporating anticapitalist points in the party program, it seems unlikely that Hitler could hope for contributions from the upper class. In fact, everything about his presentation at the Hofbräuhaus—the propaganda, the violence, the vicious anti-Semitism, and the fire-breathing oratory—would seem to have discouraged respectable support. However, there was still a great danger of another Communist revolution in Germany at the time, and if the Communist forces in all the industrial centers of Germany rose at once, the army, which simply did not have enough troops, would have difficulty in suppressing them.[45] The generals and the upper class needed a new nationalist party that would appeal to the workers and win them away from the Marxists. Very few members of the upper class would want to join such a party, but because of Hitler's method of responding to Communist violence with counterviolence it would be a useful ally. Naturally, they did not want to have violence at the meetings of their conservative parties, but if a Communist revolution were to break out they would need a patriotic workers' party that was willing to fight.

Hitler's strategy could hardly fail; he offered both the masses and the German power elite what they wanted at the same time. But the upper class did not rush to embrace this "tribune of the people." Irritated at the hostility of high society, Hitler would ask, "What have they got against me? That I have no title, that I am not a doctor or a first lieutenant! That they can never forgive me." On another occasion he declared that they were resentful of him not just because of his political views, but primarily because he was a "poor devil" who had nevertheless ventured to open his mouth.

Hitler was not a popular guest in Munich society. In spite of Eckart's help, the drawing rooms remained closed to him. It is sometimes thought that Frau Carola Hofmann, who lived in a suburban villa, was an exception to the general disdain Hitler received from "good society."[46] She heard him speak for the first time early in 1920 and was captivated. In a sense, this sixty-one-year-old woman began to take the place of the mother he missed so much. She was present for some of the early beer hall brawls of the movement, started a local party group in her neighborhood, and for a time, her country house was an unofficial headquarters for the party. However, Frau Hofmann, the widow of a headmaster, was neither socially prominent nor wealthy. She lived comfortably on her husband's savings, and though she frequently gave money to the party, these were very small sums. Her gifts to Hitler were more often home-baked cakes and cookies than cash.

A week after the meeting at the Hofbräuhaus, the German Workers' party, at Hitler's urging, changed its name to the National Socialist German workers' party (NSDAP). But the change in the party's name did little to alter its always desperate economic situation. Although people of all classes were joining the movement, by far the majority were poor. An early member who gave much of his time described some of the monetary problems that Hitler's men faced in those days.

The Nazi organization itself lived from day to day financially, with no treasury to draw on for lecture hall rentals, printing costs, or the other thousand-and-one expenses which threatened to swamp us. The only funds we could count on were membership dues, which were small, merely a drop in the bucket. Collections at mass meetings were sometimes large, but not to be relied on. Once in while, a Nazi sympathizer would make a special contribution, and in a few cases these gifts were really substantial. But we never had money enough. Everything demanded outlays that were, compared with our exchequer, colossal. Many a time, posting the placards for some world-shaking meeting, we lacked money to pay for the paste.

Instead of receiving salaries for the work we did, most of us had to give to the Party in order to carry on. Clerks and officers, except for a very few, got no pay, and the majority of members pursued their usual occupations during the day as a livelihood. Consequently, those who gave full time to Party work were a miscellaneous crew, including only two or three who had sufficient means to support themselves. The rest were chiefly recruited from the jobless men who would work for their meals.[47]

Somehow Hitler always seemed to manage to find enough money to keep the movement going from one day to the next. There was of course some money coming from right-wing army circles and the Thule Society, but both groups were contributing to numerous nationalist organizations, and there was only so much money to go around.

On March 13, 1920, extreme reactionary circles in Berlin attempted a coup. Headed by Dr. Kapp, a little-known Prussian civil servant, they were supported by the Ehrhardt Free Corps Brigade, which conducted the military part of the operation and forced President Ebert and his cabinet to flee to Dresden. The coup had virtually no popular support except for the extreme right wing of the Nationalist party, and moreover, the German upper class was against the venture. The leading industrialists condemned it, and the high command of the army refused to take part.[48] The Social Democratic party then called a general strike, and due to the political ineptitude of Dr. Kapp and his Free Corps friends, the rebel regime began to collapse.

In Munich, the conservative monarchists, who wanted a more independent Bavarian state, decided to take advantage of the situation in Berlin and carry out a coup of their own. On the night of the thirteenth, the Bavarian military authorities presented the Social Democratic government of Johannes Hoffmann with an ultimatum to resign peacefully or be suppressed. The new government, backed by the military, was headed by Ritter Gustav von Kahr, a reactionary monarchist from a family that had served the Bavarian kings for generations.

Although the Bavarian monarchists had no wish to unite forces with Berlin's new Kapp government, they did decide to send a liaison officer to Berlin to keep in touch with the regime there. Surprisingly, the choice fell on Hitler and Dietrich Eckart, rather than a high-ranking Bavarian officer.[49] A military plane was put at their disposal, and they immediately flew north in spite of bad weather. The pilot lost his way in the storm and was forced down at Juterbog, forty miles southwest of Berlin. The strikers had set up barricades along the roads; no trains were running. If the real purpose of their mission became known, Hitler and Eckart would be arrested and shot. Eckart claimed to be a paper merchant and Hitler disguised with a goatee, said he was Eckart's accountant. Allowed to continue their flight, they arrived in Berlin just as the Kapp regime collapsed five days after taking office.

Even though the liaison mission to the Kapp government proved futile, the trip to Berlin turned out to be very advantageous for Hitler. He made contact with northern German right-wing circles that had access to financial support from major industrialists like the locomotive manufacturer von Borsig. He was introduced to Free Corps leaders and officials of powerful nationalist groups like the Stahlhelm (steel helmet), a reactionary veterans' association supported by the Junkers (Prussian landed aristocrats), and extreme right-wing big business interests. The most exciting moment of Hitler's visit must have been when he was introduced to General Ludendorff, who had been the second highest ranking general in World War I and was now looked on as the senior officer of the patriotic camp. That a general like Ludendorff would shake hands with a corporal was a sign of Hitler's increasing political importance.

Dietrich Eckart, who had entrée to the higher levels of Berlin society because he had once been a drama critic for a conservative newspaper there, was also a great help in putting Hitler forward. He presented him in the homes of several wealthy upper-class families. One of the ladies who received Hitler in her salon, Frau Helene Bechstein, the wife of the piano manufacturer Carl Bechstein, was particularly struck by him.

Hitler was a bit ill at ease when he first arrived at the Bechstein residence, a great monstrosity of a house built in the 1870s in the center of the city. The interior and furnishings were all very pretentious in the style of the Berlin *haute bourgeoisie*. Frau Bechstein, who was wearing diamonds as big as cherries strung around her neck and wrist, greeted Hitler with a friendly smile. A vivacious, self-confident woman, she was intrigued by his initial shyness and tired to draw him out. As soon as the conversation turned to politics Hitler warmed up and began to speak. Before the evening was over, he had found his first socially prominent supporter. With Frau Bechstein's patronage Hitler would eventually be accepted socially in the highest circles. More important, Helene Bechstein was soon to give him sizable contributions and urge her friends to do likewise.

Hitler returned to Munich on March 31, 1920. The next

day he finally decided to leave the army. He collected his back pay and signed out of the barracks for the last time. Actually, Hitler's action was of mutual benefit to both himself and the military. Because of his recent success, people were beginning to take an interest in him, and there was always a danger that he might be labeled an army puppet.

Henceforth, Hitler was on his own; he could now devote himself entirely to political work. He rented an apartment at No. 41 Thierschstrasse, near the Isar River. He spent most of his time at party headquarters, although he took no salary in order to avoid being listed as a party employee. What he lived on was a mystery, and his enemies within the party were soon to raise this question.[50]

Under closer scrutiny, however, the mystery disappears. Hitler was able to get along without a salary only because his lifestyle was so Spartan. His "apartment" would be described as dingy at best. He had one room and the use of an entrance hall. Hitler's room was tiny, hardly nine feet wide. His simple iron military bed was too wide for its corner and projected over the windowsill. The floor was covered with a cheap worn linoleum and two threadbare rugs. On the wall opposite the bed was a makeshift bookshelf that was weighted down with heavy volumes that seemed almost out of place in these extremely humble surroundings. The only pieces of furniture in the room, with the exception of the bed, were a chair and a heavy old table. The room would have been unbearably bleak if it had not been for Hitler's drawings and watercolors, a few of which were on each wall.[51]

Members of the party who had jobs often took turns inviting him to dinner. Later, when reminiscing with some of his comrades, Hitler said: "It's crazy what economies we had to make." Small stallkeepers at the market who were sympathizers of the party used to bring him a couple of eggs. In the autumn he lived on practically nothing but Tyrolean apples because they were so cheap during that season. Occasionally, he did make a little money speaking for a small fee at meetings of other patriotic groups. But even when he did get some money, he spent it only on the bare necessities for himself. "Every mark," he said, "was saved for the Party."[52]

It was not long before Hitler allowed himself one luxury— an automobile. There were very few cars in Munich at the time, but getting one was almost an obsession with him. Frequently he would be seen in the automobile showrooms around Munich looking at secondhand cars. He said that the party needed to buy an auto for him to get around to meetings more quickly. A car would also give him a head start on the Marxists, who still went on foot or by tram. He finally obtained an old vehicle that looked like a dismantled horsecab without a top; it was all that could be afforded at the moment. Within a short time, however, Hitler purchased a secondhand Selve with funds that one party member said "he had drummed up in a mysterious way from someone."[53] This car was not much better than the first; it was a rattling monster. Those who saw it said each end of the car looked as if it were going a different way at the same time. Nevertheless, Hitler thought that having an automobile conferred a certain dignity on him and the party, and never again was he seen taking a tram or bus.

On December 18, 1920, the National Socialist party took a step that marked its emergence from the circles of fringe movements into being a viable political force: it obtained its own newspaper, the *Völkischer Beobachter*. The paper did not have a very large circulation, and it was deep in debt. This was the first occasion Hitler received a donation of a large sum of money, part of it from General von Epp, a prominent Free Corps commander who had access to secret military funds, and the balance from several wealthy businessmen. The major stockholders of the *Völkischer Beobachter* had been members of the Thule Society, so the purchase of the paper indicated that the National Socialist Party was overtaking the Thule Society in importance.

A small announcement appeared in the *Völkischer Beo-*

bachter on Christmas Day stating that the Nazi party had taken over the paper at great sacrifice "in order to develop it into a relentless weapon for Germanism." The acquisition of a newspaper with a circulation of about seven thousand represented an enormous gain for a new party that hardly had one thousand members.[54]

According to Hitler's own account, not long after the party had acquired the *Völkischer Beobachter*, he was walking along a busy street in the center of Munich when he met Max Amann, who had been his regiment's sergeant-major in the army and whom he had not seen since the end of the war. Amann claimed he was not particularly interested in politics, but at Hitler's prompting he attended a Nazi meeting and soon afterward became a party member. He was a strong, active-looking little man with a heavy head set on a short neck that was almost invisible between his shoulders. His physical appearance gave no hint of Amann's intelligence. He was a former law student and after the war had obtained a good job in a mortgage bank.

Hitler proposed to Amann that he should give up his job and become the party's full-time business manager. According to Hitler, Amann at first thought to reject the offer. He had secure career prospects and a pension to look forward to at the bank, while employment by the little Nazi party would mean a substantial cut in salary and an uncertain future. Hitler exercised his powers of persuasion on him for two hours. "What good will your pension be if someday the Bolsheviks string you up from a lamppost?" Amann pondered for three days and then finally accepted the job.

Hitler made an excellent choice in Amann. Efficient, parsimonious, incorruptible, and without personal political ambition, Amann was exactly the right man for the job. He brought a commonsense business approach to party affairs. His motto was "Make propaganda pay its own way." Hitler later praised Amann in particular for his financial management of the party newspaper: "The fact that I was able to keep the *Völkischer Beobachter* on its feet throughout the period of our struggle—and in spite of the three failures it had suffered before I took it over—I owe first and foremost to . . . Amann. He, as an intelligent businessman, refused to accept responsibility for an enterprise if it did not possess the economic prerequisites of potential success.[55]

Max Amann was a member of the Thule Society.[56] Everyone who belonged to the society was aware of Hitler's activities, and it is hardly possible that Hitler would have failed to notice one of his old army comrades among the Thule members. Certainly it is not likely that Hitler's offer was made to Amann on the spur of the moment or that Amann had much difficulty deciding whether or not to accept it.

However, this is not to say that Amann was not an excellent business manager for Hitler. In fact, because of this Thule Society connection, he was able to obtain short-term credit for the party when no one else could have. In more than one instance Amann was able to get an extension on a debt when it meant the difference between survival or bankruptcy for the *Völkischer Beobachter*. With Amann as party business manager, and Dietrich Eckart as editor of the party newspaper, the Thule Society's involvement with the Nazis was stronger than ever. But since the basic ideology of the Thule Society and the Nazi party were the same, these men could be loyal Nazis as well as members of the society.

The membership of the National Socialist party had risen to three thousand by the summer of 1921. In July of that year, Hitler went to Berlin to spend six weeks conferring with north German right-wing leaders. He stayed in the plush Bechstein villa and took elocution lessons every afternoon from a dramatics instructor in order to remedy his Austrian dialect and strengthen his voice. He met the prominent nationalist leader Count Reventlow, and the Free Corps leader Walther Stennes (who was soon to join the Nazis).

Dr. Emil Gansser, a Nazi sympathizer with important connections and a friend of Dietrich Eckart, was of considerable help.[57] A former executive of an electrical company, Gansser was well educated and cut an imposing figure. He wore stiff white collars, starched shirts, and always dressed in a black coat and striped trousers. Gansser was able to arrange for Hitler to speak at the prestigious National Club of Berlin. The impression made upon his audience of Junkers, officers, and businessmen was generally a favorable one. Only a very few, however, were particularly impressed; but among them was Admiral Schroeder, the former commander of the German marine corps.

The next day Hitler was taken to the Officers Club. Here again, he met Schroeder who, Hitler said, "made the best impression on me."[58] At that time the radical Nazi program filled most respectable people with alarm. As Hitler himself admitted: "They were even terrified lest people should know they had even heard of it!" Conservatives were particularly frightened by Nazi demands for the nationalization of large businesses, the abolition of freedom of the press, and anti-Semitism. But, said Hitler, Admiral Schroeder "accepted the whole thing without further ado."[59] Schroeder became the first real Nazi supporter in top military circles. This was quite a triumph for Hitler. In a military-oriented society like Germany it meant considerable prestige for a small new party to have a high-ranking officer among its supporters. Moreover, the admiral was of great help in propagating Hitler's views among the Prussian upper class.

While Hitler was in Berlin conferring with Admiral Schroeder and getting promises of north German support, a factional revolt directed against him erupted within the party. Some of the original members of the executive committee, who were resentful of being disregarded while Hitler ran the party as he saw fit, circulated an anonymous leaflet against him. It called him a demagogue with a "lust for power" who was trying to mislead the German people and wreck the party. The leaflet also charged that there was something unsavory in the way he supported himself, since he never answered questions on this subject but only went "into a fit of rage and excitement." The rebels wanted to know where he got the money for his "excessive association with women." It was strongly implied that he was acting as a tool for obscure financial backers. Three thousand of these leaflets were circulated, and it was printed in two Munich newspapers.

Hitler returned from Berlin at once, promptly sued the newspapers, and submitted his resignation to the party, confident that it would be rejected. Without him the party would probably shrink back to the insignificant state it was in before he brought it publicity, members, and money. Moreover, he controlled the movement's newspaper, the *Völkischer Beobachter*, because his friend Eckart was the editor. In addition, all the important supporters of the movement, such as Ernst Roehm, were on his side. When Drexler and the committee realized Hitler had the upper hand and yielded, Hitler immediately revised the structure of the party along authoritarian lines. All provisions for majority rule and parliamentary process were disregarded. He became "First Chairman," or president, with almost absolute powers. Henceforth, his decisions would be acted upon without question.

2
BILLIONS

Early in 1923 Hitler was contacted by a man who offered to sell him an arsenal of weapons. Hitler thought the moment "opportune" for such a deal, so a meeting was arranged to take place in the little town of Dachau outside of Munich. Accompanied by one of his lieutenants Hitler went to the designated rendezvous. At first they thought they had fallen into a bandit's lair. Armed men asked them for a password and then led them into the presence of a woman with a short, mannish haircut. She was surrounded by a group of men who seemed to be mostly criminal types. Hitler later remarked that they all had the faces of "gallows birds."[1]

The bargaining began. Hitler warned the woman that he wouldn't hand over any money to her until the weapons were in his possession. Finally an agreement was reached. Then Hitler was taken to a deserted military airfield at Schleissheim where the weapons were stored. There were thousands of rifles, seventeen pieces of light field artillery of various calibers, and other assorted equipment like mess tins and haversacks. Hitler said that, after it had all been put into working order, "there would be enough to equip a regiment."[2]

As soon as the payment was made, the Nazis began to cart away the arms. Then Hitler went to see General von Lossow, the commander in chief of the army in Bavaria and turned the entire stockpile of weapons over to him. He asked the general to take care of the weapons and promised that the Nazis would make no use of them "except in the event of a show-down with Communism. It was thus solemnly agreed," said Hitler, "that the material would remain in the hands of the Reichswehr as long as this eventually did not arise."[3]

To have made such a purchase his funds must have been abundant indeed, for he always considered weapons of secondary importance to political propaganda. Obviously he was no longer an employee of the army, but rather he was dealing with General von Lossow as an equal. In order to purchase a stockpile of weapons and be able to negotiate a deal with the commanding general of the army in Bavaria, Hitler must have had the backing and support of powerful, wealthy men. Who were they?

After he had acquired his own party newspaper, the *Völkischer Beobachter*, Hitler intensified his recruiting drive. The times were ideal for such a campaign. There were violent strikes, Communist uprisings, and general disorder throughout the country. The rate of unemployment remained high and wages were low. Many former soldiers were still unable to find jobs and fit themselves into an orderly civilian society.

The German economy labored under the weight of the reparations payments, which the Treaty of Versailles required Germany to make to the victorious powers. The impoverished country found it impossible to meet these large payments, since the Versailles Treaty also blocked Germany out of most export markets.[4] In addition to the international problems, inflation was already under way. The German mark, normally valued at four to the U.S. dollar, had begun to fall; by the summer of 1921 it had dropped to seventy-five to the dollar. Personal lifetime savings were rapidly becoming valueless. Fixed incomes no longer sufficed to pay for vital necessities. Many small businesses were going bankrupt. The middle class was desperate.

As Hitler's following increased, the Marxist parties became alarmed. They warned the workers to stay away from Nazi public meetings. However, Hitler's ranting denunciations of the Versailles Treaty, inflation, and Germany's humiliation by the Allies were too compelling to miss hearing. So workers, artisans, shopkeepers, and the unemployed came to hear him in spite of all the threats and warnings. Violence erupted at Hitler's meetings. He organized Nazi "defense squads" to silence hecklers and beat up disrupters. It was not long before Nazis and Communists were fighting in the streets. Important rightist leaders watched this developing struggle carefully. Hitler's party looked like the only nationalist movement capable of winning over the lower classes. If it could hold its own against the Communists, it would prove itself a party worthy of considerable financial support.

The Nazi party's "defense squads" were a poorly disciplined group of volunteer brawlers until they were reorganized in the summer of 1921 under the camouflage name "Gymnastic and Sports division." On October 5, 1921, they were officially named the *Sturmabteilung* (storm troopers), from which the title S.A. came. The S.A. uniform, the brown shirt, was somewhat accidental; it originated when the party was able to purchase cheaply a surplus lot of khaki army shirts once intended to have been worn in Africa. The structure of the S.A. was based on the tradition of the Free Corps units of ex-servicemen that in the years after 1918 had joined together to put down the Communist revolution. But beyond a general dislike for revolutionaries, the Free Corps were vague in their political objectives, whereas the S.A. were followers of Hitler's anti-Semitic ideology.

Naturally, equipping and arming a paramilitary unit like

the S.A. cost a great deal of money. Since many of the members were unemployed, they often had to be provided with food and shelter as well. Uniforms, flags, and above all weapons had to be purchased. Rent had to be paid for meeting halls and headquarters. There were transportation costs whenever the S.A. units traveled as a group. The party itself could not supply such funds because it needed every available pfennig for its own upkeep and propaganda costs. Who then financed the S.A.?

One of the principal sources of money and equipment for the S.A. was the secret paramilitary funds originally set up to finance Free Corps units. However, up to now historians have incorrectly assumed that assistance was given to Hitler with the approval of the High Command of the Bavarian Army.[5] Actually most of the aid was given to Hitler on the initiative of one officer, Captain Ernst Roehm, without the knowledge or approval of his superiors.

The year 1922 saw the German mark fall to four hundred to the U.S. dollar; the runaway inflation was beginning. Every day meant an increase in prices. Resentment against the government spread. The discontented middle class began to swell the ranks of Hitler's movement. As the German economic situation grew worse, the financial position of the National Socialist party grew stronger. More party members meant more dues, and bigger audiences at meetings meant a larger sum when the hat was passed. In November of 1921 the party had moved into a new and larger headquarters, and by April of the following year it already had thirteen full-time salaried employees. A central archive and filing system was developed under the direction of the party "business manager" Max Amann.

On the evening of November 22, 1922, a Harvard graduate, Ernst (Putzi) Hanfstaengl, whose mother was American and whose cultivated, wealthy family owned an art publishing business in Munich, attended one of Hitler's speeches on the advice of Captain Truman Smith, the assistant military attaché of the Untied States.[6] Opposed to communism and appalled by Germany's present weakness, Hanfstaengl was captivated by Hitler's oratory. A few days later he joined the party. The six-foot-four-inch Hanfstaengl, whose nickname Putzi ironically meant "little fellow" in Bavarian dialect, shared Hitler's interest in art and music and became his frequent companion.

One night as they were walking home together from a café after several hours of discussion with devoted party followers, Hitler turned to Hanfstaengl and said: "You must not feel disappointed if I limit myself in these evening talks to comparatively simple subjects. Political agitation must be primitive. That is the trouble with all the other [non-Marxist] parties. They have become . . . too academic. The ordinary man in the street cannot follow and, sooner or later, falls a victim to the slap-bang methods of Communist propaganda."[7]

Agreeing wholeheartedly, Hanfstaengl told Hitler that one of the things that gave him the most confidence in the party's eventual success was his (Hitler's) ability to speak in everyday language with "real punch" behind his words. Hanfstaengl went on to say that in some ways Hitler reminded him of the American President Theodore Roosevelt who had a vigor and courage, a vitality and familiarity with all kinds of people, and a direct style of action and speaking that endeared him to the average citizen.[8]

"You are absolutely right," Hitler replied. "But how can I hammer my ideas into the Germany people without a press? The newspapers ignore me utterly. How can I follow up my successes as a speaker with our miserable four-page *Völkischer Beobachter* once a week? We'll get nowhere until it appears as a daily."[9] Hitler then told of the great plans he had for the party newspaper if only he could find the funds.

"It must have been that evening," Hanfstaengl later wrote, "that I decided to render more substantial help."[10] About this time Hanfstaengl received partial payment for his share of the family art gallery in New York, which had been closed during the war. The money came to only $1,500, but that represented an absolute fortune when converted into depreciated marks. There were two American rotary presses for sale; if their purchase could be financed, it would mean that the Nazi party newspaper could come out as a daily in a full-size format.

"I learned," said Hanfstaengl, "that a thousand of my dollars would make up the required sum, incredible as it may seem, and one morning I went down and handed it over to Amann in greenbacks, on the understanding that it was an interest-free loan. He and Hitler were beside themselves."[11]

"Such generosity," Hitler exclaimed. "Hanfstaengl, we shall never forget this. Wonderful!"[12] Hanfstaengl was rather pleased with himself. His loan, however, was not made simply from altruistic reasons, as he pretended in his autobiography; actually he hoped to increase his own influence over the newspaper and guide it in more conservative direction.[13]

From Hitler's own style of living there was little indication that the party was growing and finding new sources of financial support. The life of the Nazi party's leader was not that of a dashing mercenary captain with plenty of champagne, caviar, and beautiful women. So, for the present, Hitler continued to wear the same old trench coat and cheap blue suit. Every night after his work was finished, he went back to the same dingy one-room apartment. The only sign of his growing importance as a political figure was that he was now accompanied everywhere by a bodyguard, a tough beer hall fighter named Ulrich Graf.

Putzi Hanfstaengl's comfortable and cultivated upper-class home was the first house of its kind in Munich to open its doors to Hitler. He seemed to feel at ease with Hanfstaengl's pretty wife and children. Putzi could play Wagner beautifully, and Hitler, who loved music, considered Wagner his favorite composer. After a while Hanfstaengl made himself a sort of social secretary to Hitler, zealously introducing him to Munich hostesses. Hitler still had an air of shyness in the presence of those of wealth and social position, yet his naïveté in social matters tempted hostesses to invite him.

Frequently he would sit in silence until the topic of politics was introduced and then dominate the conversation. However, it is a mistake to think he was so rude as to shout down the other guests or shock them with his most extreme opinions. In many instances, even though people disagreed with his anti-Semitic views, they would find themselves "amused" by his "quite witty" criticisms of the Jews.[14] He always made a point of leaving a party before the company broke up, so that the other guests would be left behind to talk about him and thus deepen their own impression.

Increasing numbers of people were turning away from the traditional political parties, which seemed unable to solve the mounting crisis. In January 1923, on the pretext that the Germans were 100,000 telegraph poles short in reparations deliveries, the French Army occupied the Ruhr. With only the small army permitted by the Versailles Treaty, Germany was incapable of defending itself, so the government ordered a campaign of "passive resistance." This involved the shutting down of all factories in the Ruhr, Germany's most highly industrialized region. During a dispute at the Krupp factory in Essen, the French opened fire on the workers with machine guns, killing thirteen men.

Along with the French occupation of the Ruhr came the total collapse of the Germany currency. The government had to pour financial support into the Ruhr for the hundreds of thousands whom passive resistance had put out of work; in order to meet this enormous obligation, more money was printed. First prices doubled, then tripled. The government told the people that inflation was an economic process over which no one had any control. In reality, however, inflation was the method chosen by the German government to push off the burden onto the middle class.

When prices doubled because more currency was being circulated, the real value of savings accounts, pensions, and bonds were cut in half, but few people realized it at the time. Financing the passive resistance in the Ruhr provided the government with the excuse it needed to begin the runaway inflation. The mark fell to ten thousand to the dollar and then to fifty thousand. Prices began to rise daily and then twice a day.

The hardest hit were the good, solid middle-class citizens who had saved for the future and suddenly saw all they had worked for wiped out overnight. Bills of increasingly higher denomination were printed. Factories began paying twice a week because the value of the money diminished so much from Monday to Saturday. On paydays the wives of the workers waited outside the factory gates. As soon as the men were paid, they rushed out and gave the money to the women, who hurried off to the nearest store to buy things before the value of the money went down further. But at least the pay of industrial workers, most of whom belonged to unions, was adjusted somewhat to the declining value of the mark. The middle class was harder hit. More than a few professional men found it impossible to support themselves on incomes eroded by inflation. They were forced to take jobs at night as cab drivers and waiters in order to survive.

Many people driven to the wall by inflation put their property up for sale at a stated price according to the value of the mark at the time. But when the legal formalities were completed and the deal closed, the worth of the mark had further deteriorated to the point where the purchaser acquired a home worth $20,000 for the equivalent of $1,000. Financiers and large companies with unlimited credit took advantage of those conditions to accumulate vast holdings at very little cost.[15] A small factory might be purchased for fifty million marks on a six months' basis. When the six months had elapsed and it was time to pay, the fifty million marks was hardly enough to buy an automobile. Big business found the inflation extremely profitable; mortgages were paid off, bonds retired, and debts wiped out with inflated marks worth only a fraction of their former real value.

"Believe me, our misery will increase," Hitler warned the

people. "The scoundrel will get by. But the decent, solid businessman who doesn't speculate will be completely crushed; first the little fellow on the bottom, but in the end the big fellow on top too. But the scoundrel and the swindler will remain, top and bottom. The reason: because the state itself has become the biggest swindler and crook. A robbers' state!"

"You have defrauded us, you rogues and swindlers," he shouted against the government. "We don't care a fig for your paper money. Give us something of value—gold!" And then Hitler told his audience that although they had thousands and even millions of marks in their pockets they would soon be starving, because the farmer would stop selling his produce. "When you offer him your million [marks] scraps of paper with which he will only be able to cover the walls of his out-house, can you wonder that he will say, 'Keep your millions and I will keep my corn and my butter.' "[16]

Hitler was one of the few politicians who correctly assessed inflation as a deliberate campaign to defraud the middle class of their savings. Representatives of the established political parties were always telling the people no one had any control over inflation, but to have confidence and the mark would not fall any lower. When Hitler's predictions about inflation began to come true, his speeches attracted bigger and bigger audiences. Because he exposed this one fraud, many people thought he was a man of honesty and sincerity. Since savings had never meant anything to him personally, he was probably just using inflation as an issue to win popularity. Nevertheless, as the value of the mark went down, the membership in the National Socialist party went up.

Almost nothing is known about the man who was the most important fund-raiser for the Nazi party during the period of inflation—Max Erwin von Scheubner-Richter.

44

There is confusion about his background, his profession, and his activities during World War I.[17] Even during his life, Scheubner-Richter was always a man of mystery. He took great pains never to appear in the limelight and always shrouded his activities in secret. Yet there is no doubt about his importance. According to a note in an official file, he succeeded in raising "enormous sums of money" for the Nazi party.[18] By 1923 his influence over Hitler was considerable, and the party was dependent on him for most of its contacts in high society.

Scheubner-Richter was a genius at procuring funds even during this time of economic crisis when money was not easy to come by in Germany. He approached Bavarian aristocrats, big businessmen, bankers, and leaders of heavy industry. Unlike other members of the Nazi party, Scheubner-Richter was a wealthy man in his own right, and since he did not ask for money for himself but for what he thought was a worthy political cause, he did it with perfect ease and notable success. Scheubner-Richter was also a close personal friend of General Ludendorff, who had been the quartermaster general of the German Army during World War I. On several occasions the general channeled money to Scheubner-Richter from industrialists.

Much of Scheubner-Richter's time and energy was spent working with the White Russian emigrés. He received large contributions from Russian industrialists, especially the oil men who had been able to transfer some part of their fortunes to Germany. Along with Scheubner-Richter's activities came an increasingly close cooperation between the right-wing Russian emigrés and the Nazis. Each group saw the other not only as an anti-Communist, anti-Semitic ideological companion but as a source of money. The Whites still hoped to be able to reconquer Russian if only they could get German help. Apparently they contributed to the Nazi party, a rapidly growing anti-Bolshevik mass movement, because Scheubner-Richter convinced them that Hitler's movement would soon have a great influence on the German government and would see that they got the necessary funds and equipment to march east.

In 1921 there were good reasons why the White emigrés refused to accept their defeat and exile as final. Millions of people were starving in Russia, industry was at a standstill, and chaos reigned through the countryside.[19] It was possible that the Soviet government might be overthrown from within, or collapse as a result of its own incapacity.

One of the most important right-wing Russians to give his unqualified support to Hitler was General Vasili Biskupsky. Not only did he play a leading part in emigré politics, but he also acted as a intermediary between Hitler and various financial backers, some of them beyond the White Russian circle. A handsome, dashing man, Biskupsky had the reputation of being an able officer and an even better gambler. When the revolution broke out, he was one of the youngest generals in the Russian Army, in command of the Third Corps in Odessa. After the evacuation of the Ukraine by the White forces, he made his way to Berlin.

In 1922 Biskupsky declared his support for Grand Duke Cyril, Romanov pretender to the Russian throne, and was appointed as Cyril's "prime minister." It was in this capacity that Biskupsky performed his greatest service for the Nazi movement. Grand Duke Cyril was a first cousin to Czar Nicholas II and therefore a rightful heir to the crown. There were, however, many monarchists who did not recognize Cyril, and bitter debates took place between his supporters and those of Grand Duke Nikolai Nikolaevich in Paris. General Biskupsky argued that Cyril's enemies were suspected of democratic and constitutional leanings and were puppets of the French.

A rather unassuming man, Cyril had served without notable distinction in the Russian Navy during the war, gone to Finland with his family after the revolution, then to Switzerland, and, in 1921, to the south of France, where they held court at the Château Fabron. Although their marital relationship was not a happy one, Cyril's strong-willed wife, Grand Duchess Victoria,* was nevertheless his closest political confidante and probably the real driving force behind his claim to the imperial throne. In 1922 Cyril and his wife moved to Coburg, Germany, where Victoria's family had its possessions. Here they lived in seclusion in the palatial Villa Edinburgh.

At Coburg, the Grand Duke Cyril, who was very handsome and somewhat of a playboy, indulged his passions for hunting, motor cars, beautiful women, and political intrigue. Cyril often left important decisions to his wife, and in fact, Victoria managed to obtain from abroad some of the funds needed for her husband's political activities; but she also collected for the Nazi party. It is said that she was even more active in her support of the National Socialists than her husband. Scheubner-Richter and his wife became close personal friends of the grand duke and duchess; and the Grand Duchess Victoria and Scheubner-Richter's wife, Mathilde, would often watch the S.A. drill in a Munich suburb and attend Nazi meetings and parades together.[20] Attracted to the Nazis' anti-communism and anti-Semitism, Victoria soon contributed some of her valuables to them.[21]

Once Hitler's cause was taken up by Russian grand dukes, counts, and generals, he automatically became more acceptable in the eyes of the upper class Germans. When Frau Bechstein came to Munich, she and her husband invited Hitler to dinner in their luxurious hotel suite. Frau Bechstein was dressed in a long, formal evening gown and covered with jewels; her husband wore a dinner jacket. "I felt quite embarrassed in my blue suit," Hitler later told a friend. "The servants were all in livery and we drank nothing but champagne before the meal."[22] That evening Frau Bechstein convinced Hitler that he was now important enough to acquire a dinner jacket, starched shirts, and patent leather shoes.

---

*Grand Duchess Victoria was the granddaughter of Queen Victoria of England and the sister of Queen Marie of Romania.

A domineering and possessive woman, Frau Bechstein thought she could tell the shy, retiring Hitler how to dress, behave, and even how to conduct his political affairs. But she, like so many women after her, made the mistake of underestimating his determination and independence. He would sit alone with her for hours explaining his political ideas. In return for her generous donations he was even willing to let her call him "my little wolf." However, the rumors that there was a clandestine romance between them are probably false. Frau Bechstein was considerably older than Hitler, and she was satisfied as long as he smiled at her, kissed her hand, and complimented her on her appearance.

In society Hitler's behavior was somewhat awkward but not unpleasant. Contrary to the stories printed in several Munich newspapers, Hitler did not throw fits in private or have the manners of a gangster. Many people, especially women, were charmed by him. Usually he would present his hostess with an extravagantly large bouquet of roses, and bow to kiss her hand in the dramatic old Viennese fashion. He was careful never to sit down before they were seated. Even his voice changed when speaking with women; its often harsh, guttural tone then assumed a certain melodious quality. He spoke to them with the accent, vocabulary, and warmth that characterized many Austrians. When talking to a woman he was able to give her the impression that he was totally interested in her and her alone. Finding themselves confronted by such a charmer instead of by the crude character they had expected, most women were overcome by speechless amazement and intense delight. "I felt myself melt in his presence," said one wealthy lady. "I would have done anything for him," affirmed another who knew him well.

Frau Elsa Bruckmann, the wife of the well-known publisher Hugo Bruckmann, was also one of Hitler's early supporters. Her husband had a great deal of influence in right-wing circles and published the books of Houston Stewart Chamberlain, one of the most popular nationalist authors at the time. Frau

Bruckmann, who was born Princess Cantacuzene of Romania, had a great deal of money and said she made it her mission in life to introduce Hitler to leading industrialists. In return, however, she was very demanding of his attention. Years later, in commenting on the strange effect he had on women, Hitler said: "One day I detected an unexpected reaction even in Frau Bruckmann. She had invited to her house, at the same time as myself, a very pretty woman of Munich society. As we were taking our leave, Frau Bruckmann perceived in her female guest's manner a sign of interest [in me]. . . . The consequence was that she never again invited us both at once. As I've said, the woman was beautiful, and perhaps she felt some interest in me—nothing more."[23]

Frau Winifred Wagner, the English-born wife of Siegfried Wagner, Richard Wagner's son, was one of the first few hundred to join the Nazi party.[24] She became one of Hitler's personal friends and a contributor to his cause. Moreover, she used the influence of her name wherever possible to help get money for the party.

On April 3, 1923, the *Munich Post* carried a story about women who were "infatuated with Hitler" and lent or gave him money. In many instances their contributions did not take the form of cash; instead, wealthy patrons presented him with valuable objets d'art and jewelry to dispose of as he saw fit. Frau Helene Bechstein stated that in addition to the regular financial support given by her husband to the leader of the National Socialist Party, she herself had made sizeable contributions, "not, however, in the form of money, but rather of a few objets d'art which I told him he could sell or do anything he liked with. The objets d'art in question were all of the more valuable sort."[25]

Usually Hitler would raise loans on the valuables presented to him by his admirers and spend the money to support his Munich headquarters. He preferred to borrow money on the valuables rather than sell them because of the length of time involved in selling antiques for a fair market value. A loan and transfer agreement concluded between Hitler and a merchant, in the summer of 1923, provides an example of the type of valuables in question: "As security for the loan (of 60,000 Swiss francs) Herr Adolf Hitler will turn over . . . the undermentioned property . . . A platinum ring set with a sapphire and diamonds . . . A diamond ring (solitaire), a 14-karat gold ring with diamonds set in silver . . . . A piece of *grosspointe de Venise*, a hand-stitched, six and a half meters long and eleven and a half centimeters wide (seventeenth century) . . . A Spanish red silk piano runner with gold embroidery."[26]

At first Hitler had considerable respect for the upper-class people he met in soliciting contributions. Germany was the most class-conscious country in Western Europe, and being from lower-middle-class origins himself, Hitler was careful to address aristocrats and officers with all ceremonial politeness. In high society his naïveté was an asset as well as a drawback. "I can still see Frau Bruckmann's eyes shining," wrote one of Hitler's lieutenants, Kurt Lüdecke, "as she described Hitler's truly touching dismay before an artichoke. 'But madam,' he had said in his softest voice, 'you must tell me how to eat this thing. I never saw one before.' "[27]

In the fall of 1922 an abrupt change in Hitler's attitude toward the upper class took place. A group of right-wing Bavarian parties and Free Corps units called the Fatherland Societies, to which the Nazis belonged, planned a putsch to take over the government. The head of the organization was a Dr. Pittinger, who was commander of one of the largest Free Corps units, the *Bund Bayern und Reich*. But when the moment for the coup finally came and the Nazis and the Free Corps troops were ready to strike, Dr. Pittinger and his staff of officers and aristocrats got cold feet.

Hitler and his men were left in the lurch. He was furious: "No more Pittingers, no more Fatherland Societies!" he shouted. "These *gentlemen*—these counts and generals—they won't do anything. I shall. I *alone*."[28] Up to this time Hitler had thought of himself simply as a sort of drummer or propagandist of the coming German reawakening that would be led by some nationalist general. But on that day of betrayal and disappointment in 1922, he began to think of himself as the "Fuehrer" [the leader]. The disgraceful failure of the Pittinger putsch, said Kurt Lüdecke, "also altered his inner regard for the 'great' people toward whom he had previously shown a certain deference and humility. But his demeanor did not change. He had found it worked to be naive and simple in a salon, to assume shyness. It was a useful pose, but now it covered scorn. 'These important people—who were they? Mediocrities! Cowards!' "[29]

If Hitler was ready to lead, the time was certainly ripe. By 1923 runaway inflation was leaving distress and chaos in its wake. Workers were making millions of marks a week and had to carry their salaries home in bags. But the price of food was rising faster than wages, and people were beginning to go hungry. A middle-class professional man or doctor who thought he had a small fortune in the bank would receive a polite letter from the directors: "The bank deeply regrets that it can no longer administer your deposit of sixty-eight thousand marks since the costs are out of all proportion to the capital. We are, therefore, taking the liberty of returning your capital. Since we have no bank-notes in small enough denominations at our disposal, we have rounded out the sum to one million marks. Enclosure: one 1,000,000 mark bill."[30] On the outside of the envelope there was a canceled stamp for five million marks.

The savings of the middle class melted to nothing; the money they had invested before the war in bonds of the government, the German states, and the municipalities were also lost. Financially the middle class was wiped out. The day that Hitler had foretold was coming to pass; the paper money was almost totally worthless now. More than three paper mills and over two thousand printing presses were operating on a twenty-four-hour basis just to supply paper money, most of which had printing only on one side. The banks were actually using the blank side of the money for scratch paper because it was cheaper than purchasing scratch pads for the purpose. A woman who took a wicker basket full of marks to the vegetable stand to buy a few potatoes sat the basket down and turned her back for a few moments while standing in line; when she turned around again, the marks had been dumped on the sidewalk and the basket stolen.

Speaking about the inflation, Hitler described a process of destruction that had already been felt by many of those in his audience. "The government," he said "calmly goes on printing these scraps, because if it stopped, that would mean the end of the government. Because once the printing presses stopped—and that is the prerequisite for the stabilization of the mark—the swindle would at once be brought to light. For then the worker would realize that he is only making a third of what he made in peacetime, because two-thirds of his labor go for tribute to the enemy."[31]

Foreign observers were shocked when Hitler shouted from the speaker's platform that the Treaty of Versailles was only "a piece of paper." But those words were not so shocking to millions of Germans who had seen their money, their savings, and their contracts become nothing more than that. With his instinct for emotional reactions, Hitler knew his words would fill them with rage. He had chosen his expression very carefully.

The runaway inflation destroyed the people's confidence in the government. The Communist party began to grow stronger; within a short time they had taken over power in the states of Saxony and Thuringia. The frightened upper class suddenly became more receptive to Hitler's pleas for money. He made several trips to Berlin to solicit contributions, and in Munich he frequently made the rounds of prominent conservative citizens.

Hanfstaengl, who was in a fairly good position to know about the party revenues during this period, wrote:

The party was permanently short of funds. In fact the conversion of the *Beobachter* into a daily, for all its propaganda value, had only made the financial situation worse in other respects, and Hitler was always on the lookout for other sources to tap. He seemed to think that I would be useful with my connections, but however interested and encouraging my friends were, they did not choose to dip into their pockets. . . . Some of the national-minded Bavarian industrialists were doubtlessly prodded into giving a check from time to time, but it was all hand to mouth stuff and there were always debts demanding payment and nothing to meet them with.[32]

Financial worries increased as the party grew larger. The initial one thousand dollars that Hanfstaengl had supplied to Hitler for the *Völkischer Beobachter* was an interest-free loan, not a gift.[33] Hitler had been obliged to pledge the entire plant of the *Völkischer Beobachter*—presses, office equipment, etc.—as security for the loan. The money was to be repaid on May 1, 1923, but of course Hitler was unable to do so. Hanfstaengl had little choice but to give him an extension until January 1, 1924. However, Putzl himself became in need of money, so he sold the claim against the paper to Christian Weber, a horse dealer and Nazi party member.

Weber was a big, rough man of enormous girth who liked plenty of good food, wine, and women. He had somewhat of an unsavory reputation. It was incorrectly reported that he had worked as a bouncer at a notorious Munich dive. The exact source of Weber's money is not clear, but only a small part of it could have come from buying and selling horses. Weber pressed Hitler to repay the money with all the tricks of a professional loan shark. He had the party automobiles mortgaged in his favor and, as one Nazi said, behaved "worse than a Jew." Such business worries were a continual irritation to Hitler, who remarked that he hoped to high heaven that the party would one day be put on "a sound footing."

Those who had access to stable foreign currency could acquire staggering sums of German money for very little and consequently live like royalty. Ernest Hemingway, who was then a reporter in Europe, wrote of spending four days at a deluxe German resort hotel with a party of four. The bill, including tips, came to millions of marks—or twenty cents a day in American money. Germany was invaded by a host of inflation profiteers. Swiss, Dutch, Czech, Italian, and Austrian money circulated freely and possessed a high purchasing power when converted to inflation marks. Hitler, by obtaining these currencies, found an excellent way to help keep the party financially afloat during this period. Comparatively small donations from sympathizers and Germans in other countries instantly became sums of importance when the stable foreign currencies were brought into inflation-torn Germany.

Switzerland was an excellent source of funds, and the Nazis played on every possible appeal to get a few Swiss francs; anti-communism; the affinity of German-speaking cultures; anti-Semitism, etc. Hitler himself went on several fund-raising tours in Switzerland. On one occasion in Zurich in 1923 he was feted at a dinner that had over twelve courses. He returned from the trip "with a steamer trunk stuffed with Swiss francs and American dollars."

Frequently Hitler spoke to German nationalist groups in Czechoslovakia and Austria. Though he received only a speaker's fee and a few small contributions, this money was worth a great deal back in Munich. When the *Völkischer Beobachter* became a daily newspaper in 1923 and moved into new and larger offices, Hitler, accompanied by Max Amann, went to buy office furniture. The clerk stared wide-eyed when Hitler, ready to pay, pulled out his wallet, which was stuffed full of Czech money. Hitler noticed this. The socialists, he said, "are always wanting to know where we get our money from. You see where it comes from: the Germans in other countries all over the world send us foreign currency because they begin to cherish hopes for Germany again, since we appeared on the scene."[34]

When Hitler was going on one of his fund-raising tours

of Switzerland, Prince Ahrenberg insisted on personally driving him part of the way. The prince, said Hitler, was "one of our earliest adherents."[35] Ahrenberg drove what Hitler said was one of the oldest Benz cars he had ever seen: "On the level the old car ran reasonably well; but at the slightest sign of a hill it blew its head off, and we were in grave danger of sticking fast. He had to change gear all the time, and so we trundled along hour after hour. At last we came to the downhill part of the journey, and there the car flew along at at least thirty miles an hour!"[36] Hitler could never quite understand why the prince did not buy a new automobile for he knew him to be a "multimillionaire."

The two men became close personal friends. It was from Ahrenberg, who had been in Africa before the war, that Hitler formed his impression of what colonial policy should be. The prince, said Hitler, "told me many interesting tales of pioneering days in our colonies. He was once sentenced to twelve years of penal servitude—and served six of them—for having killed a nigger who had attacked him!"[37] Hitler felt that Germany would have had greater success with her colonies if she had followed a strict racist policy like Britain.

By mid-1923 German economic life was grinding to a standstill, and many people were reverting to barter. Suicides were common among the middle class. Farmers were now refusing to sell their produce for the inflated paper money, as Hitler had predicted. Those who lived in cities were going hungry. The signs of malnutrition began to appear; increasing cases of scurvy were reported. Mothers who could no longer feed their babies brought them to charitable institutions frequently wrapped, not in diapers, but in paper. There were widespread strikes and riots under Communist leadership in many industrial cities. But most dangerous of all was that the Communists, who had gained control of the state governments in Saxony and Thuringia, were planning to launch a nationwide revolution from these bases.

The country, cried Hitler, "is on the brink of a hellish abyss." He alternately wept with the people in their despair and chided them for accepting it so passively. "The people are like a lot of children. You can only press million-mark notes into the hands of a childish public!" The size of the Nazi party was multiplying so rapidly it was difficult to determine the exact extent of the membership. In the fall of 1922, it was a little over 10,000; less than a year later estimates ran between 35,000 and 200,000, with sympathizers of at least ten times this number. If elections had been held at that time, the National Socialists would probably have been the second strongest party in Bavaria. It was even said that a majority of the Munich police were Nazi supporters, which is not too surprising considering that the head of the police, Dr. Ernst Pohner, was a member of the Thule Society.

In the fall of 1922, Hitler found the ideal commander for his 15,000 man S.A. unit, Hermann Goering. During the war Goering had been a fighter ace in the Richthofen Squadron and won the *Pour le Merite* (Blue Max), Germany's highest decoration. Before the war was over, he succeeded his famous commander, Baron von Richthofen (the Red Baron), and was himself appointed commander of the Richthofen Squadron.

Germany's defeat left Goering disillusioned. One evening in November of 1922 he attended one of Hitler's speeches and was almost instantly converted. The next day Goering sought out Hitler to volunteer his services for the Nazi party. The two men talked together for some time. "We spoke at once about the things which were close to our hearts—the defeat of our Fatherland, the inequities of the Versailles Treaty," Goering said later. "I told him that I myself to the fullest extent, and all that I . . . possessed, were completely at his disposal."[38]

Hitler was overjoyed with his new recruit. Goering was a great war hero, and that would bring considerable prestige to the party. He was also from an aristocratic background and was a personal friend of high-ranking officers, counts, and even princes. When one party official asked about the new recruit, Hitler replied, "Goering!" laughing and slapping his knee with satisfaction. "Splendid, a war ace with the *Pour le Merite*—imagine it! Excellent propaganda! Moreover, he has money and doesn't cost me a cent."[39]

Though Goering came from a wealthy family, Germany's defeat and the inflation had left him virtually penniless. He was, however, living comfortably on the money of his wife, former Swedish countess Carin von Kantzow, who turned out to be of great prestige value to the party. The presence of this beautiful, aristocratic lady at Nazi rallies and storm trooper parades made a good number of wealthy people reexamine their first impression of the Nazi party. If such a dignified, noble woman is a supporter of Hitler, perhaps he isn't a danger to respectable people after all, they said to themselves.

The Goerings' villa in Obermenzing, a suburb of Munich, became a gathering place for the leaders of the National Socialist party. Hitler, who liked pretty women, was charmed by Carin Goering. She in return embraced the Nazi cause with all the fervor of her emotional temperament.

There is no evidence in her letters to her relatives in Sweden that she had any objections about Hitler or the other Nazi guests in her home.[40] When her sister, the Countess von Wilamowitz-Moellendorff came for a visit, she described the atmosphere of the villa:

On the ground floor was a large attractive smoking room, with an alcove lit from outside by a bull's-eye window. A few steps down from it was a wine cellar with an open fire, wooden stools and a great sofa. Here came together all those who had dedicated themselves to Hitler. . . . late in the evening Hitler would arrive and you would see around him all the early devotees of the Party, Dietrich Eckart, Hermann Esser, Hanfstaengl, etc. After the earnest conferring would come the warm, cheerful hours which filled Carin with so much joy. Hitler's sense of humor showed itself in gay stories, observations, and witticisms and Carin's spontaneous and wholehearted reaction to them made her a delightful audience.[41]

Among the other visitors to the Goering villa was a man of the greatest importance, General Erich Ludendorff. Goering and his charming wife played a key role in getting the general to back Hitler. It is impossible to overestimate the prestige of Ludendorff's name in nationalist circles at the time. During the war he had been the quartermaster general of the German Army with the virtual power of dictatorship over the country. Although he no longer held any official military post, Free Corps leaders and representatives of many rightist groups came to him for advice and guidance. Initially, Count Reventlow, a well-known nationalist leader and editor of an anti-Semitic weekly, had presented Hitler to Ludendorff and recommended that the general support this rising tribune of the masses. The political ideas of the general and ex-corporal were alike in many respects; they were both nationalists and anti-Communists, they were against the Versailles Treaty, the Jews, and the Bavarian separatists. At a "German Day" rally in Nuremberg on September 1 and 2, 1923, before almost 100,000 people, Ludendorff announced his support of Hitler's party.

General Ludendorff himself had little money, but many prominent, wealthy men looked upon him as Germany's senior military officer and consequently the true leader of all nationalist forces. There were industrialists and businessmen who wanted to support the anti-Communist forces but knew very little about politics and still less about the strengths and weaknesses of the numerous right-wing groups; consequently, they gave their money to Ludendorff, a man whose honesty they could trust and whose judgment they relied on, telling him to divide it among the nationalist forces as he saw fit.[42] By 1923 a considerable portion of this money was finding its way to Hitler.

In the fall of 1923 Fritz Thyssen, heir of the Thyssen steel empire and chairman of the board of the United Steel Works

(Vereinigte Stahlwerke), the greatest German steel combine, attended one of Hitler's rallies. Thyssen, a man with strong right-wing sympathies, was impressed. "I realized his oratorical gifts and his ability to lead the masses," Thyssen said. "What impressed me most was . . . the almost military discipline of his followers."[43] The revolutionary uprisings of 1918–1919 had thoroughly terrified Thyssen. For a few frightening days he was in the custody of the revolutionaries; and even after the "Red terror" was crushed, he had no faith in the institutions of the Weimar Republic to maintain "law and order." "The impression which those agitated days left upon me has never been blotted out," Thyssen recalled. "During an entire year, 1918–1919, I felt that Germany was going to sink into an anarchy."[44]

In 1923, Germany was once again in a state of extreme political tension. Economic difficulties caused by inflation and political strife produced problems in industry that bordered on class warfare. The result was increasing social distance between the classes that hardened to open "class hostility." Most of Germany's great industrialists, Thyssen among them, realized that if economic conditions were not improved soon and class antagonism smothered, they would find themselves engulfed by the tide of a Communist revolution. In such a turbulent atmosphere, a charismatic nationalist leader like Hitler seemed like the man of the hour. "We were at the worst time of the inflation [October 1923]," said Thyssen. "The money . . . sank in value from one day to the next. In Berlin the government was in distress. . . . Authority was crumbling. In Saxony a Communist government had been formed. . . . Amidst all this chaos . . . my first meeting with Hitler took place."[45]

However, Thyssen's support or even sympathy for Hitler at this time should not be overrated. Later in October, during a visit to the home of General Ludendorff, Thyssen gave 100,000 gold marks* to the general to distribute between the

---

*These were not inflated paper notes, but mark gold coins worth about $250,000 in today's money.

Nazi party and the Free Corps Oberland. Although this sum amounted to a fortune in the inflation-torn country, the fact that the money was to be divided between the National Socialist party and the Free Corps Oberland indicates that even Thyssen was supporting Hitler only as one among many nationalist forces.[46]

By November 1923 inflation reached nightmare proportions. The mark soared to astronomical figures: a dollar was officially worth five trillion marks, unofficially seven trillion. Banks could no longer afford to count million-mark notes; they were simply weighed in bundles or measured with a ruler. Yet, there was no way to measure the human misery caused by inflation. The ruined middle class went hungry and suffered from malnutrition; some were actually starving. The political atmosphere was on the verge of exploding.

When Hitler and the Free Corps leaders learned von Kahr, the leader of the conservative Bavarian government, was planning to declare Bavaria independent, they moved to forestall the separatists with a putsch of their own. On the evening of November 8, von Kahr was speaking to an audience of three thousand respectable people at the Bürgerbräu, a first-class beer hall on the outskirts of Munich. Arriving shortly after 8:00 P.M., Hitler and some of the Nazi leaders pushed their way into the tightly packed hall where von Kahr was droning on and on with a boring speech. While waiting for all the Nazi troops to arrive, Hanfstaengl bought several beers, at a price of one billion marks apiece, for Hitler and the other Nazis. Meanwhile six hundred S.A. men surrounded the hall from the outside. At 8:30 the elite guard of the S.A. arrived. Goering with twenty-five Brownshirts burst into the hall and quickly set up a machine gun at the entrance. During the uproar Hitler jumped up on a chair and fired a shot into the ceiling. "The National Revolution has begun," he shouted. "This hall is surrounded by six hundred heavily armed men. No one may leave the hall."

Hitler then invited von Kahr, General Lossow, the commander of the army in Bavaria, and Colonel Seisser, chief of the State Police, to come to a side room to discuss plans for overthrowing the German government in Berlin. They refused to comply with his proposals until the arrival of General Ludendorff, who was successful in pressuring them to join Hitler's coup against the government in Berlin. Triumphantly Hitler led the group back into the hall where they all made short speeches. The audience went wild with excitement.

But the victory gained was soon to be lost. Informed of difficulties between some S.A. men and army troops, Hitler left, leaving Ludendorff in charge at the Bürgerbräu. Ludendorff accepted the "word of honor" of von Kahr, Lossow, and Seisser to be loyal to Hitler and told them they were free to go. Of course none of the three had any intention of supporting Hitler's coup; so they proceeded to call for reinforcements from the outlying army garrisons.

As soon as Roehm received the news of the successful coup, he announced it to his troops, who were assembled in the Löwenbräu beer hall. The police spies who were listening rushed off to report to headquarters. As Roehm's motorcycle courier zoomed away to spread the word of the putsch, the police were still waiting on the corner for a street-car, as they had no other means of transportation. In contrast the putschists had adequate transportation for their troops. Trucks belonging to the Nazi party were supplemented by rented trucks and even taxicabs.

During the rest of the night disorganized troop maneuvers continued, yet the leaders of the putsch failed to make any decisive actions or to take any further control of the key centers of the city. Instead guns were taken out of hidden vaults to be distributed, and Jews were rounded up in their underwear as hostages. Trucks carrying storm troopers from the suburbs rumbled into the city all night long. Most of the Nazis stayed around the Bürgerbräu; some tried to sleep in the corridors and halls while others stood guard outside in the cold wet snow. There were hardly any civilians on the streets, except for a few small groups of revelers out squandering their inflation money.

On the gray morning of November 9, at six o'clock, a line of trucks with Gregor Strasser's unit of 150 S.A. men from Landshut came rolling through Munich. One of the men said, "What kind of a revolution do you call this? People are going to work as usual. Something's wrong."[47]

Early that morning Hitler had ordered the confiscation of paper money from the Parcus and Muhlthaler printing firms. Hanfstaengl returned sometime after eight o'clock to the Bürgerbräu: "The air was thick with cigar and cigarette smoke," he later recalled. "In the anteroom there was a little orchestra platform and on it, in a pile about five feet high, thousands of million- and billion-mark notes in neat banker's bundles, which the Brownshirts had 'requisitioned.' . . . I could have done with a few of them myself, for my hospitality the night before had left me without a penny in my pocket, but evidently they were to be expended in a legal and formal fashion whatever their origin."[48] Some of this money was later passed out to pay the troops. Free beer had been provided for the men in the Bürgerbräu, but they all had to pay for their own food.

By this time Hitler knew that von Kahr, Lossow, and Seisser had betrayed him. He and Ludendorff desperately tried to think up a plan that would save the putsch from impending failure. They decided on a public march through Munich to link up with Roehm's forces, which were holding out in the War Ministry building.

Shortly after eleven o'clock the march of over two thousand S.A. men and Free corps members started from the Bürgerbräu, across the Isar River, through the center of the city, and finally down the narrow Residenzstrasse. In the front of the column marched Hitler, Scheubner-Richter, and Ludendorff. Most of the troops carried weapons; some even had machine guns. At half past twelve the putschists encountered a cordon of police at the end of the narrow street. Almost instantly a shot rang out, which was followed by a hail of bullets from the police. Sixteen Nazis, including Scheubner-Richter, were killed. Ludendorff marched straight through the firing into the ranks of the police; Goering was badly wounded; and Hitler dislocated his shoulder when he fell to the ground. The young S.A. doctor, Walter Schulz, guided Hitler back to a side street where they hopped into a car and raced out of the city toward the mountains. Two days later, Hitler was arrested and imprisoned. His treason trial turned out to be one of the most blatant cover-ups in judicial history, not for his sake, as is often assumed, but to protect the "good names" of those who financed him, supported him, and intrigued with him.

Once the putsch began, money was of little importance. Hitler's men were well enough equipped, but they were disorganized and lacked training to face the regular army. The putsch failed because von Kahr, Lossow, Seisser, and the officers of the Bavarian Army were willing to oppose it. No amount of money could have bought their loyalty.

Looking back at the financing of Hitler's political activities from 1919 to 1923, one thing is particularly interesting. Many historians have contended that the National Socialist party was financed and supported by "big business."[49] Yet as has been seen, only one of Germany's major industrialists, Fritz Thyssen, gave anything to the Nazi party during these early years. Donations came from some conservative Munich businessman who gave at the height of the Communist danger, as well as small Bavarian factory owners. But none of these men, in spite of their personal wealth, could fit properly in the category of "big business."

There is absolutely no evidence that the really big industrialists of Germany, such as Carl Bosch, Hermann Bucher, Carl Friedrich von Siemens, and Hugo Stinnes, or the great families such as the Krupps and the leading bankers and financiers, gave any support to the Nazis from 1918 to 1923. Indeed, few of them knew this small party from Bavaria even existed. Most of Hitler's donations came from individuals who were radical nationalists or anti-Semites and contributed because of ideological motivation. To a certain extent, the wealthy White Russians fit into this category; they could also be looked on as the one real interest group that hoped to gain a definite political-economic objective from their aid to the Nazis.

There was one other important industrialist (in fact the world's largest) who gave to Hitler during this period, but his story must be dealt with in a separate chapter, for he was not a German, but an American.

3
FORD AND HITLER

"That Henry Ford, the famous automobile manufacturer, gave money to the National Socialists directly or indirectly has never been disputed," said Konrad Heiden, one of the first biographers of Hitler.[1] As startling as this statement may seem, there is considerable evidence to support such a conclusion. In the 1920s, Henry Ford financed the circulation of more anti-Semitic propaganda than Hitler. Ford had always admired Germans, thus, given his hatred of Jews, it did not take much to get him to contribute money to Germany's leading anti-Semite. Naturally Ford's money was not given openly but transferred through a network of agents who traveled between Detroit and Munich. How Henry Ford, the all-American businessman, came to be involved with Hitler can be traced back to Ford's utopian effort to end World War I.

In 1915 Henry Ford chartered a ship at his own expense and sailed to Europe with a group of supporters in an effort to end World War I by negotiating a compromise peace. On board the ship, Ford told the well-known pacifist Madame

Rozika Schwimmer: "I know who started this war—the German Jewish bankers."[2] Ford later said to the Florence, Alabama, correspondent of *The New York Times:*

> It was the Jews themselves who convinced me of the direct relationship between the international Jew and war. In fact they went out of their way to convince me. On the peace ship were two very prominent Jews. We had not been at sea 200 miles before they began telling me of the power of the Jewish race, of how they controlled the world through their control of gold, and that the Jew and no one but the Jew could end the war. I was reluctant to believe it, but they went into detail to convince me of the means by which the Jews controlled the war, how they had the money, how they had cornered all the basic materials needed to fight the war and all that, and they talked so long and so well that they convinced me.[3]

Slapping the pocket of his coat, Ford told Madame Schwimmer, "I have the evidence here—facts! I can't give them out yet because I haven't got them all. I'll have them soon!"[4] Needless to say, his peace mission failed and left him somewhat bitter. Years later, Ford reflected on his fruitless efforts: "The whole world laughed at my Peace Expedition, I know." But Ford was far from discouraged, and the world and Hitler were soon to be deluged with evidence of Ford's anti-Semitic feelings.

At the end of 1918, Ford bought a typical country newspaper called the *Dearborn Independent.* When Ford announced his publishing plans, he justified his actions by saying: "I am very much interested in the future not only of my own country, but of the whole world, and I have definite ideas and ideals that I believe are practical for the good of all and I intend giving them to the public without having them garbled, distorted or misrepresented."[5] He must have had something serious in mind, since he said that, if need be, he was willing to spend $10 million (approximately $100 million in today's money) to finance the publication.[6]

The *Independent* was not to be a medium for publicizing the Ford company; in fact, the editors were told specifically to avoid any mention of Ford's industrial enterprise. Unlike most newspapers, it had no advertisements. Ford didn't want any commercial influence interfering with his editorial program. Initially, the basic tone of the *Independent* was antiprofiteer, antimonopoly, and antireactionary; on the positive side, it supported Wilsonian ideals of postwar reconstruction at home.

Ford had apparently been planning an attack on the Jews for some time, but he kept his plans to himself, although a few of his assistants and close associates had picked up hints. Ford's first editor of the *Dearborn Independent*, Edwin Pipp, said that Ford "was bringing up the Jews frequently, almost continually in conversation, blaming them for almost everything. . . . At first he talked only about 'the big fellows' and said he had nothing against Jews in ordinary walks of life. Later he stated: 'They are all pretty much alike'. . . . We had not published the paper more than six months before [Ford] commenced to talk persistently about a series of articles attacking the Jewish people. He said that he believed they were in a conspiracy to bring on war for profits."[7]

A year after Ford had purchased the *Independent*, he was questioned about his experiences on the peace ship by one of his company's executives.

"What did you get out of that trip, Mr. Ford? What did you learn?" the man asked.

"I know who makes wars," Ford responded. "The international Jewish bankers arrange them so they can make money out of it. I know it's true because a Jew on the peace ship told me."

Ford said that this Jew had told him that it was impossible to get peace his way. However good his intentions, no argosy such as the peace ship could accomplish anything unless he saw the right people, and the "right people" were certain Jews in France and England.

"That man knew what he was talking about—[and] gave me the whole story," Ford said. "We're going to tell the whole story one of these days and show them up!"[8]

Suddenly on May 22, 1920, the *Independent* lashed forth with a violent attack on the Jews. The boldface headline on the front page was a blunt and concise summation of the editorial's thesis: "The International Jew: The World's Problem." The first paragraph began: "There is a race, a part of humanity which has never yet been received as a welcome part." "This people," the article continued, "has ever been fouling the earth and plotting to dominate it. In order to eventually rule the Gentiles, the Jews have long been conspiring to form an international super-capitalist government." This racial problem, the *Independent* said, was the "prime" question confronting all society.

The following ninety-one articles covered a wide field of paranoid topics related to the international Jew. Ranging from Jews in a world government to Jews in American finance, in communism, theater, movies, bootlegging, and song writing, the articles had slanderous titles, such as "The Jewish Associates of Benedict Arnold," "The Gentle Art of Changing Jewish Names," "What Jews Attempted When They Had Power," "The All-Jewish Mark on Red Russia," and "Taft Once Tried to Resist the Jews—and Failed."

In many of the articles, Ford accused the Jews of causing a decline in American culture, values, products, entertainment, and even worse, of being the instigators of World War I. Serious charges were leveled against several well-known Jews. Bernard M. Baruch was called the "pro-counsel of Judah in America," a "Jew of Super-Power," and "the most powerful man" during World War I. When asked by news reporters to comment on these charges, Baruch replied, tongue in cheek, "Now boys you wouldn't expect me to deny them would you?"[9]

But understandably, most Jews reacted without the humor

of Baruch. Riots took place in Pittsburgh and Toledo, and in Cincinnati, vigorous protests by Jewish citizens influenced the city council to establish a ban. Street sales of the *Independent* were so reduced by opposition that Ford had to obtain an injunction. In some of the larger cities, people threatened and assaulted the newspaper's salesmen. In 1921, the theatrical producer Morris Gest filed a $5 million libel suit against Ford, but soon dropped it. Some public libraries barred the *Independent* from their collections, and a resolution of protest was introduced in Congress. Representatives of almost all national Jewish organizations and religious bodies issued a common declaration denouncing the Ford campaign.

One hundred and nineteen prominent Christians, including Woodrow Wilson, called upon Ford to stop his "vicious propaganda." President Harding, after an appeal by Louis Marshall, president of the American Jewish Committee, privately asked Ford—through his friend, Judson C. Welliver—to halt the attacks. William Fox, president of Fox Film Corporation, threatened to show choice footage of Model T accidents in his newsreels if the industrialist persisted in attacking the character of Jewish film executives and their motion pictures. When the Jews of Hartford were preparing for a four hundred-car parade in honor of Dr. Chaim Weizmann and Albert Einstein, they drew nationwide publicity by ordering "Positively no Ford machines permitted in line."[10]

Soon many Jewish firms and individuals boycotted Ford products.*

---

*Unfortunately the boycott made the innocent suffer along with the guilty. One man alone—Henry Ford—was responsible for the anti-Semitic campaign, not the whole Ford Company. The workers, executives of the company, and members of Ford's family were in no way involved; indeed, some even expressed their disapproval of the articles to Ford. It is only fair to mention that after the death of Henry Ford, the Ford Motor Company has maintained a good relation with the Jewish public. In fact, the company has given generous contributions to Jewish organizations and causes. Likewise, the Ford family has deservingly gained the esteem of the Jewish community.

The drop in orders for cars was most severe in the eastern metropolitan centers of the country, and within a few months Ford competitors began to gain the edge. Officials high in the company later agreed that during the run of the anti-Semitic articles the company lost business that was never regained, but nevertheless, because of the large postwar market the boycott was not strong enough to cripple the Ford industry.

In 1921, Ford and his friend (and fellow anti-Semite) Thomas Edison were on their way to inspect the Muscle Shoal's power plant when an Alabama reporter got through the crowd to ask Ford how long his anti-Semitic articles would continue. Ford replied that his "course of instruction on the Jews would last five years."*

Despite all of the attempts to silence Ford's campaign, his racist ideas spread quickly throughout the world. Within a year and a half, Ford had turned the *Independent* into a notorious, mass-circulated, anti-Semitic propaganda sheet. From 1919 to 1923 the *Independent*'s nationwide circulation exceeded a quarter of a million, and from 1923 to 1927 it reached the half-million mark. (This figure included copies given away free.)[11] Reprints of the articles that appeared in the *Independent* were published in a four-volume set (1920–1922) that gained a considerable circulation in the United States. Entitled *The International Jew*, this compilation was distributed widely and translated into sixteen different

---

*Since the first edition of this book new information has come to light indicating that Thomas Edison may have been at least partly responsible for Henry Ford's anti-Semitism. Edison was one of the few men Ford looked up to. The relationship was almost one of pupil and mentor. In October of 1914 Edison told a reporter that the rise of German commercial power was the cause of the war [World War I]. The Jews, he said, were largely responsible for German business success and "the militarists which govern the country [Germany] do their bidding." After an outcry of public protest, Edison apologized, claiming he never meant to accuse the Jews of starting the war. However, the evidence seems to indicate that Edison remained an anti-Semite and even encouraged Ford's anti-Semitic campaign. [See: Albert Lee, *Henry Ford and the Jews* pp. 152–55.]

languages, including Arabic.[12] It was published in Europe, Asia, and South America.[13]

From France to Russia, anti-Semitic and nationalist groups eagerly bought up the publications of the famous American. A prominent Jewish attorney, after completing a world tour in the mid-1920s, stated that he had seen reprints and translations from *The International Jew* in the "most remote corners of the earth." He maintained that "but for the authority of the Ford name, they would have never seen the light of day and would have been quite harmless if they had. With that magic name they spread like wildfire and became the Bible of every anti-Semite."[14]

If *The International Jew* was the Bible, then to the Nazis Henry Ford must have seemed a god. His anti-Semitic publications led many Germans to become Nazis. Baldur von Schirach, leader of the Hitler Youth movement, stated at the postwar Nuremberg War Crimes Trials that he had become an anti-Semite at the age of seventeen after reading *The Eternal Jew* (title of *The International Jew* translated for the German editions). "You have no idea what a great influence this book had on the thinking of German youth," von Schirach said. "The younger generation looked with envy to the symbols of success and prosperity like Henry Ford, and if he said the Jews were to blame, why naturally we believed him."[15] One of Hitler's lieutenants, Christian Weber, boasted that Ford would be "received like a king" if he ever came to Munich.

Hitler's admiration for the auto magnate, *The New York Times* reported, was made obvious by the large picture of Henry Ford on the wall beside Hitler's desk in his Munich headquarters. In an adjoining room there was a large table covered with books, most of which were copies of the German translation of *The International Jew*.

When news of the Jewish boycotts reached the Nazis, Hitler declared that "the struggle of international Jewish finance against Ford has only strengthened the sympathies of the National Socialist party for Ford and has given the broadest circulation to his book, *The International Jew.*[16] And in 1923, when Hitler learned that Ford might run for president, he said, according to the *Chicago Tribune*, "I wish that I could send some of my shock troops to Chicago and other big American cities to help in the elections. . . . We look to Heinrich Ford as the leader of the growing Fascist movement in America. . . . We have just had his anti-Jewish articles translated and published. The book is being circulated to millions throughout Germany."[17]

Theodore Fritsch, editor of the Leipzig anti-Semitic publishing house, *Der Hammer*, produced six printings of *The International Jew* between 1920 and 1922; by late 1933 Fritsch had issued twenty-nine printings, each of which lauded Ford in the preface for the "Great service" that he had done America and the world by attacking the Jews."[18] After 1933, the book became a stock item of Nazi propaganda; every schoolchild in Germany came into contact with it many times during his education. *The International Jew* had the backing of the German government and, as the Nazis said, was an important factor in "educating" the nation.[19]

Not only did Hitler specifically praise Henry Ford in *Mein Kampf*, but many of Hitler's ideas were also a direct reflection of Ford's racist philosophy. There is a great similarity between *The International Jew* and Hitler's *Mein Kampf*,[20] and some passages are so identical that it has been said Hitler copied directly from Ford's publication.* Hitler also read Ford's autobiography, *My Life and Work*, which was published in 1922 and was a best-seller in Germany, as well as Ford's book entitled *Today and Tomorrow.*[21] There can be no doubt as to the influence of Henry Ford's ideas on Hitler. Not only do Hitler's writings and practices reflect *The International Jew*, but one of his closest associates, Dietrich Eckart,

---

The International Jew was first published by Ford in 1920. Hitler did not begin to write *Mein Kampf* until 1924.

also specifically mentioned *The Protocols of the Elders of Zion* and *The International Jew* as sources of inspiration for the Nazi leader.[22]

Ford and Hitler both charged the Jews with an unlimited number of false accusations and used them as a scapegoat for all the ills of the modern world. As will be seen in the following pages, Ford and Hitler claimed the Jews were an "inferior race" with no culture. However, these same "inferior" Jews were charged with masterminding a conspiracy to conquer the world through the control of international banking and finance. Finally, the Jews were blamed for being behind communism, controlling the news media, and promoting jazz and cheap movies. The obvious unreasonableness of these charges never bothered Ford or Hitler because neither they nor their followers ever examined them in the light of rational logic.

Unlike the traditional religious and social anti-Semitism that had flared up at various times since the Middle Ages, *Mein Kampf* presented a theory of racial anti-Semitism. A distinguished group of historians, including Sidney B. Fay, William Langer, and John Chamberlain, who edited the American edition of *Mein Kampf*, claimed that the use of racial anti-Semitism as the integral part of a political program was Hitler's "Copernican discovery."[23] However, this harsh new philosophy was first propagated to the general public, not by Adolf Hitler, but by Henry Ford.*

In *The International Jew* it is clearly stated: "Neither directly nor by implication is it held . . . that the Jewish question is a religious question. On the contrary, supported by

---

*The purpose of this section is not to discuss the falsity and unjustness of Hitler's and Ford's accusations, but rather to compare the similarity of their thinking. Because their anti-Semitic beliefs are today known to be false, there is no need to refute them here at length. For a thorough analysis disproving the entire anti-Semitic concept of a Jewish world conspiracy, see Norman Cohn, *Warrant for Genocide: The Myth of the Jewish World Conspiracy and the Protocols of the Elders of Zion*. Also see Hermann Bernstein, *The History of a Lie*.

the highest Jewish authorities, it is firmly stated that the Jewish question is one of race and nationality."[24] Quotations from many prominent Jews are taken out of context and cited as proof of this contention.

In contrast to the Jews, who are presented in *The International Jew* as a race "that has no civilization to point to, no aspiring religion . . . no great achievement in any realm . . ." the Anglo-Saxons are portrayed as explorers, nation builders, and thinkers. As Ford was fond of telling people, it was the Anglo-Saxons who overcame all odds to establish a great new civilization on the American continent. Their accomplishments throughout the centuries, Ford said, have proven that the Anglo-Saxon race is destined to "master the world."

Echoing Ford's concept of the superiority of the Anglo-Saxons, Hitler described the "Aryans" as the only race capable of creating great civilizations. Interbreeding with the lower races caused the decline of these civilizations. North America, "the population of which consists of the greatest part of Germanic elements," was given as an example of Aryan conquest and civilization of a continent once inhabited only by an inferior race. "The Jew forms the strongest contrast to the Aryan," Hitler wrote.[25] The Jewish people, despite their "apparent intellectual qualities," are nevertheless without any "true culture" of their own. The "sham culture" that the Jew possesses, Hitler said, is taken from other people and is mostly spoiled in his hands. But the alleged lack of true Jewish culture was not the main thrust of either Ford or Hitler's anti-Semitism.

Ford's primary complaint is clearly stated in *The International Jew:*

We meet the Jew everywhere in the upper circles, literally everywhere where there is power. And that is where the Jewish question begins—in very simple terms. How does the Jew so habitually . . . gravitate to the highest places? Who puts him there? . . . What does he do there? . . . In any country, where the Jewish question has come to the forefront as a vital issue, you will discover that the principal cause is the outworking of the Jewish genius to achieve the *power of control*. Here in the United States is the fact of this remarkable minority attaining in fifty years a degree of control that would be impossible to a ten times larger group of any other race.[26]

Both Ford and Hitler believed in the existence of a Jewish conspiracy—that the Jews had a plan to destroy the Gentile world and then take it over through the power of an international super-government. This sort of plan had been described in detail in *The Protocols of the Learned Elders of Zion*. Despite evidence against the genuineness of the *Protocols*, Ford continued to defend its authenticity, saying, "The only statement I care to make about the *Protocols* is that they fit in with what is going on . . . They have fitted the world situation up to this time. They fit it now."[27]

Hitler's attitude on the *Protocols* is quite congruous with Ford's, as can be seen in a private and revealing conversation he had with Hermann Rauschning, a high Nazi official. Hitler said he was "appalled" when he read the *Protocols*: "The stealthiness of the enemy and his ubiquity! I saw at once we must copy it [the conspiratorial strategy outlined in *The Protocols*]—in our way, of course." He continued on to say the fight against the Jews was "the critical battle for the fate of the world!" Rauschning objected: "Don't you think that you are attributing rather too much importance to the Jews?" "No, No, No!" Hitler shouted. "It is impossible to exaggerate the formidable quality of the Jew as an enemy." But, Rauschning contested, "the *Protocols* are a manifest forgery. . . . It couldn't possibly be genuine." "Why not?" Hitler replied. He said he didn't care whether the story was historically true; if it wasn't, its intrinsic truth was all the more convincing to him. "We must beat the Jew with his own weapon," he said. "I saw that the moment I had read the book."[28] Echoing Ford, Hitler said, "The best criticism applied to them is reality. He who examines the historical developments of the past hundred years . . . will . . . immediately understand the clamor of the Jewish press [against the *Protocols*]. For once this book has become the common property of a people, the Jewish danger is bound to be considered as broken."[29]

The conspiracy theory described the Jews as a people who lack any original creative ability; their only skills were knavery, cunning, and trickery. Lacking other alternatives, and being psychologically oriented toward getting money rather then making or producing goods, the Jews throughout history had acted as middlemen and merchants. In other words, the theory continues, they make their living by financial manipulation. Because many Jews were financiers, bankers, and stock brokers, Hitler and Ford jumped to the erroneous conclusion that the Jews had a controlling influence over the flow of international money.

"The finances of the world are in the control of Jews; their decisions and devices are themselves our economic laws," the *Dearborn Independent* stated.[30]

Ford clashed with the Wall Street financiers not only in the pages of his newspaper and books, but in reality as well. Authorities say that many of his ideas about Jewish financiers came from unpleasant personal experiences with bankers; a conflict between Ford and the financiers occurred early in 1921. At that time, rumors claimed that Ford was in difficult financial straits. Due to a lack of capital, Ford was forced to curtail production for several months.

As Ford was the world's most prominent industrialist, it was only natural that German businessmen would pay a certain amount of attention to what he said on the topic of business, even if they disregarded his political opinions. Like many conservative members of the middle-class who had rural origins, Ford deplored "the lack of moral standards" in modern commerce and blamed this on the Jews. Ford told one reporter: "When there's wrong in a country, you'll find Jews . . . The Jew is a huckster who doesn't want to produce but to make something of what somebody else produces."[31] Nothing irritated the industrialist more than the idea of somebody getting something for nothing.

One evening during a private dinner conversation with his friends, Hitler spoke of the lack of standards in modern commerce and, like Ford, blamed such conditions on the Jews.[32] He compared the financial probity and honesty of the merchants of the Hanseatic League (mid-1200s to the 1800s) to the knavery and cupidity of the Jewish merchants. Each tradesman who possessed the approval seal of the Hansa was obligated to maintain the standard price and to produce only high-quality goods; if he failed in his obligation, retribution followed. A baker, for example, who cheated on the quality of flour was ducked several times in a basin filled with water in such a way that he came close to drowning. But "as soon as the Jews were allowed to stick their noses out of the ghetto, the sense of honor and loyalty in trade began to melt away." Hitler went on to explain how the Jews made the fixing of prices depend on the law of supply and demand rather than on the intrinsic value. European commerce had been dragged down to such a level that a remedy was needed urgently; and the first step of the remedy, Hitler said, was "to do away with the Jews."[33]

The attack on "Jewish financiers and middlemen" by Ford and Hitler shows their ignorance of economics. In the above quotation, by Hitler, he blames the Jews for basing price on supply and demand; in other words, for developing a modern capitalistic economy. Price based on intrinsic value became obsolete after the Middle Ages. But what Ford and Hitler both really wanted was to turn the clock back to a village economy.

"Quick turnover and quick profit," was the essence of Jewish business, according to *The International Jews*. It was "the old Yiddish game" of changing the styles to speed up business and make people buy. "Nothing lasts any more," bemoaned Ford's *Dearborn Independent*. "It is always something new to stimulate the flow of money to the pockets of the Jews."[34] Ford himself often grumbled about the decline in the quality of items produced by industries that had "fallen into the hands of Jews."

One night an office worker at Ford's Dearborn factory bit into a candy bar and quickly thumbed through the pile of his accumulated mail. He had just returned from Washington that evening and had gone to the office on the way home to see if anything had taken place during his absence. The train had been so crowded he had not been able to get into the diner. So on the way to the factory he had picked up a couple of candy bars to tide him over until he got home for dinner. He had been sitting there at his desk only a few minutes when he noticed a face pressed against the glass panel of the door, and the knob turned.

"What's up that you're here at this hour?" asked Ford, perching on a corner of the desk.

The executive said he was cleaning up odds and ends and catching up on the work he'd missed while out of town. Ford helped himself to a piece of candy. He munched on it for a while and frowned.

"This stuff isn't as good as it used to be, is it?" he remarked, putting the untouched remainder back on the tinfoil.

"Don't you think so?" the executive replied without looking up from his work.

"The Jews have taken hold of it." Ford shook his head in disgust. As he slid off the edge of the desk, he said, "They're cheapening it to make more money out of it."[35]

Ford apparently proposed milder remedies to the "Jewish question" than Hitler. Ford said the only invincible course was to return to "the principles which made our race great. Let businessmen go back to the old way when a man's word was his bond and when business was service and not exploitation. Learn to test quality in fabric and food."[36]

In the years following World War I, American jazz and

Hollywood movies were all the rage in Europe. As might have been expected, Hitler denounced the "degenerate Negro music" and the immoral themes of the "Jewish dominated" cinema. But it was Henry Ford's publications, not Hitler's, that first announced to the world that the export of modern American "Jewish" culture was a part of a deliberate conspiracy.

After examining the names of actors, screenwriters, directors, and producers, the *Dearborn Independent* came to the following ridiculous conclusion: the motion picture industry of the Untied States and the whole world "is exclusively under the control, moral and financial, of the Jewish manipulators of the public mind."[37] The Jews used the movies and theater to poison the American people with sensuality, indecency, appalling illiteracy, and endless liberal platitudes. *The International Jew* stated that the use of vulgarisms and slang in the movies was so extensive that Shakespeare wouldn't have recognized his own language.

Jazz and "popular music" were anathema to the ears of Ford and Hitler. "Monkey talk, jungle squeals, grunts and squeaks camouflaged by a few feverish notes"—this was the way Ford described it. *The International Jew* said that this kind of music was not really "popular," rather an artificial popularity was created for it by high-pressured advertising. The Jews had supposedly created the popularity of the African style to destroy the moral fabric of the white race. In Ford's opinion, the beat of the jungle and other "congo compositions" degenerated into more bestial sounds than the beasts themselves made.[38]

Both Ford and Hitler believed that Jewish capitalists and Jewish Communists were partners aiming to gain control over the nations of the world. Their views differed somewhat, but this was mainly a result of their contrasting positions and nationalities. Ford placed more emphasis on Jewish financiers and bankers because as an industrialist he naturally came into close contact with them. Hitler, on the other hand, was more concerned with "the Jew's use of

communism as a weapon," since communism was a powerful opposition force to the Nazis in Germany at that time.

Ford was, however, frightened by the Russian Revolution
and the rapid spread of communism through other countries. If Marxism established itself in America he would obviously be one of the first to suffer. The Communist threat
was one of the first topics he discussed in his autobiography.

In the minds of Ford and Hitler, communism was a completely Jewish creation. Not only was its founder, Karl Marx,
the grandson of a rabbi, but more importantly Jews held
leading positions, as well as a high percentage of the membership, in the Communist parties throughout the world.
The International Jew deceptively stated that since the time of
the French Revolution Jews had been involved in numerous
movements to overthrow ruling regimes. If the Jews were
not always visible in these revolutionary activities, it was
concluded, without any proof, that they were operating behind the scenes, planning and manipulating the forces in
their hands. "Revolutions are not spontaneous uprisings, but
carefully planned minority actions, and the subversive elements have been consistently Hebrews."[39] In *Mein Kampf*
there is a similar discussion of the Jews sneaking in among
nations and subverting them internally by the use of lies,
corruption, and liberalism. The most modern weapon in the
Jewish arsenal was communism: "In Russian bolshevism,"
said Hitler, "we must see Jewry's twentieth-century effort
to take world domination unto itself."[40]

According to *The International Jew*, the Russian Revolution
was financed in New York by Jewish bankers. No evidence
is given to support this accusation, which of course was
completely false. Jacob Schiff of Kuhn, Loeb and Company
is the only Jewish financier mentioned in this connection.[41]
It is impossible to determine if Henry Ford sincerely believed that Jewish bankers financed communism or if the
accusation was just being used to slander the Jews. It is
true that a few wealthy Jews did actually give some small
contributions and loans to revolutionary movements in Rus-

sia, because of a hatred of the anti-Semitic policies of the czarist government.[42] However, the revolutionaries they gave to were generally Mensheviks (moderate socialists) rather than Bolsheviks (Communists). This important distinction could have been missed by people like Henry Ford who were not knowledgeable of the Russian political situation and automatically labeled all left-wing movements as "Communist."

As far as its influence on upper-middle-class Germans was concerned, what was said in *The International Jew* about the German revolution of 1918 was probably even more important than what Ford said about the Russian Revolution.[43] In the early 1920s when Hitler was still an obscure agitator, his charges that the Jews were responsible for the revolution in Germany in 1918 and the subsequent loss of the war were taken seriously by many people who would have ignored them if Ford's publications had not stated the very same arguments. The Jew is the "world's Bolshevist and preeminently Germany's revolutionist," Ford's *Dearborn Independent* claimed.[44] In *The International Jew* there appeared over one entire page of names of Jews who gained high government positions during or after the German revolution. These Jews "would not have gained these positions had it not been for the Revolution, and the Revolution would not have come had not they brought it."

The influential factors that destroyed the German people's morale and encouraged defeatism in 1918 were directed by the Jews; furthermore, *The International Jew* said, "the Jews of Germany were not German patriots during the war."[45] That same false accusation was later made by Hitler: "Almost every clerk a Jew and every Jew a clerk," he said. "I was amazed by this multitude of fighters of the Chosen People and could not help comparing them with the few representatives they had on the front."[46] Summing up the principal Jewish influences that supposedly caused the downfall of Germany, *The International Jew* listed the following three reasons: "(a) the spirit of Bolshevism which masqueraded under the name of German Socialism, (b) Jewish ownership and control of the Press, (c) Jewish control of the food supply and the industrial machinery of the country."[47] Compared with Hitler's comments and conclusions about the revolution, Ford's ideas appear uncannily parallel.

The democratic political system in Germany began only in 1918 as a result of the revolution and was never very popular with many people of the upper classes. The fate of democracy hung by a slim balance. But even the German Right was hesitant to turn to the kind of authoritarian system advocated by Hitler. They feared foreign disapproval, which would be reflected in the international money market and could cause a collapse of the fragile Germany economy. The fact that Henry Ford, the leading American industrialist, condemned Germany's democratic government almost as strongly as Hitler must have been seen by some German businessmen as an indication that America would have no fundamental objection to Germany's becoming an authoritarian state. Even later, after Hitler became chancellor, protests by American journalists and politicians against the abridgement of the human rights of the Jews were disregarded by the Germans, to some extent because they thought the real powers in America, the industrialists, like Ford, secretly approved of their policies.

Some people believed Ford did not write *The International Jew*. They contended that Ford was unaware of the anti-Semitic rampage encouraged by his own newspaper because it was written by someone else. Their contention, like most cover-ups, contains a grain of truth; Ford did not write the book word for word. Actually his editor Bill Cameron transcribed Ford's ideas onto paper, but Ford's secretary, Ernest Liebold, stated that "the *Dearborn Independent* is Henry Ford's own paper and he authorized every statement occurring therein."[48] When the first articles from *The International Jew* were published, a public statement, marked "Authorized by Henry Ford," was released and signed by E. G. Liebold. It stated: "The Jewish question, as every businessman knows, has been festering in silence and suspicion here in the United States for a long time, and none has dared discuss it because the Jewish influence was strong enough to crush the man who attempted it. The Jews are the only race whom it is 'verboten' to discuss frankly and openly, and abusing the fear they have cast over business, the Jewish leaders have gone from one excess to the other until the time has come for a protest or a surrender."[49.]

Throughout the 1920s Henry Ford continued to publish anti-Semitic articles in his *Dearborn Independent*. Then in 1927 he became involved in a lawsuit with Aaron Sapiro, a prominent Chicago attorney. Sapiro charged Ford with libel for saying that he was involved in a plot with other Jewish middlemen to gain control of American agriculture. The case was settled out of court when Ford published a personal apology to Sapiro and a formal retraction of his attacks against the Jews.

But publishing his accusations against the Jews apparently was only the first step for Ford. There is evidence that shortly after he began the anti-Semitic articles, Ford took stronger action by financing the global anti-Semitic campaign. He struck at the Jews where they would later prove to be the most vulnerable.

Throughout the 1920s there were numerous leaks of information about Ford's financing Hitler. The U.S. ambassador to Germany, William E. Dodd, said in an interview that "certain American industrialists had a great deal to do with bringing fascist regimes into being in both Germany and Italy."[50] The *Manchester Guardian,* one of the outstanding liberal British newspapers, reported that Hitler received "more than merely moral support" from an American who sympathized with anti-Semitism and thought that Hitler would be of assistance in the battle against international financiers.[51]

The New York Times reported in 1922 that there was a widespread rumor circulating in Berlin claiming that Henry Ford was financing Adolf Hitler's nationalist and anti-

Semitic movement in Munich. In fact, the rumor was so rampant that the Jewish-owned *Berliner Tageblatt,* one of the largest newspapers in Germany, made an appeal to the American ambassador, Alanson B. Houghton, requesting an investigation of the issue and of American interference in order to prevent any further financial support for Hitler,[52] but the outcome of this request has never been determined.

It should be pointed out that there is no evidence that any money from the Ford Motor Company was ever given to Hitler. In fact, it would have been in Henry Ford's own interest to see that any money he gave Hitler came from his personal funds, and not from an account of the company. Ford was aware that most of the Ford Motor Company executives and Ford dealers across America were strongly opposed to his anti-Semitism and would not quietly tolerate the company's being involved in financing a foreign anti-Semite like Hitler. Furthermore, Ford's son, Edsel, who owned 41 percent of the company stock, was very much against his father's anti-Semitic activities. Actually, it was Edsel and several other Ford executives who finally convinced Henry Ford to drop his anti-Semitic campaign in the late 1920s. The Ford Motor company's New York sales manager, Gaston Plaintiff, who was a personal friend of Henry Ford, persistently argued with him about the damage his anti-Semitism was doing. Plaintiff played a significant role in getting Henry Ford to stop his attacks on the Jews.

Ford's major motivation for financing the Nazis was his desire to support an organization that would further the fight against the Jews. Since America and Germany were the two largest industrial powers, Ford thought that the influence of the Jews would be greatly shaken if there were strong anti-Semitic factions in these two countries. Ford's financial support and his well-known book against the Jews would gain him recognition and respect in the ranks of the Nazi party. And if this party did eventually become an influential political force in Germany, then Ford's philosophy would play an important role in the battle against the Jews.

There was also a point in the Nazi program that was advantageous to Ford's economic interests. Hitler's vehement protests against the injustices of the Versailles Treaty were secretly applauded by the American industrialist. Not only did the trade restrictions set up by the Versailles Treaty hurt Germany, they also hurt American businessmen who operated in foreign markets, such as Ford. America could benefit from trade with Europe only if Europe recovered from the destruction of World War I, and as the economist J. Maynard Keynes said, Europe could be made prosperous only by making Germany prosperous. But as long as the Versailles restrictions were wrapped around Germany's neck, there could be no hope for her recovery.

As a boy Ford had worked for a toolmaker from Germany who taught him many useful things. He liked Germans because "they are talented and thrifty people." In the 1920s Ford wanted to set up a factory in Germany where he could benefit from the availability of skilled labor.

In 1921 a Ford executive was sent to tour the defeated and occupied Germany to locate a possible site for a Ford automobile factory, but because of the financial restraints the Versailles Treaty placed on the German automotive industry, the Ford plant could not possibly be built. That year (1921), Ford had sold only three Model T cars and trucks and six tractors in all of Germany. Ford thought that if Hitler and the Nazis could bring pressure to bear upon the Berlin government, and therefore on the Allied governments, perhaps the Versailles restrictions would be lifted and the automobile business would improve.

In the early 1920s there was nothing illegal about the Nazi party, so Ford had every right to give his support openly. However, just as most political funding is secretive, it was obviously more prudent for Ford that there be no evidence linking his name with a radical anti-Semitic party. The State Department would not have appreciated his interference in the internal affairs for a foreign country. The Nazis also had a very good reason for wanting the source of funds to remain anonymous. If the German people found out that Hitler was financed by Ford, he would be accused of being the puppet of a foreign capitalist.

Tracing covert political funding is difficult under any circumstances. Naturally, it is even more difficult after the passage of more than seventy years. Although there is no presently known documentary evidence that Henry Ford financed Hitler, the abundance of circumstantial evidence from reliable sources makes it extremely likely that such financing did indeed take place. At one time, documentary evidence may have existed. In the early 1920s Erhard Auer, the vice president of the Bavarian Diet (state Parliament) stated in a report to President Ebert: "The Bavarian Diet has long had information that the Hitler movement was partly financed by an American anti-Semite . . . Henry Ford." Unfortunately, Auer did not produce his evidence at the time.* Any documents he may have had were probably destroyed by the Nazis after 1933.

However, a lack of documentary evidence is not unusual in cases of covert funding. In such situations money is often transferred in cash, so there is never any documentary evidence to begin with. If Ford had not financed Hitler, he would probably have published a vigorous denial of such accusations when they occurred in the 1920s, particularly *The New York Times* article of December 20, 1922.

From the extensive circumstantial evidence, the statements of reliable contemporary observers, and a knowledge of Henry Ford's motives and how he· operated, it is possible to reconstruct how his covert funding of Hitler probably took place.

The best way of disguising the origin of the money was to channel it through a middleman or agent who had contact with Ford and indirectly with Hitler. Of course there was a

---

*Auer was a very reliable witness. Although a staunch anti-Nazi he had opposed a motion of the Bavarian Diet to deport Hitler to Austria, on the grounds that it would be an infringement on political freedom.

myriad of possible ways in which funds could have been transmitted, ranging from a single courier to a more complex chain of middlemen.

Fortunately, in the Ford-Hitler case there is enough evidence to reduce the numerous possibilities to two or three probable channels through which money flowed. Rather than taking the risk of giving one lump sum of money, Ford seems to have broken it up into several deliveries.

The primary intermediaries between Ford and Hitler were the White Russians. Shortly after Ford made himself known as an anti-Semite, a small cluster of White Russians started to work for him. One of these emigrés was Boris Brasol. Born in Russia in 1885, Brasol as a short man with sharp features and piercing eyes who closely resembled Joseph Goebbels. He had the same aquiline nose, receding forehead, same shape of mouth, and the same cunning and ruthless look in his eyes. Trained as a lawyer, Brasol had gained investigative experience serving as the assistant of the anti-Semitic Russian minister of justice, Schegolitov, who organized the infamous Beiliss trial against an innocent Jew accused of ritual murder. When Brasol came to America in 1917, he was the chairman of the Association of Russian Army and Navy officers, and may have been on a mission to get financial support for the organization.

In 1918, Brasol was employed by the United States government for secret service work, a job that gave him an opportunity to introduce American intelligence officers to the *Protocols*.[53] During the next two years he worked hard to promote the publication and circulation of the *Protocols* in the United States. In 1920 he was hired as a member of the writing staff of Ford's *Dearborn Independent* where he provided much of the false historical background to support Ford's accusations against the Jews. His experience as an investigator for the czarist secret police made him the ideal sort of man to be involved in a covert funding operation. No one seemed to notice his frequent trips to Germany during the 1920s and 1930s to confer with high Nazi authorities.

During these trips, Brasol had plenty of opportunity to convey substantial sums of Ford's money to Hitler. Norman Hapgood, the well-known journalist and later U.S. ambassador to Denmark, wrote a number of articles on Henry Ford's shady political connections. In one of the articles, he stated that the former head of the Russian constitutional government at Omsk said, "I have seen the documentary proof that Boris Brasol has received money from Henry Ford."[54] With Ford's and Hitler's reputation as well as his own at stake, Brasol was fully aware that direct delivery of money was highly imprudent. He had to be discreet. He had to have a plausible reason for transporting money to Germany—which he did. Boris Brasol was the U.S. representative of Grand Duke Cyril Vladimirovich, the first cousin to the last reigning czar, Nicholas II, and one of the rightful pretenders to the Russian throne. Grand Duke Cyril had asked Brasol to collect funds for the Russian monarchist cause in America.

In 1921, Kurt Lüdecke, one of Hitler's lieutenants, visited Boris Brasol in the United States and was given a letter of introduction to Grand Duke Cyril, whereupon Lüdecke went to Nice, France, where Cyril and his wife, Victoria, were living in the Château Fabron. Lüdecke, who was received "with all due formality,"[55] quickly discovered that the Grand Duchess was "an intelligent, artful, and ambitious woman . . . [who] ruled over her husband." By stressing the advantages that would come to the White Russians if Hitler came to power, Lüdecke hoped to gain their cooperation, but due to their "stiff-necked" reaction Lüdecke did not even bother to ask for money, "as it was obvious that every rouble they had rescued from the Red Terror was desperately needed to keep up their regal charade."[56] If the duke and duchess were so short of money, how could they have contributed to Hitler? Nevertheless, between 1922 and 1923,

Cyril and Victoria gave General Ludendorff an "enormous sum" for the German right-wing extremists.

In 1939 General Biskupsky, a Russian monarchist leader, tried to get back this money for the White Russians. He argued that the Nazis were obliged to repay to the Russian emigrés the money Cyril had provided when he was living in Munich in the early 1920s. Biskupsky wrote to Nazi official Arno Schickedanz, "Here I must note that the Grand Duke Cyril and his wife gave General Ludendorff a sum of nearly half a million gold marks in 1922–23."[57] These were not the ordinary inflated marks, but marks that were backed with gold. It seems apparent that the half million gold marks in question had been supplied by Henry Ford, with Boris Brasol acting as the intermediary. Of course, the Grand Duchess Victoria did give Hitler some of her jewels and Cyril perhaps also contributed some financial aid, but not the "enormous sum" described by Biskupsky, for the very good reason that Cyril and his wife did not have that much money to spare.

After the failure of the 1923 putsch the close cooperation between the White Russians and the Nazis ended. Hitler had to make a new effort to reestablish contact with Henry Ford. Just how the Nazis went about doing this in 1924 provides an excellent example of their fund-raising techniques. A detailed account of this appeal to Ford is extremely significant because during the conversation with Frau Wagner, who was helping raise money for Hitler, Ford admitted that he had given money to Hitler in the past. This is the only known acknowledgment Ford ever made of having funded the Nazis.

On January 28, 1924, a typical cold, gray day in New York City, Siegfried and Winifred Wagner checked into the old Waldorf Hotel. The next day they would leave New York for a tour on which Siegfried was booked to conduct the music composed by his father, Richard Wagner, in the principal cities of the United States. While Siegfried was visiting Detroit, Baltimore, St. Louis, and other towns, Winifred would give lectures at various exclusive ladies' clubs along the way. The main mission of their tour was to collect enough financial contributions, about $200,000, to be able to reopen the yearly Bayreuth festival in Germany. Bayreuth, a small picturesque town in southern Germany surrounded by rolling hills and deep forests, was the site chosen by Richard Wagner in 1872 for his theater, known as the Festspielhaus, and for a home for his family.

The outbreak of the war in 1914 put an end to all performances, and even after the signing of the Versailles Treaty, Bayreuth remained a ghost town. The Festspielhaus remained empty; no foreigners were interested in traveling to hear German music, and the German people were still struggling to survive in the wake of destruction left by the war. At the height of the anti-German war hysteria, Wagnerian operas were either shelved in the Allied countries or at best performed in modified translations while mobs demonstrated against the treason of playing German music at all. Even the war brides had to find substitutes for the *Lohengrin* wedding march. All music needs patronage, and since Wagnerian opera was held in such disrepute, Siegfried was in serious financial difficulty. In order to restore a good image and hopefully to reawaken interest in the annual Bayreuth festival, the Wagners had come to America; even if they did not find many contributors, at least the concert fees would be of some help.*

It was more than a coincidence that the Wagners were accompanied by Kurt Lüdecke, who had come to America to collect funds for Hitler. The Wagners, Lüdecke said, "were here on a mission not very different from mine."[58] In his autobiography, Lüdecke mentioned his discussion with the Wagners in their hotel suite: "So here I sat, talking with the man for whose nursing the incomparable 'Siegfried Idyll' had been composed—and we scarcely mentioned music! . . .

---

*There is no evidence that any of the money the Wagners collected from music patrons was ever given to Hitler.

We were discussing money. More particularly, we were speaking of the chance of interesting Henry Ford (to Europeans the incarnation of money in its alluring bulk) in the Nazi movement." Winifred was a very active woman who managed her husband's business affairs, and Lüdecke said, "she now took a hand in mine."[59]

Winifried Wagner often helped with her husband's concert tours. But she also had interests of her own; one of these was sponsoring Adolf Hitler. She originally had heard of Hitler in the Munich home of her guardian, Herr Bechstein, the piano manufacturer whose wife contributed to the Nazis and was a close friend of Hitler. In 1920 or 1921, Winifred joined the Nazi party, and Hitler became a frequent visitor in Bayreuth during the twenties. Siegfried had no objections to his wife's young friend. According to Winifried, his attitude to Hitler was that of a benevolent uncle: "The young man had some bright ideas—good luck to him if he could bring them off."[60]

As they sat in their hotel room discussing various maneuvers, the Wagners and Lüdecke finally decided to pin their hopes on Mrs. Ford's interest in and hospitality toward celebrities. The hours slipped past midnight as they continued to debate whether Mrs. Ford could be relied upon to extend an invitation. Lüdecke laughingly said that, in the case of Mr. Ford, perhaps it would have been better to present their case through some hillbilly fiddler, as his musical tastes were "intensely folksy." Before going to bed, the trio concluded their planning with the hope that Ford's wife and son would be eager to meet the Wagners, if only for the change of hearing tidings of the world outside Detroit. If fortune ceded this much, Lüdecke said, "The rest of the plot was obvious—A word in Mr. Ford's presence, a hint, a request."

Before leaving New York, Frau Wagner sent a letter to the Fords inviting them to attend the Wagnerian concert in Detroit on January 31 as her personal guests. The Wagners and Lüdecke then took the train to Detroit, arriving there early on Wednesday, January 30. Despite the bone-chilling winter weather, their spirits were greatly lifted when they checked into the Statler Hotel and the Wagners found an invitation from the Fords already waiting.

The next afternoon, Thursday, January 31, the Wagners went to the Fords' home for an early supper. Ten miles from Detroit, driving west on Michigan Avenue, just beyond its junction with Southfield Road, the Wagners turned into a driveway heading northwest through an area wooded with old towering oaks and elms. This was Fair Lane, the two thousand-acre estate of Henry Ford. They were stopped briefly at the iron entrance gate, where a guard was always stationed to make sure that Ford could enjoy his privacy and to keep out uninvited visitors. From the gates the driveway stretched a mile through the forest to the large, gray stone house overlooking the calm Rouge River.

The Wagners were greeted by their hosts and then escorted into the sitting room. At first the conversation was very light, combining comments on the weather and the beauty of Fair Lane. But soon the discussion became more serious, leading logically from one topic to another—music, Wagner, Bayreuth, Germany, and finally politics in Germany. After a simple but good meal of salad, fresh vegetables, and a very skimpy portion of meat (of which Ford disapproved because of his basically vegetarian health program), the conversation again rolled around to politics.

In their discussion about the Jewish question and the Nazis, Frau Wagner and Ford did most of the talking while Siegfried only added an appropriate comment now and then. At first, Frau Wagner was a bit surprised that Ford could express himself so well on political topics. He told the Wagners that "the Jews had a tremendous power in America and that their influence was growing every day." He was trying through the articles in the *Dearborn Independent*, he said, to provide a "course of instruction" for the American people on the "conspiracy of the Jews." Then they spoke about the threat of communism in Europe, the Versailles

Treaty, and the "power of the Jews over the press." "The philosophy and ideas of Ford and Hitler were very similar," Frau Wagner later recalled.[61] Winifred and Ford began to talk about Hitler and the Nazi party. She was amazed to find that "Ford was very well informed about everything that was going on in Germany. . . . He knew all about the National Socialist movement."[62] But before Frau Wagner had time to bring up gently the subject of Hitler's need for money and suggest the possibility of a contribution, Ford himself mentioned the matter. "Ford told me," Frau Wagner recalled, "that he had helped to finance Hitler."[63] At her charming best, Winifred then suggested that Hitler was now more in need of money than ever. Ford smiled and made a vague comment about still being willing to support someone like Hitler who was working to free Germany from the Jews. Finally, Frau Wagner asked if a special representative sent by Hitler, Kurt Lüdecke, might be given an appointment to talk with Ford and discuss the matter of further cooperation between Hitler and Ford in detail. Ford nodded his assent and said he would be very interested to talk with the fellow.

After a pleasant evening the Fords and Wagners drove back to Detroit together for the concert that night. A quick change into evening clothes in their hotel room and the Wagners were ready to go to Orchestra Hall. The concert began at eight-thirty. While the orchestra tuned up, Lüdecke joined Winifred in her box. Even before she told him the good news, Lüdecke recalled, "her charming smile told me she had been successful."[64] He was to see Ford the next day to explain any further details about the Nazi party that Frau Wagner had been unable to supply, and if possible get a definite commitment for more financial support.

The next morning at nine, Liebold, Ford's secretary, picked up Lüdecke at the hotel and drove him out to meet Ford. Lüdecke was rather nervous at first, for Ford rarely received visitors, but as soon as Liebold left him in an office Ford entered with an alert step and a cheerful greeting. Lüdecke described as "the *Dearborn Independent* in the flesh! His clear, bright eyes and his strong face, almost free from wrinkles, did not betray his more than sixty years." After shutting the door, Ford eased himself into a big armchair, put one foot up on the desk and clasped his hands over his knee. Lüdecke observed his friendly gray eyes, his firm, pleasant voice, his lean figure, and "well-shaped head," which he said showed "character and race."

Lüdecke opened the conversation with a brief outline of the aims of the Nazi movement in relation to the critical political situation in Germany. As soon as Hitler came to power, Lüdecke explained, one of his first acts would be to inaugurate the social and political program that had been advocated in the *Dearborn Independent.* But it was urgent that Hitler be successful soon or "the Jews would destroy Aryan solidarity" by drawing corrupt politicians into a war between the countries of the white world. Ford listened attentively. Money, said Lüdecke, was the only obstacle that stood between the Nazis and the fulfillment in Germany of Ford's and Hitler's mutual views. He explained that the time was not ripe to unseat the Jews from their positions of power in the United States but that Germany—because of her geographic position, her historic past, and the terrific pressure of her present suffering—was the country that was to become the "torch-bearer of liberation from the Jews."

At various points in the discussion Ford would interject curt remarks, such as "I know . . . yes, the Jews, these cunning Jews . . ." Encouraged, Lüdecke continued to elaborate on the fact that Hitler's success or failure was a world issue, involving the future of America as much as that of any other nation. Anyone who helped the Nazis now would benefit from a business standpoint as well, Lüdecke said. Agreements could be arranged that would guarantee concessions in Germany as soon as Hitler came to power. Since a Nazi regime in Germany might led to a change in the Russian situation, the reopening of that vast market would bring tremendous business rewards to those who had befriended Hitler.

Lüdecke's memoirs indicate that this long-winded discussion was all in vain. He says that Ford made no definite commitment of financial assistance, but considering that Lüdecke was a Nazi, one would certainly expect him to deny that Ford gave any money to Hitler. A promise from the Nazis to keep silent about the financial contribution would probably have been part of the bargain. Despite Lüdecke's denial of any transfer of money at that time, he carefully pointed out that Ford's reputation was at stake: "No man in the public eye can endow an insurgent revolutionary movement as casually as he would contribute to . . . [a] Home for Homeless Animals."[65] The Jewish boycott, Lüdecke said, "pinched him [Ford] in the ledgers where even a multimillionaire is vulnerable."[66] If Ford was willing to reach in his pocket for the Nazis, they would have to be willing to keep the secret.

Henry Ford's reward from Hitler finally came in July 1938, when on his seventy-fifth birthday he was awarded the Grand Cross of the Supreme Order of the German Eagle. Ford was the first American and the fourth person in the world to receive this medal, which was the highest decoration that could be given to any non-German citizen. Benito Mussolini, another of Hitler's financiers, had been decorated with the same honor earlier that year.[67]

The presentation was made in Ford's Dearborn office by the German Consul of Cleveland, Karl Kapp, and Consul Fritz Hailer of Detroit. Kapp placed the red silk sash over Ford's right shoulder. The Sash was worn in a diagonal line from the right shoulder to the left hip where it was clasped with a gold and white cross. Kapp then pinned a large, shining star-shaped medal on Ford's white suit. The decoration was given "in recognition of [Ford's] pioneering in making motor cars available for the masses." Hitler's personal congratulatory message accompanied the award.[68] At Ford's birthday dinner on July 30, 1938, the citation was read aloud by Kapp to the 1,500 prominent Detroiters in attendance.

American Jews and the press voiced strong objections to Ford's acceptance of the award from Nazi Germany. During a speech to a women's Zionist organization, the Jewish entertainer Eddie Cantor called Ford "a damn fool for permitting the world's greatest gangster to give him a citation." He told his audience, "the more men like Ford we have, the more we must organize and fight."[69]

But the most bitter criticism came from Harold L. Ickes, secretary of the interior. Speaking to the Cleveland Zionist Society, he denounced Ford and other Americans "who obsequiously have accepted tokens of contemptuous distinction at a time when the bestower of them counts that day lost when he can commit no new crime against humanity."[70]

Despite all the objections, Ford was determined not to give in to their demands. He told a friend: "They [the Germans] sent me this ribbon band. They [the critics] told me to return it or else I'm not an American. I'm going to keep it."[71]

4
THYSSEN GIVES A BIG CONTRIBUTION

In mid-November 1923, about a week after the fiasco of the beer hall putsch, a handful of Nazi leaders gathered clandestinely in Salzburg, which was then blanketed with a deep layer of snow. The group of exiles included Hermann Esser, the young, fanatical anti-Semite; Gerhard Rossbach, the daring Free Corps leader; Kurt Lüdecke, the Nazis' foreign representative who had missed the putsch because he was in Italy soliciting funds; and Putzi Hanfstaengl, who had made a quick getaway when the bullets started to fly and was now slinking through the shadows with his coat collar turned up and his hat pulled down, fearing that the police were after him. They were a somber, disheartened group of souls commiserating with one another about their dire situation. Putzi moaned on and on about the thousand dollars he had lent the party: "What good is it now to have a receipt and a mortgage on the office furniture."[1] Since no one in the group had more than a pittance of money, they had to put their heads together to figure out how they could obtain funds to start to reorganize the party.

There could be no hope for financial support from the members, many of whom were now unemployed, arrested, or in hiding. And it would indeed be difficult to persuade anyone else that the Nazi cause still had a future. "If we only had our hands on the money you seized in Munich!" Lüdecke lamented aloud. He was referring to the money that the others told him they had seized on the night of the putsch. A detachment of storm troopers had invaded the publishing plant of the Parcus brothers, who were Jewish, and "in the name of the nationalist regime" confiscated several stacks of freshly printed inflation money. The total sum was 14,605 trillion marks, for which the Parcus brothers demanded a receipt, and got it. The money was hauled to the beerhall and distributed at the rate of two trillion marks, or two dollars. When the putsch collapsed, the authorities recovered the money, most of which was still tied in neat bundles.

Fortunately for the Nazis, Hitler had better ideas than his lieutenants on how to raise money. He had had time to do considerable thinking while he was in Landsberg prison, and he realized that if his party were ever to come to power, he would need not only the financial backing of wealthy people, but even more important some "friends" among the key people of the German upper class. But with the sudden end of inflation in 1924, and the economy improving, there was little reason for any industrialist to continue to support an extremist party whose leader was in jail.

Yet Hitler's original faithful supporters remained true to him even when he was imprisoned. He received a continuous profuse supply of gifts from women admirers: flowers, chocolates, cakes, and books. After visiting Hitler, Hanfstaengl said: 'The place looked like a delicatessen . . . You could have opened up a flower and fruit and wine shop with all the stuff stacked there. People were sending presents from all over Germany and Hitler had grown visibly fatter on the proceeds."

Hitler was released from prison the day before Christmas

of 1924, and he immediately set about reorganizing the party. Several thousand followers remained loyal to him. The official refounding of the Nazi party was a major news event, and the publicity naturally drew some new supporters, among them a Munich businessman, Albert Pietsch, the director and principal owner of a chemical company, who contributed one thousand marks to the National Socialist party. Pietsch later said that he was attracted by Hitler's fascinating oratory and his uncompromising attitude toward socialism and communism. He continued to give similar contributions to Hitler from time to time, but no larger amounts of money were ever mentioned.[2]

The German economy was improving steadily. The mark was stable, the unemployment rate was dropping, the people were generally content. In fact, the years between 1924 and 1928 are now referred to by historians as the German "period of prosperity." The Nazis were able to attract few new members under such conditions. But if new recruits were scarce in 1924, money was even harder to come by. In those days, the major sources of party revenue were still the members' meager dues of a mark a month, collections and charges of admission for meetings, and the small profit earned from the party newspapers and the publishing house.

How then was Hitler to win some support from the upper class and big business? During the period of prosperity following the time of inflation, there seemed to be little he could do at first to make the industrialists take notice of his existence. In 1926, however, a new domestic issue appeared that aroused political passions. The question concerned the expropriation of the property of the many royal dynasties that had ruled the German states up to 1918. These princely rulers, such as the king of Bavaria and the duke of Württemberg, had not only governed local affairs but also had owned vast lands, palaces, and castles.

In 1918 the revolution had failed to settle the question of the deposed dynasties' properties. They were neither confiscated nor were any other arrangements made officially. The settlement had been left to the individual state governments. A few of them took over the property of the princes but "only in order to keep it secure pending negotiations." Prussia, for example, confiscated the Hohenzollern property and "temporarily" put it under the administration of the state.* Kaiser Wilhelm immediately dispatched a letter to the Prussian government in which he said: "I have renounced the throne in the manner which had been suggested to me by the government. Doing this, I had expected that the government . . . would free my own and my family's property."[3]

However, once the Weimer Constitution was ratified, its Article 153 established the rights of private property and also made the property of the dynasties safe from expropriation. Then in 1926 the Communists and socialists introduced a bill in the Reichstag demanding expropriation of the princely dynasties without compensation and further demanded the issue be settled by a plebiscite. Big business was generally indifferent if not opposed to the interests of the princes. However, the crucial question of the plebiscite for them was the protection of private property. Most non-Marxist parties saw the socialist-Communist bill as an attack against the right of property. Thus, by opposing the expropriation of the princes, the nonsocialist parties were primarily acting to protect private property.

In order to have any hope of ever getting support from wealthy individuals, the aristocrats, or big business, Hitler had to oppose the expropriation of the princes. Yet the matter was not so simple because a considerable number of Nazis, led by Gregor Strasser, were in favor of expropriation.

Strasser was a big, powerfully built man, a reasonably

---

*Before the unification of Germany, Kaiser Wilhelm's Hohenzollern ancestors were the kings of Prussia. Thus most of the property owned by the Hohenzollerns was located in Prussia. After the unification in 1871, Berlin, which had been the capital of Prussia, also became the capital city of all Germany.

good speaker, and very able organizer. After Hitler, Strasser was the second most powerful man in the Nazi party. In many ways his background was similar to that of Hitler's. Strasser was born in Bavaria, the son of a petty official. He volunteered for the army during World War I and was awarded the Iron Cross, First Class. Following the war, he fought under the command of General von Epp against the Munich Soviet Republic in May 1919. The next year, he got married and opened his own pharmacy in the small town of Landshut. His hatred of the Communists led him to organize the town's veterans into a military battalion. At the end of 1920, he joined the Nazis and soon became the district leader of the party in Lower Bavaria. He was arrested for participating in the Munich putsch but was released when he was elected to the Bavarian Landtag (state congress). Due to his organizational abilities and his skill as a writer and speaker, Strasser was appointed by Hitler as the leader of the Nazis in the north of Germany.

Strasser's good sense of humor, friendly personality, and willingness to compromise were balanced by a ferocious determination, conviction in his beliefs, and willingness to fight. As a speaker, he could roar like a lion and intimidate those who stood in his way. He was always proud to tell how he confronted the representative of the soldiers' soviet in Landshut when returning from World War I with his troops:

> "There he stood, the lousy bum, and chattered and clattered on with his stupid swine grunts that he had learned by heart about the International, the victorious proletariat, the bloodthirsty generals and warmongers, the sweat-squeezing capitalists and stockbrokers. I sat up there on my nag, which I secretly nudged against the guy so that he was always having to step backward again and again, and I said nothing and slowly collected a whole mouthful of spit. Finally the guy got to the end and screamed out: 'Deliver up your weapons! Rip up your flags and insignia!

Vote for the Soviet of Soldiers!' And by then I was ready: I let him have the whole mouthful of spit right in the middle of his face; I flooded the bum away. And then I gave the order 'Battery . . . trot!' and we marched back into Landshut the same way we had marched out in 1914."[4]

Early in 1925 Strasser gave up his pharmacist's practice in Landshut and devoted himself exclusively to building up the Nazi movement in northern Germany and the industrial cities of the Rhineland.[5] With the help of his brother Otto, who was a talented journalist, he made rapid progress. Hitler quickly recognized that the growing influence of Gregor Strasser was a threat to his control over the party. Moreover, the Strassers were inclined to take the "socialist" part of the party program rather seriously, advocating the nationalization of heavy industry and large landholdings. Hitler, for both strategic and ideological reasons, was against this movement to the left. He did not want to spoil his chances for an alliance with the ruling elite.

On November 22, 1925, Strasser called a meeting of the party gauleiters of northern Germany in Hanover.* Along with most of the gauleiters, Strasser was restive under the control of Munich and was opposed to Hitler on many important questions. Feelings against Hitler were running high and crystallized around the question of whether or not the property of the former German royal houses should be expropriated. Strasser and the north German leaders wanted the Nazi party to stand behind the Social Democratic government's move to expropriate the princes' property. This view clashed with statements Hitler had already made to the effect that the party was against the government's plan because the possessions of the deposed royal houses were their own private property. Hitler had called the move for

---

*A GAU was a party district. These districts basically corresponded with the thirty-four Reichstag electoral districts. The Nazi party leader in each district was called a gauleiter.

expropriation a "Jewish swindle." The fact that many Jews, being property owners, favored the side of the princes meant nothing to him.

All those present at the Hanover meeting voted to follow Strasser's policy in favor of expropriation, except Gottfried Feder, the party ideologist, and Dr. Robert Ley, gauleiter of Cologne. Hitler responded to the challenge of Strasser and his followers by summoning a conference of the entire party leadership, on February 14, 1926, in the Bavarian town of Bamberg. Otto Strasser gave an account of this conference, asserting that February 14 was a weekday and therefore none of the north German and Rhineland leaders except Gregor Strasser and his assistant, Joseph Goebbels, were able to attend.[6] But the assertion is false; the fourteenth was a Sunday, and everyone who was anyone in the north German movement was there, including all the rebellious gauleiters who had met in Hanover a few months before.[7]

Chosen especially by Hitler as the site of the meeting, Bamberg was a picturesque little medieval town in northern Bavaria. The population of the region was generally conservative, so the Nazis would not have to worry about disruptions from the socialists. To impress the northern delegates Hitler transported hundreds of storm troopers and party supporters from Munich. As they arrived at the railroad station, the delegates were greeted by an S.A. band and a Brownshirt unit. Outside the station there were several party automobiles decorated with swastika banners waiting to drive them to the meeting. Strasser's followers were not used to such treatment; they normally took the streetcar or walked where they were going. Outside the meeting hall itself enthusiastic crowds cheered and uniformed S.A. men stood at attention along the street. Everywhere delegates looked there were red swastika flags fluttering in the breeze.

The party representatives from northern Germany were impressed, as Hitler had planned. They were rarely able to wear their brown shirts or display the swastika flag, and usually they even had to hold their meetings in some quiet out-of-the-way place to prevent an attack by the Communists.

Now Hitler was ready to come to grips with all his opponents within the party, but only Gregor Strasser spoke up against him. The two protagonists fought out their differences in a daylong debate on socialism versus nationalism, and the expropriation of the princes' property.

In a speech that lasted several hours Hitler denounced the advocates of expropriation as deceitful because they never mentioned expropriating the property of "the Jewish lords of banking and the stock exchange." He admitted the princes should not receive anything they had no right to, but what justly belonged to them should not be taken from them. The National Socialist party stood for the concepts of private property and justice. His south German followers applauded these sentiments and were hesitantly joined by a few north Germans. Then Hitler began to tear up the whole leftist program of the Strasser group point for point, by comparing it with the party program of 1920. Could any true Nazi deviate from the founding document of the party?

Since they had given public endorsement to expropriation, Gregor Strasser and Goebbels were humiliated. After the meeting Goebbels wrote in his diary: "What kind of a Hitler is this? A reactionary? Amazingly clumsy and uncertain. Russian questions: altogether beside the point. . . . Our duty is the destruction of Bolshevism. Bolshevism is a Jewish creation!! . . . a question of not weakening private property (sick!). Horrible."[8] Although the left-wing Nazis were distraught by the results of the meeting, they bowed to Hitler's will.

Hitler's success in stifling dissent and debate within the Nazi party turned out to be more important for him than the results of the plebiscite. To pass the proposed bill, approval of a majority of all eligible voters (approximately 39½ million votes) was necessary. But when the people went to the polls on June 20, 1926, only 15,551,218 votes instead of the required majority were registered in favor of expropriation without compensation. However, the fact that the Nazis opposed expropriation was hardly noticed by big business, because the Nazis had the support of very few people compared to the established moderate parties. Of course, if Hitler had not been able to control the left-wing Nazis on the expropriation issue, he might well have lost the help of the few wealthy individuals whose support he had.

All evidence seems to indicate that Hitler's campaign to win support among the industrialists from 1926 to 1928 was not very successful. During these years the National Socialist party was, for the most part, financed by membership dues, collections at speeches, and the sales of party newspapers. In other words, Hitler's hard core of fanatical followers kept the movement going by contributing generously from what little they had. So the financial position of the party remained desperate throughout this period. Even by the end of August 1928 there were debts amounting to over 14,000 marks, and most of the Gau organizations suffered from similar monetary problems.[9] Schwarz, the party treasurer, was able to balance the books only by such questionable methods as listing dues of expected membership increase on the credit side of the ledger and subtracting forty marks per month from the salary of each Nazi legislator.

Despite the party's financial difficulties, it should not be thought that Hitler himself was living in poverty. His personal income after 1925 was said to have come primarily from the royalties he received on his book and the fees from articles he wrote for the party press. The first volume of *Mein Kampf* was published in June 1925. It cost twelve marks, double the price of the average German book, but despite the high price Max Amann, the director of the Nazi party publishing house, claimed to have sold 23,000 copies in the first year. (This sales figure is probably exaggerated and includes the copies given away free.)[10] Hitler's income tax file and correspondence with the government tax agents show that he had an income of 19,843 marks in 1925.[11] The largest item on his expense account was 20,000 marks for an automobile, a supercharged Mercedes that he bought shortly after his release from prison. He accounted for this expenditure by saying he borrowed the money from a bank.

Being driven at top speeds was a great passion of Hitler's. Before the 1923 putsch he had owned an old Selve touring car, then a Benz, which the police seized after his arrest. Almost as soon as he was released from Landsberg, he began looking around for a new car. He believed that an impressive automobile was an important prop for a politician and was able to talk an automobile agency into selling him one of its most expensive Mercedes on generous credit terms, at a time when he could hardly afford such a luxury. In spite of his interest in automobiles, Hitler never drove himself; even in 1925 he employed a chauffeur. In fact, it aroused the suspicion of the tax agents that Hitler could afford to pay his private chauffeur two hundred marks a month.

The source of Hitler's income during this period was the subject of rumor and gossip in Munich. His income tax returns do little to clarify the picture, for he reported as personal income only the payments he received from his writings.[12] Is it to be assumed that he had no other income? Were all the gifts known to have been given to him personally by people like Helene Bechstein, the wife of the wealthy piano manufacture, turned over to the party treasury? Where did he get the money to pay off the bank loans that he received between 1925 and 1928, which he reported in his tax returns? Where did he get the money to rent and furnish the luxurious apartment on the Prinzregentenplatz in 1929 and staff it with servants? Where did he get the money to lease and maintain the Villa Wachenfeld at Berchtesgaden? These questions remained unanswered. The only possible conclusion is that Hitler had sources of money that remain unknown even today.

By the beginning of 1929 there was an obvious change in Hitler's financial fortunes. He suddenly seemed to have plenty of money. Such funds must have come from an almost limitless source. And indeed they did, for Hitler now had the backing of one of the richest men in Germany, Fritz Thyssen.

Fritz Thyssen is remembered as the man who gave more money to Hitler than any other individual, yet the reasons for both his fervent adherence to and later dispute with Nazism arc generally unknown. Until he was fifty-three years old, Fritz Thyssen was the "Crown Prince" of the Thyssen steel empire located in Muehlheim-on-the-Ruhr. He knew all the frustrations common to sons of dominant fathers. Old August Thyssen kept his son Fritz busy attending advanced technical schools all over Europe, partly to keep him away from the business, which he himself insisted upon administering almost until his death. The old man seemed almost relieved when the son, finding himself all but useless, went on extensive travels to the Far East, India, and North and South America.

Although he was a small, wiry, self-made man who grew up on a farm, August Thyssen was a practical hardheaded businessman. His firm was everything to him, and his intellectual horizon extended no further than the boundaries of his industrial empire. He was eighty-four years old when he died in 1926. That same year Germany's greatest steel trust, the United Steel Works, came into being. The Thyssen interests were the principal component in the merger. Fritz Thyssen was chosen as chairman of the board of the new combine, a position he held until 1936. His job was not to be an easy one, for the German steel industry was in severe financial trouble after 1918; in fact, the formation of the United Steel Works was more a defensive measure by the steel industry than a movement of expansion.[13]

Unlike his father, over whom he towered with his six foot height, Fritz Thyssen was the contemplative type. He was always philosophizing and pondering. He was sensitive to matters of religion and conviction, and always seemed to be looking for causes that he might advance. Still, he was not really a man of superior intellect or penetration, a fact of which he was painfully aware. Nevertheless, his personality was generally well balanced. He was a hard worker who was in his office punctually at nine o'clock every morning, but people meeting him for the first time were usually surprised by his "charming" personality. He had an excellent sense of humor and was an unusually witty conversationalist. He loved good food and the best wines and was often known to spend three hours over lunch.

Thyssen served as an officer in World War I. He shared the sufferings and the hopes of all the soldiers at the front. When he came home on leave he saw that the civilian population was growing weary of the hardships of the war economy. In the Rhenish-Westphalian industrial region where his father's factories were located, the fires of revolution had been smoldering for a long time. In 1917 there had been strikes and serious disorders. A great number of demonstrators had been arrested in the various industrial centers of the Rhine. The strikers were principally motivated by a lack of food and other material hardships, but political agitators took advantage of these causes to fan the flames of class hatred.

In Muehlheim the situation was tense in the fall of 1918. Although the local workers' and soldiers' councils that now held power had posted notices that excesses and looting would be punished, the streets were no longer safe. Gradually the moderate elements that had at first held a majority in the councils were pushed aside by radical agitators.

At this time, Hitler was still a common soldier in Munich, watching the revolution develop there. Being an unknown man without property, he was essentially in no danger from the revolution and so could study its developments from the sidelines. His studies of anti-Communist political parties in Vienna had prepared Hitler intellectually for the 1918 revolution. Although a fervent nationalist, he had no strong loyalty to monarchy as a political system and so was already thinking of alternative systems of government. Thyssen and the men of his class, on the other hand, found themselves completely lost. They had been loyal monarchists up to 1918 and, unlike Hitler, had never thought of any alternative method of government. They and their property were under direct attack from the revolution, but none of them had any ideas of how to meet it. They attempted compromise, but Hitler was already certain the Communists would have to be confronted by something stronger than compromise.

On the evening of December 7, 1918, a group of men armed with rifles pounded on the door of the Thyssen villa. They had come to arrest Fritz Thyssen, but they also decided to take away his father, despite his advanced age. Along with four other industrialists, the Thyssens were thrown into the prison at Muehlheim. In the middle of the night, they were awakened by a dozen rough-looking men carrying rifles and wearing red armbands. They pushed the six prisoners down a narrow corridor and into a dark courtyard illuminated by the glare of a single spotlight. The industrialists were ordered to line up against the wall. "I thought they were going to execute us," said Thyssen. There they waited. The moments seemed like hours.

Then, finally, the silence was broken. One of the guards shouted something; the prisoners would be taken to the railway station to catch the train for Berlin. The industrialists were placed in a third-class car and their guards took up posts near the doors in order to prevent any attempted escape. There was no heat in the train and it was very cold. Fortunately the elder Thyssen had been able to take a blanket with him. The train arrived at the Potsdam station in Berlin the following evening. On the platform a Red guard detachment was waiting. The Muehlheim Communists handed their prisoners over to them and jeered at the "capitalist pigs," who they said would soon meet their fate. Old August Thyssen, who had left his blanket in he train, politely asked one of the guards wearing a red armband if he could go and get it for him. "What are you talking to me for?" the man responded indignantly. "I am the chief of police of Berlin."

They later learned that this was Emil Eichhorn, whom

Fritz Thyssen described as "a dangerous Communist agitator in the service of Soviet Russia." During the early days of the revolution the radical socialists had nominated Eichhorn chief of the Berlin Police. He had transformed the central police station into a fortress known as the "Red House" and had picked his personal bodyguard from the Berlin proletariat. Some of them were political prisoners who had been released from prison only a few weeks earlier. At the time, said Thyssen, it was rumored that "Eichhorn had ordered the arrest of many political enemies and officials of the old regime, and that he had had them executed in the courtyard of the police headquarters without trial."* Naturally the Thyssens and their companions again feared for their lives.

Eichhorn's men took the prisoners from the Potsdam station to police headquarters for "interrogation." The prisoners were assembled before Eichhorn. "You are accused," he said, "of treason and antirevolutionary activities. You are enemies of the people and have asked for the intervention of French troops in order to prevent the socialist revolution." The industrialists all protested that they had no contact with the French Army of occupation.

Eichhorn interrupted insolently: "Don't try to deny it. I am well informed. The day before yesterday you had a conference at Dortmund with other industrialists and you have decided to send a delegation to the French general asking him to occupy the Ruhr. This is treason. What have you to say, gentlemen?"

The prisoners looked at one mother in astonishment. None of them had gone to Dortmund. Thyssen and his father said they knew nothing of such a conference. Moreover, they had an alibi. Neither of them had left Muehlheim for a week; numerous witnesses could affirm this.

"Those witnesses! All bourgeois! Their statements have

---

*The rumor was false. There is no evidence Eichhorn ordered any illegal executions, but of course, Thyssen did not know this at the time.

no value whatever," Eichhorn shouted brutally. "Take 'em away."[14]

As they were led out of Eichhorn's office the industrialists again trembled for their fate. Had they escaped death at Muehlheim only to be shot in Berlin? After a short time their guards were told that there was no more room for prisoners at police headquarters. "Take them to Moabit," a Communist leader growled. Moabit was the main prison of Berlin. At the gate of the Red House a prison van was waiting for the industrialists. Through the bars of the van they could see the agitation in the Berlin streets as they drove along. Near the Alexanderplatz machine guns were set up and an armored car was on patrol. After about twenty minutes, the van entered the prison yard. An official came out to meet the industrialists and said: "I don't know anything about this affair. At any rate, it is perhaps much better for you to be here. With me at least you are safe."

The director of the Moabit prison was an old official who was responsible to the Prussian state administration and not to Eichhorn.* Thyssen's father was placed in the infirmary because of his age. He endured everything with the utmost calm. "Never mind," he said, "at my age no great accident can befall me."[15] The other industrialists and Fritz Thyssen were placed in regular prison cells.

On the fourth day, Thyssen and his father were freed along with the four other industrialists. Eichhorn had had their statements verified and had no evidence against them. His position in Berlin was precarious at the time, so he decided it was better to release them.

It is easy to see how a close call with execution would have a traumatic effect on anyone. To a great extent Thyssen's later association with and financing of Hitler was motivated by his dread of the "Red Terror." Although none of Hitler's other financial supporters were actually put through

---

*The city of Berlin was located in the state of Prussia, hence some prisons in the city were controlled by the Prussian state government.

the agonizing mental torture of being stood up against a wall in the middle of the night, to a certain extent they all feared for their lives during the revolutionary days of 1918 to 1919. They read daily in the newspapers of the brutal murders of the Russian upper class by the Bolsheviks. Then in Germany itself, twelve upper-class hostages were shot down in the courtyard of a school in Munich. The friends of those killed became some of Adolph Hitler's first supporters.

After their harrowing experience, the Thyssens returned home only to face another crisis. At the nearby town of Hamborn, where the Thyssens also owned a factory, the radicals had gained power.[16] Thyssen believed the man behind this trouble was Karl Radek, a Russian Communist agitator.[17] On Christmas Eve, a strike was proclaimed at Hamborn. Alarmed, the mayor of Hamborn called Thyssen on the telephone and asked him to come over and attempt to settle the dispute. However, Thyssen replied that Hugo Stinnes, one of the most powerful industrialists in the Ruhr, had already negotiated an agreement with the trade unions in the name of all the industrialists of the Rhineland. He told the mayor he would not conclude any separate arrangements beyond what Stinnes had agreed upon.[18]

Early the following morning five armed Communist workers arrived at the Thyssen villa in Muehlheim. They had come to take Thyssen to Hamborn by force. "I did not fancy the prospect of repeating my recent Berlin experience," Thyssen recalled. He told the butler to let the men know that he was dressing and ask them to come in and take some coffee while he was getting ready. While they were drinking coffee, Thyssen warned his wife and told her to take their daughter and go to Duisburg, which was occupied by Belgian troops. In the meantime, Thyssen himself was to go and warn his father, who was living about eight miles from Muehlheim in the castle of Landsberg on the Ruhr. Leaving by a secret passage and a hidden door, Thyssen proceeded to Landsberg. He told his father what had happened, and they left immediately on foot along the road.

Fortunately, they were soon given a ride in a passing car, which saved the elder Thyssen a painful walk of about seven miles. "We had good reason to fear that we would be arrested once more," recalled Fritz Thyssen. "Already the rumor was spreading that well-known personalities had been shot by Communist bands. . . . The impression which those agitated days have left upon me have never been blotted out," said Thyssen. "I have spent my life among workers. My father had worked with them at the beginning of his career. Never have the workers of our factories shown us any kind of hostility, still less of hatred . . . all disorders and excesses have almost always been due to foreigners."[19]

Thyssen believed that the organizers of the strikes and riots were professional political agitators and agents of Moscow. "Radek . . . Leviné . . . Axelrod . . . these were the men responsible for the riots and murders," Thyssen said. All the revolutionary leaders Thyssen came in contact with or mentioned were Jewish. Although he later denied being an anti-Semite, he certainly felt the Jews were one of the principal forces behind communism. Without doubt, Thyssen's experiences in 1918 to 1919 made him ripe for Hitler's anti-Semitism.

Despite their completely different backgrounds, the thinking of Hitler and Thyssen was shaped by the events of 1918 in a very similar way. Although Hitler was already an anti-Semite, the major role Jewish leaders played in the November revolution was probably more important than any other factor in confirming his anti-Semitic beliefs. Certainly blaming the Jews for the revolution was completely unfair, for only a small percentage of the total Jewish population were Communists; but one would hardly expect someone like Hitler to view the matter fairly. However Thyssen, of all people, should have known better because he was personally acquainted with prominent Jewish industrialists, such as Walter Rathenau and Paul Silverberg.

In contrast to Thyssen's suspicions about the Jews, he thought the Social Democratic party consisted of "reasonable and moderate" people. When the miners went on strike in January of 1919 he took part in the negotiations with the strikers. "They understood the difficult position of the industrialists," he said. The owners in return tried their best to ease the food shortages of the workers' families that resulted from the continuation of the Allied blockade. The agreement made between the Ruhr industrialists and their workers broke down only because of the intervention of radical outside agitators.

"Strikes followed one another without either motive or results," said Thyssen. During that chaotic period, it seemed impossible to reorganize industrial production. The mining of coal had come almost to a standstill. There was even fear that saboteurs might destroy the machinery of the mines. "No one was any longer assured of his individual freedom," recalled Thyssen. "Or even of the safety of his life. A man could be arrested and shot without any reason."

"It was then," said Thyssen, "that I realized the necessity—if Germany was not to sink into anarchy—of fighting all this radical agitation which, far from giving happiness to the workers, only created disorder. The Social Democratic party endeavored to maintain order, but it was too weak. The memory of those days did much to dispose me, later on, to offer my help to National Socialism, which I believed to be capable of solving in a new manner the pressing industrial and social problems of . . . Germany,"[20]

In the late spring and summer of 1919 Fritz Thyssen served as an economic advisor to the German delegates at the Versailles Peace Conference. He stayed nearly three months at Versailles and left in mid-June to accompany the German delegates back to Weimar, where the government and the National Assembly were in session. He tried to convince the deputies of the Catholic Center party, whom he knew, that it would be an error to accept the conditions of the Allies. Most of the deputies realized that the terms of the treaty could not be fulfilled, but they felt there was no choice but to sign. Thyssen thought this was a mistake. By signing, the Germans pledged themselves to the treaty. Yet they knew fulfilling the conditions of the treaty was impossible.[21] The dilemma the German leaders found themselves in was a tragic one. Rejection of the treaty would mean surrendering the country to immediate foreign occupation and revolutionary upheaval.

President Ebert and the Social Democratic party decided in favor of signing. They were supported by the Catholic Center party and its leader, Matthias Erzberger, whose political style was one of compromise and subtle maneuvering. Thyssen and his father, who were Catholics and probably the wealthiest members of the Catholic Center party, dropped out of the party when Erzberger agreed to sign the Versailles Treaty. Signing this humiliating treaty, said Thyssen, "condemned a whole nation to a sort of economic slavery." The conditions of the treaty were made even more insulting by forcing the Germans into an admission of "war guilt." The revolutionary upheavals and the humiliation of the Versailles Treaty that followed gave rise to a violent nationalist reaction that gathered momentum throughout the country.[22]

The fight against the Versailles Treaty was a key issue of Hitler's program. In time Thyssen would be in complete agreement with Hitler on this point, for both political and economic reasons. Again, he was personally involved in the issue. He saw for himself the intransigence of the French and how the articles of the treaty were designed to rob Germany and put her in an economic straitjacket. Although he was completely unaware of it then, one by one Fritz Thyssen's personal experiences were bringing him closer and closer to Hitler. First there was his fear of communism, then his suspicions of the Jews being behind Marxism, then his determination not to accept the Versailles Treaty.

In March of 1920 the extreme reactionaries attempted to seize power in the Kapp putsch. Although Free Corps troops supporting the conservative politician Wolfgang Kapp took

Berlin with ease, a general strike called by President Ebert forced them to yield. In the Rhineland the consequence of this clumsy counterrevolution was a new Communist insurrection. In Essen, Duisburg, Düsseldorf, and Muehlheim, Communist revolutionary committees seized political power under the pretext of the general strike proclaimed by the Ebert government. The radicals immediately organized a well-armed workers' militia.

As soon as the trouble began, Thyssen left Muehlheim with his family and proceeded to Krefeld on the left bank of the Rhine where the occupation troops were preventing any disorders. The bridge over the Rhine was guarded by Belgians, who allowed Thyssen and his family to pass. The German industrialists were very apprehensive about the new revolutionary movement, which again disorganized the whole economic life of the region. The insurrection lasted about two weeks. Finally the army was obliged to intervene to reestablish order. Bloody battles took place at Duisburg and Wesel between the army and the revolutionary militia. The abortive Kapp putsch and the wave of revolution that followed it had lasting repercussions in the Ruhr. There was a feeling of antagonism that could no longer be calmed. During the following year more strikes and street battles occurred in many industrial cities.

The recurrence of revolutionary uprisings resulted in a strong yearning for political stability on the part of the upper class. Thyssen told some of his friends that he wanted law and order "at any price." That was just what Hitler was offering. Thyssen never completely endorsed Hitler's authoritarian ideas, but he wanted a "strong state" enough that he was willing to sacrifice a few freedoms to get it.

When the French occupied the Ruhr in 1923, Thyssen, unlike some other industrialists, remained at his factory and helped organize the passive resistance.[23] The German coal syndicate called a meeting in Hamburg. Thyssen attended along with other prominent industrialists, such as Stinnes, Krupp. Kirdorf, and Kloeckner. His opinion was that the coal owners should resist the delivery of goods demanded by the French.

On January 20, Thyssen and several other mine owners were arrested by the French and transferred to the military prison at Mainz. He was charged with inducing organized labor to resist, and with disobeying French military orders under martial law. When they heard the news of his imprisonment, the workers of the Thyssen factories became agitated. At his trial, Thyssen's defense culminated in the fearless sentence: "I am a German and I refuse to obey French orders on German soil." Several clashes between the people and the French Army of occupation had already occurred. In the face of this unrest among the workers, the French government decided it was best to be lenient. Instead of condemning Thyssen to five years' imprisonment as had been expected, the court-martial imposed a fine of 300,000 gold marks.

The humiliating treatment he received from the French left a permanent scar on Thyssen's character. Up to that time he had been relatively international in his thinking, but now he became intellectually and emotionally ready for Hitler's sort of extreme nationalism. When Hitler argued that Germany had to rearm to protect itself against the aggressive French Army camped on the Rhine, many men like Thyssen reluctantly agreed that he was right.

As he left the court, the population of Mainz and the delegations of workers who had come from the Ruhr staged a great demonstration in Thyssen's honor. He was carried to the railway station in triumph. When he returned to Muehlheim, Thyssen began in earnest to organize the passive resistance that was Germany's only defense against the occupation. The German government had forbidden coal deliveries to the Allies and had instructed all the workers to refuse to obey the orders of the French authorities. The railroad employees went on strike. Navigation on the Rhine came to a standstill. As a result, the French themselves had to provide the means for transporting all passengers and freight. The coal accumulated in great mountains at the mouths of the mine pits because no train or boat would transport any of it to Belgium or France.

Although the passive resistance in the Muehlheim region was organized by Thyssen, he had the absolute cooperation of the whole population, including the trade-union leaders. His experiences during the passive resistance campaign led Thyssen to believe that Germany could still have a bright future if only the class hostility between the workers and employers could be put aside in the name of nationalism.

Thus Thyssen began to think, as Hitler had already, of the possibility of a patriotic, nationalist workers' party that would win the lower classes away from Marxism. When this idea was combined with the beliefs that Thyssen drew from his unpleasant personal experiences since 1918, the result was amazingly similar to Hitler's basic political program.

In October 1923, just a month before Hitler's ill-fated beer hall putsch in Munich, it looked as if there was about to be another Communist revolution in Germany. Thyssen decided to visit General Ludendorff, the World War I hero who was viewed as the senior officer of all right-wing forces, and ended up giving him 100,000 gold marks to distribute between the Nazi party and the Free Corps Oberland, another right-wing paramilitary group.[24] On November 9, 1923, Hitler's' attempted putsch was brought to an abrupt halt.

For the next five years the Nazis heard nothing from Thyssen. Then in the fall of 1928, Hitler became desperate for money to finance the purchase of his new palatial party headquarters. Rudolf Hess, Hitler's private secretary, approached the wealthy pro-Nazi Emil Kirdorf for the money. Kirdorf was a reactionary coal tycoon who had contributed heavily to the Nazis the previous summer. At that time, during the summer of 1927, the Nazi party was almost bankrupt, and Kirdorf's money helped pay off some of the outstanding debts and made the party solvent again. However, by the fall of 1928, Kirdorf himself was short of cash. He told Hess he was unable to raise on such short notice the money Hitler needed to finance the purchase of the new headquarters. He suggested that Hess try Fritz Thyssen. With Kirdorf's assistance a meeting was arranged. Hess, who was well educated and from a good background, presented Hitler's case with considerable skill. Thyssen decided it was once again time to help the Nazis.

Thyssen arranged for a loan of the required sum (which he later claimed was only 250,000 marks) through a Dutch bank. The exact terms of the deal are not known, but it is clear that Thyssen expected Hitler to repay at least some of the money. There are also strong indications that by obtaining the money for Hitler, Thyssen hoped to be able to exercise an influence over Nazi policy. He later said, "I chose a Dutch bank because I did not want to be mixed up with German banks in my position, and because . . . I thought I would have the Nazis a little more in my hands."[25]

According to Thyssen's account, the Nazis repaid only "a small part" of the money.[26] He then had no alternative but quietly to pay the balance due the Dutch bank. This supposedly amounted to 150,000 marks (or about $360,000 in today's money). However, the modest sum of 150,000 marks would not even have covered the downpayment on the Barlow Palace (Brown House). One leading Nazi estimated that just the remodeling of the palace, which Hitler directed himself, cost over 800,000 marks (or about $2 million in today's money).[27] Naturally, Thyssen may have later tried to give the impression that he gave less to the Nazis than he actually did. But when the Barlow Palace was transformed into the splendid new Nazi party headquarters, the Brown House, there could be no doubt that Hitler now had considerable funds at his disposal.

The Brown House was located on the Briennerstrasse in the most aristocratic neighborhood of Munich. The building itself was three stories high, set back from the street between narrow, fenced gardens. When one Nazi saw the Brown House for the first time, he said: "Only the swastika flag floating over the roof convinced me that this was not a cardinal's palace or a Jewish banker's luxurious residence."[28] The former palace was elegantly remodeled according to Hitler's own plans. He transformed great halls into moderate-size rooms by constructing new walls and intermediary floors.

The result was impressive. The visitor entered through two huge bronze doors where two S.A. men were always on guard. He would then pass into a large hall decorated with swastika flags. A grand staircase led to the second floor, where the offices of Hitler and his staff were located. The interiors of these rooms were decorated with dark wood paneling and rich red leather armchairs. "Everything had that air of richness which comes only from expensive materials," said a visitor. One of the distinctive features of the building was a cozy beer-cellar restaurant in the basement. Here a fat, jolly chef and his wife prepared meals to suit every taste from Hitler's vegetarian dishes to Goering's gourmet feasts.

After Thyssen financed the purchase of the Brown House for the Nazis, his relationship with Hitler became much closer. Hitler and Hess were invited to spend the weekend at one of Thyssen's Rhineland castles.[29] And whenever Thyssen was in Munich he tried to arrange to have lunch or dinner with Hitler, during which they discussed current political events.

It was also during this period that Thyssen developed a close personal friendship with Hermann Goering. "He [Goering] lived in a very small apartment in those days, and he was anxious to enlarge it in order to cut a better figure. I paid the cost of this improvement," said Thyssen. "At that time Goering seemed a most agreeable person. In political matters he was very sensible. I also came to know his first wife, Carin, who was a Swedish Countess [sic] by birth. She was an exceedingly charming woman."[30]

Thyssen frequently visited Goering in Berlin. Before long, he gave him money not only for political expenses but for his personal financial needs as well. According to Thyssen's own statements, he made three donations to Goering at this time of 50,000 marks each. Whenever Goering was in the Rhineland he was invited to stay with Thyssen. The two men shared a common passion for gourmet food and works of art. Goering walked through Thyssen's palatial home admiring the old master paintings, dreaming of the day when he too would have fine artwork like his industrialist friend.

"I saw something of Fritz Thyssen in 1929 and 1930," wrote the well-known journalist R. G. Waldeck, "when we both used to take the cure at a spa in the Black Forest." According to Waldeck, Thyssen had already "staked everything on Hitler." It was widely rumored that the United Steel Works would soon be facing bankruptcy. Economic motives were to become increasingly important for Fritz Thyssen as the depression began, but they were not enough to account for his support of National Socialism. During their long walks through the cool pine woods, it became obvious to Waldeck that Thyssen "believed in Hitler and liked Goering." He spoke of them "with warmth" and explained that they were a kind of "new men" who would make Germany united and strong again and put an end to the threat of communism. To his more apprehensive fellow industrialists, Thyssen would say, slightly irritated: "None of *us* can get the country out of the mess!" And he would shrug off that part of Hitler's program that advocated discrimination against the Jews. Hitler himself did not mean it, he assured Jewish friends. As for Hitler's socialism: "Good God, a leader of the masses on the make has to say many things." The revolution was to be strictly a national revolution, not a social one. He had Hitler's word for it.[31]

5

WHAT DID BIG BUSINESS WANT?

Because the crimes Hitler committed later in his career were so monstrous, historians have naturally concentrated on the negatives of his program even in the 1920s. True, even then anti-Semitism, authoritarianism, and militarism were an important part of Hitler's philosophy and propaganda. However, the issues that meant the most to middle-class Germans and businessmen at the time were Hitler's anti-communism and his fight to overcome the injustice of the Versailles Treaty.

From the beginning, anti-communism was one of the major points of Hitler's program. Naturally he wasn't the only anti-Communist politician in Germany, but he differed from the others in two important respects. First, his appeal to the common people offered a chance to win the working class away from communism. Second, unlike the traditional middle-class politicians who only wanted to mention the evils of socialism in hushed tones for fear of a violent confrontation, Hitler wanted to smash the skulls of the Marxists, to physically fight with them in the streets. This violent approach had a strong appeal to the people who were fed up with being terrorized by Red mobs.

No one had forgotten the Communist revolution in Germany that briefly controlled Berlin, Munich, and a number of the German cities. The German Communists were supported by Lenin and the Russian Communists, who were eager to export their revolution and get control of German industry.

The German middle and upper classes were justifiably terrified during this period when revolutionary mobs called for the confiscation of private property and the establishment of workers soviets to control business. Armed bands of disheveled, hungry young men, wearing red armbands, smashed store windows and erected barricades of overturned trolly cars and automobiles in the streets. Rifle shots rang out in the night as mutinous soldiers and sailors, Marxist fanatics, and escaped convicts roamed the streets. For a while it seemed Germany would suffer the same fate as Russia, which had just fallen to Communist tyranny. To people shaken by all this chaos, Hitler's disciplined columns of Brownshirt storm troopers were a reassuring sight.

As much as anti-communism was the key to Hitler's domestic appeal, so his strident opposition to the Versailles Treaty was the key to his foreign policy. In fact, he elevated attacks on the treaty to a fine art form, full of drama and passion. He played on the stark contrast between the Allies words—Wilson's Fourteen Points, which promised freedom and self-determination—and the Versailles Treaty itself, which saddled Germany with an occupation army and denied Germans the right of self-determination.

"When in the gray November days of 1918," said Hitler, "the curtain was lowered on the bloody tragedy of the Great War . . . the views of the President of the United States [Wilson] reached the ears of the world . . . in Fourteen Points. No people succumbed more completely to the magic power of this fantasy than the Germans . . . That peace, which was intended to be the final stone laid on the tomb of war, turned out to be the seed for new struggles! . . . It was the spirit of revenge . . . the spirit of hatred!"

The Versailles Treaty was designed to emasculate Germany not only militarily but economically as well. Hence the major preoccupation of German business leaders during the 1920s was to find a way to escape the economic strangulation of the Versaille Treaty. At first, they tried to compromise with the Allies, but when this failed some of them became more susceptible to the one politician who was the most vocal opponent of the treaty: Adolf Hitler. Preeminent among the German industrialists was Gustav Krupp, who had more reason than most to hate the Versailles Treaty. His experiences were typical of his peers in the business community; although they tried the path of moderation, every day brought them a little closer to Hitler.

In 1902 young Bertha Krupp, the daughter of Friedrich Krupp, became the sole owner of one of Germany's largest steel firms. Her father had been at the head of the third generation of Krupps to rule over the family's industrial empire, but he died leaving no sons, meaning that the Krupp name would die out with the fourth generation. Then a young Prussian aristocrat named Gustav von Bohlen und Halbach,* who was engaged to Bertha Krupp, was permitted after the marriage to precede his family name with his wife's, and in 1906 the young bridegroom became Gustav Krupp von Bohlen und Halbach.

He was a man of medium height and build and was no doubt always somewhat embarrassed that his wife was taller than he was. His face rarely displayed emotion. The small tight mouth, domed forehead, and Spartan nose were always frozen in the same stern look. He always wore the right clothes for every occasion, but there was a rigid overdone neatness in his dress. Without any experience in busi-

---

*Gustav von Bohlen, incidentally, was the great-grandson of the General William Bohlen who was killed in the Battle of the Rappahannock in 1862 while fighting on the Union side in the American Civil War.[1]

ness, he was suddenly placed at the head of a huge firm in a very competitive industry. His business colleagues were either men whose fathers or who themselves had created their companies or men of great managerial skill who after years of hard work had been appointed president of their firms.

Gustav Krupp saw himself not as an entrepreneur but as an administrator of his wife's fortune. He learned to manage the Krupp firm the hard way, by familiarizing himself with a business that was new to him and by regulating his life in such time-clock fashion that he sometimes gave the impression of being an automaton rather than a human being. The fact that he considered himself merely the trustee of the Krupp family fortune and not an industrial tycoon in his own right led him to be extremely cautious. He shied away from anything that might in the long run damage the Krupp interests.

As a product of the rigid German civil service, he had a very strong respect for authority and duty. His first and foremost duty as he saw it was to his country, but his patriotism was not of the narrow ideological type. Once in the early 1920s, during a reception at the Krupp home, the name of President Ebert, a Social Democrat, was mentioned in a discussion. In an effort to ridicule the president, a gentleman of rightist sympathies commented on Ebert's humble origins with a disparaging remark about "that saddle maker Ebert." (As a young man Ebert had worked as a saddle maker.) Krupp, who usually exhibited perfect self-control, immediately flared up and declared he would not stand for an insult to the chief of state.[2]

Next to his duty to his Fatherland was his obligation to the Krupp family, the Krupp tradition, and the Krupp workers and employees. He carried on, and even expanded the famed Krupp social projects, such as workers' insurance, pensions, medical care, and housing. This patriotic philosophy of duty also turned out to be excellent for business. From 1906 to 1914 Germany was arming rapidly, and the

Krupp firm prospered. During World War I they were the leading German manufacturer of big guns and armaments. Then disaster came in 1918.

The kaiser abdicated and fled to Holland; a Social Democratic government was formed in Berlin under President Ebert. When the German people heard the news, some responded differently from others. In a military hospital, Corporal Adolph Hitler cursed these Social Democrats as traitors to the Fatherland. In Essen, Gustav Krupp immediately sent a telegram to Berlin to find out what the new government wanted him to do. Krupp did not believe in democracy, and he had always respected Kaiser Wilhelm, but he felt his first duty was to the German State, whoever might be governing at the time.

On November 10, 1918, there was trouble at the Krupp factory in Essen. Crowds gathered in the streets. There were demonstrations and speeches by socialist agitators. Over 100,000 families in Essen directly depended on the Krupp firm for their livelihood. If there were no more armaments orders, everyone would be unemployed; so the workers were in an ugly mood. Gustav was so frightened that he armed all the servants in the Krupp home, the massive Villa Hügel, which sat high on a hill above Essen. But no angry mobs came storming the hill. However, for Krupp and the other German industrialists, the worst, the Treaty of Versailles, was yet to come.

Before sunrise on May 7, 1919, messengers scurried throughout Paris to deliver copies of the Versailles Treaty to the Allied officials. Because no one had yet seen it in its finished form, it came as a shock to many of them. Herbert Hoover, at that time chief of the Allied Food-Relief Services and a senior American economic advisor, was awakened from a sound sleep at 4 A.M. to receive his copy. Still bleary-eyed, Hoover read the document and was horrified by its severity. Too upset to go back to sleep, he dressed at daybreak and walked the deserted Paris streets. After walking only a few blocks, he met General Smuts of South Africa, and then John Maynard Keynes of the British delegation. "It all flashed into our minds," Hoover said, "why each was walking about at that time of morning." Even Woodrow Wilson thought the Versailles Treaty was too harsh; he said; "If I were a German, I think I should never sign it."[3]

The Treaty of Versailles was finally signed by the representatives of the German Social Democratic government on June 28, 1919, after the resignation of several German officials who refused to sign their names to such an "unjust" treaty. The terms of the treaty made it impossible for Germany to regain economic stability. Territorially, Germany lost twenty-five thousand square miles in Europe inhabited by over six million people, and all her colonies, which totaled more than a million square miles. In raw materials, she lost 65 percent of her iron ore reserves, 45 percent of her coal, 72 percent of her zinc, 12 percent of her principal agricultural areas, and 10 percent of her industrial establishments. The German Army was limited to 100,000 men with no reserves, the navy was reduced to insignificance, and the air force was totally abolished. In the atmosphere of economic chaos and depression that followed the treaty's enactment, radicalism of both the Left and Right flourished in a way that would have been impossible in a stable society.

Despite the antagonisms that divided Germany on most political questions, the Versailles Treaty was one issue on which general agreement could be reached. It was almost universally condemned. Newspapers, irrespective of party affiliation, attacked its terms and called for its rejection. The democratic *Frankfurter Zeitung* wrote in bold headlines "UNACCEPTABLE!" It then commented that the terms "are so nonsensical that no government that signs the treaty will last a fortnight . . . Germany is crushed." The socialist *Vorwärts* demanded rejection. The *Berliner Tageblatt* predicted that if the treaty was accepted, "a military furor for revenge will sound in Germany within a few years, and a militant Nationalism will engulf all."[4]

Protest meetings made up of people from all classes were

held throughout Germany. In the industrial section of Berlin, workers dressed in grimy overalls assembled outside their factories to protest. At the University of Berlin the student fraternities, dressed in their colorful Renaissance uniforms, some covered with gold braid and others with great white plumes in their caps, marched carrying shiny sabers and signs calling for an honorable peace.

The Versailles Treaty was an example of the disastrous economic rivalry between sovereign nation-states. Britain and France designed the treaty as a weapon to forever weaken Germany, their number one industrial competitor. The objectives of most of the provisions of the treaty were economic in nature, rather than being outbursts of a desire for revenge or heavy-handed stupidity, as was popularly believed. In addition to losing some of her richest provinces, much of her natural resources, and her colonies, Germany had to forfeit all rights, trade concessions, and property in foreign countries. The treaty provided that in these areas the Allies reserved "the right to retain and liquidate all property and interests of German private nationals or companies." Naturally, the Allies did not fail to take advantage of Germany's departure.

In addition to limiting Germany's potential to move into expanding overseas markets, the Allies obtained a virtual blank check from Germany in terms of reparations. The Allies claimed that since Germany was responsible for the war she was liable for the costs and damages incurred by the victors. The total indemnity was to be set at $32 billion, plus interest. The schedule of payments would be a fixed annuity of $550 million, plus a 26 percent tax on exports (another technique to make Germany less competitive in world markets). Upon threat of invasion, the German government accepted the terms. But the annuities would not even cover the interest charges, so the indebtedness would increase every year no matter how faithfully the payments were made.[5]

In retrospect it is clear that the Versailles Treaty was one of the primary causes of the failure of German democracy. It completely discredited the moderate leaders who for months had insisted that only a new democratic German government could count upon a just peace from the Allied democracies. It made little difference that President Ebert denounced the treaty and only told the German delegates to sign under protest to avoid a French invasion, or that Philipp Scheidemann, one of the most important moderate Social Democrats, resigned from the cabinet because he refused to sign this "death warrant." The clearest indication of popular dissatisfaction would come with the elections of June 6, 1920. The Social Democrats and the Catholic Center party, who led the drive to sign the treaty, would lose a total of eleven million votes, with three million going to the Nationalists. These parties would never recover sufficiently from this blow to gain the majority needed to rule effectively.

Was the Versailles Treaty designed simply to protect the world from the threat of German militarism, or was the treaty deliberately planned to strangle Germany's economy and make her uncompetitive in world markets? To answer this question it is only necessary to look at the treatment of nonmilitary German shipping. Understandably the Allies would have wanted to restrict the size of the German Navy in the interest of their own defense, but what was the military significance of the German merchant marine? Certainly, the military importance of unarmed vessels was very slight, yet their economic significance was very great.

By 1900 Germany was rapidly becoming the world's greatest industrial power. In order to gain new export markets and obtain vital raw materials, Germany built up a large merchant marine to develop trade in all parts of the world. In fact, Germany's bid for industrial and commercial supremacy was based in large part on her great merchant fleet. "It was that particular form of German rivalry," said American economic reporter Ludwell Denny, "that perhaps threatened British supremacy most, and for which, had there been no other reason, Britain went to war. Therefore it was not surprising that Britain in dictating the peace terms took away from Germany virtually all her merchant marine."[6] The treaty called for the confiscation of Germany's entire oceangoing fleet, with the exception of some small craft under 1600 tons (fishing boats). All German freighters and great passenger liners were handed over to the Allies. "That," said Denny, "was one of Britain's major war gains."[7]

Britain and France claimed that Germany was being forced to forfeit her nonmilitary fleet simply to pay for war reparations, but everyone knew that without a merchant fleet Germany would only have a more difficult time paying reparations. Thus, in terms of shipping alone, the Versailles Treaty gave Britain and France a stranglehold over German export trade.

Yet in spite of the Versailles Treaty, with hard work and ingenuity, German business gradually began to recover, so other ways were found to restrict Germany from foreign markets. High tariff barriers became one of the principal weapons used against Germany. No foreign-made goods could successfully compete with English goods in the British Empire. France put outright quotas (in addition to high tariffs) on the importation of German iron and steel products, textiles, and electrical equipment.[8]

The tariff barriers themselves were often given a more severe effect by the method of their enforcement. This administrative attack was directed in particular against certain kinds of German goods. For example, there was the practice of customs inspectors checking any German imports. To discourage import they would open a crate of one hundred radios, and instead of examining ten, they would examine each of the one hundred separately. The goods were thus tied up for weeks, and the importer was unable to make his scheduled deliveries.

The process of tariff classifications by customs officials was also used as a weapon of commercial warfare against German exports. For example, under the McKenna Tariff,

Britain had a duty of 33⅓ percent on all foreign automobiles. A German toy manufacturer sent to England a shipment of toy dogs and dolls that moved by a clockwork mechanism. These toys were taxed as automobiles on the implausible argument that they moved under their own power. This made it impossible for the German exporter to maintain his contract price, so the shipment was sent back.[9]

If the Versailles Treaty had been based on President Wilson's Fourteen Points, as the Allies had originally promised, the Germans might have accepted it as a just peace and complied with its regulations. However, because it was so obvious to the leading German businessmen that the treaty was designed simply to enslave them economically, their first thought was of clandestine evasion. Gustav Krupp wrote:

> In those days, the situation seemed hopeless. It appeared even more desperate if one remained as firmly convinced as I was that "Versailles" could not represent the end
> If there should be a resurrection for Germany, if ever she were to shake off the chains of Versailles, then Krupps would have to be prepared. The machines were demolished; the tools were destroyed; but one thing remained— the men, the men at the drawing boards and the workshops, who in happy cooperation had brought the manufacture of guns to perfection. Their skill would have to be saved [along with], their immense resources of knowledge and experience. I had to maintain Krupps as an armament factory for the distant future in spite of all obstacles.[10]

Gustav Krupp's reactions to the revolutionary upheaval, the Versailles Treaty, and rearmament are significant not only because they are the personal experiences of a prominent industrialist, but because they also reflected the political attitude of most German business leaders. Industrialists like Krupp acknowledged the authority of the new government of the Weimar Republic and cooperated in every possible way with the moderate Social Democrats, but the Versailles Treaty was something they could not live with.[11]

This was a question of economic survival for German business, not of ideological passion. They had to have access to foreign markets and they could no longer afford to pay the high taxes caused by reparations. The leaders of the German business community decided it was best to deal with the problem of Versailles in two ways: they would give full support to Chancellor Stresemann's attempts to negotiate with the Allies for reasonable reform, but at the same time, in case the Allies refused to see reason, they could carry out a secret program of rearmament.

Up to the last days of World War I, Germany had been an absolute monarchy. Most big businessmen, such as Gustav Krupp, were completely loyal to their sovereign, yet they hoped for liberal reforms that would gradually bring about a true parliamentary government and a constitutional monarchy. In Imperial Germany big business, although influential and indispensable, was subordinate in actual power to the traditional political elite, which was made up of a complex power structure of monarchy, nobility, officer corps, and high bureaucracy.

In the great glittering reception salons of the kaiser's court, people were always received in order of their rank. First came the higher nobility, princes and dukes, in regal uniforms covered with gold. Next came the army officers in blue and white uniforms that were only slightly less splendid, with military medals and decorations of every conceivable sort sparkling on their chests. They were followed by the diplomats and civil servants, who were also entitled to wear a uniform, though it was not nearly as chic as that of the army. Last came the civilians, dressed in black. Industrialists and businessmen, regardless of their wealth, were placed in this category. Socially, they ranked lower than the most humble young lieutenant. The military collapse in 1918 distressed business leaders as much as anyone else, but to a certain extent they blamed the collapse on the incompetence of the old political rulers and their mismanagement of the war economy. Many of Germany's most important businessmen regarded the passing of the old regime with ambivalent feelings and a sense of opportunity.

Carl Duisberg, the founder of I.G. Farben, the great chemical trust, and the president of the National Association of German Industry (Reichsverband) from 1925 to 1930, expressed this viewpoint in a letter he wrote to a colleague in October 1918, three turbulent weeks before the Republic officially came into existence: "From the day when I saw that the [Imperial] cabinet system was bankrupt, I greeted the change to a parliamentary system with joy, and I stand today, when what is at stake is what I consider to be of the highest value, namely the Fatherland, behind the democratic government, and where possible, I work hand in hand with the unions and seek in this way to save what can be saved. You see I am an opportunist and adjust to things as they are."[12]

Fritz Ebert, a moderate Social Democrat who had been chosen president of the Republic, had worked constructively with the army and government throughout the war. A short man with a double chin and a large stomach, Ebert was the perfect image of a cautious bureaucrat. Like the rest of his colleagues, he had neither wanted nor planned a revolution. Indeed, he would have been willing to accept Prince Max of Baden as regent (ruler in absence of the king). The maximum demand made by the Social Democrats in their ultimatum of November 8 was for the abdication of the kaiser and the Crown Prince.

On the dark night of November 9, 1918, as revolutionary mobs roamed Berlin, Ebert sat alone in the chancellor's office afraid the Communists were about to overthrow his moderate socialist government.* Although the windows were closed and the thick velvet curtains drawn, the noises of the

---

*Ebert was appointed chancellor in November of 1918 to succeed Prince Max of Baden. On February 11, 1919 Ebert became the president of Germany.

demonstrators in the streets still could be heard. Ebert had no military unit on which he could depend to enforce his authority. Suddenly the ringing of the telephone on the desk drowned out all other sounds. It was General Groener, who had succeeded General Ludendorff as quartermaster general of the German Army, calling on the secret line from the military headquarters at the front. The general and Ebert were in complete agreement as to the necessary action to be taken.[13] They agreed on the desirability of getting rid of the radical socialists from the government, eliminating the soldiers' and workers' councils from any position of influence, and getting the army out of the revolutionary atmosphere as soon as possible.

Although most businessmen would have preferred a government oriented more toward laissez-faire economic principles than Ebert and the moderate Social Democrats, they realized that it was necessary to make some concessions to the working class in order to avoid a radical social revolution. The general staff of the army went along with this strategy because they realized that only by this means could Germany comply with President Wilson's prerequisites for peace; furthermore, they secretly welcomed the existence of a moderately "revolutionary" government in Berlin that would take the odious responsibility of negotiating and signing the peace treaty.

Among that segment of society generally classified as "big business" there were many different political points of view. For example, although Krupp and Duisberg both supported the Weimar Republic, they backed different political parties. For the most part the political differences between big business groups were based on economic interests rather than personal preferences.[14] In order to understand more clearly the political goals of "big business," it is necessary to identify its limits as a group, and its component parts, each of which had different political objectives. Actually the term "big business" does not imply a homogeneous entity. Various groupings within it—industry (heavy and light), commerce, and finance—have different economic interests. Such groupings are closely interrelated, and the lines of demarcation between them are not always very sharp; but this by no means prevents the existence of antagonisms. One must be aware of these groupings to pinpoint where and how Hitler was able to utilize divisions within big business to his own advantage.

To the average person all factories must have looked alike. From the Ruhr to Hamburg their tall smokestacks all belched the same sooty clouds. It might also have been said that, like the factories, German big businessmen all looked alike. From appearance alone, it would have been difficult to tell the difference between a mine owner and a banker. They all were middle-aged, portly gentlemen wearing dark blue or gray pinstripe suits and riding in long black Mercedes limousines. But just as their wealth was dependent on different goods, so they needed different political conditions, taxes, tariffs, and wage laws to give them advantages over their competitors. The need for these advantages, of course, would become more acute if business was not good.

From 1918 on, the conflicts within German big business centered primarily around two groups, heavy industry (iron, steel, and mining, etc.) versus light industry (electrical, chemical, textiles, etc.). The magnates of heavy industry and their bankers were struggling to regain their former markets and economic position: consequently, they wanted to take back many of the concessions made to the workers in 1918 to 1919. Light industry, producing consumer goods for the most part, adopted a policy of collaboration with organized labor.

Light industry and commerce (department stores, retail merchants) wanted an economic policy that would restore prosperity by restoring the purchasing power of the people. Heavy industry, of course, did not want to see the purchasing power of the lower classes wiped out completely; they simply wanted lower labor costs that would give them an advantage in world markets.

Light industry, which was gaining an increasingly significant role in the economy, rebelled against the dominant position of heavy industry, which forced it to pay monopoly prices for the raw materials and machines it needed. The aftermath of the war and the obligations of the Versailles Treaty impelled heavy industry to favor a foreign policy that would recapture its lost markets and sources of raw material, particularly in eastern Europe, and shake off reparations, which added greatly to their production costs.

Under the kaiser's' rule, heavy industry, which earned a significant portion of its profits from the munitions orders of the German government as well as "friendly powers," favored an imperialistic foreign policy. An immediate return to such a policy was impossible after the defeat in 1918, and from 1924 to 1929 a strategy of international collaboration was needed because the reorganization of German industry was carried out largely on foreign capital. However, with the onset of the depression, foreign loans ceased, and there was no longer any motive for collaboration. Heavy industry then saw no other alternative than to return to its old expansionist program in order to obtain the raw materials it needed, while at the same time it sought to defend its home market by protectionist tendencies.

Faced with such harsh determination on the part of the victors to restrict Germany from world markets, it is not surprising that most German business leaders had only limited faith in the possibility of peaceful revision of the Versailles Treaty, and turned to rearmament as the only alternative. The Versailles Treaty had placed the German economy in an even tighter straitjacket than it had been in before World War I.

Prior to World War I, Germany had become the number one industrial power in Europe, yet after the war, she had been cut off from foreign markets by the empires of Britain, France, and the other Allies. By 1929, German industry had been modernized and rebuilt and was under considerable pressure to open up new markets for itself abroad; however, because of the restrictions of the Versailles Treaty, it was not able to obtain prewar foreign trade levels. Economic rivalry among the industrialized nations of Europe, the ultimate source of the dangerous tensions that had led to World War I, was not liquidated but continued to exist and was even intensified.

Big business was committed to a policy of "national liberation" and expansion by economic necessity. However, if Germany were to overcome "the Versailles system" and regain equality with the other powers, the rearmament program would ultimately have to be directed by the army; the industrialists could not do it alone.

The task of "neutralizing the poison contained in the disarmament clauses of the Versailles Treaty,"[15] as he put it, was carried out primarily by General Hans von Seeckt, the commander in chief of the Reichswehr from 1920 to 1926. At first glance General von Seeckt seemed to be a typical Prussian officer, but despite his neat, precise, military appearance, Hans von Seeckt was well traveled, well read, and had a very keen intellect. When he wanted to be, he was a warm and fascinating conversationalist, but when the occasion demanded he could also present a very cold exterior that led people to call him "the sphinx with the monocle."

During his period as commander in chief of the army, von Seeckt concentrated all his energies on two primary objectives: (1) reorganization of the army within the restrictions imposed by the treaty, but with such a high level of technical efficiency that in due course it could be expanded into a mass national army, and (2) preservation of the Prussian military traditions despite the same treaty restrictions. In other words, he wanted to evade the treaty without openly violating it. Unlike most of his military colleagues, von Seeckt had a clear understanding of politics; it was said that he was one of the few German generals with an appreci-

ation of the political and economic aspects of war. The real
secret of von Seeckt's political and military genius was his
ability to take the long view.

Von Seeckt understood, above all, the vital fact that the
intellectual demilitarization of Germany was more important for the Allies and consequently more dangerous for the
Germans than the mere limitation of the army. Hence, in
the early 1920s he believed it was best to support the Weimar Republic and operate behind a facade of democracy for
the next few years at least. On this matter his opinion agreed
with that of a rising nationalist politician in Munich, one
Adolf Hitler, who told his audiences that it was spiritual
and intellectual rearmament that counted; if only Germany
had the *will* to defend herself, all else would follow
naturally.

General von Seeckt admired Hitler's ability to win the
masses for the cause of nationalism, for he envisaged the
day when such a surge of patriotism would be necessary
for "national liberation." The two men met for the first time
on March 11, 1923, in Munich; von Seeckt was favorably
impressed but did not show it at the time. Later he made
the very revealing comment: "We were one in our aim; only
our paths were different."[16]

The Nazi party certainly played a part in the rearmament
program. Until the army could openly increase its size, Hitler's S.A. was a kind of military reserve. When the storm
troopers would first begin to assemble in some remote field
to drill, they did not look very impressive in their ski caps
and baggy brown shirts; but when the sergeant-major
barked out the command to "fall in," the rowdy group of
street fighters suddenly became a disciplined body of men.
True, their arms were haphazard, and they had no heavy
weapons, but these could always be provided by the army
in time of national emergency.

Almost a year before the Treaty of Rapallo officially reestablished diplomatic relations between Germany and Soviet

Russia,* General von Seeckt was instrumental in formulating a secret agreement of Russo-German military collaboration. Germany would help train the young Red Army and build up the Russian arms industry; in return, the agreement provided Germany with a place to train its officers and build its arms industry beyond the watchful eyes of the Allied disarmament commission. On the vast, empty plains of Russia, where the eye could see to the horizon, there was no one to hear the whistle and whine of bullets or the dull thud of artillery shells as the Reichswehr tested its new weapons. This accord with Soviet Russia would also be of considerable benefit to German big business. Large orders were received by German industrial firms, which would not only bring them financial profit, but would also permit them to expand their plants, to progress scientifically and technically in arms building, and to maintain the thousands of specialized workers necessary for the secret rearmament program soon to be carried out within Germany itself.

The little army that von Seeckt was in the process of perfecting for future expansion had to be matched by an economic organization, equally capable of expansion, that could equip and maintain the military might of Germany once it had been restored. A highly secret office was set up in November 1924 under the direction of the army to act as a kind of economic general staff. Von Seeckt believed the outcome of the "war liberation" would ultimately depend upon the work of this office. In the meantime, its task was to prepare plans for the economic mobilization of Germany, and for equipping and maintaining an army of sixty-three divisions. In addition, this office was to obtain the cooperation of industry in establishing "spear-head organizations" that would concentrate on the development of economic and industrial rearmament not only within the Reich but also in

---

*At Rapallo, Italy, in 1922 Russia and Germany made a treaty by which they renounced all claims of war damages against each other and agreed to resume all normal relations.

Austria, Italy, the Netherlands, Spain, Sweden, and Switzerland. A study was made of foreign raw materials and industries that would be particularly useful to Germany, and special emphasis was placed in training military officers in economic affairs.

The activities of this secret economic planning office were received with enthusiasm in the leading circles of German industry. One of the goals was to replace the machines and property demolished by orders of the Allied disarmament commission. Property of the Krupp firm, for example, worth millions of dollars, had been destroyed in 1920. About 9,300 machines weighing over 60,000 tons were demolished; 801,520 gauges, molds, and other tools with a total weight of almost 1,000 tons, along with 379 installations such as hardening ovens, cranes, oil and water tanks, and cooling plants were smashed.[17]

This so-called dismantling demanded by the Versailles Treaty had been a very bitter experience for many German industrialists and undoubtedly played a part in their later willingness to accept Hitler. Thyssen, Krupp, Kirdorf, and other executives had stood helpless as they watched the work of generations senselessly destroyed. Even years later, Gustav Krupp was incensed by the memory of the "uncouth, irreconcilable attitude of the Allied Control Commission."[18]

The plans for economic and industrial mobilization proposed by the army's secret economic staff received the approval of big business and of almost all political forces, with the exception of the Communists, and these plans were pushed forward as part of the general industrial development of the country. From 1924 to 1927, the emphasis was placed on planning and designing prototypes.[19] With the departure of the Allied Control Commission on January 31, 1927, the second phase of German rearmament began, and factories were adapted for the mass production of the prototypes built abroad. The budget of the army increased rapidly from 490 million marks in 1924 to 827 million marks in 1928.

The size of the army's budget and its key role in directing rearmament should not, however, lead to the conclusion that it was all-powerful. Von Seeckt had opposed any security pact with the Western powers, preferring instead to maintain his secret accord with Moscow; but by the mid-1920s big business viewed his continued hostility to the West as a hindrance to the economic advantages offered in the Dawes Plan.* Gustav Stresemann, the German foreign minister who was supported by the business community, turned against von Seeckt and carried his policy to a successful conclusion, the Locarno Agreement, in spite of the general's resistance.† By the fall of 1926 von Seeckt was forced to resign his post as commander in chief of the Reichswehr.

The secret rearmament program does not necessarily prove that Germany was planning aggressive warfare or that the German character was instinctively militaristic. Too often it goes unnoticed that the Germans were not the only ones to violate the Versailles Treaty. The preamble of Part V of the Treaty of Versailles, introducing the limitations on Germany's military and naval powers, read: "In order to render possible the initiation of a general limitation of the armaments of all nations, Germany undertakes strictly to observe the military, naval and air clauses which follow." The disarmament of Germany, however, did not ease the nerves of the world, because it was a method of political

---

*From January to April 1924, a committee of experts under the chairmanship of the American banker Charles G. Dawes met in Paris. The plan provided that a large international loan of $200 million would be made to the German government. Although the total amount of reparations was unchanged, it was made payable in annual installments over an indefinite period of time. Also, the French agreed to remove their troops from the Ruhr within a year.

†By the Locarno treaties of 1925, the Franco-German border and the Belgian-German border were guaranteed. England and Italy promised to fight whoever violated the frontier. France and Germany agreed to seek arbitration to settle their disputes. In return, Germany was accepted as a member of the League of Nations.

and economic oppression rather than a sincere step toward universal disarmament. Hence the Allies, particularly France, violated the spirit of the Versailles Treaty by never even attempting a "limitation" of their own armaments.

While the Germans were secretly drawing plans for new tanks and making one or two prototypes, France was producing thousands of them. The German Army was limited to 100,000 men with no reserves, while France maintained a standing army of 612,000 men with an active reserve of 3,488,000. Germany was forbidden to have any tanks, while France had 3,500. All the planes of the German Air Force were destroyed in 1919 and building any new ones was strictly outlawed, while France, who was not alone in steadily increasing the size of her military forces, had 2,800 planes. Even Poland, for example, had a standing army of 266,000 men, over twice the size of Germany's, and an active reserve of 3,200,000 men, and an air force of 1,000 planes.

One of the best justifications of Germany's rearmament was stated in an article written by Gustav Krupp in 1932 entitled "Objectives of German Policy." He protested that the Germans were being treated as second-class members of the world community: "The vital rights of national defense enjoyed by all other peoples are withheld from them. Not *increase* in armaments but *equality* of armaments must therefore be the aim of every German government . . . As a businessman, I am of the opinion that international disarmament must be the general aim."[20]

Regardless of their particular party loyalties, the gaining of national independence was the real aim of all the Weimar governments. Political and economic as well as military equality were to be reestablished relative to the other great powers. Thus, the ultimate goal was the restoration of Germany as an imperial state. The only disagreement among the German power elite was on the question of how national resurgence would be accomplished. Light industry favored a policy of international cooperation; heavy industry wanted complete rearmament; agricultural interests, commerce, and

labor all had their pet programs; but for all, the objective
was basically the same.

Germany was just beginning to make some headway
toward recovery when the depression began. With the coming of economic collapse rivalries and hostilities intensified.
As the possibility of sinking into ruin became very real,
everyone began to think only in terms of saving himself.
Germany's options narrowed: national recovery would have
to come quickly, before internal collapse.

The advocate of drastic measures, the one politician who
had predicted the economic collapse and prepared himself
for it, was waiting in the wings. Stirring up the nationalistic
passions of the people and motivating them with the concepts of duty, honor, and self-sacrifice was Hitler's specialty.
A police report of one of Hitler's meetings in 1927 illustrates
the patriotic, militaristic atmosphere of the Nazi party and
how it copied symbols from Mussolini's "movement of national revival" in Italy: "From the entrance come roars of
'Heil' . . . Then a trumpet blast." Amid cheers from the
spectators, disciplined columns of Brownshirts march into
the hall, led by two rows of drummers and the bright red
swastika flag. "The men salute in the Fascist manner, with
outstretched arms. The audience cheers them. On the stage
Hitler has also stretched out his arm in salute." Then two
brass bands begin to play a military march. "The flags move
past, glittering standards with swastika inside a wreath, and
others with eagles modeled on the ancient Roman military
standards. About 200 march past . . . the flagbearers and
standard bearers occupy the stage."[21]

Although Hitler's methods and tactics were more blatant
and extreme than those of the industrialists, generals, or
politicians of the established parties, his primary goal, at
least in the matter of foreign policy, was the same. "The
aim of German foreign policy today," he said in *Mein Kampf,*
"must be the preparation for the reconquest of freedom for

tomorrow."[22] From the beginning Hitler had a unique grasp of the harsh realities of international power politics.

On April 10, 1923, shortly after the occupation of the Ruhr by the French, he delivered a speech in Munich that was a strange combination of insight into the decisive elements of the relations between states and the most vicious kind of rabble-rousing:

> No economic policy is possible without a sword, no indus-trialization without power. Today we no longer have a sword grasped in our fist—how can we have a successful economic policy? England has fully recognized this pri-mary maxim in the healthy life of states; for centuries England has acted on the principle of converting economic strength into political power, while conversely political power in its turn must protect economic life. . . . Three years ago, I declared in this same room that the collapse of German national consciousness must carry with it into the abyss the economic life of Germany as well. For libera-tion something more is necessary than an economic policy, something more than industry: If a people is to become free it needs pride and willpower, defiance, hate and once again hate.[23]

Gustav Krupp encountered Hitler in the late 1920s, just before the beginning of the depression, when the Nazi leader was making a propaganda tour of the Rhineland. While in Essen, Hitler decided it might be both interesting and of propaganda value to visit the famous Krupp factory.

At the main gate a huge sign blocked the path of Hitler and his staff:

IT IS REQUESTED THAT, TO PREVENT MISUNDERSTANDING,
NO APPLICATION BE MADE TO VISIT THE WORKS,
SINCE SUCH APPLICATION CANNOT BE GRANTED
UNDER ANY CIRCUMSTANCES WHATSOEVER.

Nevertheless, Hitler demanded a tour of the factory. He was, however, restricted from entering the workshops, "because he was too unknown to be trusted." Instead, the company tried to pacify him with a visit to the firm's historical exhibit. "Even there he displayed a sense of theater," wrote William Manchester. "Recognizing the political value of any association with Krupp, he had signed the exhibit register with a flourish and underscored his signature as though he knew that soon the Krupp destiny would be inextricably entangled with his own. The name was still there, slashed across the guest book like a jagged prophecy: *Adolph Hitler.*"[24]

On June 7, 1929, a committee of experts appointed by the Allied powers under the chairmanship of the American banker Owen D. Young, and hence called the Young Committee, signed a report that required the Germans to pay reparations for another fifty-nine years, that is until 1988. However, the annual payments were considerably lower than on the Dawes Plan (2,050 million marks a year as compared to 2,500 million). Direct international control over Germany's economy was to be removed as well, and the total sum demanded in payment was less than the 132 billion gold marks originally claimed by the Allies.

Within Germany the new agreement encountered boisterous opposition. Nationalist crowds carrying signs and waving flags gathered to protest outside the Reichstag in Berlin. Even those with a realistic understanding of the Reich's difficult international position were disappointed. There was an element of cruel mockery in forcing Germany to agree to payments for the next fifty-nine years when she could not afford to make even the first few annual payments. Over two hundred prominent men, including many liberals and moderates, such as Hans Luther, the former chancellor, Carl Duisberg of I.G. Farben, and Konrad Adenauer, then mayor of Cologne, issued a public statement of concern against the agreement. Eleven years after the end of the war, the Young Plan once again exposed the Allies' merciless attitude toward the defeated.

Although the terms of the Young Plan were far stiffer than Foreign Minister Stresemann had hoped for, he decided to accept them, confident that he could then secure the evacuation of the remaining zones of the occupied Rhineland. Finally he succeeded in persuading the French to begin the withdrawal of their troops in September, five years before they would have been required to do so by the Versailles Treaty. This was to be the last of Stresemann's triumphs. Until his death on October 3, he was very ill, worn out by the exertions of public office. Before he died, he had succeeded in overcoming the opposition of the French, but the Germans still remained to be convinced. The parties of the Right, including the Nazis, were in close conference, planning a united campaign of rejection against this new reparations settlement. Any rightist coalition against Stresemann's policy would undoubtedly be led by the powerful German Nationalist party. Only they had the money, the press, the deputies in the Reichstag, and a large enough party to make such a campaign a success.

A national committee was formed on July 9, 1929, to organize a campaign for a plebiscite rejecting the Young Plan and the "lie" of German war guilt, which was the "legal" basis of the Allies' claims. For the next nine months the press and parties of the German Right united in a vicious campaign to defeat the government's reparations policy. The leader of the campaign against the Young Plan was Alfred Hugenberg.* Dr. Bank, a Nationalist political financier from Dresden, had introduced Hitler to Hugenberg in June at the Deutscher Orden, a Nationalist club in Berlin. Hugenberg had tried to persuade Hitler to join his alliance against the Young Plan. He already had the support of the Nationalist party, the Stahlhelm (Germany's largest veterans organization), and the Pan-German League. In addition, he could count on the financial backing of many important aristocrats

---

*Hugenberg was the leader of the conservative Nationalist party. He owned a chain of newspapers, cinemas, and a major movie studio.

and industrialists and of course his own media empire; but what he needed was someone who could arouse the masses, someone who could win over the lower middle class and at least a few workers. True, Hitler's party was not of significant size in 1929; they had only twelve representatives in the Reichstag and 120,000 members. However, these members were all well-disciplined, devoted fanatics who could be used as propaganda shock troops. They could be counted on to work day and night pasting up billboards, marching, and holding rallies, things that the "respectable gentlemen" of the Nationalist party would never dream of doing.

Hugenberg also thought the campaign against the Young Plan would give him a chance to assert his leadership over the divided forces of the Right, including the Nazis. The more conservative elements of the upper class might even be able to regain their lost initiative. With all the arrogance of an upper-class gentleman toward a man of the masses, Hugenberg was confident he could make use of Hitler. He would use the ex-corporal's gift for agitation to lead the masses back to conservatism. At least Hugenberg was intelligent enough to see that the traditional spokesmen of the conservative cause were isolated by their own class-consciousness. But he foolishly believed that he would know how to put Hitler back in his place when the time came.

Hitler could not allow himself to be easily persuaded to join the alliance because he knew the party radicals, including Strasser, who was looked on as the leader of the more socialistic-minded Nazis, would be opposed to working with the reactionary Hugenberg and would denounce the move as a sellout to the industrialists. However, the advantages of being able to draw on the big political funds at Hugenberg's disposal and the possibilities of using his vast media network were too tempting to resist.

On July 9, 1929, when the committee was formed for the purpose of organizing the plebiscite, the membership of this committee showed clearly the delineation of the new national unity front: Hugenberg of the Nationalist party;

Seldte, the leader of the Stahlhelm; Heinrich Class, chairman of the Pan-German League; and Adolf Hitler, the leader of the National Socialist party. This committee appealed to the German electorate with a demagogically formulated "Law Against the Enslavement of the German People," which denounced the war-guilt clause of the Versailles Treaty, demanded the immediate end of all reparations payments, and stated that the chancellor and the members of the cabinet should be liable to prosecution for treason if they accepted the Young Plan.

At a meeting of Nazi party leaders that followed the alliance with Hugenberg, Strasser acted as the spokesman for the critics. Hugenberg's hopes for the alliance were Strasser's fears: the National Socialists would no longer be able to fight against the "respectable" elements of the Nationalist party; they would be overwhelmed by the other's superior financial strength; they would now be nothing but a pawn of the stronger party. Hitler remained unmoved by Strasser's arguments. He was not about to lose his chance to profit from an alliance with the established order. This opportunity meant a great deal to him, for his plans still called for following Karl Lueger's example of utilizing the existing implements of power.* Moreover, Strasser had personally underestimated Hitler, who did not become anyone's "pawn." Hitler responded to his critics with a lengthy speech, much of which included the usual emotional phrases about the Versailles Treaty and the Jews. Yet in concluding he made a statement that should have been clear even to the thickest heads among his listeners: "We shall carry on our propaganda at the expense of the others . . . at least we are gaining access to the funds which up to now have been reserved for the German Nationalists."[25]

In order to submit the "Freedom Law" to the Reichstag,

---

*Dr. Karl Lueger was the leader of the anti-Semitic Christian Socialist party and mayor of Vienna (1897–1910). When Hitler lived in Vienna, from 1908–1913, he greatly admired Lueger.

the German Right needed to secure the support of 10 percent of the electorate. This was accomplished on October 16, when their bill received a little over four million votes (10 percent). The bill, however, received less support in the Reichstag, when even some members of the Nationalist party refused to vote for it and broke with Hugenberg.

In a last, desperate attempt, the bill was submitted to a national plebiscite. Since the bill had received only four million votes in the elections on October 16, there was little chance of receiving a majority in the plebiscite. Nevertheless, it provided the nationalist forces with a good opportunity to bring their cause before the public. The Nazis used every propaganda trick they knew as they ranted about those who were enslaving the nation to foreign capitalists, crippling national survival for the next two generations, and turning Germany into a "Young colony." Every speech made by Hitler and other Nazi leaders was carried by all the newspapers in Hugenberg's chain. Millions of Germans who had hardly ever heard of Hitler before now became interested in him, since he was given such good publicity in the "respectable" press. Thousands of newsboys across Germany selling Hugenberg papers shouted: "Herr Hitler says, 'Young Plan means Germany's enslavement'."[26]

"The Young Plan," Fritz Thyssen later wrote, "was one of the principal causes of the upsurge of National Socialism in Germany."[27] Thyssen had not been opposed to the Dawes Plan, since it called for a system of reparations payments to be made primarily in material goods. But under the Young Plan the German reparations payments were to be made entirely in cash. Thyssen felt the financial debt thus created was bound to disrupt the entire German economy. He then decided to use his influence to help bring together the Nazis and the traditional Nationalists in opposing the Young Plan. "I turned to the National Socialist party," Thyssen said, "only after I became convinced that the fight against the Young Plan was unavoidable if a complete collapse of Germany was to be prevented."[28]

The Young Plan, according to Thyssen, would have the effect of pledging Germany's entire wealth as security for the reparations obligation. American capital was bound to flood into Germany. Thyssen was angered that some industrialists who supported the Young Plan were attempting in advance to free their property from this huge mortgage by transferring their stock to foreign holding companies. Thyssen felt this meant the beginning of the financial liquidation of Germany.

A considerable portion of the money Thyssen gave to the anti-Young Plan campaign went directly to the National Socialists. He knew of this and approved. "I financed the National Socialist party," said Thyssen, "for a single definite reason: I financed it because I believed that the Young Plan spelled catastrophe for Germany. I was convinced of the necessity of uniting all parties of the Right."[29]

The money that respectable businessmen like Thyssen placed at the disposal of the Nazis was used to pay for an unparalleled campaign of propaganda and demagoguery. In addition to the coverage given them in Hugenberg's newspapers and newsreels, the Nazis staged continuous rallies and protest demonstrations throughout the country. Noting that under the Young Plan Germany would have to continue reparations payments until 1988, Nazi speakers ranted about "fifty-eight years of bondage" for a generation of Germans not yet born.[30] In order to strike fear into the masses, Goebbels designed a poster showing a powerful clenched fist throwing its menacing shadow over a child. In despair, the child, representing Germany's next generation, raises its tiny arms as a shield, a cry of fear distoring its mouth. By the child's side is his father, a German worker with bowed head, worn out. But a storm trooper, upright and virile, shakes him with an outstretched arm, points to the threat, and shouts at him: "Father, rescue your child! Become a National Socialist!"

Hugenberg and Hitler needed twenty-one million votes to win; they received less than six million. With the defeat of the plebiscite, Hugenberg's last hope was that President von Hindenburg would refuse to sign the legislation embodying the Young Plan. Some Nationalist friends tried to influence Hindenburg, but he refused to be pressured by the extremists even though they were personal friends and members of his own party. On March 13, 1930, the president signed the laws to carry out the Young Plan. Hugenberg's campaign had been a dismal failure, an obvious defeat for the powerful Nationalist party. But a defeat for Hugenberg did not mean a defeat for Hitler. Hitler did not consider his part in the campaign a failure because in the past nine months he had succeeded in breaking into national politics for the first time and demonstrating his skill as a propagandist.

Most people felt that whatever success had been won in the campaign against the Young Plan was due to Hitler. He had criticized the conservative parties of the Right for years for their "respectable" inhibitions. Now he had demonstrated, on a larger scale than ever before, what he meant by propaganda aimed at the masses. Once the Young Plan became law, Hitler broke with the Nationalist party and blamed them for the failure of the campaign. He said their support for the campaign had been halfhearted; after all, some of their own members had split and refused to go along with Hugenberg. Such arguments carried weight with many of the more extreme Nationalists.

This alliance with Hugenberg was the first success in an extraordinary series of political maneuvers, tactical compromises, and manipulative alliances that brought Hitler to his goal. The campaign against the Young Plan also provided him with connections among many industrialists who had supported Stresemann's foreign policy over the years but who now felt the Young Plan went too far. As the economic situation worsened, some of the men who controlled the political funds for big business and heavy industry began to look around for political alternatives. Of course, Hitler had not yet succeeded in winning them over to his side, but for the first time they became fully aware of his remarkable gifts as a propagandist.

The campaign against the Young Plan brought the Nazi party an increase in general revenues in addition to the funds they received from Hugenberg. The income of the party unit in the Schwabing district of Munich, for example, was 388 marks for the first ten months of 1929; in the last two months of the year the same unit collected 803 marks.[31] For the first time since 1923 the National Socialists began to receive some contributions from the well-to-do middle class. At party headquarters names were collected for a special S (sympathizer) file of wealthy persons and firms who could be counted on to contribute to the support of the party.[32] By mid-1930, several months before their great election victory, the party was operating on a reasonably firm financial basis.

PART 2

6

DEPRESSION

In the spring of 1929 the prices of German agricultural products fell drastically, impoverishing peasant and landlord alike. Misery began to spread among the farmers; many went bankrupt and were driven from their homes when they could no longer pay on their mortgages. This was one of the first symptoms of the approaching world depression. As economic disaster began to cast its shadow over the land once again, Hitler, the prophet of doom, prepared to receive his due.

In America the prices on the New York Stock Exchange crashed in October 1929. This was the beginning of the great depression which, in a few months, would spread to all continents. The Wall Street crash marked the end of American loans to Germany, thus cutting off the flow of foreign exchange, which had enabled her to pay her debts. By the end of the year the economic crisis was starting to affect all segments of German society.

As early as the fall of 1928, there was cause for a certain uneasiness about the German economy. Though conditions steadily worsened throughout 1929, it was not until the approach of 1930 that people came to realize that the country was teetering once more on the edge of an abyss. One of the best indexes for the social consequences of the depression is the rate of unemployment. The number of registered unemployed in Germany rose from 1,320,000 in September 1929, to 3,000,000 in September 1930; it was up to 4,350,000 in September 1931 and 4,102,000 by September 1932. In the first two months of 1932 and again in 1933, the figures climbed over the six million mark. (The actual number of unemployed was much higher than the "registered" figures, which did not take into account those who could find only part-time jobs and those who failed to register for one reason or another.) "Translate these figures," said Alan Bullock, "into terms of men standing hopelessly on the street corners of every industrial town in Germany; of houses without food and warmth; of boys and girls leaving school without any chance of a job, and one may begin to guess something of the incalculable human anxiety and embitterment burned into the minds of millions of ordinary German working men and women."[1]

Although Hitler was no economist, he was acutely aware of the social and political consequences of economic events that, like the inflation of 1923, affected every man, woman, and child in Germany. As the economic crisis became more serious, the population grew restive.

During the period of prosperity German farmers had been encouraged by the government to increase their production. By 1929, their crops could no longer compete on the world market. In order to maintain themselves and their families, the peasants borrowed money from the banks and mortgaged their farms. Within a short time the rate of interest doubled. In spite of the agricultural crisis, the high taxes on German farms were not reduced.

Unable to pay the interest on their loans or the taxes on their farms, many peasants went bankrupt. Foreclosures began. Families were driven from their homes and their property was put up for auction. The desperate farmers responded with open rebellion; they refused to pay interest and taxes and in some areas gathered into armed mobs throwing stones at the tax offices. In several towns there were clashes between the police and crowds of club-wielding peasants. The Communists, rigidly following Marxist principles of class struggle, tried to incite the small peasants against the large landholders. In this they followed Lenin's Russian example, which was totally unsuited for export. In Germany their propaganda met with no success because the big landowners and the peasants had the same interests: higher prices on produce and lower interest rates on loans. Unlike Russia, the only "land hunger" among the German peasants was a hunger to keep the land they already had.

The National Socialists had a far better understanding of the agrarian struggle. Convinced that the most fertile field for agitation was now in rural rather than urban areas, Hitler proclaimed a new agrarian policy for the party. The farmer was to be the hero and the innocent Jew the scapegoat. "The country people are the chief bearers of hereditary and racial wealth, the people's fountain of youth, and the backbone of our military power," he said.

> The preservation of an efficient peasant class constitutes a pillar of National Socialist policy. . . . German agriculture must be protected by tariffs and state regulation of imports. . . . The fixing of prices for agricultural produce must be withdrawn from the influence of stock exchange speculation, and a stop must be put to exploitation of farmers by large middlemen. . . . The high taxation cannot be met out of the poor returns for labor on the land. The farmer is forced to run into debt and pay usurious interest on loans. He sinks deeper and deeper under this tyranny, and in the end forfeits his house and farm to the moneylender, who is usually a Jew.[2]

But the Nazis did more than just talk about the problems of the peasants. When a farmer would be forced to declare bankruptcy and his home and property would be put up for auction, Nazi party members would turn up in large numbers for the sale. They would interrupt the auctioneer with ridiculous questions and ask if the poor farmer's family was to have their home taken away from them "just so some Jew could make a fat profit." They would outbid serious buyers only to say later they misunderstood the price and could not pay. If all else failed, the storm troopers present would start a fight and in the process break up everything in sight. Thus by one means or another, the foreclosure sales on many farms were interrupted by the Nazis, and they gained the reputation of being the protectors of the impoverished farmers.

The increasing success of the Nazis at the polls was a direct reflection of the economic conditions, which had impoverished the peasants and were beginning to spread to other sectors of the economy. In the 1928 Reichstag elections, Hitler's party had won a mere 2.8 percent of the votes. In May 1929, the National Socialist party won 4.95 percent of the vote in the state elections in Saxony, and five out of ninety-six seats in the Landtag (state congress). On October 17, 1929, the Nazis received 6.98 percent of the votes in the Landtag elections in Baden. Less than a month later Hitler's party won 8.1 percent of the vote in the municipal elections in Lubeck. The citizens of Thuringia went to the polls on December 8, 1929, to elect their state Landtag, and 11.3 percent of them cast their ballots for the Nazis.

As a result of their success in the Thuringian elections in December, the Nazis held the balance of power in the state legislature. Hitler accordingly demanded that a National Socialist become a member of the right-wing coalition cabinet that was to take office. For the post he proposed Wilhelm Frick, one of the few Nazi leaders with governmental administrative experience. However, the other right-wing parties in the coalition, particularly the German People's party

(DVP), objected to taking a Nazi into their government. Hitler then showed his skill in political manipulation by pressuring the leaders of the German People's party from behind the scenes with a direct appeal to their financial backers.[3]

The industrialists decided that the National Socialists should be given a chance. The politicians quickly yielded to the power of money, and Wilhelm Frick became the first Nazi minister of a state government.

People were puzzled as to why so many respectable middle-class farmers would vote for a radical party like the Nazis. But it must be remembered that many of them were desperate, and when neither government nor any of the established parties seemed able to solve their problems they turned to Hitler. "He was our last hope," they said. "We thought we might at least try it with him."[4]

Although the farmers who voted for Hitler were now impoverished, many of them came from middle-class backgrounds, and hence, unlike the workers or very poor, they had relatives and friends who still had money and were converted to National Socialism by their example.

In explaining why he joined the National Socialist party, a young businessman told a story full of paranoia and anti-Semitism of his attempt to save his family's farm "from a Jewish moneylender":

> One day my brother visited me and told me that despite all diligence and frugality could do, my parents' homestead became more heavily indebted each year. It was then, when our plot of native soil seemed in danger, that I roused myself from my middle-class complacency. I had to forestall the catastrophe that threatened our homestead. My sisters wanted to marry, but they had no dowries. Consequently my father proceeded to mortgage the farm. At first he found the money-lenders willing and ready to help him out at the rate of 10 percent or more interest. The instant he was unable to pay all the interest and amortization debts, however, it would be all over for him. The

Jew threatened to drive him from the soil his ancestors had tilled for over three hundred years.

I was struck by the terrible realization that the government sought to seize all farms through the granting of credit. The Jew at the bottom of it all had to tame the farmer in order to achieve his plans. After this shocking realization, it occurred to me that these facts had long been exposed by the preachers of National Socialism without my having paid any attention to them. I went to ask the advice of my party (Nationalist) leaders. But their shrugs and discouraging attitude taught me that no rescue could be expected from that quarter. . . . I then tried to contribute as much as I could out of my modest income, in order to avert the worst. In 1930 I turned my back on the Deutschnationale Volkspartei [German Nationalist party], and after attending National Socialist party meetings regularly, I was won over to National Socialism.[5]

Within a year the depression that had ruined German agriculture began to affect industry. In the inflation of 1923, money had lost its value. Now in 1930, work began to lose its value; three million men could no longer sell their labor, and millions more could expect to lose their jobs in the near future. However, the economic effects of the depression were not limited to the working class but also struck the middle class and small businessmen almost as sharply. The small shareholders in Thyssen's Steel Trust saw their stock fall to a third of its original value; landlords were unable to collect their rents; and mortgage holders received no interest payments.

Everyone got some idea of just how serious the world economic crisis had become when news arrived from South America that the fire boxes of the locomotives had been adapted to burn coffee beans instead of coal. The Germans could no longer afford to buy South American coffee, so naturally the South Americans had no foreign exchange with which to buy German coal or locomotives; the vicious downward cycle of the depression was just beginning.

Germany suffered far more heavily from the world economic crisis than the other advanced industrialized nations. Her industrial production dropped by approximately half.[6] Neither the United States, Britain, nor France were affected so severely. It was a matter of decisive importance whether the crisis struck an economically strong and socially stable country or whether it struck one that was already badly shaken, and therefore highly vulnerable. Unlike Britain and France, which possessed large foreign investments, Germany was a debtor country. When the crash came and the creditors began to demand repayment of their loans, Germany had nothing to fall back on and thus quickly found the situation becoming catastrophic.

The German government decreased wages by decree and lowered prices, but not enough to compensate for the wage cuts. Despite the shrinking salaries and all the sacrifices of those who were still employed, more and more workers were discharged every day. The official unemployment figure was over three million in the spring of 1930; but the actual number was more than that, as German industry had a tendency to give its workers partial employment in hard times. So this unemployment figure reflected graver economic distress than it would have in other countries. The huge smelting furnaces of Fritz Thyssen and the German Steel Trusts, which were capable of producing twice as much steel as England, now stood useless, cold and still. Coal found no buyers, so it lay in great piles around the mines; meanwhile, the unemployed miners spent the winter with their families in unheated rooms.

In the woods around Berlin tent colonies sprang up; here lived those unemployed who could no longer pay their rent in city tenements. There were community soup kitchens in the tent camps, and the residents shared tasks such as garbage removal. Despite the poverty, discipline and order prevailed. Yet in the potato fields around Berlin the peasants had to post guards with loaded rifles, because large groups of starving men came from the city and carried away all their sacks would hold, even in broad daylight while traffic went by on the roads. Young men who had seen the last of their families' property dwindle away and had never learned the meaning of work now wandered through the countryside in famished bands of desperate marauders often literally singing with hunger. Residential sections resounded with the terrible songs of poor people who had never dreamed they would someday be singing for bread.

It was still "good times" for those unemployed who could stand in the long, shabby lines along the sidewalk outside the employment office. Slowly they moved forward and finally presented a little booklet at a window, where a clerk pasted in a stamp certifying that they had presented themselves in vain to ask for work. This entitled them to unemployment benefits, which amounted to as much as seventy marks a month. Soon the gray, disheveled mob had swollen beyond measure. After thirteen weeks of unemployment a person was transferred to another category where the benefits were much smaller and actually based on a kind of state charity. Originally what the unemployed worker received had been an insurance benefit that he had paid for in good times by compulsory deduction from his wages, but after a time it became a gift from the state. According to a popular joke, the optimist predicted: Next winter we will all go begging. The pessimist asked: From whom?

The mass discontent caused by the depression frightened many industrialists. With poverty and unemployment stalking the land, communism was on the rise again. Fritz Thyssen and a considerable number of his colleagues wanted the paramilitary organizations of the Right to unite in case they were needed to suppress a Red uprising. With this end in view Thyssen proposed to Hitler that the Nazi S.A. unite with the powerful rightist veterans group, the Stahlhelm. The negotiations for an alliance between the two organizations were directed by Thyssen himself.[7] The union would open up almost unlimited money and other resources to the Nazis.

Although the Stahlhelm was closely affiliated with the German Nationalist party, it was an independent organization of considerable strength and prestige. Reactionary monarchism, nationalism, and anticommunism were the political creeds of the organization.

President von Hindenburg was an honorary member of the Stahlhelm, and the army regarded it as a vast reserve and school for military training. Financing was never a problem for the Stahlhelm; they had abundant funds from both the aristocratic landlords and the industrialists. Nevertheless the dominant voice in the organization belonged to retired Junker army officers.* The commanders of the Stahlhelm were two former officers of the Imperial Army, Lieutenant Seldte and Lieutenant Colonel Duesterberg.

The organization was structured along military lines and divided into battalions, regiments, and brigades. Its members wore a field gray uniform and a cap with an emblem of a steel helmet. They were obliged to drill regularly and attend frequent exercises, consisting of day and night marches, map reading, marksmanship practice, and reconnaissance work. Their flag was the old Imperial standard, white with a black Iron Cross and the Hohenzollern eagle in the center.

The imposing outward strength of the Stahlhelm concealed an inner flaw, which Hitler was quick to recognize. The officers of the organization were mostly reactionary monarchists of the old school, but some of its younger members were radical nationalists who in their desperation might have been susceptible to Nazi propaganda. This division of political views within the Stahlhelm would provide Hitler with an opportunity to take it over from within. Once the S.A. and the Stahlhelm were united, Hitler felt his superior

---

*The Junkers were Prussian aristocrats. They had a strong tradition of serving as officers in the German Army and dominated its upper ranks.

skill as a propagandist would quickly win for him the allegiance of the younger men, and for a paramilitary group these were the ones who counted most.

Unaware of Hitler's secret ambitions, Thyssen tried to persuade the leaders of the Stahlhelm to accept an alliance with the S.A. He conferred with Lieutenant Colonel Duesterberg for a whole night, promising larger financial subsidies from industry if the two groups united. But all efforts were in vain. The leaders of the Stahlhelm sensed that their old-fashioned monarchist principles would not be able to compete with Hitler's skill as a demagogue. Furthermore, the aristocratic-agricultural interests, which provided a major portion of the funding for the Stahlhelm and controlled it through the Junker officer corps, were afraid that industrialists like Thyssen, who ultimately had much more money than they, would come to exercise a decisive financial influence over the organization. In spite of the fact that the proposed alliance came to naught, Hitler profited from the incident because Thyssen believed that Hitler had been ready to compromise and subordinate his own goals to those of a united nationalist movement.[8] A few years later when the question would arise whether or not Hitler should be taken into the government, Thyssen would cite the case of the negotiations with the Stahlhelm as proof that Hitler was a reasonable individual willing to compromise.

Hermann Mueller, the last Social Democratic chancellor of Germany, resigned in march 1930 because his government, based on a coalition of democratic parties, could not hold together on the dispute over the unemployment insurance fund. He was replaced by Heinrich Bruening, the parliamentary leader of the Catholic Center party, who as a captain had won the Iron Cross during the war and was known for his conservative political views.

The three political parties that had been responsible for the adoption of the Weimar Constitution—the Social Democrats, the Catholic Center and the Democrats—never again obtained a majority after 1919. In order to govern they had had to take other parties into the coalition, thus making any firm policy almost impossible. The party leaders were absorbed in bargaining and maneuvering for party advantages, "cattle trading" as the German politicians called it. Many were not at all displeased with the situation. Weak governments suited them because it made those in power more accessible to party pressure and economic interests. In the economic crisis, which intensified after March of 1930, it became impossible to assemble a coalition government that could be sure of a majority vote in the Reichstag. Instead of coming together, facing the depression, and forming a government of unity, each economic interest group—the labor unions, the farmers, the small shopkeepers, the Junkers, and the industrialists—demanded sacrifices from the others while seeking state aid for itself.

As soon as he took office, Chancellor Bruening was confronted with the same problem as his predecessor: he had to rely on precarious Reichstag majorities laboriously reassembled for each piece of legislation. There were continual disputes over where the economic burdens were to be placed, whether wages and unemployment insurance were to be cut, or taxes raised or tariffs increased. The debating became so turbulent that the government was unable to accomplish anything by parliamentary methods. By July, Bruening could see no way out of the deadlock, so he asked President von Hindenburg to dissolve the Reichstag. Hindenburg agreed, and new elections were called for September 14, 1930.

Although Heinrich Bruening was an able man, he was not appointed chancellor and granted such sweeping powers by President von Hindenburg on his merits alone. Behind Bruening stood a very powerful sponsor, General von Schleicher, who was to play a major role in the downfall of the Weimar Republic. Bruening had been made chancellor simply because von Schleicher "suggested" his name to Hindenburg as a man who could solve the economic crisis.

Bruening's sponsor was a man of mystery; only a very few Germans had ever heard of him. Actually, General Kurt von Schleicher had a high post behind the scenes in the elaborate hierarchy of the Germany Army.[9] The remarkable success of his military career was due to two factors: an unusual talent for organization and intrigue; and the good will of highly placed patrons. Schleicher came from a noble Brandenburg family and, like most young men of his class, was sent to a military academy. His excellent record at the academy attracted the attention of a general staff officer, Wilhelm Groener (later minister of war), who was so impressed with young Schleicher's ability that he made him his protégé. When Schleicher received his officer's commission he entered President von Hindenberg's old regiment, the Third Foot Guards, and had the good fortune of becoming the close friend and messmate of Hindenburg's son, Oskar. Schleicher was a frequent guest at the Hindenberg home. He was very clever, a good conversationalist, and could be charming whenever it suited his purpose.

During World War I, Schleicher served on the general staff. When General Groener succeeded Ludendorff as the first quartermaster general of the German Army, he appointed Schleicher, who was then only thirty-six years old, as his personal aide-de-camp. In 1919 Groener had his protégé transferred to the Ministry of War. In his new capacity, Schleicher helped to plan the foundations for the new Reichswehr. During the next few years, he made the most of his social contacts to push himself forward, and his progress continued, the result of his smoothness and his capacity for patient, meticulous work. His goal was the highest: to make himself the behind-the-scenes director of the Reichswehr.

What Schleicher wanted was power without responsibility. Hindenburg's election to the presidency brought him closer to his goal. Through Oskar, who now served as his father's personal adjutant, Schleicher was able to gain admittance to the presidential palace whenever he wished. The old president was impressed by the intelligence of his son's friend. Schleicher got to know all the members of Hindenburg's entourage. Before long, Oskar von Hindenburg, Schleicher, and State Secretary Meissner formed the so-called palace camarilla (a group of secret advisers), which exerted a tremendous influence over Hindenburg and eventually controlled him completely.

In 1928 the man who was appointed the new minister of war was none other than Schleicher's patron, General Groener. A few months later, Schleicher was made a major general, and a special post was created for him in the Ministry of War. His official title was "chief of the ministerial office," and his functions were similar to those carried out by the secretaries of state in other ministries. The new post carried with it broad authority and enormous power. It put Schleicher in control of the military intelligence services and of all relations between the Reichstag and the armed forces. As time went on, the scope of the post expanded and Schleicher's influence behind the scenes grew with it. He established contact with the leaders of many political parties, including the Social Democrats and the Nazis, but was careful never to identify himself publicly with any particular group. The political careers of General von Schleicher and Hitler paralleled each other as they both progressed steadily in the late 1920s and early 1930s. Ultimately they would be rivals for the leadership of Germany.

Because he was a general, Schleicher had no trouble keeping a balance between his friendship with conservatives and socialists, industrialists and labor leaders. Hitler, on the other hand, was criticized by the socialist elements in the Nazi party because of his contacts with what they called "the reactionary forces of big business." This simmering dispute broke into the open in April 1930 when the trade unions in Saxony went out on strike. Otto Strasser, Gregor's brother, who controlled several Nazi newspapers in northern Germany, came out in full support of the strike. Strasser's newspapers had for some time maintained a radical socialist line, which irritated and embarrassed Hitler. Even those industrialists who were sympathetic to the Nazis had always been afraid of the party's socialism: now they made it clear that unless Hitler immediately repudiated the stand taken by Strasser there would be no more subsidies.

Being able to count on the loyalty of the gauleiter of Saxony, Hitler ordered that no party member could take part in the strike. However, he was unable to silence Strasser's papers; the time for a showdown with this "rebellious individual" was clearly at hand. On May 21, 1930, Hitler, acting with his characteristic suddenness, arrived unannounced in Berlin with his staff. Shortly after their arrival, Hess telephoned Otto Strasser and invited him to come to the Sans Souci Hotel to discuss his disputes with Hitler. The only account of this discussion, which was held before a very small group of party leaders, is Otto Strasser's; nevertheless, it is probably basically accurate because it was published by Strasser shortly afterward and Hitler never challenged it.

Hitler reprimanded Strasser for deviating from the party line; his purpose, however, was persuasion rather than coercion. He tried to bribe Strasser by offering to put him in charge of all Nazi newspapers throughout Germany. Only after such appeals failed did he threaten to run Strasser and his supporters out of the party if they refused to submit. A long debate followed, extending over into the next day. Strasser insisted vehemently on five points: a thorough revolution, opposition to bourgeois capitalism, real socialism, no coalitions with the reactionary parties, and no attacks against Soviet Russia. Hitler countered by accusing Strasser of advocating democracy and Bolshevism.

The next day the debate was taken up again. Strasser began by demanding the nationalization of industry. "Democracy has laid the world to ruins," commented Hitler with scorn, "and nevertheless you want to extend it to the economic sphere. It would be the end of the German economy. . . . The capitalists have worked their way to the top through their capacity, and on the basis of this selection, which again only proves their higher race, they have a right to lead. Now you want an incapable Government Council or Workers' Council, which has no notion of anything, to have a say: no leader in economic life would tolerate it." Lowering his voice a bit, Hitler said that the economy of Germany depends upon cooperation between the industrialists and the workers. A factory owner is dependent on his workmen. If they went on strike, then his so-called property would become utterly worthless.

At this point he turned to Amann (the party business manager) and said: "What right have these people to demand a share in the property or even in the administration? Herr Amann, would you permit your typist to have any voice in your affairs? The employer who accepts the responsibility for production also gives the working people their means of livelihood. Our greatest industrialists are not concerned with just the acquisition of wealth or with good living, but above all else, with responsibility and power." Hitler then mellowed a bit. "But socialism," he explained, "does not mean that factories must be socialized, only that they may be when they act contrary to the interest of the nation. So long as they do not, it would simply be a crime to disturb business. . . . Just as the Fascists have already done, so in our National Socialist State we will have employers and workers standing side by side with equal rights."

Not satisfied, Strasser asked: "What would you do with the Krupp industries if you came to power?"

"Why nothing," Hitler replied. "Do you think I am so senseless as to destroy Germany's economy? Only if people should fail to act in the interests of the nation then—and only then—would the State intervene. But for that . . . you do not need to give the workers the right to have a voice in the conduct of the business: you need only a strong State."[10]

Hitler was forced to tread a narrow path because he needed both the support of big business interests, who had the money to finance the party, and the support of the masses, who had the votes. In origin the National Socialist party had been to a certain extent truly "socialist." This anticapitalist part of the Nazi program was not only taken seriously by many loyal members, but also was becoming increasingly important as the depression spread unemployment and poverty across the land.

Neither Hitler's threats nor pleadings had succeeded in convincing his rebellious lieutenant. Strasser was more certain than ever that Hitler was only the pawn of "reactionary" interests, working hand-in-hand with the "Jewish Stock Exchange" to uphold capitalism. For over a month the issue was left unfinished. Then, in the provincial elections of Saxony, held in June 1930, the Nazi representation rose from five to fourteen deputies, making them the second largest party in Saxony, in spite of Hitler's repudiation of the strike a few months earlier. Much of the Nazi election victory was due to support from the small- and medium-size firms of Saxony. Now Hitler felt safe to run Otto Strasser out of the party. In a General Assembly, on June 30, Strasser was bitterly attacked by Dr. Goebbels and ejected from the meeting. On July 1, Strasser telegraphed Hitler in Munich, demanding an explanation within twenty-four hours. None came. Strasser then seceded from the party and established "the Union of Revolutionary National Socialists," better known as the "Black Front." But the response among party members was very small; even his own brother Gregor remained loyal to Hitler.[11]

As the fall Reichstag elections of 1930 approached, the dominant sectors of heavy industry were using their influence in an effort to strengthen the moderate parties of the center. They tried to force Hugenberg and the Nationalist party to be amenable to compromise and cooperate with the moderates rather than retreat into a negative opposition. Thus, when the election campaign began, the leading heavy industrialists were still willing to work with the democratic, parliamentary system.[12]

Much of the election campaign consisted of the moderate bourgeois parties attacking the "Marxism" of the Social

Democrats, which they saw as the main issue. As it turned out, Hitler and the Nazis tapped a deeper vein of public opinion, a basic distrust of the whole democratic system.

The Nazi party organization, which Hitler had long been preparing for just such an occasion, moved quickly to saturate the cities and rural areas with propaganda. Anxiety and resentment formed the mood of the time. The people wanted some explanation for their misfortunes. It was the Allies, especially the French, who were to blame, Hitler said. The Versailles Treaty had enslaved the German people and destroyed their economy. The Republic, with its corrupt self-seeking politicians, money barons, monopolists, and speculators, was no better. There were the Marxists, who fostered class hatred and kept the nation divided, and above all the Jews, who grew rich on Germany's poverty. There was only one hope, insisted Hitler. Germany must turn to new men and find a new movement that would restore security, prosperity, and dignity to her people. The old gang of politicians and their parties could offer no solutions because they were part of the system that had brought about the collapse in the first place.

There was little need for Hitler to attack the Social Democrats; that was already being done for him by the moderate bourgeois parties. This left him free to concentrate his attack on the moderate parties themselves. He accused Chancellor Bruening and bourgeois politicians generally of being out of touch with ordinary people, and there was just enough truth in this accusation to make it stick. The Social Democrats were also under attack from the Communists, who accused them of betraying Marxism. Almost no one bothered to reply to Hitler's campaign; the professional politicians refused to believe the Nazi party was of any significance.

The hard-pressed middle class saw the Nazis as something new and different. One fifty-year-old white-collar worker later recalled his participation in the 1930 elections:

> I had been unwilling to join any of the old parties. I usually voted for the moderate candidates, but never had any

real faith in "politicians." Before the elections, the people were always right, but after the balloting the voter was just a nuisance. The so-called representatives of the middle class would then proceed to make every sort of shady deal with the stock exchange barons and the representatives of the Marxist parties.

A few weeks before the 1930 elections I attended my first National Socialist meeting at the urging of a friend. The speaker said the old parties had betrayed the German people. He talked about the November criminals, the Versailles Treaty, the inflation and finally the mass unemployment. Hitler, he said, provided the only hope. Then he mentioned the Jewish question and their conspiracy. I had never thought about the Jews or the racial issue before, but that night I couldn't get to sleep. Thinking back, I remembered that the Jews I met at work never seemed concerned about Germany's problem, but if the Jews were involved in any issue, whether it be in Russia or Palestine, they got very excited. . . . A few days before the election I became so involved in the campaign that I even offered to give one-fourth of my meager week's salary to help buy extra propaganda literature.[13]

To audiences overwhelmed with a sense of helplessness, facing poverty and the bread line, Hitler cried: "If economic experts say this or that is impossible, then to hell with economics. What counts is the will and if our will is strong enough we can do anything. We must renew the old German virtues of discipline, and self-reliance. Not so long ago Germany was prosperous, strong, and respected by all." Hitler would then pause for a second, as if to look each member of the audience in the eye. With a tone of sincerity he assured them: "It is not your fault that Germany was defeated in the war and has suffered so much since. You were betrayed in 1918 by Marxists, international Jewish bankers, and corrupt politicians; and these same forces have exploited you ever since, prospering on Germany's misery. All we need to do is clear out the old gang in Berlin."

Only the Communists could rival the Nazis in methods of agitation, but they deliberately limited their appeal to the working class. They were also hampered by the rigid beliefs of Marxist doctrine. Unlike the Communists, the Nazis could appeal to the powerful sentiment of nationalism, which provided an almost unlimited audience. Hitler intended to unite the discontented of all classes.

In the last days of the campaign, Hitler made almost impossible demands on his party members, most of whom had never been involved in politics before. They threw themselves into the contest with winner-take-all spirit. The vigor and zeal of the National Socialists sharply contrasted with the dull routine way in which the established parties went through the motions of an election campaign. Being, on an average, much younger than the members or leaders of rival parties, the Nazis had a purely physical energy and militancy that the middle-aged bureaucrats of the bourgeois and socialist parties could not match. Two days before the election the National Socialists held twenty-four mass rallies in Berlin alone. Almost every wall and fence in the city was covered with their shrieking red posters.

Where did all the money for this huge Nazi election campaign come from? True, unlike the bourgeois parties, most of the Nazi campaign workers received no salaries and paid their own expenses; nevertheless, the costs were tremendous. Big business gave very little, aside from the usual contributions from Thyssen, Kirdorf, the coal tycoon, and a few other wealthy Nazi sympathizers. Some small firms that were being ruined by the depression looked favorably on Hitler, but the Nazis' chances of winning any sizable number of votes were still too unsure to lead such financially overburdened firms to contribute.

A considerable portion of the campaign funds were produced by the party treasurer, Franz Xavier Schwarz. A skilled accountant, Schwarz juggled the party books to produce money that literally wasn't there. He delayed the payment of party salaries and the bills for regular day-to-day expenses. He mortgaged some of the party automobiles and whatever other items of value he could find, those that were not already mortgaged, that is. Due to his reputation for thoroughness, he was also able to obtain extensive credit for campaign literature, posters, renting of meeting halls, and other expenses.[14] Schwarz's methods had only one flaw: if the party did not gain a substantial victory it would be bankrupt.

On September 14, 1930, almost five million new German voters went to the polls; most of them were young people representing an entirely new force in politics. The majority of them did not want to be counted as belonging to any definite social class, and many of them had never really had a class. This was the generation born in the early 1900s, which grew up in an age when employment was rare, when the economic crisis had thrown millions out on the streets; the youngest in particular could find virtually no jobs at all. A very young man beginning his adult life in Germany in 1930 faced a dismal future. Between the ages of fifteen and seventeen he might have learned a trade, or if his parents had the money he might have stayed in school until he was twenty-two; but in both cases there was a strong possibility that he would then sit idle without work. Those lucky ones who were able to find a job received no more than a subsistence wage.

Many young people openly admitted that they were for Hitler—at least he represented something "new and different." Yet only a few days before the elections no one foresaw the extent of the coming Nazi success. It was obvious that the party had made quite a bit of progress since 1928, but even the most optimistic Nazis themselves were discussing the possibility that with luck they might win as many as fifty seats in the new Reichstag. In spite of his understanding of mass psychology, Hitler himself had little expectation of the breakthrough on the horizon.

On the evening of September 14, 1930, all Germany waited with anticipation as the election results began to trickle in. By about three o'clock in the morning the historic significance of the occasion was becoming apparent. Everyone, including Hitler, listened in amazement as the news of the Nazi landslide was announced. This was the turning of the tide. Adolf Hitler, who only a few days ago had still been considered an extremist political crank, was now one of the nation's key political figures. His triumph signaled the Republic's doom. It would not collapse immediately, but its death agony had begun.

The National Socialists polled 19 percent of the electorate, which meant 6,409,600 votes compared to 810,000 in 1928. They won 107 seats in the Reichstag, compared with 12 in 1928, and had suddenly become Germany's second largest political party, with only the Social Democrats still ahead of them. Although the Communists' gains were not quite as spectacular, they received 4,592,000 votes and increased their seats in the Reichstag from 54 to 57. This was actually convenient for Hitler because a strong Communist party terrified the upper class, and Hitler presented himself as the only man capable of saving Germany from Bolshevism.

The two parties that had openly campaigned for the overthrow of the existing regime, the National Socialists and Communists, had together won almost a third of the votes and seats in the new Reichstag. The Communists primarily took votes away from the Social Democrats, whose representation fell from 152 to 143. Hitler, on the other hand, increased his strength by eroding the moderate and the conservative parties. The three moderate bourgeois parties—the People's party, the German State party (Democrats), and the Economic party—lost well over a million of their 1928 votes. The biggest losers in the election were Hitler's right-wing rivals, the Nationalists, whose vote fell from 4,381,600 in 1928 to 2,458,300 in 1930. It was clear to all that Hugenberg's party was in decline; their lost voters had gone over to the National Socialists. Hitler, who commanded 107 deputies compared to 41 for the Nationalists, was now the undisputed leader of German nationalism. A future indication of the radicalization of German politics was seen in the fact that an overwhelming number of the new voters supported either the Nazis or the Communists; thus the youth of Germany was drifting into the hands of the extremists.

Literally overnight, Hitler had become the force to be reckoned with in German politics. The Nazis registered spectacular gains in all electoral districts, and increases of over eight times the 1928 vote were not uncommon. However, the best showings were among the farmers and lower-to-middle-class voters in the rural and Protestant areas of northern Germany. Relatively less impressive, though still formidable, were the returns from Catholic areas and the working-class districts of the large industrial centers. The National Socialist vote in Berlin was typical of the percentages they received throughout the country; in Wedding, a working-class neighborhood, the Nazis received 8.9 percent of the vote; in Steglitz, a middle-class area, 25.8 percent of the vote; and in Zehlendorf, a middle-to-upper-class neighborhood, 17.7 percent of the vote.[15]

Until now, the majority of Hitler's supporters were individuals who were totally opposed to the democratic values of the Weimar government. But in the 1930 election many middle-class people with otherwise moderate political views cast their ballots for Hitler, not because the agreed with everything he said, but because they hoped he could save them from the miseries of the depression. To be sure, it was not the *haute bourgeoisie* or the new rich who supported Hitler, but those whom the economic crisis had squeezed to the wall: the clerks, office workers, small shopkeepers, and farmers.

The notion of a genuine social revolution as proposed by the Communists was anathema to these "respectable," though impoverished, members of the middle class, yet they were profoundly dissatisfied with the existing political and economic system. The tension between their desire to preserve their status and their equally fervent desire to alter radically the established system was resolved by Hitler's appeal for patriotic revolution, which would revitalize the nation without revolutionizing its structure. Ultimately the Nazi revolution was the ideal nationalist revolution; it was a "revolution of the will," which actually threatened none of the vested economic interests of the middle class. However, Hitler's struggle against the Jews, who were unfairly stereotyped as the speculator, internationalist, and big banker, provided a revolutionary outlet and scapegoat for the more radical among his followers.

After the great Nazi victory no one knew exactly what to expect from Hitler. Would he use the Nazi deputies in the Reichstag to discredit democracy and bring the government to a standstill? Would he then seize power by force? Or did he think that his popularity would continue to grow in landslide proportions, enabling him to come to power legally as a result of election victories and to postpone any revolutionary action until after he had gained control of the machinery of the state? In public, at least, he was still expounding the same policy he had before the election: "It is not parliamentary majorities that mold the fate of the nations. We know, however, that . . . democracy must be defeated with the weapons of democracy."[16]

Hitler considered the various alternative strategies. He certainly planned to have his revolution, but it would have to wait until after he came to power. Why risk defeat in the streets, as he had in November 1923, when the party was making more progress than ever before? The sudden entrance of the National Socialists into the ranks of the major parties was immediately reflected in the movement's membership and financial status. The very fact that other political parties took the National Socialists seriously for the first time since 1923 lead to a bandwagon effect and rapid increases in the membership rolls. Special clerks in Munich had to work a 6 to 11 P.M. shift to process the applications that poured into party headquarters. The flow of application fees and the simultaneous influx of business advertising revenue for the *Völkischer Beobachter* and other party newspapers put the National Socialist party on a reasonably firm financial footing and wiped out most of its staggering debts.

One of the biggest sources of day-to-day income for the Nazi party now came from the subscriptions sold for the *Völkischer Beobachter*. The printing of this paper and other propaganda literature also constituted a large expenditure from the party budget. This was all carried out under the financial management of Max Amann, the former party business manager, who was now the director of the Nazi party publishing house. The occasional donations from wealthy sympathizers, and the big collections from rallies where Hitler spoke, were a welcome but irregular source of income. The circulation of the party newspaper was a more consistent gauge of success, for it provided a significant sum that the party administration could count on.

The *Völkischer Beobachter* had been operating on a sound financial footing since 1926, but after September 1930 it began to produce a substantial profit. Quite rightly Hitler credited this accomplishment to the "exemplary industry" of Max Amann. "Thanks to a quite military discipline, he has succeeded in getting the very best out of his colleagues, suppressing particularly all contact between the editorial and administrative staffs. I don't know how often Amann, when telling me of the great financial development of the newspaper, begged me to make no mention of the fact in front of Rosenberg, the editor in chief, or of the other members of the editorial staff. Otherwise, he used to say, they would plague him for higher salaries."[17]

After the September elections of 1930, the party newspaper also earned a large revenue from advertising. Once in anger, Hitler wrote an open letter to an innkeeper reproaching him for the commercial demagoguery of the big brewers, who pretended to be the benefactors of the little man, struggling to ensure him his daily glass of beer. The next day Amann came to Hitler's office "completely overwhelmed" to tell him that some of the big beer halls were canceling their advertising contracts with the newspaper. This meant an immediate loss of 7,000 marks, and of 27,000 over a longer period. "I promised myself solemnly," said Hitler, "that I would never again write an article under the domination of rage."[18]

The one businessman on whom the Nazi party was most dependent was not a great industrialist who contributed money to the movement, but the Munich printer Adolph Mueller. He was not a Nazi but a member of the Bavarian People's party, and he printed most of the political newspapers in Munich. In appearance, Mueller looked more like a tavern keeper than a press magnate. He was a short, stout man and almost completely deaf. He had done business with the Nazis since before the putsch. When Hitler wanted to start publishing the *Völkischer Beobachter* again after his release from prison in 1924, Mueller advanced the editor's wages and supplied the paper on credit. According to Hitler, Mueller was a man of "infinite flexibility" in his political views. Several Communists worked for his firm, and he was in the habit of saying to them that if anything displeased them with the activities of the company he would make the changes they wished, provided that in return he could pay them their week's wages in orthodox opinions instead of money. Mueller, who was a self-made man, had a great admiration for Hitler, and the two became close personal friends.

In spite of their long association, Hitler continually haggled with Mueller over his prices: "The best trick I played on him," said Hitler, "was the adoption of the large format for the *Völkischer Beobachter*. Mueller had thought himself the cunning one, for he supposed that, by being the only man who possessed a machine corresponding to our new format, he was binding us to him. In reality, it was he who was binding himself to our newspaper, and he was very glad to continue to print for us, for no other newspaper used our format. Mueller had become the slave of the machine."[19] After the beginning of the depression, however,

Mueller was glad to have the Nazis as customers because their newspaper was the only one that did not have a drop in circulation.

The exact details of all the Nazi party's business and financial affairs were worked out under the direction of party treasurer Schwarz. "It's unbelievable what the Party owes to Schwarz," said Hitler. "It was thanks to the good order which he kept in our finances that we were able to develop so rapidly."[20] Schwarz had started to work for the Nazis in 1924; before, he had been employed in the Munich City Hall and had been the treasurer for the right-wing "Popular Block." Coming to see Hitler in Landsberg prison, the fat, bald, bespectacled Schwarz said that he was fed up with working for the petty individual who controlled the "Popular Block" and would be pleased to work for the Nazis for a change. "I was not slow to perceive his qualities," said Hitler. "As usual, the man had been stifled by the mediocrities for whom he worked."

> Hitler said, Schwarz organized, in a model fashion, everything that gradually became the Party's gigantic [financial] administration. . . . He had the fault—and what luck that was!—of not being a lawyer and nobody had more practical good sense than he had. He knew admirably how to economize on small things—with the result that we always had what we needed for important matters. It was Schwarz who enabled me to administer the Party without our having to rely on petty cash. In this way, unexpected assets are like manna. Schwarz centralized the [financial] administration of the Party. All subscriptions [monthly membership dues] are sent directly to the central office, which returns to the local and regional branches the percentage that's due to them.[21]

Schwarz's centralization of the party's financial affairs was an important instrument of control in Hitler's hands and useful in controlling rivals such as Strasser.

All the data concerning the sources of the Nazi party's income was assembled in Schwarz's office. Every pfennig was booked as to its origin with meticulous care. Treasurer Schwarz's accounts have never been found. This is one of the greatest mysteries surrounding the last days of the Nazi regime. Hitler trusted Schwarz completely and consequently told him the source of even "anonymous" contributions so the name of the donor could be recorded and he could be approached again in the future. Which industrialists contributed to Hitler before 1933? Precisely how much did they give? These questions would undoubtedly have been answered in detail by the books of the party treasurer, just as the party membership records, which were also kept in Brown House, revealed every individual who belonged to the party.

It is not unlikely that all of Schwarz's records were purposely destroyed as the Allied armies neared Munich. We do know that as far as the party membership files were concerned, they were taken to a Munich paper plant with orders to tear them to shreds, to be recycled for new paper. But the owner of the paper factory had them dumped on a huge, empty floor in one of his warehouses; and to hide them from discovery by Gestapo agents, he had them covered with miscut pages, smudgy castoffs from pages of books in the process of being printed, and other wastepaper. When the American Army entered Munich, the paper manufacturer reported to the U.S. security offices the important records hidden in his warehouse.

It is probable, therefore, that some other firm was given orders to destroy the records of the party treasurer, and that this company obeyed.

7

HITLER'S AGENTS IN
HIGH AND LOW
PLACES

Naturally Chancellor Bruening was appalled by the victory
of the Nazis in the September elections. Rather than getting
a more manageable Reichstag he was now faced with one
in which it was almost impossible to form a working majority. One possibility would have been for him to attempt
to "tame" the Nazis by giving them posts in a coalition
government. Some tentative moves were made in this direction, probably through Fritz Thyssen, who had close connections with the Catholic Center party. According to the
official government version, Hitler insisted that his party,
which would be the largest in the coalition, should have the
key posts of minister of interior and minister of defense.
Bruening considered such a proposal out of the question.
However, Thyssen later wrote that an "accommodating offer
had been made by the National Socialists to the cabinet of
Chancellor Bruening. They [Nazis] were willing to tolerate
Bruening, without being represented in his cabinet, if the
Chancellor would be prepared to say that he would part
company with the socialists [Social Democrats]."[1] Thyssen

makes it clear that he thought Bruening should have accepted the offer, but it was refused.[2]

When the attempted compromise with Bruening failed, the 107 National Socialist deputies in the Reichstag became anxious to test their strength. On October 14, 1930, at the behest of Strasser and other left-wing leaders in the party, the Nazi faction introduced a bill to limit the interest rate to 4 percent; furthermore, "the entire property of the bank and stock exchange princes [wealthy financiers] . . . must be expropriated without indemnification for the welfare of the German people as a whole" [In other words, the banks would be confiscated by the government without any payment to the owners or shareholders.]; the same would be done with the property of all eastern Jews; and "the large banks must be taken over by the state without delay."[3] This was actually nothing new; Strasser and Feder had submitted this same proposal to the Reichstag before and no one had paid any attention to the radical little group. But this time, 107 deputies, a sixth of the Reichstag, were demanding the expropriation of the banks. The upper class and Hitler's financial backers were shocked: this was communism!

Hitler was furious. He tried to put his financial backers at ease by ordering the Nazi deputies to withdraw their bill for the expropriation of the banks. They obeyed with silent rage. Then the Communists indulged in a clever trick by reintroducing the bill exactly as it was worded by the Nazis. Hitler commanded his followers to vote against their own bill and reluctantly they did so, to the great amusement of their enemies. However, what looked like an embarrassing situation to the general public was actually a triumph for Hitler. Business leaders, even those who had no sympathy for the Nazis, remarked with amazement at the absolute control Hitler had over his followers. The wealthy supporters of the party who feared its left-wing elements were now reassured.

Not only did Hitler have to contend with his financial

backers, but he also had to worry about assuring the army of his good intentions. As early as 1927, the army had forbidden the recruitment of National Socialists in its 100,000 man force and even banned their employment as civilian workers in arsenals and supply depots. In spite of this, it had become obvious by 1930 that Hitler's propaganda was making headway in the army, especially among the young officers who were attracted by his promises to restore the size and glory of Germany's fighting forces. The Nazi infiltration into the army became so serious that the minister of defense, General Groener, issued an order on January 22, 1930, warning the soldiers that the Nazis were only trying to woo the army because they were greedy for power. He said that the National Socialists were trying to convince the army that they alone represented the national interests, and he requested all troops to refrain from politics and "serve the state" aloof from political strife.

A few months later three young lieutenants from the garrison of Ulm were arrested for spreading Nazi propaganda in the army. They had also allegedly committed the more serious offense of trying to persuade their fellow officers to agree that in case of a Nazi putsch they would not fire on the insurgents. This offense would ordinarily have been considered high treason, but General Groener did not wish to publicize the fact that treason existed among the officer corps, so he attempted to hush up the matter by trying the three lieutenants on the charge of a simple breach of discipline. When one of the defendants smuggled out an inflammatory article to the *Völkischer Beobachter*, General Groener's plan became impossible. Shortly after Hitler's victory in the September elections of 1930, the three officers were brought before the Supreme Court at Leipzig on charges of high treason.

Hans Frank, the Nazi defense lawyer, arranged to call Hitler as a witness. This was a calculated risk. It would be embarrassing for Hitler to disown the three young officers whose activities were proof of the growth of pro-Nazi feelings in the army. And yet, the prosecution had charged that the National Socialist party was a revolutionary organization intent on overthrowing the government by force. Hitler had to deny this charge if anyone was to believe his policy of legality. However, he also had a more important objective to accomplish. As the leader of the second largest political party, which had just scored a stunning popular victory at the polls, he wanted to assure the commanders of the army that they had nothing to fear from National Socialism.

It was not the accused who occupied the limelight at the trial, but Adolf Hitler. He made good use of this opportunity. Every statement was designed to have a particular effect, not on the Court, but on the army. He went out of his way to reassure the generals that he did not intend to set up the S.A. as a rival to the army.

> They [the S.A.] were set up exclusively for the purpose of protecting the Party in its propaganda activities, not to fight against the State. I have been a soldier long enough to know that it is impossible for a political party to fight against the disciplined forces of the army. . . . I did everything I could to prevent the S.A. from assuming any kind of military character. I have always expressed the opinion that any attempt to replace the Army would be senseless. . . . My only wish is that the German State and the German people should be imbued with a new spirit. . . . We will see to it that, when we come to power, out of the present Reichswehr a great German People's Army shall arise. There are thousands of young men in the Army, of the same opinion.

Full of self-assurance, Hitler brazenly stated his intentions. It is amazing how exactly his plan, as he described it before the Court, was to be realized in years to come.

The president of the Court asked: "How do you picture

the establishment of the Third Reich?"* Hitler: "The Constitution prescribes the theater of war but not its goal. We shall gain control of the Reichstag and in this way make our Party the decisive factor. Then, when we control the constitutional bodies, we shall pour the State in the mold we consider correct."

The president of the Court then referred to a Nazi handbill that declared: "Reform is only half. Revolution is all."

Hitler: "The German people are being intellectually revolutionized by our propaganda. . . . Our movement does not require violence. The time will come when the German nation will get to know our ideas. Then thirty-five million Germans will stand behind us. It makes no difference to us whether we join a government today or remain in opposition. The next election will turn the hundred and seven National Socialists in the Reichstag into two hundred. . . . It is in our opponents' interest to represent our movement as inimical to the State, because they know that our goal is to be attained by legal means. Of course, they also see that our movement must lead to the complete reshaping of the State."

The president of the Court asked: "Only by constitutional means, then?" Hitler answered loudly: "Certainly!"

The president of the Court: "How do you interpret the expression 'German National Revolution'?"

Hitler: "The concept of a 'National Revolution' is always taken in a purely political sense. . . . When we have had two or three more elections, the National Socialist movement will have a majority in the Reichstag, and then we shall pave the way for the National Socialist Revolution. . . . Germany is muzzled by the peace treaties. The whole of Ger-

---

*The previous two German empires were called the First and Second Reich. The First Reich was the Holy Roman Empire, which was founded in 962 A.D. and theoretically lasted until Napoleon's invasion in 1806. The Second Reich was founded by Bismark in 1871 and lasted until the fall of the kaiser in 1918. In the 1920s, Hitler began talking about founding another great German Empire, or Third Reich, that would last 1,000 years.

man legislation is nothing but an attempt to anchor the peace treaties on the German people. The National Socialists look on these treaties not as law, but as something forced on us. We will not have future generations which are completely guiltless burdened with them. If we defend ourselves against them with every means, then we shall be on the way to revolution."

The president of the Court asked timidly: "Also with illegal means?"

Hitler: "I am assuming now that we shall have triumphed, and then we shall fight against the treaties by every means, even though the world looks on these means as illegal."

All of this was intended for the generals, but there was also the party to be considered, so Hitler added with sinister ambiguity: "I can assure you that, when the National Socialist movement's struggle is successful, then there will be a National Socialist Court of Justice too; the November 1918 revolution will be avenged, and heads will roll."[4] With this closing comment, the public gallery broke into cheers.

No one could say that Hitler did not give fair warning of what he would do if he came to power; however, the audience in the courtroom apparently welcomed it, for they applauded the threat loud and long. It made a sensational headline in the newspapers throughout Germany.[5] Lost in the excitement of Hitler's testimony was the actual case at hand. The three young lieutenants were found guilty but were given the mild sentence of eighteen months fortress detention. This was of little importance to Hitler; his primary concern was the effect of his comments on the army. As he had hoped, the generals now felt reassured. The opinion of many of the army's leaders was expressed by General Jodl, who would become one of Hitler's highest ranking generals, when he later stated that it was the Leipzig trial that changed his mind in favor of Hitler. After all, the army probably suffered from the Versailles Treaty more than anyone else, so the Officer Corps could hardly object to a revolution that intended to destroy the treaty, as long as it did not threaten their power or plunge the nation into civil war.

The Officer Corps of the army was one of the most important groups of the German ruling class. The German Army was nonpolitical only in the sense that it usually did not interfere in the disputes within the establishment. If the establishment were threatened by an outside force, such as the Communists or Nazis, the army probably would have become "political." The German Army, like any other modern army, had close connections with the industrialists and munitions makers, but it was an independent force to a far greater degree than the British or American armies. Naturally the Officer Corps was nationalistic and adamantly opposed to the Versailles Treaty, which limited the size of their force to 100,000 men. Thus they favored the same sort of foreign policy that big business did, which would eventually free Germany from the restrictions of the Versailles Treaty. On this point they agreed with Hitler. Most members of the Officer Corps were also Junkers (Prussian aristocrats), so there was a considerable overlap of interests between this group and the army. The political views of the Junkers were primarily represented by the Nationalist party, which had already demonstrated its willingness to cooperate with the Nazis.

Henceforth, Hitler's struggle for power was waged on two levels. Outwardly, there was his propaganda effort to increase the size of the party and his popular support among the masses. At the same time, behind the scenes, he would try to convince the key individuals of the German power elite that he did not threaten their economic interests and thus should be appointed chancellor, a position to which his mass following entitled him. In this quiet but highly important campaign, he employed a strategy of ambivalence. First he swore his loyalty to the constitution, then he promised that heads would roll. In one breath, he would give some encouragement to Strasser's socialist wing of the party, and in the next, he would severely rebuke them. All this ambiguity was primarily intended for those who controlled the levers of power, especially Hindenburg and those around him. On the one hand, Hitler was making an offer of alliance, and on the other warning them what might happen if they weren't willing to compromise with him.

From 1928 on, Hermann Goering was living in Berlin with his aristocratic Swedish wife. Although he complained of always being short of money, he lived well, dining in the city's most exclusive restaurants almost every night. He still considered himself a Nazi, but he had not been active in the leadership of the party for some time. From time to time, he tried to win over a few of his upper-class friends to the Nazi cause. Goering was a man comfortable in both the world of the drawing room and the company of beer hall fighters. Once, while dining at Horcher's, Berlin's most exclusive restaurant, he gestured toward the room full of well-fed faces surrounding him and said: "One day we will sweep all this away, and bring justice back to Germany. It is time we cleared out these bloodsuckers and fed the German people, instead."[6]

Goering's first real chance to regain a leadership position in the Nazi party came when Hitler asked him to stand for the party in the 1928 Reichstag elections. In spite of the fact that Goering was ultimately intended to be a contact man with the upper class, he waged a rough and rowdy election campaign aimed at the masses. Having modeled his style of speaking closely after Hitler's, Goering was an effective rabble-rouser. He had a talent for exchanging insults and challenges with the Communist hecklers who followed him from meeting to meeting. Considering his background and upbringing, he had a surprisingly good ear for vulgar slang and popular humor. When his mood was at its most sarcastic he seemed to have the best rapport with his audience.

"All Berlin has election fever," Carin Goering wrote home to her mother, Baroness von Fock, on May 18, "and it will be settled on Sunday. They have already begun to shoot each other dead. Each day Communists with red flags with hammer-and-sickle on them drag their way through the city, and always there are clashes with Hitler-men carrying their red banners with swastikas on them, so then there is strife, killings, and woundings. We have to wait to see how the election goes on Sunday."[7]

As one of the twelve Nazis elected to the Reichstag in 1928, Goering received a letter from the Kaiser's eldest son, Crown Prince Wilhelm, congratulating him on his victory: "Your extraordinary talent, your skill with words, and your bodily strength are just what are needed for your new profession of people's representative."[8] What did the prince mean? Carin Goering asked her husband. He laughed and said that Wilhelm was anticipating the fights between the young Communist agitators in the Reichstag and the Nazis. "Hermann is now so terribly busy," Carin Goering wrote in June of 1928, "that I only see him when he pops in and out. But he gives me all his free time and at least we can eat together. But I don't think there is a single meal we have had alone, there are always people there."[9] The "people" were businessmen, politicians, aristocrats, and bankers. Some had come to talk about the Nazi party and some simply to do business with Goering. Eventually, however, all of them were given a sales pitch about Hitler.

Even after Goering became a Nazi representative in the Reichstag, he continued to pursue his own personal business activities as an agent for several aircraft manufacturers.[10] In fact, the two occupations blended well and complemented each other. He was also representing several parachute manufacturers and traveling frequently to Zurich and Bern to give lectures and demonstrations of parachutes.[11] After one such visit to Switzerland, Goering's wife acted as hostess at a luncheon in Berlin for a group of Swiss generals and colonels who had come for further conversations with Goering on the development of an air force.

Hitler assigned Hermann Goering the task of making the Nazi party look more respectable and "civilized" to the upper class and the aristocracy, whose power had been only slightly diminished by the fall of the monarchy. The most important individual to succumb to Goering's persuasion was Prince August Wilhelm, the second son of the Kaiser. Within a short time, Goering was even calling the prince by his nickname, Auwi. Through this royal connection, the social world of the Goerings widened, and soon the names of those on the guest list for their dinners were to be found in either the *Who's Who in Germany* or in *Almanac de Gotha* (a book listing members of the German nobility). The fact that he often had some of the wealthiest people in Germany as guests did not stop Goering from making his home a kind of headquarters for any member of the party, no matter how humble his origins, who happened to be in Berlin looking for a place to stay and a free meal. It became the talk of Berlin society that at the Goerings', a princess might find herself with a farm laborer as a dinner partner. This demonstration of social equality emphasized to Goering's guests and their friends the democratic policy of the Nazis; and, of course, it did no harm to Goering's reputation among the rank-and-file party members.

Goering's campaign among the upper class was not the only activity of the Nazis in Berlin. When Dr. Joseph Goebbels was first appointed as the party leader in the capital in 1926, almost all the members were from the lower and lower middle classes. The Berlin party headquarters was in a filthy basement and was better known by the Nazis as "the opium den." "The rays of the sun never penetrated down there," said Goebbels, "and the electric light was left burning day and night. As soon as you opened the door the smell of stale cigarette smoke overwhelmed your nostrils. . . . All corners of the place were stuffed with heaps of old newspapers. . . . There was complete confusion. The finances were in a mess. The Berlin Gau then possessed nothing but debts."[12]

Nazis who were unemployed usually devoted all their time to party work. They could get their meals from the S.A.

soup kitchen, but the burden of supporting their families fell upon their wives. "My wife," said a Nazi with a large family, "underwent untold hardships throughout those years. To enable me to pay my Party dues, and spend an occasional penny, she worked hard at sewing, constantly harassed to provide a meager living for me and the family. Frequently, if I returned late at night from a meeting or a propaganda trip, I still found her bent over her work, happy to see me come home unharmed. This went on for weeks, months, and years. But she willingly endured it, for she too could not be robbed of her faith in the ultimate victory of National Socialism."[13]

The only activity of thousands of young Nazis without jobs was to sit day after day in the "S.A. centers" found throughout Berlin and in most every other major German city. The "centers" were usually back rooms of beer halls where both the proprietor and customers were loyal National Socialists. There in their "headquarters" sat the unemployed S.A. men in their coarse khaki uniforms. They would sit for hours over half-empty beer mugs and at mealtimes would be fed for a few pfennigs on soup from a large iron kettle. Often their uniforms were their only suit of clothes, and even they had been sold to them on credit from the S.A. field ordnance department. Twice a week they would spend a few hours in line at their "employment office," and with the dole they received from the state they paid for their uniforms and meals.

But when the shrill sound of a whistle was heard in the back room of the beer hall and the squad leader shouted "Attention!" then these men rotting in inactivity sprang up, formed ranks, and stood at attention. The squad leader would then announce: "In the name of the Fuehrer, it has been ordered that . . ." and then they would march off.

One night a Berlin S.A. unit was given orders by Dr. Goebbels to undertake an unusual mission. Free theater tickets were distributed among the men. This had never happened before; being short of funds, the party was not in the

Hitler speaking at a Nazi mass rally. The Nazis always passed the hat whenever Hitler spoke and the contributions provided a steady source of income.

Hitler attempting to use his "Austrian charm" on a woman. One of the most mysterious things about Hitler was his dual personality: the hate-filled demagogue one day could become a polite charmer the next. Many of the Nazi party's most important contributors were women who had been personally won over by Hitler.

Hitler speaking at a torch light rally. Hitler preferred to speak at night whenever possible because he felt the audience became more emotionally involved in the speech at night than during the day.

Hermann Goering (left) and Prince August Wilhelm (right). Goering was Hitler's representative among the upper class and one of the most successful Nazi fund-raisers. One of his notable accomplishments was bringing Prince August Wilhelm, the son of the former kaiser, into the Nazi movement.

Franz von Papen and General Blomberg (seated first and second from left) at the opera with Hitler. Papen and Blomberg played a key role in bringing Hitler to power. This photo was taken after January 1933. Prior to that time they tried to keep their dealings with Hitler secret and would never be seen in public with him.

Hitler and General Blomberg. Blomberg represented a radical ultra-nationalist element in the officer corps that was planning an expansionist war.

Captain Ernst Roehm was the founder and commander of Hitler's private army, the Brownshirts, or S.A. He was known to be homosexual, and for years there were rumors about the nature of his relationship with Hitler.

General Kurt von Schleicher was a decent and cultured man who disliked Hitler and was morally opposed to anti-Semitism. Nevertheless, he secretly funneled army funds to the Nazis in an attempt to use their mass following.

habit of providing the S.A. with free entertainment. But when small boxes in which something seemed to be moving were also distributed, the S.A. hooligans began to grin, having some idea as to what their mission might be. Dr. Goebbels explained that their assignment was to secure a ban against the "pacifist" film *All Quiet on the Western Front*, which had been adapted from the German novel by Erich Maria Remarque. The group leaders then explained what each unit was to do. In an optimistic mood the Storm Troopers set out. The Nazis entered the theater and waited until the film began. Then in the darkness the signal was given; white mice and snakes were released and a few stink bombs were set off for good measure. With hundreds of mice running through the theater women jumped up on the seats and railings while a snake slithered its way down the center aisle. The police were called, but by the time they arrived no trace of the culprits could be found. Everyone present merely stated that he wanted to see the film. The following day, the government banned the film as being likely to cause more disturbance.

The activities of the Berlin S.A. were usually not so harmless. The traditional domination of the capital city by the Marxist parties provided an excellent reason why it had to be taken. Gauleiter Dr. Goebbels was determined to "smash the Reds" in the very center of their strength. Berlin's East End had been in a virtual state of seige since May 1, 1929, when open hostilities broke out between the Storm Troopers and the Red Front Fighters. The basement taverns and corner cafés served as bases for the rival armies and were described by S.A. men as "fortified positions in the battle zone." For days at a time, whole rows of streets were in the grip of a new kind of urban guerrilla warfare that raged through the tenement districts and the grim terrain in the networks of alleys between the tall old buildings. Only massive intervention by the police was able to temporarily quell the fighting in which nineteen were killed and forty were seriously injured.

In spite of his proletarian background and his familiarity with the workers of Berlin, Dr. Goebbels also made his coup in high society. This triumph did not come through influential friends or from having persuaded an industrialist to contribute, but by way of a romance. One evening a beautiful and elegant lady, attracted by the sound of military music and the excited faces in the large crowd that was pushing its way to the box office, decided just out of curiosity to attend a Nazi meeting at the Sportpalast. Ten thousand people cheered Dr. Goebbels as he walked across the platform past an honor guard of burly young storm troopers wearing brown shirts. The front of the stage was lined with red swastika flags. Goebbels began to speak; there was perfect silence in the hall. A torrent of words poured down on the enemies of the people, the bosses and the November criminals; the eyes of the speaker flashed. He then spoke of Adolf Hitler, "the savior of the German people who will lead them out of their misery." The people jumped up, shouted, and were beyond themselves with ecstasy. The beautiful young lady, who at first had felt out of place among these rough, fanatical people who smelled of sweat, sat fascinated by what she had heard and the man on the platform. Her name was Magda Quandt. She was twenty-nine years old, divorced, and bored with a life that seemed to her monotonous and senseless.

Magda Quandt offered her services to the local party group in west Berlin, which was overjoyed to enlist such a refined lady. She was asked to take charge of the local party's women's group. This was hardly a fitting job for Frau Quandt, since the members of the group even in this fashionable neighborhood belonged mostly to the lower classes. Among them were servants, concierges, and the wives of small grocers. Magda didn't put up with that for very long and soon went to the Berlin headquarters of the party to offer her services as a volunteer. By now, the main party office in Berlin was anything but the "opium den" where Goebbels had begun a few years ago. The beautiful, elegant new member, from a class all too sparsely represented in the party, and who needed no pay, was naturally greeted with open arms. Magda soon generously offered to contribute one tenth of her monthly income (four hundred marks) to the party. It was not long before she was noticed by Dr. Goebbels himself. When Goebbels got to know her better, he put her in charge of his private files. Both met daily and got to know each other more and more intimately. He was fascinated by her beauty and her elegant manners. It took some time for the two to become lovers, but by the summer of 1930, they had become engaged.

Hitler met Magda Quandt for the first time in the fall of 1930 at a small party. Despite Goering's warning that Magda was "Goebbels's lover," Hitler took an immediate liking to her. He was charmed by her refined appearance and her beauty. For a time, it almost looked as if Magda would have her choice between Hitler and Goebbels. But in the end, Hitler encouraged her to marry Goebbels, for Hitler was already deeply involved with Eva Braun.

Magda's family was horrified with the prospect of her marriage to Dr. Goebbels. Her mother, her father, and also her ex-husband, with whom she now enjoyed a much better relationship than she had had during their marriage, tried to discourage her. But their opposition simply strengthened her determination. On December 19, 1931, she and Goebbels were married at the country estate of her ex-husband in Mecklenburg. There was an elaborate party after the ceremony. Hitler attended both the religious services and the party that followed.

The next day, Goebbels gave up his small bachelor's quarters in the lower-middle-class Steglitz District and moved into Magda's splendid apartment. Magda, however, lost her four thousand marks monthly allowance. By marrying, they had no doubt worsened their financial condition. Goebbels earned only one thousand marks from his two jobs as a member of the Reichstag and Berlin gauleiter. But Hitler immediately raised his income to two thousand marks. In the long run, the marriage was financially advantageous to the party. Although the party leader in Berlin was not acceptable in high society, his wife was. Because of her finishing school background and the wealth and social standing of her former husband, Quandt, she was invited even to the most exclusive parties, where she had the opportunity to find more than a few wealthy supporters for Hitler.[14]

On March 23, 1930, Hermann Goering began a speaking tour of East Prussia and the Rhineland with Prince August Wilhelm as his companion. Carin Goering wrote that the prince was now "a real and true Hitler-man . . . so modest, helpful, obedient, and hard-working."[15] The fact that Prince August Wilhelm had joined the Nazi party and was openly campaigning for Hitler was indeed a triumph for Goering. The monarchists were still a very powerful force in Germany, enjoying tremendous social prestige and popularity among the upper class. The two largest conservative political parties, the German People's party and the Nationalist party, were promonarchist. Moreover, the monarchists had access to tremendous financial resources: the fortunes of the various royal and princely families, the money of the aristocracy, and the support of a considerable number of conservative industrialists who still considered themselves loyal subjects of the kaiser.

Kaiser Wilhelm and his sons were actively plotting for a restoration of the monarchy. They had the support of a majority of the Officer Corps, but what they lacked was a following among the masses. Now that the Nazis had become the largest non-Marxist party in the Reichstag, it became imperative to seek their cooperation.

In light of his achievements, Goering was appointed by Hitler as the chief political spokesman for the Nazis in the Reichstag. There were, however, those within the Nazi party who objected to Goering's "courting" of the aristocracy. Soon Goering was complaining to Hitler that each time he was about to bring another industrialist or count into the party ranks, the left-wing elements of the party around

Strasser would spoil everything with a prosocialist newspaper article or a demonstration against some factory.

In the fall of 1930, Hitler was looking for a new commander for the S.A. after the dismissal of Captain Franz Pfeffer von Salomon. It was a job that Goering had once held and wanted again. He realized that it was the most powerful post in the party. But instead of appointing Goering, Hitler wrote a letter to Bolivia to Ernst Roehm, asking him to return to Germany at once and take over the command of the S.A. Dismissed from the army after the 1923 putsch, Roehm had become disenchanted with conditions in Germany and in 1928 had gone to South America to be an instructor for the Bolivian Army.

As Hitler and Goering both knew, Roehm was a homosexual. Actually he had never made any particular secret of his sexual preferences, but the moment he replied to Hitler's letter, saying that he was leaving for Germany, a series of scandalous stories began appearing in the German press. Some letters that he had sent from South America to his friends, complaining of the Bolivian ignorance of "my kind of love," were printed. Someone had learned that Hitler intended to appoint Roehm chief of the S.A. and had leaked the letters to the press. This someone could only have been an individual inside the Party, and no one could have been more interested in sabotaging Roehm's chances than Hermann Goering, who wanted the S.A. commander's post for himself. Hitler, however, refused to be swayed in his judgment. Goering had no choice but to swallow his dissatisfaction and accept Roehm's appointment with good grace.

On Christmas Day, 1930, the Goerings gave a party for their intimate friends. In spite of the fact Carin Goering was ill with tuberculosis, the atmosphere was very festive, with a Christmas tree, candles, and presents for everyone. Prince August Wilhelm and Dr. Goebbels came. Many of the other guests were prominent people in Berlin society. "In the dining room sat 14 guests!" wrote Carin Goering. "[Prince] August Wilhelm arrived bringing some lovely gifts, a great bucket of white lilies and a huge camel-hair rug, light as a feather, for me, as well as many other little things, a silk shawl, a Dürer Madonna, writing blocks, etc. I had stitched or painted things for everyone, and I think they were pleased with them, and Hermann had gathered together his own presents for the guests."[16]

By 1931 Goering was receiving money from Fritz Thyssen, the pro-Nazi steel tycoon, who found the ex-air ace "a sensible [and] most agreeable person." With the financial backing of this new sponsor, Goering was now able to entertain on a more lavish scale, and Thyssen himself became a frequent guest at the home of Hitler's Reichstag spokesman. With his aristocratic charm and ebullient manner, Goering began to exercise a strong influence on Thyssen. Just how significant this influence was is illustrated by an incident that took place shortly after Hitler became chancellor. After every important reception given for Hitler, a list entitled "Contributions for the Party" was placed at the door of the reception room. One evening the industrialists decided on a plan together. No one was to sign for more than twenty thousand marks. Thyssen was the first to leave. He wrote down twenty thousand marks. Then Goering suddenly appeared and, with a laugh, slapped him on the back. "What's all this, Herr Thyssen? You know everybody expects you to write down 100,000 marks tonight."[17] Thyssen gave a weak smile and corrected the figure.

Yet in spite of the fact that Goering was suddenly receiving substantial sums of money from Thyssen, it must be admitted that he did not abandon his friends who were stricken by the depression, or neglect his duty as a Nazi leader. Some idea of the desperation of the times is conveyed in the following letter, which Carin Goering wrote to her mother.

Yesterday we had a small tea party here, and while we were sitting there a certain Count X arrived with his wife for a visit, quite unannounced. She is Swedish by birth. He is a young man, really pleasant, two children, he without employment, the whole family living dispersed among relatives, and he looking for work and here to ask Hermann's help. All poor Hermann could do was show him a list of applicants with over a hundred names on it. On Christmas Eve, twenty-eight people shot themselves because of want and hunger and despair. Among them was a young officer, a flier well known during the war. On Christmas morning, Hermann received a letter which began by saying: "My true comrade and friend, by the time this letter is in your hands I shall be no more." He went on to write about his fight to keep himself, his son, and the small estate where his family had lived for over 600 years. Now he was completely penniless, and the only way for his wife and son to save the house was for him to shoot himself and allow them to collect on his small life insurance. Hermann telegraphed at once by express telegram: "Don't be too hasty, I'm hoping to help you," but his wife telegraphed back that he was already dead.[18]

While Goering was soliciting the support of industrialists and aristocrats, his rival, Captain Ernst Roehm, who was now chief of the S.A., was trying to work out an accord with the army. This project was facilitated by Roehm's friendship with General Kurt von Schleicher, a military intriguer who was a close confidant of the minister of defense, General Groener. After having several talks with Schleicher, who was playing an increasingly important role in German politics, Roehm was able to convince him that the Nazis were eager to cooperate with the army. In the meantime, Schleicher had been doing some thinking of his own. Impressed by the Nazi success in the September elections and their nationalist program, he began to play with the idea of somehow winning Hitler's support for the Bruening government and changing the National Socialist movement with its mass following into a prop of the existing regime, instead of a legion marching against it. Schleicher began to woo the

Nazis by removing the ban on the army's employment of National Socialists in arsenals and the prohibition against their enlistement in the army.

Observing the increasing sentiment of discontent among the masses, Schleicher wanted to establish a strong government as soon as possible. He recognized the weakness of the Weimar system, in which political coalitions bargained for special advantages for the groups that elected them, and the national interests be damned. If a stable government did not appear soon to master the political and economic crisis, Schleicher was afraid that the army would be forced to intervene to suppress the discontented population. He thought he had found a possible way out of the crisis when he persuaded Hindenburg to appoint Bruening as chancellor and allow him to govern by the president's emergency powers. But in the September elections of 1930, it became obvious that Bruening had failed to win the confidence of the German people. It was the two extremist parties, the Nazis and the Communists, that had won the most spectacular successes at the polls. This worried Schleicher; he was afraid that, as in 1923, Nazi and Communist uprisings might break out simultaneously. If such a situation did occur, foreign powers, especially Poland, would have an opportunity to extend their borders even farther, at Germany's expense, while the German Army would be fully occupied dealing with uprisings. With few other alternatives, Schleicher approached the Nazis, with whom he thought he might be able to compromise because of their nationalist views.

In April of 1931, Germany announced the formation of a customs union with Austria. Despite German assurances that this was not a step toward political union (which was clearly forbidden in the Versailles Treaty), Paris, Rome, and Prague protested that Austrian independence would be jeopardized by the move. Austria, a country without appreciable natural resources, where the peasants barely made a living on their stony mountainsides, was even more deeply shaken by the economic crisis than Germany. The customs union was an emergency move to allow exhausted Austria to enter into an economic partnership with impoverished Germany. In this way an enlarged economic market was to be created and an even larger one was planned for all the Danubian countries southeast of Austria—Hungary, Yugoslavia, and Romania—all of which lived on the sale of their agricultural products to Germany. Germany and Austria offered to take them into their new economic union. This was to be Bruening's first step in his peaceful policy of "liberation."

France wanted to keep Germany economically weak and thus argued that such a union was illegal under the terms of the treaties of Versailles and Saint Germain, by which Austria had promised to maintain its independence from Germany. The dispute was referred to the World Court, but in the meantime, in order to discourage the union, France recalled all short-term loans from Austria and Germany. Both countries were vulnerable to the French economic pressured. Austria was quickly brought to her knees; the slow economic decline turned into a bank crash. The Austrian banks called in all the funds they had in German banks. Then some German banks began to collapse.

In this new crisis, the Reichsbank lost almost 200 million marks of its gold reserves and foreign exchange in the first week of June, and about 1,000 million by the end of the next week. The discount rate (interest rate) was raised as high as 15 percent without stopping the loss of reserves; however, this did "succeed" in bringing the activities of German industry to a standstill.[19] The German banking crisis rapidly became more acute. The Bruening government could find no means of preventing bank crashes, other than proclaiming a bank holiday. Several banks were placed under state control and the flow of money halted; salaries and wages were paid in dribbles or not at all.

The worse the economic disaster, the better for the National Socialists. Or, as Gregor Strasser had written: "Everything that is detrimental to the existing order has our support. . . . The collapse of the liberal system will clear the way for the New Order. . . . All that serves to precipitate the catastrophe of the ruling system—every strike, every governmental crisis, every disturbance of the State power, every weakening of the system—is good, very good for us and our German revolution."[20]

In the summer of 1931, Thyssen began giving money to Walther Funk, who had become one of Hitler's advisors earlier in the year, and who began publishing a newsletter on economics for the Nazis. Thyssen expected Funk to encourage "sound" economic thinking within the National Socialist party and act as a counterweight to the semisocialistic radicalism of Gottfried Feder, who was regarded as a sort of economic thinker by the left-wing Nazis. The money given to Funk was not intended merely to help the Nazis, but rather to exercise an influence on them.

Later, when he was tried as a war criminal at Nuremberg by the Allies, Funk admitted that he became a contact man between Hitler and a number of important men in big business. Several of his friends who were officials in the big Rhineland mining concerns had urged him to join the National Socialist movement, said Funk, "in order to persuade the Party to follow the course of private enterprise. . . . My industrial friends and I were convinced that the Nazi Party would come to power in the not-too-distant future." Explaining his work with the Nazis in greater detail, Funk said:

At that time the leadership of the Party held completely contradictory and confused views on economic policy. I tried to accomplish my mission by personally impressing on the Fuehrer and the Party that private initiative, self-reliance of the businessmen, the creative power of free enterprise . . . [should] be recognized as the basic economic policy of the Party. The Fuehrer personally stressed time and again during talks with me and industrial leaders to whom I had introduced him, that he was an enemy of state economy and so-called planned economy and that he considered free enterprise and competition as absolutely necessary in order to gain the highest possible production.[21]

After the Nazis came to power, Funk was rewarded on his birthday for his services when he was given an estate in Bavaria by a group of industrialists.

Funk and his industrialist sponsors wanted what they called "organized capitalism." In fact, the German economy was ready to be taken over by a strong man. Under the Weimar Republic, prices of raw materials were controlled; government loans were made to owners of the great Prussian estates; key public utilities, the railroads, telephone, telegraph, gas and water supplies were government owned; agriculture was supported by subsidies and tariffs; and government funds were made available to private banks that had no capital left after the 1923 inflation. The big banks and large corporations controlled much of German private industry through the great vertical trusts and 2,500 cartels.* Most all businessmen looked to the state to revive the economy during the depression.

Funk's testimony at the Nuremberg trials threw some light on the relationship between heavy industry and the Nazi party. He stated that the big German firms, like big business in other countries, gave contributions to competing parties whether or not they approved of all of their principles, and the amount given to the National Socialists was less than the sums given to some of the other parties, in particular the German People's party and the Nationalist party. According to Funk, even the Social Democrats were heavily supported by big business. In the early 1930s an increasing number of executives of big corporations were

---

*Vertical trusts were monopolies that controlled a product through all stages of production and distribution. Cartels were formed by a number of corporations agreeing to control prices to establish a monopoly.

becoming interested in Hitler. By then, said Funk, "some" of the directors of Germany's largest firms were pro-Nazi.

On July 9, 1931, Hitler himself went to Berlin to meet Alfred Hugenberg, the Nationalist party leader. Their meeting was a success, and afterward they issued a statement saying that they would henceforth cooperate to bring about the downfall of the existing "system." This new alliance did not bear fruit until August, when Hitler and Hugenberg jointly demanded a plebiscite for the dissolution of the Prussian Diet. The Nazis and Nationalists united in an effort to throw out the coalition of Social Democrats and Catholic Center party, which dominated Prussia, by far the most powerful of the German states. The Communists continued to denounce their more moderate "Marxist" rivals, the Social Democrats, and ordered their supporters to vote along with the Nazis and reactionary Nationalists. During the plebiscite, the police dispersed a crowd of Nazis in the city of Koenigsberg, using their clubs; it so happened that Prince August Wilhelm, a son of the former kaiser, was in the crowd. A member of the National Socialist party and an S.A. man, the prince wrote to his father about his new experience. Kaiser Wilhelm answered from his place of exile in Holland: "You may be proud that you were permitted to become a martyr for this great people's movement."[22] However, even with the sympathy of the kaiser and the aid of the Communists, Hitler and Hugenberg were unable to arouse enough people against the Prussian government. They won 9,800,000 votes (35 percent), far short of the majority they needed.

As might have been expected, the Nazis and the Nationalists blamed each other for the failure in the Prussian plebiscite. So the alliance cooled off for a while.

In the fall of 1931, General von Schleicher arranged an interview between Hitler and President von Hindenburg in an attempt to persuade the Nazis to support the Bruening government. The field marshal and former corporal met for the first time on October 10. Hitler was nervous and unsure of himself in his first encounter with this tradition-bound old Junker. Unable to face the field marshal alone, he wired Goering, who was in Sweden at the deathbed of his wife, whose long illness was reaching its termination. Like Hitler, Goering thought the meeting might be a turning point in German history; even his dying wife agreed and urged him to go. Leaving Sweden, Goering met Hitler in Berlin, and together they went to see President Hindenburg.

Hindenburg was not at all anxious to meet Hitler, whose followers had repeatedly insulted and vilified him. They said that he was not true to his duty, did not love his Fatherland, and had no sense of honor. But his advisers, his son, and his secretary of state insisted that he speak with the leader of the second largest political party; so he yielded. There was a fundamental difference of character that stood between the two men. Hindenburg had a rigid and fixed formula for conversation with people he met for the first time. "Where were you born? What was your father?" This rigid pattern of conversation was useless in this case, Hitler's flood of words tore down every fixed traditional barrier.

There are no complete accounts of what was actually said at the meeting. However, Secretary of State Meissner said afterward that the meeting lasted an hour and a quarter and Hitler had spoken for an hour. A cataract of words bore down on the old man of eighty-two without hindrance and without interruption. It is probable that Hitler spent much of the time on the theme that only the National Socialists could save the country from communism. He certainly complained of how his "patriotic" followers were being persecuted by the government, and he threatened that under such circumstances, no spirited resistance by his men could be expected if the Poles were to overrun the eastern border.

The meeting ended in failure. Schleicher claimed Hindenburg grumbled afterward that such a strange fellow would never make a chancellor, but at most a minister of posts (equivalent to postmaster general in the United States). Obviously, Hitler had made the mistake of talking too much in an effort to impress the old man; instead he had bored him.

The day after his interview with President von Hindenburg, Hitler hastened off to Bad Harzburg, a Thuringian resort town nestled in the Harz Mountains. On October 11, 1931, this picturesque setting was the scene of a great patriotic rally. Represented were the National Socialists, the Nationalists, the Stahlhelm veterans organization, the Junker Landbund, a conservative agricultural group, the Bismarck Youth, which was a conservative youth group, and the Pan-Germans, a racist-nationalist party. On hand too were several members of the royal families, representatives of industry and big business, and generals and admirals. It was the largest right-wing political gathering that had ever taken place in Germany. Among the notables present were Fritz Thyssen, Alfred Hugenberg, Franz Seldte, one of the leaders of the Stahlhelm, Hjalmar Schacht, former president of the Reichsbank, and two sons of the kaiser—Prince August Wilhelm and Prince Eitel Friedrich. The purpose of the meeting was to unite all rightist elements in a common effort to oust the Bruening cabinet and set up a "national Government."[23]

In December of 1931, Hitler stepped up efforts to win support among the industrialists by forming a circle of business advisors for the party. This project, one that he had been working on since the summer of 1931, was part of a deliberate campaign to make inroads into the worlds of industry and finance.[24] He asked Wilhelm Keppler , a depression-stricken small industrialist who had been advising him on economic matters, to take charge of this effort. "During a conversation which I had with the Fuehrer in December 1931," Keppler related, "the Fuehrer said: Try to get a few economic leaders—they need not be Party members—who will be at our disposal when we come to power."[25] Hitler's general plan was for Keppler to ask about twelve prominent businessmen to form a "Circle of Friends from the Economy" for the purpose of discussing economic affairs informally, with no minutes taken. The Circle was to discuss and advise Keppler primarily on two things: how to solve the problem of unemployment and how to revive German industry. Keppler, in turn, would communicate what he had heard to Hitler. At this time, according to Keppler, Hitler had no ideas on prospective members other than Dr. Schact and Albert Voegler, the director general of the United Steel Works. The choice of the rest of the members was left to Keppler.[26]

Hitler now had several representatives working for him in business circles. On December 11, 1931, Walther Funk met with Baron Kurt von Schroeder, a Cologne banker, who had many connections with reactionary industrialists. Schroeder was interested in finding out the real views of Hitler on certain questions affecting the international banking business. Later, events seemed to indicate that Funk was able to satisfy Schroeder.

8

HITLER'S FOREIGN FINANCIERS

Contact between the Italian Fascists and the Nazis began in September of 1922 when Kurt Lüdecke, Hitler's foreign representative, met Mussolini for the first time. Mussolini did not make his march on Rome until October 29, 1922, but the Nazis were able to foresee that a showdown was coming. It was Lüdecke's assignment to size up the Italian Fascists, estimate their chances for success, get Mussolini's opinions on certain issues, and find out how the Nazis and Blackshirts might cooperate.

Upon arriving in Milan, Lüdecke telephoned Fascist headquarters. He said he wanted to speak with Signor Mussolini because he had traveled from Munich to bring him an important message from important people. Within a few moments Mussolini was on the phone and expressed his agreement to set up an interview with Lüdecke at three that very afternoon.

When Lüdecke arrived at the "office" of the *Popolo d'Italia*, the Fascist newspaper, he found that it occupied an entire building of immense size, quite a contrast to the miniature headquarters of the Nazis. A Blackshirt showed him the way to Mussolini's office on the second floor. As Lüdecke walked up the steps, he tried to visualize what Mussolini would look like, as he had never even seen a picture of him. Would he have the countenance of a typical Italian, or would he resemble Verrocchio's statue of Colleoni, whose face is full of force and brutality?

These preconceived images vanished from his mind as soon as Lüdecke crossed the threshold. At a desk in the farthest corner of the room sat a square-cut man, in a dark shabby suit and rumpled shirt, with a high dome of bald forehead, and piercing, almost frightening, eyes. Mussolini welcomed him in a pleasant, resonant voice. After Lüdecke conveyed the greetings of General Ludendorff and Adolf Hitler, they sat down to talk. Since Mussolini spoke only a few words of German, and Lüdecke only a smattering of Italian, they conducted the discussion in French. Although the Italian Fascist leader had an unhealthy appearance due to a sallow complexion, a tired sagging mouth, and finger-nails bitten to the moons, his strong gaze and his powerful, eloquent manner of speaking made a favorable impression on the young Nazi.[1]

Lüdecke recalled that he had to explain the German political situation from the beginning, as Mussolini had never even heard of Hitler. While Lüdecke gave a brief, but thorough explanation of the goals of the Nazi movement, Mussolini listened with obvious sympathy and understanding, asking many astute questions. He agreed that the Versailles system was impossible for Germany and for all concerned; he therefore thought it would not last much longer. The two men then talked about bolshevism, fascism, and liberalism. When Mussolini described the internal chaos in Italy and the advance of his Blackshirts, his eyes sparkled with pride.

Judging from the confidence with which Mussolini was able to answer all questions, and from his eagerness to assume the reins of government, Lüdecke was certain that the Fascists would soon make their bid for power. "Signor

Mussolini," Lüdecke asked, "in case the government does not yield, are you prepared to resort to force?" Without hesitation, he answered: *"Nous serons l'état, parce que nous le voulons!"* ("We shall be the state because we will it.")[2] On this note their discussion concluded; it was after seven in the evening. Mussolini was not a man to spend four hours discussing something he did not think was important.

Returning from Italy, Lüdecke telephoned Nazi headquarters; Hitler said that he would like to hear a detailed report of the interview with Mussolini as soon as possible. Within a few minutes they were sitting together at a table analyzing the Italian situation. Lüdecke pointed out the numerous similarities between nazism and fascism: both were extremely nationalist and anti-Communist; both were dedicated to a radical new order; both had leaders who were men of the people, veterans, self-made, and outstanding political speakers. These likenesses would help to build the foundation for a solid relationship between Hitler and Mussolini in the future.

The discussion then moved to the important role of Italy in Nazi foreign policy. Hitler asserted that the natural future ally of Germany should be England, and thus when the Nazis came to power they would try to alienate England from France. But at the present time the Nazis were not in a position to manipulate or bargain with England, or with any of the major foreign powers. If there was any hope of finding an ally in Europe, it would be Italy—that is, if Mussolini came to power. Both Hitler and Lüdecke considered the repercussions the Italian struggle might have on the Nazis. They felt that, if only for the psychological effect, it would be a great advantage to have a fascist group in another country defeat Communism and parliamentary liberalism. The more they talked about Mussolini's imminent role in European affairs, the more evident it became that the Nazis' struggle for political supremacy was not merely within Germany itself, but also in foreign spheres from which any support would greatly facilitate the progress of the Nazis in their own country.

As Lüdecke had predicted, Mussolini became the prime minister of Italy on October 29, 1922. Most Nazi leaders believed that Mussolini would give them his sympathetic, although silent, support. But not until the Nazis initiated some action could he be expected to commit himself. As a prime minister and statesman, he first had to consider if such a commitment would be useful to Italy. In another meeting with Hitler, Lüdecke said that if the Nazis could prove their strength, Mussolini probably "would go a long way with us." Hitler agreed enthusiastically: "Good, good! I believe you are right and that your most valuable work lies ahead of you in Italy. . . . Will you go to Rome at once?" It was decided that Lüdecke's mission would have four goals:

(1) Obtain the sympathy of the Italian press and their consent to use the Nazis as their source of German news rather than the Berlin news agencies.
(2) Weaken the influence of the Berlin government and use every opportunity to further the prestige of the Nazi party.
(3) Assure Mussolini that Nazi Germany would not claim any interest in the area of the South Tyrol.
(4) *"And finally, if possible, to get money."*[3]

That evening, Hitler, Lüdecke, and some other Nazi officials had a little party in the old Austrian town of Linz, where Hitler had lived as a child, to celebrate the Italian venture in advance. The next day, Hitler and Lüdecke climbed to the top of the Poestlingberg, a towering peak that rises abruptly out of the fields and woods. From the mountaintop there was a magnificent panorama of the Danube stretching into the distance and the farms and villages scattered across the plain. As they gazed over the vast landscape, Hitler spoke about the future of the Nazi party. He seemed certain of the National Socialists' ultimate victory. But one of the main prerequisites for victory was money. Lüdecke later wrote of Hitler: "He wanted money, because money paves the road to power."[4]

When it was time for farewells, Lüdecke was still feeling inspired from Hitler's talk on the mountain. Just after the small group of Nazis had wished him good luck and he was turning away, Hitler shouted to him a final command so brutal that it made even the unscrupulous Lüdecke shudder: "*Fetzen Sie aus Mussolini heraus, was Sie Können!*" (Rip out of Mussolini whatever you can!).[5]

Following a short business trip to Budapest,[6] Lüdecke traveled to Milan at the end of August 1923. Mussolini was scheduled to arrive there the next day; it would be his first visit to the city since he had become prime minister. Mussolini's brother, Arnaldo, who had taken over the position of editor of the *Popolo d'Italia*, told Lüdecke that Mussolini would stop by the office at three that afternoon.

The moment that Lüdecke stepped forward to greet the dictator, Mussolini recognized him instantly. He chatted with Lüdecke in a very friendly tone but was slightly more aloof than in their first encounter. The improvement in his appearance was quite noticeable; with a healthy bronze tan, normal-looking fingernails, and an energetic spring to his step, he now looked like a dictator. Mussolini examined the credentials stating that Lüdecke was a representative of the National Socialists and then suggested, this time speaking in fairly good German, that they continue their conversation on his train to Rome that evening.

At each station on the route, the dictator's train was cheered enthusiastically by large crowds. Not until 4 A.M. was Lüdecke informed that Mussolini would be able to see him, and then only for a short time. So Lüdecke tried to make his message brief and impressive: the political crisis in Germany was on the verge of exploding; the Nazis would take action very soon. Thus the aim of his trip was not to admire the Italian countryside, nor the artwork; rather it was to increase Italy's knowledge of Hitler and its sympathy with his goals. Courteous, but very tired, Mussolini seemed to miss the urgency of the Nazi's plea. Lüdecke asked for another meeting in Rome, and Mussolini nodded his approval.

The moment Lüdecke had finished unpacking his luggage, he began to draw up a schedule of all the interviews and public relations meetings to be arranged to advance the acceptance of the Nazi party. His first aim was to gain the support of the Italian newspapers. This would be no easy task. There were many well-known German journalists in Italy representing great newspapers of international reputation, such as the *Frankfurter Zeitung* and the *Berliner Tageblatt*. In contrast, Lüdecke had no experience in journalism and represented only the *Völkischer Beobachter*, the small radical Nazi paper. Although the Italian newspapers had some reporters in Germany, they usually took their interpretation of German news items from the most important German newspapers like the *Frankfurter Zeitung*. The idea that one lone foreigner could oppose the entire German press and news media and succeed in having major Italian papers accept his view of German news seemed almost too incredible to be true. Nevertheless, this is exactly what happened.

At this time many large Italian newspapers were beginning to fall under the increasing influence of the Fascist party. Using this to his advantage, Lüdecke began his work by talking with editors and journalists about the similarities between the Nazis and Fascists. The change to Lüdecke's rightist interpretation of the news would be additional propaganda for the new Fascist Italian government.

As soon as Lüdecke had formed good relations with the large newspapers, the tone of the news changed to favor the Nazis. Compared with a few months earlier, Hitler's name began to be much better known and carried greater authority.[7] Special interest was focused on the German political scene. Interviews and articles appeared that transformed the

Italian people's ideas about the strength of the Nazis and their opposition to the Berlin government.

Lüdecke requested another appointment with Mussolini, but the Duce [the leader, Mussolini] was too busy with political problems at home and instead arranged for Lüdecke to meet with Baron Russo, the secretary of foreign affairs. Baron Russo was very attentive while Lüdecke told of the Nazis' difficulties, but "no help or special commitment was offered at this time." Of course, Lüdecke explained, since Mussolini was legally prime minister of Italy and in friendly relations with the Berlin government, he could not "officially" recognize the representative of a party opposing the government.

Having no reason to reveal the Nazis' financial supporters, Lüdecke claimed that the Italian government gave no "official" aid to the Nazis. Yet, his use of the word "official" makes his statement ambiguous enough to be interpreted to mean that there were "unofficial" ties between them. Lüdecke wrote this denial about receiving any money in 1938, when Mussolini was still somewhat concerned about the world's opinion of him. Therefore, not wanting to hurt Mussolini's reputation, Lüdecke hedged by making the clever and partially true excuse that Mussolini did not "officially" give any money.

His denial that any Italian aid was given to the Nazis seems even more dubious when considering the treatment that Lüdecke was accorded by the Italian government. When a limited number of invitations were sent out for Mussolini's first reception with the king at the Palazzo Venezia, many important foreign representatives were excluded. Yet one of these sought-after invitations was sent to Lüdecke—the representative of a radical party that did not hold even one seat in the Reichstag. If the Nazi ambassador was acceptable enough to be part of a formal government occasion, then why would his party not be worthy of "unofficial" support?

Covert funding to sponsor international fascism was an essential policy of Mussolini's government. Adrian Lyttelton, a renowned Oxford historian, wrote that "Mussolini's secret, personal policy gives . . . concrete proof of his desire to disrupt the European order."[8] Thus, contributions were made not only for ideological motives, such as the brotherhood of fascists, but also in order to increase Mussolini's influence in the countries of Central Europe, especially Austria, Yugoslavia, and southern Germany.

Mussolini realized that discretion and covert methods were necessary to weaken his enemies from within. The "fondness for tactics of internal subversion and intrigue with foreign political movements was a marked feature of Fascist policy from the beginning," Lyttelton said.[9] Mussolini provided military supplies for the Hungarian nationalists and the German Army.[10] Italian aid was also sent to the rightist revolutionaries in Corsica, Malta, Macedonia, and Croatia. In 1928, the Duce agreed to back the Austrian conservative paramilitary organization, the Heimwehr, with weapons and money.[11] During the Spanish Civil War, Mussolini sent fifty thousand troops, seven hundred planes, plus supplies to help Franco. It is also rumored that Mussolini financed fascist organizations in Britain.[12]

Three top-level sources, men who had access to highly classified secret intelligence information, confirmed that Mussolini gave financial aid to Hitler. André François-Poncet, who was the French ambassador to Germany in the 1930s, an expert on German foreign policy, and a master of diplomatic intrigue, wrote in his account of prewar diplomacy that the Nazis received financial backing from the Italian Fascists.[13] S.S. General Karl Wolff, an intelligence mastermind, who was Himmler's personal chief of staff and who served as one of the top commanders of the German Army in Italy during World War II, said that he was certain that Mussolini had given money to the Nazis before they came to power.

The fact that François-Poncet, a French diplomat, and Wolff, an S.S. general, who represented the opposite poles of the political spectrum, both confirmed the donor-recipient relationship between Mussolini and Hitler greatly adds to its credibility. There was also confirmation from a high official of the government of the Weimar Republic, Otto Braun, minister president of Prussia, who indicated he had evidence that the Nazis received funds from the Fascists even after the 1923 putsch. Braun told Hermann Ullstein of the famous publishing company that Mussolini contributed money that helped Hitler to win his early electoral successes.[14]

The numerous reliable sources which have stated that the Nazis received financial support from Mussolini are more than enough evidence for a sound conclusion. Alan Cassels, a well-known historian of Italian Fascism and an astute scholar who has made a thorough study of the relation between Mussolini and the Nazis, stated: "Certainly Hitler was the recipient of Italian money."[15]

As has been seen, there is considerable evidence that Mussolini gave financial aid to the Nazis before the 1923 putsch and that he may have done so again in the early 1930s. However, just because it is known that he gave to the Nazis on these occasions does not mean that he was ready to contribute whenever they asked for money. Mussolini gave only when it suited his purposes and the interests of Italian foreign policy.

During 1924, Kurt Lüdecke was in America visiting Henry Ford* and campaigning in the large cities for more funds from German-Americans. Before leaving for the United States, Lüdecke received credentials verifying him as a representative of the National Socialist party in the United States, and authorizing him to collect money for the party. Hitler, still in prison, wrote a letter thanking Lüdecke for his work in Italy and approving of his plans for a trip to America:

---

* For Henry Ford's financial support to Hitler, see Chapter 3.

Much Esteemed Herr Lüdecke: Dated 4, Jan. 1924
    First expressing my heartiest thanks for your representation of the movement in Italy, I ask you to solicit in the interests of the German Liberty movement in North America and especially to assemble financial means for it. I ask you to receive these means personally and, if possible, to bring them over in person. Thanking you in advance for your efforts, I greet you most heartily.
                                (signed) Adolf Hitler[16]

This letter was typed on the stationery of Hitler's lawyer, who then brought it in person to Lüdecke before his departure. There is special significance to this document because Hitler always refused to admit that he ever solicited—let alone accepted—money from abroad.

After meeting with Ford in Detroit, Lüdecke took the train to Washington, D.C., where a German society had invited him to address a meeting. His heartrending speech described how desperately the Nazis needed money. Most of the people in the audience had never heard of Hitler; so they listened with wide-eyed amazement to the story of the beer hall uprising. Judging from the looks on their faces, Lüdecke thought he would collect a good-size sum. But suddenly someone started to shout out in opposition; a fat blond man, who was the perfect image of the typical cartoon German, stood up to denounce the Nazis' racial, political, and economic program. He concluded with an insulting attack on Lüdecke. As he spoke, the change in the crowd's attitude was obvious. He was one of the respected leaders of the community and easily turned the people against the Nazis. After he sat down, Lüdecke tried to win back the ground he had lost, but to no avail. In fact, the crowd became so hostile, they almost threw him out of the hall.

In Pittsburgh, Cleveland, Chicago, Milwaukee, St. Louis, and other cities, Lüdecke met with similar disappointments. The minority of German-Americans who sympathized with the Nazi viewpoint were outnumbered by the majority, who condemned it. But Lüdecke didn't blame himself for his lack of success: "Had the Sirens themselves sung my cause, results would have been just as negative. The eloquence I wasted might easily have raised a fund to rescue moths from the sun; but Hitler and the Nazis rated nothing better than a perpetually empty collection plate. I was howled down in derision each time I spoke of him as a coming world power."[17]

After leaving Washington, D.C., in the spring of 1924, Lüdecke stopped off in England before turning to Germany. Although he claimed that he hadn't received any financial contributions, he admitted the "real profit" was the personal contacts he had made with wealthy, influential men whose power with the media and the government might be of much greater importance to the Nazis than a contribution.

One of the British elite who went down in Lüdecke's book of achievements was the Rt. Hon. Lord Sydenham of Combe, a former governor of Bombay and the author of the radical pamphlet *The Jewish World Problem*. He was known in the House of Lords for his attacks against the British mandate over Palestine, which he described as the "mad policy of protecting the Jews against the Arabs in Palestine with the help of English bayonets, which cost the British taxpayer five hundred thousand pounds a month." If Sydenham was not generous to Lüdecke with his money (although it seems likely that he might have been), he was overflowing with advice and recommendations for a fellow anti-Semite. Sydenham urged him to read the novels by Disraeli in order to "grasp the Jewish problem." Of more importance to Lüdecke were the introductions into British high society arranged by Lord Sydenham. Other Nazis were soon to exploit the connections Lüdecke had made.

In the fall of 1931, Alfred Rosenberg, Hitler's representative, arrived in London to meet with Montagu Norman, the governor of the Bank of England.[18] Norman was the Gibraltar of the British financial community. A revered symbol of the establishment, he was beyond reproach: he was seen as being incorruptible and infallible. In Mach 1920, when he was selected as the governor of the bank, the position was already one of vast autocratic power. During his twenty-four-year reign he exercised this power ruthlessly and fastidiously. No governor had held office for such a long period during the two and a half centuries since the founding of the bank.

All who met Norman were impressed by his appearance. Émile Moreau, head of the Bank of France, said: "He seems to have walked out of a Van Dyck canvas; the long face, the pointed beard, and the big hat lend him the look of a companion of the Stuarts."[19] According to his biographer, Norman's princely Mephistophelian image, dramatized by his black silk hat and cloak, was carefully contrived in order to give an air of aloofness and omniscience.

But why did Norman want to meet Rosenberg? Well, for one reason, the governor was "instinctively pro-German."[20] Ever since his stay in Dresden, as a young student, he'd had a special liking for Germany. Thus, while head of the Bank of England, he was determined to do everything within his power to relieve Germany from the oppressive burden of the Versailles Treaty. The sooner the guilt and punishment in the form of the reparations was removed, the better Germany and Europe would be. Norman argued that there could be no advantage to France nor any of the Allied countries in forcibly demanding repayment on the belief that blood could somehow be extracted from stone.

Although this policy of "economic lunacy" drove Norman to despair, he never openly opposed the decisions of the government and the politicians. Perhaps time would show them the folly of expecting more than bitterness from their economic strangulation of Germany. If anyone was guilty, he thought, it was Germany's political rulers, not her industrious merchants, bankers, and workers. The Bank of England and the unstable British economy were affected both directly and indirectly by the financial chaos in Germany. If Germany was restored to normal economic conditions, then, Norman said, the Allies would also benefit. When the French invaded the Ruhr in January 1923, Norman called it a typical act of "French madness." This move confirmed his disdain for France and his favoritism for Germany.

But just because he was pro-German one cannot jump to the conclusion that there was a connection between Norman and the Nazis; however, the fact that he also hated Jews arouses suspicion even more.

Ernest Skinner, the governor's devoted private secretary for thirteen years, said that Norman "had some fundamental dislikes . . . the French, Roman Catholics, Jews."[21] His disdain for Jews was also noticed by Émile Moreau: "M. Norman . . . appears to be full of contempt for the Jews. He speaks of them in very bad terms."[22]

Moreau soon became aware of Norman's hatred of the French during a conversation in which Norman said, "I want very much to help the Bank of France, but I detest your government and your treasury. For them, I shall do nothing."[23] In contrast, Moreau noticed, Norman had a strong sympathy for the Germans. In fact, one of his best friends was the well-known German banker, Dr. Schacht. Moreau seemed suspicious of their closeness: "He [Norman] sees him [Schacht] often and together they hatch up their secret plots."[24]

This brings us to one of the connections tying Norman to the Nazis—Dr. Hjalmar Schacht, the president of the Reichsbank. From their first meeting in 1924 until Norman's death in 1945, they maintained a close personal and business relationship. On the eve of World War II, Norman went to Berlin to attend the christening of Schacht's grandchild, named Norman in his honor.[25] This was seven years after Schacht had started to give support to the Nazis; so Norman was on friendly terms with a Nazi representative from 1932 onward. After Hitler came to power, Norman and Schacht conferred on arrangements for loans to Germany. In May 1934, a private meeting took place between the two bank presidents. Then on June 11, a "secret conclave" took place at Badenweiler, in the Black Forest, where Norman again saw Schacht for an "unofficial discussion." Early in October, they met once more at the same Black Forest rendezvous and gain undertook the secret negotiations for loans to Nazi Germany.

Did Norman help finance the Nazis before they were in power? His biographer John Hargrave thought so: "It is quite certain that Norman did all he could to assist Hitlerism to gain and maintain political power, operating on the financial plane from his stronghold in Threadneedle Street."[26] Naturally Norman did not supply Hitler with money from the Bank of England; but there is evidence that he played a significant role in helping to arrange financing of the Nazis.*

Before Rosenberg left England, he saw Lord Beaverbrook, the owner of the *Daily Express*, the *Sunday Express*, and the *Evening Standard*. Beaverbrook didn't given Rosenberg any money, but his merely meeting with Hitler's representative gave a certain recognition to the Nazis that they didn't deserve. Furthermore, pro-Nazi articles in the British press played an important role in helping the Nazis look more respectable to the German upper class. As has been seen, the German industrialists, aristocrats, and bankers were all very sensitive to how foreign opinion would regard the Nazis. When even moderate Germans were debating about the merits of joining the Hitler bandwagon, a favorable comment or two in the respectable, neutral British press could be very influential.

Like Norman, Lord Beaverbrook was opposed to the Versailles Treaty and was a staunch advocate of the British Empire. On December 6, 1931, he wrote to his friend Arthur Brisbane (who was also a close friend of Henry Ford) about

---

* Norman's assistance to the Nazis did not have the approval of the Bank of England.

his recent meeting with the Nazi: "I had a call from Hitler's man, who came here to find out if the success of the Conservative-Liberal and petty-Labour Coalition should be attempted in Germany.

"I advised him that a strong policy is damaged by coalition. Plainly, he had already come to that conclusion; and got the advice he was seeking. He went off to telegraph to his master.

"He is a strong anti-Semite, is Hitler's representative, and like many another man who is opposed to the Jews, he has their racial marks upon him."[27]

The whole tone of Beaverbrook's letter is very strange. He expressed no disapproval of Hitler's policies, including anti-Semitism, yet it is obvious he was aware of them. Also, he advised the Nazis not to enter a coalition government, because *"a strong policy"* is damaged by it.

Although no record exists to show that Rosenberg met with him, there was one powerful press lord who was much more favorable to the Nazis than Beaverbrook. In fact, he was so pro-Hitler that there was really little need for Rosenberg to see him. The wealthy newspaper magnate Viscount Rothermere gave the Nazis an abundance of praise and accolades. There is also some indication that Rothermere gave actual financial support to Hitler through Putzi Hanfstaengl, the Nazi's foreign press chief,[28] but the publicity he gave Hitler was worth more than money.

Shortly after the Nazis' sweeping victory in the election of September 14, 1930, Rothermere went to Munich to have a long talk with Hitler and, ten days after the election, wrote an article discussing the significance of the National Socialist's triumph. The article drew attention throughout England and the Continent because it urged acceptance of the Nazis as a bulwark against communism:

These young Germans have discovered, as I am glad to note the young men and women of England are discovering, that it is no good trusting to the old politicians.

Accordingly, they have formed, as I should like to see our British youth form, a Parliamentary party of their own. . . . We can do nothing to check this Movement [the Nazis] and I believe it would be a blunder for the British people to take up an attitude of hostility towards it. . . . We must change our conception of Germany. . . . The older generation of Germans were our enemies. Must we make enemies of this younger generation, too? If we do, sooner or later another and more terrible awakening is in store for Europe.

Let us consider well before we lay our course toward that peril. If we examine this transfer of political influence in Germany to the National Socialists we shall find that it has many advantages for the rest of Europe. It sets up an additional rampart against Bolshevism. It eliminates the grave danger that the Soviet campaign against civilization might penetrate to Germany, thus winning an impregnable position in the strategical center of Europe.[29]

Rothermere went on to say that if it were not for the Nazis, the Communists might have gained the majority in the Reichstag. The tremendous success of the Nazi "German Party of Youth and Nationalism should receive the closest possible attention from the statesmen of Britain," Rothermere advised.

Lord Rothermere was a man of large stature, with a high forehead and such an extreme conservative political attitude that some people said he was "very near to being unbalanced on the issue of Communism."[30] Although he was not the only one with an obsession about the dangers of communism, he was one of the few who devoted so much money to the anti-Communist cause. In England, he was a well-known backer of the British Union of Fascists, whose members wore black shirts.

A reviewer for the *Sunday Times* once tried to explain Rothermere's political viewpoint: "He saw Hitler as a sincere man who had defeated Communism in his own country and whose programme was now to reverse the *Diktat* of Versailles. He did not see him as a conqueror whose ambitions for world power inevitably mean, if not conflict with, then hostility to, the British Empire."[31] In fact, Rothermere hoped that England and Germany would be allies. Hitler said that the "Beaverbrook-Rothermere circle" came and told him: "In the last war we were on the wrong side." In one of his conversations with Hitler, Rothermere explained that he and Beaverbrook were "in complete agreement that never again should there be war between Britain and Germany."[32]

Hitler was known to have many sympathizers in British high society, but there was one individual whose importance stood far above the others. This was the Prince of Wales, who later became King Edward VIII, and finally after his abdication was known as the Duke of Windsor. The prince's affinity for Germany had been strong since he was a youth. Many of his relatives were German (his mother was a German princess before she married King George V), and he often spoke German in private. As soon as all the courtiers had left the room, closing the heavy, carved oak doors behind them, then the prince would relax and start to converse in German with his mother.

In June 1935, the prince gave a speech at the annual conference of the British Legion. He said he felt that the Legion was the most appropriate organization of men to "stretch forth the hand of friendship to the Germans," whom they fought in World War I. This speech was regarded by many in England and Germany as "the seal of the friendship agreement between the two countries."[33] He was reprimanded by his father, King George V, for speaking about political matters without prior approval of the Foreign Office. Indeed the speech did bring wide repercussions. Sir Henry Channon, chronicler of the period and a Conservative member of Parliament, wrote in his diary shortly after the speech: "Much gossip about the Prince of Wales' alleged Nazi leanings."[34] When the prince became Edward VIII,

Channon wrote of the new king: "He, too, is going the dictator way, and is pro-German, against Russia and against too
much slip-shod democracy. I shouldn't be surprised if he
aimed at making himself a mild dictator."[35]

Legend has it that Edward was compelled to abdicate in
1936 due to his refusal to give up "the woman he loved."
However, this issue was used as a facade to conceal the
more critical objection that the government had with the
king—namely, his pro-Nazi attitude. Once Baldwin, the British prime minister, realized the king was serious about his
political opinions he [Baldwin] decided to force the monarch
out, since it was not likely that the king would cooperate
with the prime minister's anti-German policy.[36]

Hermann Goering was certain that Edward VIII had lost
his throne because he wanted an Anglo-German agreement
and did not share his government's disdain for the Nazis.
The so-called unsuitable selection of Mrs. Simpson for his
wife was only a pretext to get rid of him, according to Goering.[37] Hitler thought the "real reason for the destruction of
the Duke of Windsor was . . . his speech at the old veterans'
rally . . . at which he declared that it would be a task of his
life to effect a reconciliation between Britain and Germany."[38] Anthony Eden, the foreign secretary, was reported
to have said that if King Edward continued to speak inde-
pendently on foreign affairs, there were "ways and means of
compelling him to abdicate."[39] Hugh Dalton, a Labor M.P.,
mentioned the "widespread rumors that he [the King] was
unduly sympathetic to the German Nazis, and a general
feeling that, for a constitutional monarch, he was inclined
to hold and express some dangerously personal views."[40]
The duke affirmed the suspicions that he looked with admiration upon the Nazis when he spoke at a meeting in Leipzig, Germany, in the fall of 1937. The former king told his
audience: "I have traveled the world and my upbringing
has made me familiar with the great achievements of mankind, but that which I have seen in Germany, I had hitherto
believed to be impossible; one can only begin to understand

it when one realizes that behind it all is one man and one will, Adolf Hitler."[41]

Considering the abundant amount of evidence from various sources it can hardly be denied that the king was pro-Nazi. Certainly this does not mean he financed Hitler; however, his opinions did encourage many important Englishmen and Germans to back the Nazi leader. In the early 1930s the influence of the monarch on the British upper class was still very great. Members of the British ruling class tried consciously or subconsciously to please the sovereign. Although Edward was not yet king at the time of Rosenberg's 1931 visit, men like Norman, the governor of the Bank of England, and Rothermere, the press lord, were undoubtedly aware of Edward's pro-German feelings, and this gave them a certain amount of moral support for their own beliefs. Likewise, German industrialists and businessmen were impressed by Edward's favorable view of Hitler. In fact, most Germans believed that the British royal family held the reins of political power in their hands.[42] Thus, when they heard that the heir to the throne was pro-Nazi, the Germans mistakenly thought that the English government would accept his viewpoint as soon as he became king. This was one more reason why the Germans thought that a Nazi government would be welcomed by Britain.

In May 1933, Rosenberg made his second and last trip to England. Although his mission was not an outstanding success due to his tactless anti-Semitic remarks, which were reported in the press, there was one noteworthy event during this trip. One weekend Rosenberg stayed at Sir Henri Deterding's palatial country home at Buckhurst Park, Ascot, only about a mile from Windsor Castle. Two newspapers reported that they had reliable information that verified the Rosenberg-Deterding meeting. *Reynold's Illustrated News* stated: "In the light of the present European situation, this private talk between Hitler's foreign advisor and the dominant figure in European 'oil politics' is of profound interest. It supports the suggestion current in well-informed political circles that the big oil interests have kept closely in touch with the Nazi Party in Germany."[43] This was not Rosenberg's first meeting with Deterding: they had met as early as 1931.[44]

Who was Sir Henri Deterding and why did he invite a Nazi to his estate? Deterding was one of the wealthiest men in the world. His clandestine meetings with Hitler's representative gave little indication of the plots, intrigues, and secret transfers of money that were taking place between Deterding and Hitler.

The son of a seaman, Hendrik August Wilhelm Deterding was born in Amsterdam in 1866. Fascinated by the swaying ships in the busy harbor, the young Hendrik dreamed of becoming a sailor. But due to his father's death when Hendrik was only six years old, the boy's career had to be something more practical and profitable that could help the family's failing finances. After finishing his schooling, he got a job for six years as a bank clerk. Bending over ledgers filled with columns of figures was grueling, monotonous work; nevertheless, he was quick to learn how business transactions were made and the importance of good investments. Soon he found a better job with the Netherlands Trading Society, and finally in 1886, Deterding joined the Royal Dutch Petroleum Company. Within four years he was managing director of Royal Dutch-Shell, an international combine created as a result of his successful efforts to merge the British Shell Oil Company with Royal Dutch.

Whether Deterding should be considered Dutch or English is a debatable question. The *Wall Street Journal* printed a statement by Richard Airey, president of the Asiatic Petroleum Company, a Royal Dutch subsidiary, claiming that even though Deterding was made a knight of the British Empire in 1920, "he was born a native Dutch subject . . . and will remain so until his death."[45] However, the British embassy in Washington said that "to the best of its knowledge" Deterding was a naturalized British citizen. Despite his national origin, he lived in England, he wore finely tailored English clothes, he rode in English hunts, and he spoke English perfectly, although with a slight accent.

One could not determine his nationality from his appearance; he just looked like a wealthy European industrialist. Sir Henri was a short, stocky man with an ambitious, energetic, and effervescent personality. His rather large head seemed closely set on his body. Despite a headful of white hair and a bristly, trimmed white mustache, he seemed younger due to his ruddy complexion and black flashing eyes.

Each day he sat behind his large, carved wooden desk with the row of telephones at one end. These were Sir Henri's links with his worldwide business and political informants. Each ring of a phone would bring reports from important outposts, news of production, movements of oil tankers, fluctuations in the stock market, activities of his competitors, or the latest information about political tremors that might affect his investments.

By 1913, Deterding possessed the controlling interest in the oil fields of Romania, Russia, California, Trinidad, the Dutch Indies, and Mexico. He was also pumping oil out of Mesopotamia and Persia. Deterding was acknowledged as a man who had the sole executive rule over a large portion of the world's "black gold." One English admiral described him as "Napoleonic in his audacity and Cromwellian in his thoroughness."[46]

Before the Communist revolution in 1917, Deterding had large investments in the Russian Baku oil fields, as well as holdings in the Grozny and Maikop oil fields. When the British Army withdrew from Baku in the spring of 1920, the Red Army moved in, and Moscow nationalized the oil fields. To add insult to injury, the Communists started to export oil in 1922, and their competition became a serious threat to Deterding.

From this point onward, Deterding aimed to destroy bolshevism. His hatred drove him to support every anti-Communist or White Russian organization that he heard of. In

1924, he married a lady who was the daughter of a White Russian general. As a tireless enemy of the Soviet regime, he would always give his financial backing to anyone who proposed a plan that might have a chance of overthrowing the Communist rulers.

Deterding was often accused of encouraging armed uprisings in Soviet Russia, such as the Georgian-Caucasian rebellion in 1924. This was the location of many of Russia's oil fields, and if the rebellion had succeeded it would have greatly weakened the stability of the Moscow government. A *New York Times* correspondent wrote an article appearing on September 13, 1924, that stated: "It is understood, according to well-informed persons, that the revolution is being financed [by] . . . former proprietors of Baku oil wells." Essad Bey, a member of the White Russian community, claimed that it was Deterding who supplied the money for the rebellion.

On January 5, 1926, the British newspaper *The Morning Post* published a vituperative letter by Deterding, denouncing the Soviets as thieves. "What else is it [communism] but lawlessness and an attempt to go back to the prehistoric world of right by force and brutal force only." Besides his own anti-Communist writings, Deterding financed the quarterly English publication of the Society of Ukrainian Patriots—an organization whose aim was to break the Ukraine away from Soviet Russia.

Georg Bell, a mysterious German of Scottish origin who had many useful business and political connections, was said to be an agent of Deterding. He had attended a number of the Ukrainian Patriots meetings in Paris as a representative of both Hitler and Deterding. Because he knew Rosenberg and was a close friend of Roehm, the chief of staff of the S.A., Bell was an excellent contact for Sir Henri to have with the Nazis. In 1931, the same year as Rosenberg's first visit, Bell came to London with orders signed by Roehm. His mission was to further the existing ties between England and Germany for a future alliance against Russia. The *Morn-*

ing Post somehow found out that Bell's instructions were "the same in substance as those carried by Herr Rosenberg on his recent visit to London."

Johannes Steel, a German writer and former agent of the German Economic Intelligence Service, gave evidence at the inquiry into the Reichstag fire that Sir Henri Deterding was giving money to the Nazis. Almost as soon as Steel had finished his indictment of Deterding, the former editor of an important German newspaper jumped up quickly to remind the members of the board that these facts linking an English businessman with Hitler could not be mentioned publicly, since it might embarrass the British government. A vote was then taken confirming the decision to keep the facts secret.

A *Daily Telegraph* reporter believed that Bell and Rosenberg met an international magnate in London and "big credits for the Nazis followed."[47] The Dutch press stated that Deterding sent to Hitler, through Georg Bell, about four million guilders.[48] Some said Sir Henri gave the Nazis money in exchange for their agreement to give him preferred standing in the German oil market when they came to power.[49] In 1931, it was reported that Deterding made a loan of £30 million to Hitler in return for a promise of a petroleum monopoly. Some claimed the loan was as much as £55 million.[50] Louis Lochner, former foreign correspondent for the Associated Press and authority on the relation between Hitler and big business, mentioned an alleged "ten million marks" contribution by the Dutch oil lord to the Nazis.[51]

With so many sources agreeing on the matter, there can be little doubt that Deterding financed Hitler. All that remains uncertain is the exact sum of money; nevertheless, one would not be injudicious to say it was substantial. Deterding had much to gain by financing the Nazis. They were a strong anti-Communist party that was planning to eventually attack Russia and throw out the Bolsheviks.[52] But even if the Nazis did not come to power, Deterding had much to gain; as the largest party in the German Reichstag, the Nazis could use their influence to push the German government in an anti-Soviet direction.

Bavaria had always been one of the most powerful German duchies; however, in 1806 Napoleon made it a kingdom as a reward for its being his ally against Austria . Maximilian, head of the Bavarian royal house of Wittelsbach, was crowned king. To further strengthen the tie between Bavaria and France, Napoleon arranged a political marriage between his stepson Eugene and Princess Augusta, daughter of Maximilian.

For several centuries, one of France's major aims in foreign policy was the containment of her continental rival, Germany. After World War I, when America and Britain had refused to join in a pact against any future German aggression, France was forced to make her own defense. Besides agreements with Belgium and Poland, France formed an alliance with Czechoslovakia, Romania, and Yugoslavia in 1921 known as the "Little Entente." These states were given financial assistance and promises of French military support against the Germans. France was searching madly for any other possible way to emasculate Germany. One plan was to promote and finance separatist groups in the German states, especially in the Palatinate (located on the Rhine near the French border), Württemberg, and Bavaria.

This plot was no secret to the Germans. In August 1920, King Ludwig III of Bavaria was informed that France was favoring a federated Reich and in it a Bavarian monarchy.[53] If Germany had refused to sign the Versailles Treaty, the French military was prepared with plans for an attack on Berlin. However, Marshal Foch, the supreme allied commander during World War I, said the Allies would have made separate and *lenient* treaties with certain German states, such as Bavaria and Württemberg, in order to break them away from the main German government.[54] Toward the end of the war there was a faction in Bavaria that wanted to make a separate treaty with the Allies in order to get better terms than the rest of Germany.[55]

Proud of their historic traditions and Catholicism, Bavarians regarded themselves as being distinctly different from the Protestant Prussians. Most of the enmity between them resulted from the Bavarians' resentment of being ruled by the German central government in Berlin. Due to the basically agrarian economic structure of Bavaria, its people were also more conservative politically than the industrial workers of northern Germany. When the Republic was formed in 1919, the new constitution took away Bavaria's authority on all issues dealing with the military, the state treasury, the postal system, and railroads. This aggravated the Bavarians even more.

As a result of these factors there were several monarchist and anti-Weimar political parties in Bavaria. The Bavarian People's party, which was the largest party in the Diet, had a very pro-Wittelsbach, federalist program. Some of its members broke away to form the more radical Bavarian Royalist party[56] There were accusations that a few Bavarian separatist leaders were receiving money from the French. In the murky underworld of rightist paramilitary politics in Bavaria, separatist sympathizers came in frequent contact with the Nazis.[57] Although the separatists and the Nazis hated each other, they hated the Social Democratic central government in Berlin even more. If French money was given to some separatists, they may in turn have passed part of it on to Hitler in an attempt to gain control over the Nazis.[58]

Throughout 1923, French intelligence was trying to stir up a revolution in Bavaria against the Berlin government.[59] In 1921, the Nazi *Völkischer Beobachter* wrote of the French people, "whose essential nobility we ungrudgingly recognize and honestly esteem." In 1922, Hitler said that the French had been incited against Germany by the Jews who aimed "to stir up and exploit the conflict."[60] Therefore, he concluded, that the Germans should hate the "November Criminals"* not the French.†

Then in early 1923, Hugo Machhaus, the former editor of the Nazi paper the *Völkischer Beobachter*, conspired with French assistance to separate Bavaria from Germany. But the plot was uncovered by the government and the intriguers were arrested. Before the trial took place, Machhaus was found dead in his cell, hanging by his own belt. It was questionable if suicide was the cause of his death because most prisoners are not allowed to keep their belts for this very reason.

It must be pointed out that there is no concrete evidence to show that Hitler knew of Machhaus's dealings with the French. Hitler, of course, denied ever having received any foreign funds. As one Nazi official remarked, "The legend that Hitler was in French pay . . . kept cropping up for years and gave him grounds for a number of lawsuits against various newspapers and individuals."[61]

But there is further warrant for suspecting the Nazi-French connection. In October 1923, a socialist member of the English parliament, E. D. Morel, came to Munich to see Dr. Gustav von Kahr, the conservative leader of the Bavarian government. Morel revealed some startling news: "I should like to tell you that some highly placed Paris friends of mine have definitely assured me that a large part of the money received by Hitler is derived from a French source." Kahr refused to believe it; he said he knew that Hitler was a German nationalist, not a separatist nor a monarchist. So Morel continued: "One of my informants is a member of the French cabinet. The money passes through eight or nine

---

*"November Criminals" was a sarcastic term used by the Nazis to describe those supposedly responsible for the Communist revolution in November 1918, and Germany's defeat in the war.

†It is difficult to determine why Hitler would seem to be favoring the French. It was probably because he wanted to concentrate all hatred on his enemies in Germany.

places across the occupied area."[62] Morel's testimony is a strong indictment against the Nazis. It is possible, even if Morel was right, that Hitler was unaware of the source of the money coming into the Nazi treasury. If he had known, he probably would not have accepted the money for fear of being labeled a French puppet and traitor.

Two of Hitler's top money seekers—Lüdecke and Rosenberg— were sitting in the office of the *Völkischer Beobachter* in 1932, talking about the accusations of Hitler being in foreign pay. Rosenberg thought it was a "very delicate affair." Speaking in a 'voice of veiled irony accompanied by a suggestive smile," he said, "You know, of course, that Hitler has declared in court that we never receive foreign pay from any source and never even asked for it."[63]

What was the total sum that Rosenberg's smile was suggesting? Perhaps it is inestimable, because Italy, America, England, and France were not the only countries from which money was given to the Nazi party. As was seen earlier, contributions also flowed in from Austria, Hungary, Switzerland, Finland, and Czechoslovakia, and this does not complete the list.[64] Hitler had many other wealthy admirers who probably favored his party, but as of now, no definite proof of their contributions has been found. Two notable people in this category were Queen Marie of Romania and King Ferdinand of Bulgaria. Queen Marie is known to have "rather admired" some of Hitler's policies, and King Ferdinand was often seen wearing a swastika pin encircled with diamonds in his lapel.

In time, more evidence will undoubtedly turn up and the contributors and the sums they gave can be cited more precisely, but the basic picture of the Nazi party's primary sources of foreign money given here will remain much the same.

9
HITLER RUNS FOR PRESIDENT

In the early autumn of 1931, a young man named Dr. Otto Dietrich was appointed "Chief of the Press Bureau of the National Socialist Party." Newspapers throughout Germany reported that Dr. Dietrich was the "Liaison man of Rhineland heavy industry."[1] It was also stated that he had previously negotiated the support and financing of the Nazis by the "coal barons" and had now been called to Munich by Hitler in order to establish closer links between him and the industrialists.

After the war, Otto Dietrich flatly denied this account and stated in his memoirs that he "had nothing whatsoever to do with heavy industry."[2] The truth, however, was not so easily concealed. In 1928, Dietrich had been a business and commercial editor of a conservative newspaper. He also happened to be the son-in-law of Dr. Reismann-Grone of Essen, the owner of the *Rheinisch-Westfälische Zeitung*, a newspaper considered to be very friendly to heavy industry. Reismann-Grone was also the political advisor of the Mining Association, one of the wealthiest employers' associations in

Germany. Although Dietrich was only thirty-one years old at the time, through his father-in-law, he had gotten to know most of the important Ruhr industrialists and was on especially friendly terms with old Emil Kirdorf, who was an important contributor to Hitler.

Dietrich's postwar denial of having had anything to do with heavy industry even contradicts what he himself wrote in 1934 about the part he played in helping win over the tycoons of heavy industry for Hitler. According to Dietrich, in 1931, most big businessmen were still opposed to the Nazis except for "some praiseworthy exceptions."[3] Unfortunately, he does not elaborate on who these "praiseworthy exceptions" were. In his account, entitled *With Hitler on the Road to Power*, Dietrich does, however, describe in detail Hitler's efforts to gain contributions and support from big business.

Hitler, said Dietrich, "realized that, besides striving to gain the support of the broad masses, he must make every possible appeal to the economic magnates, the firmest adherents to the old system." In the summer of 1931, in Munich, he suddenly decided to concentrate systematically upon convincing the influential economic magnates "who, through their financial power, controlled the moderate non-Marxian parties." "These prominent men," wrote Dietrich, "formed the main resistance [against the Nazis] and Hitler thus hoped, step by step, to break them away from the existing system of government."[4]

In the next few months, Hitler and Dietrich traveled from one end of Germany to the other in a big black Mercedes, "holding private interviews with prominent personalities." Some of these meetings were so secret that they had to be held in "some lonely forest glade." "Privacy was absolutely imperative," said Dietrich; "the press must have no chance of doing mischief. Success was the consequence. The pillars of the government began to crumble. This seemed alarming [to the democratic politicians] yet indiscernible—incomprehensible. The 'Deutsche Volkspartei' [German People's

Party] was alienated from the government. . . . Adolph Hitler was satisfied."[5]

At first there were some Nazi leaders, such as Gauleiter Albert Krebs of Hamburg, who complained of Dietrich's appointment to an important party post as a sign of the growing influence of big business within the party. In fact, Otto Dietrich openly acknowledged that he was a double agent. This is not to say that he was betraying anyone; he simply had a double mission: to help Hitler gain business support and to report to big business on Hitler's real strength and economic program.

From the first Dietrich was impressed with the devotion of Hitler's followers. Young and old, men and women, all with faces full of enthusiasm, they were always crowding around their "Fuehrer" wherever he went, trying to shake his hand and speak with him. It soon became obvious to Dietrich that Hitler could claim the allegiance of the masses of people in a way that the leaders of the traditional parties never could.

Even the sophisticated Dietrich was impressed by an incident that took place while he was accompanying Hitler on one of his campaign tours. On his way to a rally at Stralsund, Hitler's plane was forced down in the night by a storm and had to make an emergency landing far from its original destination. His usual caravan of cars was not at the landing place, so different automobiles had to be secured. It was already late, so this took some time. Hitler realized that at best he would be several hours late for the rally, which had been scheduled for eight o'clock, but he decided to proceed nevertheless in the hope that the crowd would wait for him. Shortly after the caravan of rented cars departed, the powerful headlights of Hitler's Mercedes flashed upon it from the opposite direction; the wireless message sent ahead from the emergency landing place had reached the drivers. On the dark highway Hitler and his staff quickly changed cars and drove off at top speed. But there was another delay before they reached Stralsund.

"Anxious adherents stopped us in a small village," said Dietrich, "and warned us that danger lay ahead. A forest close by through which we had to pass was occupied by armed Communists in ambush, and ready to waylay us." Hitler ordered his caravan to proceed with caution. "As we came to the forest," recounted Dietrich, "we saw police scouring the countryside with loaded rifles. They had already pounced upon the Communists." A light rain was falling as they finally drove through the deserted suburbs of Stralsund at 2:30 A.M. They had almost abandoned hope of even the most devoted followers waiting so long in the rain and cold. But an imposing sight met their eyes. Said Dietrich: "In the open air, and in the pouring rain, we met the crowd drenched to the skin, weary and hungry, just as they had gathered over the night, and patiently waited. . . . We stood amidst the mighty assembly, as the red streaks of morning appeared in the sky. . . . The night had been long and the way to Stralsund far, but now we had forgotten all inconveniences." Hitler spoke to the audience as the day slowly dawned. "Was there ever such a spectacle—a gathering of 40,000 people at four o'clock in the morning?" Dietrich asked himself. "Was there ever a finer proof of devotion and boundless faith"[6]*

Dietrich's industrialist friends regarded Hitler's tremendous popularity with interest. But what did Dietrich think of Hitler's plans and ideas? Was he responsible? What kind of economic programs did he have? These were some of the questions German business leaders wanted answered.

Being a young man, Dietrich was more aware of the economic misery caused by the depression than were the older industrialists of his father-in-law's generation. He believed that some social welfare measures like those proposed by Hitler were absolutely necessary if the lower classes were

---

* Although Dietrich's fawning language seems almost ridiculous today, it illustrates the hero worship that was an important part of the Hitler mystique created by Nazi propaganda.

to be kept from turning to communism.[7] Dietrich himself was undoubtedly attracted to Hitler's policy that national recovery would be achieved only along with social measures. Hitler proposed the creation of a classless state by establishing a "racial people's community," by eliminating the evils of class warfare and the party system. The guiding principle of this national folk community was to be "'common good before the good of the individual."

Big businessmen were undoubtedly interested in Hitler's social welfare policy and his views on the Jews, but what concerned them most was the question of capitalism and free enterprise. At first, Dietrich himself was disturbed by the Nazi slogans about "eliminating unearned income" and "smashing the bondage of interest." After discussing economic matters with Hitler at some length, Dietrich was reassured. He later wrote: "Hitler accepted private property and the role of capital in modern economic life because he recognized these as the economic foundations of our culture." He opposed only the abuse of capitalism, but not capitalism in principle. Although 'smashing interest slavery" was one of the points of the Nazi program, Hitler recognized that he could not eliminate the system of interest from the economy, "without undermining his own political existence."[8]

Hitler's political offensive for 1932 began at midnight on New Year's Eve. While others partied and celebrated, Hitler was addressing his followers in Munich: "In twelve months, the road to German freedom will be open! . . . Let us march into this new year as fighters, so that we may leave it as victors."[9] Hitler had every reason to be optimistic. In the last year and a half his party had mushroomed in size. Up to the fall of 1930, the Nazis were little more than a noisy fringe party; but in the September elections of that year, they won 18 percent of the vote and 107 seats in the Reichstag. Throughout the year Hitler consolidated his support and tapped new sources of money from the traditional supporters of the conservative parties. He recognized that as the depression grew worse, his support could only increase.

Chancellor Bruening hoped to be able to hold out until economic conditions improved. Whether or not he would be able to do so depended on the reelection of Hindenburg as president at the end of his term in office, since under the German constitution the president had the power to appoint or dismiss the chancellor. Hindenburg was eighty-four years old and in failing health, so no one could tell how long he would last. Only with great difficulty had Bruening prevailed on the old man to agree to serve on if parliament prolonged his term, thus making it unnecessary for him to have to shoulder the burden of a bitter election campaign. Bruening realized that an election campaign for the presidency during a time of such economic hardships could only benefit the radical parties. He made every effort to avoid this alternative, and so he invited Hitler to come to Berlin for new negotiations.

The chancellor's telegram arrived while Hitler was conferring with his lieutenants Rosenberg and Hess in the *Völkischer Beobachter* offices in Munich. He read it with satisfaction and then slammed down his fist, saying: "Now I have them in my pocket! They have recognized me as a partner in their negotiations."[10]

Hitler met with General Groener, the minister of defense, on January 6, for negotiations, and on January 7 he conferred with Chancellor Bruening and General von Schleicher, Groener's assistant. Essentially, the chancellor repeated the proposal he had made in the fall; Hitler was asked to agree to an extension of Hindenburg's term as president for a year or two until economic conditions began to improve and the problems of reparations and armaments had been settled. In return, Bruening agreed to resign as soon as the Allies had canceled the reparations. Hitler listened politely and then asked for time to consider his reply. He then went back to the Kaiserhof, the big hotel in the Wilhelmstrasse opposite the Reich Chancellery, where the suite that served as his Berlin headquarters was located.

The most important Nazi leaders were waiting for Hitler when he arrived at the Kaiserhof. Strasser was in favor of accepting Bruening's proposal, arguing that if the Nazis insisted on an election, Hindenburg would undoubtedly win it. Goebbels and Roehm argued that it would be a fatal mistake for the party to appear to avoid this chance of letting the people decide, especially after the recent Nazi successes in the provincial elections. A long debate followed. Goebbels wrote in his diary for January 7: "The presidency is not really in question. Bruening only wants to stabilize his own position indefinitely. . . . The contest for power, the game of chess, has begun. It may last throughout the year. . . . The main point is that we hold fast, and waive all compromise." The night before he had written: "We discuss the state of affairs within the Party. There is one man . . . whom nobody trusts . . . Gregor Strasser."[11]

Hitler knew that an election campaign against Hindenburg would be a considerable risk, but he was not about to strengthen Bruening's hand by giving the Republic a breathing spell. He rejected Bruening's proposal but was subtle enough to do so in such a way as might drive a wedge between the chancellor and the president. He addressed his reply to Hindenburg over Bruening's head, warning him that the chancellor's plan was unconstitutional. He offered, however, to support Hindenburg as the presidential candidate if he would dismiss Bruening, form a "national" government of Nazis and Nationalists, and call new elections for the Reichstag and the Prussian Diet.

Hindenburg refused to agree to Hitler's conditions. The Nazis and even the conservative Nationalists who were angered by Bruening's cooperation with socialists and the labor unions responded by refusing to support the prolongation of his term in office. Feeling that he had been betrayed by his friends and supposed supporters, the Nationalists, Hindenburg finally agreed to stand for reelection. In addition to his resentment against the right-wing parties for refusing to spare him the strain of another political campaign, the old president was now displeased with Bruening, who he felt had fumbled the whole affair and was forcing him into conflict with the same nationalist forces that had elected him president in 1925. Poor Hindenburg could be reelected only with the support of the socialists and the labor unions, for whom he had always had a certain contempt.

Hitler, however, was faced with a difficult decision. Was he, himself, to risk running against Hindenburg for the presidency? Hindenburg seemed unbeatable. He was the ideal candidate, the legendary hero of the World War, whom many people on the Right would probably support for sentiment's sake alone. His position as the defender of the Republic against extremists would win the support of the moderate parties and even the Social Democrats, who had been against him in 1925. By running against the old field marshal, the Nazis would risk their reputation of invincibility, which had been built up in one provincial election after another since their great triumph in September 1930. But if Hitler wished to continue convincing people that National Socialism was on the threshold of power, could he risk evading such a contest?

Fortunately for Hitler, he had several weeks to make up his mind. There were many question to be considered; for one, how were the Nazis to finance such a massive campaign? By now, Hitler had several agents working for him in big business circles, soliciting contributions and trying to win the support of wealthy individuals. Funk and Dietrich, who both had worked for conservative newspapers and had good connections in the business community, and Keppler, a pro-Nazi industrialist, all reported limited success. Later, when questioned after the war, each could honestly say that they knew of only a few industrialists who supported the Nazis. However, this was only because Hitler never let any of his agents know what the others were doing. "Hitler knew how to keep silent," said Dietrich. "With rigid strictness he carried out the principle that nobody needs to know more about important matters than is absolutely necessary for the performance of his duties. If only two persons need to know about something no third person is to hear of it."[12] Yet, in spite of the efforts of all his agents with upper-class contacts, the party was deep in debt.

On January 5, Dr. Goebbels wrote in his diary: "Money is wanting everywhere. It is very difficult to obtain. Nobody will give us credit. Once you get the power you can get the cash galore, but then you need it no longer. Without the power you need the money, but then you can't get it."[13] However, a little over a month later, on February 8, he was much more optimistic: "Money affairs improve daily. The financing of the electoral campaign is practically assured."[14] Perhaps one of the reasons for Goebbels's more encouraging reference to money matters was a speech that Hitler delivered to the Industry Club in Düsseldorf on January 27.

At seven o'clock on the evening of January 27, over six hundred members of the Industry Club assembled in a large ballroom at the Park Hotel in Düsseldorf to hear Hitler's speech.

The audience feared communism more than anything else. Realizing this, Hitler made the danger of Marxism the central theme of his speech. He discussed the topic with rational logic and made some startlingly accurate predictions about its future development. He said it was no use dismissing communism as a mere delusion of misguided manual workers.

"Bolshevism today is not merely a mob storming about in some of our streets in Germany, but it is a conception of the world which is in the act of subjecting to itself the entire Asiatic continent, and which today in the form of a State (Russia) stretches almost from our eastern frontier to Vladivostok.

"Bolshevism, if its advance is not interrupted, will transform the world as completely as in times past did Christianity. . . . Today, we stand at the turning point of

Germany's destiny. If the present course continues, Germany will one day land in Bolshevist chaos."[15]

Hitler had hardly uttered his last word when the audience broke into "long and tumultuous applause."

However, the question remains: did the speech have any lasting effect? Did it bring any large contribution from industry into the Nazi treasury? The mere fact of Hitler's appearance before so distinguished and important a group as the Industry Club added to his prestige. Gustav Krupp, the munitions king, did not attend Hitler's Industry Club speech. Instead, he sent a high-ranking member of his board of directors, who was also a member of the club, with instructions to bring back a complete report. The emissary returned with more; he himself had been converted, and his report was full of passages of National Socialist propaganda. Krupp, who had always been against Hitler, now began to waver: "The man must have something," he said.[16] Fritz Thyssen, the pro–Nazi steel tycoon who had helped arrange the speech, later wrote: "As a result of the address, which created a deep impression, a number of larger contributions from heavy-industry sources flowed into the treasury of the Nazi Party."[17]

Although the Nazis may have received enough contributions to help them finance their coming election campaign, there was no "flow" of money from industry. The industrialists continued to give most of their contributions to the moderate parties, as they had always done. In fact, the Nazi party was nearly bankrupt again at the end of the year. But the speech was certainly a great victory for Hitler because many of the industrialists no longer saw him as a radical but as a reasonable politician with whom they could work and who might be needed to save them from the Communists.

Throughout most of January and February of 1932 Hitler tried to make up his mind whether or not he should run for the presidency. Hindenburg still seemed unbeatable.

Should he risk a defeat, just when the party seemed to be doing so well? Dr. Goebbels tried to persuade him to announce his candidacy. They traveled to Munich together on January 19, and that night Goebbels wrote in his diary: "Talked over the presidency question with the Fuehrer. . . . No decision has as yet been reached. I strongly urge him to come forward as a candidate himself."

Goebbels went over his estimates of the votes with Hitler on February 12. He admitted it was "a risk" but one that had to be taken. At almost the last moment a cavalry captain who represented the Crown Prince made contact through Gregor Strasser. The Crown Prince indicated he was considering offering himself as the Nazi candidate for the presidency.[18] Naturally this produced a sensation in the party. Negotiations began at once. There would be three definite advantages to having the Crown Prince as the Nazi candidate: (1) The party would have access to the vast wealth of the monarchists; (2) Hugenberg's Nationalist party would undoubtedly also support the Crown Prince; and (3) contributions to the campaign would flow in from the aristocracy. But the disadvantages might outweigh the advantages. The revolutionary Nazi party could hardly afford to be too closely associated with the reactionary forces of monarchism. Would not the Crown Prince with his extreme arrogance try to take over the leadership of the party himself? And furthermore, what guarantee was there that he would be able to win the vote of the common people in the election?

Hindenburg formally announced his candidacy for the presidency on February 15. Goebbels was jubilant: "Now we have a free hand." But by February 21, Hitler still had not made up his mind. Goebbels wrote: "This everlasting waiting is almost demoralizing." Then the next day, February 22, negotiations with the Crown Prince were broken off: "At the Kaiserhof with the Fuehrer . . . we once more go into the question of the presidential candidate. The chief thing now is to break silence. The Fuehrer gives me permission to do so at the Sportpalast tonight. Thank God!"

That night, Goebbels recorded: "Sportpalast packed. . . . Immense ovations at the very outset. When after about an hour's preparation, I publicly proclaim that the Fuehrer will come forward as a candidate for the presidency, a storm of deafening applause rages for nearly ten minutes. Wild ovations for the Fuehrer. The audience rises with shouts of joy. They nearly raise the roof. An overwhelming spectacle!"[19]

It was Goebbels who set the tone of one of the most bitter election campaigns Germany had ever known, when in the Reichstag he branded Hindenburg as "the candidate for the party of deserters." He was expelled from the chamber for insulting the president. Nevertheless, the Nazis knew they were fighting against heavy odds, so they spared neither the president nor anyone else in their attacks against the "system." Traditional party and class loyalties were upset in the confusion of the campaign. Hindenburg, a conservative Prussian monarchist and Protestant, was supported by the Social Democrats, trade unions, the Catholic Center party (Bruening's party), and the other moderate parties. The conservative middle and upper classes of the Protestant north voted either for Duesterberg, the candidate of the Nationalist party (to which Hindenburg formally belonged), or for Hitler, the hero of the lower- to middle-class masses. The Communists denounced the Social Democrats for "betraying the worker" by supporting the "reactionary" Hindenburg and ran a candidate of their own, Ernst Thaelmann, the party's leader.

A few weeks before the election campaign began, it was reported that Hitler had gained the support of Ludwig Grauert, the executive director of the Northwest German Employers' Federation. On the surface this seemed to be a triumph for the National Socialists. However, Grauert's "support" of Hitler was a far more involved matter than was stated in the press. One day in early January, Walther Funk, one of Hitler's economic advisers and fund-raisers, called on Fritz Thyssen of Düsseldorf, requesting a donation of 100,000 marks (about $24,000) for his newspaper, the *National Socialist Economic News*. Thyssen agreed to the request, hoping that Funk's conservative ideas might have an influence upon the party and counteract the thinking of men like Gottried Feder, the left-wing Nazi who advocated ridiculous economic ideas like abolishing interest income.[20]

However, the steel tycoon was momentarily short of cash, so he asked Ludwig Grauert to make this sum available to Funk. Because of Thyssen's powerful position within the Federation, Grauert complied with his request. But when this contribution was reported to the full board of the Federation, it was sharply disavowed. Grauert was reprimanded and threatened with dismissal, which was averted only when Thyssen agreed to repay the sum in question. A resolution was then passed that no further political contributions would be made from funds of the Federation.[21] The Grauert incident was a clear indication that Hitler would receive support from only a very few heavy industrialists during the presidential campaign.

Although most of the leaders of the German business community supported Hindenburg for the presidency, they did so reluctantly.[22] The old field marshal was not popular with the industrialists because they saw him as being too closely associated with reactionary Junker interests. The old president had little understanding of or appreciation for the problems of big business. In October 1931, former Chancellor Wilhelm Cuno, then head of the Hamburg-American Shipping line, met secretly with Hindenburg to suggest that some of Germany's most prominent businessmen be brought together in a special economic council on the depression. It quickly became obvious to Cuno that Hindenburg did not even recognize the names of most of the industrialists on the list.

From the beginning, businessmen had disliked Hindenburg. In 1925, the industrial spokesmen of both the Nationalist party and the German People's party had opposed his nomination for the presidency, but the power of the old field marshal to attract the vote of the average citizen was something that could not be ignored. Now, in the middle of the depression, the ability of Hindenburg to inspire the confidence of the people was more important than ever before. Millions were desperate and longing for a strong leader, but other than the members of the Nazi party, who would vote for Hitler rather than Hindenburg? To answer this question it is necessary to examine closely the existing social and economic conditions in Germany in February of 1932.

In Germany the winter of 1931 to 1932 was generally acknowledged "the hardest winter in one hundred years." But it wasn't just the record low temperatures and heavy snowfall that made the situation so severe. The frigid weather struck Germany in the depths of the depression when only a few people could afford warm clothes or coal for their furnaces. Including the families of the unemployed, the total number of Germans living on public assistance in February 1932 was approximately 17.5 million, almost one-third of the population.

The average unemployed German received fifty-one marks a month for himself and his family, on the government dole. After paying the usual tenement rent, the money left for food rations was just about enough for one poor meal a day. It was enough to live on—in the sense that it might take ten years to die on it. When asked what kind of food she could buy for her family on the few marks her unemployed husband received from the state, one German woman replied: "Bread and potatoes; mostly bread. On the day we get the money we buy sausage—can't resist the temptation to have a little meat. But the last two days of the week, we go hungry."[23]

An iron screen guarded the buffet of a Berlin restaurant; behind it lay a platter of fried horse meat and a pair of horse meat sausages. The guests were hungry. They sat at their tables gazing through the screen at the horse meat.

Even though it was dinnertime, they ordered nothing. Their hunger had nothing to do with dinnertime; it had been with them for months. There were about forty customers in the restaurant, but only two had anything on their table. Between one old man and woman stood a mug of malt beer. First he would take a sip, sit the mug down and stare at the horse meat. Then she would take a sip, sit the mug down, and stare at the horse meat. They were the liveliest guests in the room until a tall young man came in. His skinny neck was sticking awkwardly out of a tattered overcoat that flapped about his ankles. He wandered through the room holding out a dress shirt that had once been white. He was willing to trade the shirt for the price of a horse meat sausage but found no takers.

The restaurant was the Zum Ollen Fritz (at the sign of Old Fritz), and the seal of Frederick the Great was on its door, even though it was located in the almost solidly Communist neighborhood of Wedding. Here in densely populated north Berlin, one could see German poverty in its most acute form. In the Zum Ollen Fritz there were plenty of witnesses who could explain why the capital city of Germany had more Communists than any city outside Russia.

There was a sign on the wall at the Zum Ollen Fritz that read, MEN'S HOME—BED 50 PFENNIGS. Beneath the sign sat a half dozen men with their heads resting on the table, sleeping. "Why don't they go to the men's home and get a decent sleep?" a stranger asked.

"Because they haven't got fifty pfennigs," (about twenty U.S. cents) answered the waiter. In another Berlin restaurant, the Meadow Spring, twenty or thirty men and a few women sat and watched as several young couples danced to the snaggled tune of an old phonograph. It was still dinnertime and signs on the wall advertised, IF YOU WANT TO WHIP MAX SCHMELING, EAT OUR GOULASH—35 PFENNIGS, but few had anything on their tables. "How do these proprietors get along?" asked an American journalist. "They don't," was the reply. "They're not much better off than their customers."

Since the September elections of 1930, there had been a political landslide in Germany toward the two extremist parties, the National Socialists and the Communists. Throughout the country the extremist vote went hand in hand with unemployment. Two-thirds of the Communist vote and one-half of the National Socialist vote in the 1930 elections came from regions containing much less than half the population of Germany but where the percentage of unemployment was considerably above that of the whole country. The centers of unemployment and the strongholds of communism were the same: Berlin and its industrial environs, the giant chemical works of Merseburg, the mill towns of Thuringia Saxony, the steel and coal regions of the Ruhr, and the mines of Silesia.

Which region was the most impoverished in Germany? That was difficult to say. "We drove through the Forest of Thuringia on a winter afternoon," wrote American journalist H. R. Knickerbocker, who was touring Germany. "The smokeless stacks of abandoned glass works threw occasional shadows across the snow-decked roads, and the gaping windows of deserted factories eyed us coldly. All the 75 miles from Jena we passed not a half dozen automobiles, although the towns and villages crowded one upon the other. We were not the only travelers, but the others were on foot."[24] This was the Thuringian Forest, the traditional home of Europe's most famous glassblowers. Here, in a series of communities whose average population numbered about 6,000 men, at least 5,500 of them were unemployed. This degree of poverty, which existed in the most highly industrialized country in Europe, was unparalleled in history.

Thuringia may have been the most impoverished region in Germany, but things were almost as bad everywhere else. In 1932, it was said that the population of Saxony had a Bible in one hand and a public assistance ticket in the other. Half of the textile mills and lace factories in the Saxon town of Falkenstein were closed. The other half only ran three days a week. In one of the textile factories, open prayers could be heard in a back room at noon. There, most of the workers were gathered praying for help. Of the 15,000 inhabitants of Falkenstein, 7,500 were unemployed or dependents of the unemployed. Of the other half of the population, 2,500 were workers still employed but those wages had been cut to the point where they were barely more than the unemployed received from public assistance.[25]

The owners of the factories, however, were not much better off. Half of the villas outside the town were for sale, and some of the former owners were now on public charity along with their former workers. Small factories and businesses, which were so numerous in Saxony, were even more vulnerable to the depression than large industry. Facing bankruptcy, the owners of such enterprises were easily tempted by the promises of Hitler. Angry and frustrated with the traditional parties in which they had once placed their confidence, they now contributed to the National Socialists in the vague hope that Hitler could somehow make Germany strong again and bring back the good old days. Individually their contributions were small, but when taken together the sum of such donations was substantial.

Saxony and Thuringia were poverty-stricken, but what of the industrial heartland of Germany, the Ruhr? Here mountains of coal sat waiting for market. Ten million tons, nearly a year's normal production, were heaped outside the pitheads in the Ruhr. In the winter of 1932, millions of German families huddled together, shivering from the cold, unable to afford to heat their homes and apartments, yet the coal just sat, unable to find any buyers.

In Essen there were smokestacks on the horizon as far as one could see—smokestacks in rows, smokestacks in clusters, a whole forest of smokestacks. But less than half of the smokestacks were belching the sooty brown smoke they were noted for; the others were idle. This was the most highly concentrated industrial area in the world: the home of German heavy industry.

The Communist party was strong in the Ruhr and among

the unemployed workers in Essen. Communist agitators denounced the lords of heavy industry who oppressed their workers. But what was the winter of 1932 really like for Germany's big capitalists? Germany's wealthiest family, the Krupps, who lived in Essen, were losing so much money during the economic crisis that they were forced to close down over half the rooms of their home, the palatial Villa Huegel, and confine themselves to the sixty rooms of its "small wing." The big capitalists were still able to afford caviar and champagne, but many of them lived in fear—fear of Communists, of the economic crisis, and that the economic crisis would create more Communists.

With Germany still in the depths of the worst depression in history, Hitler began his first campaign for the presidency in late February 1932. The weather was still bitter cold; the impoverished masses would not easily forget the miseries they had gone through for the past three months when it came time to cast their votes on March 13. Hitler realized this and launched the Nazi party on a campaign that was a masterpiece of organized agitation, attempting to take the country by storm. Every constituency down to the remotest rural hamlet was canvassed. The Nazis sent some of their best speakers to the little Bavarian village of Dietramszell, where the old president spent his summer holidays, to win 228 votes against 157 for Hindenburg, a clever propaganda stunt. They plastered the walls of the cities and towns with over a million screeching colored posters, distributed eight million pamphlets and twelve million extra copies of their party newspapers. Introducing two innovations into German politics, the Nazis sent trucks with loudspeakers through the streets spouting forth from gramophone records that had been distributed in mass numbers, and films of Hitler and Goebbels were shown everywhere.

However, the major Nazis effort was based on propaganda of the spoken word. The leading party speakers, Hitler, Goebbels, Gregor Strasser, and others, crisscrossed the country, addressing several mass meetings a day, working their audiences into a state of hysterical enthusiasm by the most unrestrained mob oratory.

Hitler threw himself into the campaign with furious energy. By car and train he conducted a speaking tour that rocked the rival parties and exhausted companions and opponents alike. From one town to another, from one mass meeting to another, Hitler covered the entire country as no politician had ever done before. He usually traveled in a convoy of cars and was accompanied by his staff. With Hitler's big black Mercedes in the lead, the cars were usually met on the outskirts of a town by a guide sent from local party headquarters to take them through the back streets to the meeting hall. Sitting in the front next to his chauffeur, Hitler left nothing to chance and always had a map on his knee ready to find a quick escape route if necessary. The precaution was probably not superfluous, since the Communists were always anxious for a chance to attack the hated Nazi leader.

On two different occasions, in Breslau and Cologne, wrong turns took the convoy into "Red" controlled neighborhoods, which they got through only after a foray and general uproar. The Communists were a strong and violent force in the winter of 1932. In "Red cities" like Chemnitz, people did not even dare display Christmas trees in working-class neighborhoods for fear of being attacked by fanatics. Driving through Bamberg late one night, two of the cars in Hitler's convoy had their windshields shattered by revolver shots. In Nuremberg, a bomb was thrown from the roof of a house onto the car of Julius Streicher, the vicious Nazi anti-Semite, which, fortunately for him, had only his chauffeur in it at the time. Several times during the campaign, Hitler's convoy was attacked by "Red mobs" throwing everything from rotten eggs to rocks. On such occasions, Hitler would berate the local gauleiter at the top of his voice for not having anticipated the action of the Communists.

In spite of the fact that the Communists were Hitler's most vocal and violent opponents, the only other serious contender for the presidency was Hindenburg. Chancellor Bruening worked tirelessly to win the election for the old field marshal. For once he was ruthless enough to reserve all radio time for his own side, and although this tactic infuriated Hitler, it later gave him an excuse to do the same thing. Hindenburg spoke only once, in a recorded broadcast on March 10: "Election of a party man, representing one-sided extremist views, who would consequently have a majority of the people against him, would expose the Fatherland to serious disturbances whose outcome would be incalculable."

The organization that bore the burden of Hindenburg's election campaign was the Social Democratic Iron Front, the reorganized version of Reichsbanner, the old paramilitary unit of the Social Democratic party. Naturally, Hindenburg also had the support of the moderate bourgeois parties, which were more to his liking. German big business financed the old field marshal's campaign, and three important industrialists, von Siemens, Duisberg, and Bosh, belonged to the Hindenburg Reelection Committee. Almost all of the prominent industrialists and bankers came out in support of the old president.

However, the moderate nonsocialist parties that big business had financed so heavily were rapidly losing contact with their following among the masses, so the number of votes they could deliver was doubtful. The presidential election campaign clearly illustrated that Hugenberg's Nationalist party was not the party of big business. Duesterberg, the Nationalist candidate, was supported by the aristocrats, the big landowners, and the agricultural associations. With the agrarian forces for Duesterberg and both capital and organized labor for Hindenburg, who would be left to vote for Hitler? His following was estimated in the millions, but every major newspaper in the country was against him.

Late on the evening of the elections, many of the Nazi

party leaders sat in the living room of Goebbels's Berlin home, "confident of victory." Goebbels himself was skeptical. He wrote in his diary:

> We listened to the results of the election on the wireless. News comes slowly trickling through. Things look queer for us. At about ten o'clock the situation receives a summing up. We are beaten; awful outlook for the future! We have not so much miscalculated our own votes as underrated those of our opponents. . . . We have gained 86 percent since September 1930; but that is no consolation. The Party is deeply depressed and discouraged. Only a bold stroke can retrieve matters.
>
> Phoned the Fuehrer late at night. He is entirely composed and is not at all upset."[26]

The results of the elections were astounding:

Hindenburg	18,651,497	49.6%
Hitler	11,339,446	30.1
Thaelmann (Communist)	4,983,341	13.2
Duesterberg (Nationalist)	2,557,729	6.8

The Nazi vote had risen from slightly less than 6.5 million in September 1930 to almost 11.5 million, an increase of 86 percent, giving Hitler approximately one-third of the total votes in Germany. But all the Nazi efforts still left them more than 7 million votes behind Hindenburg. The Nazis were disappointed; they had gotten used to landslides since September 1930 and had actually expected Hitler to win. However, Hindenburg's supporters were also disappointed, for they had fallen just .4 percent short of the absolute majority needed to win, and so had to face a runoff election. The Communists did not do as well as might have been expected in the middle of a depression, but they did receive two and a half times as many votes as they had seven years before. The only notable Communist success was in Berlin, where they received 28.7 percent of the vote against Hitler's 23 percent.

At midnight on March 13, Hitler was sitting in the Brown House in Munich with other party leaders and officials. Dr. Otto Dietrich, one of Hitler's contact men with big business and his press adviser, was present. He recorded the reactions of the gathering as the election results came in:

After the publication of the first figures declaring the final results, deep despondency seized those whose hopes were naturally fixed far too much upon their own desires during the heat of the battle. Already, there were loud cries of abandoning the Reich presidential campaign as hopeless, and instead of bleeding to death in a second [runoff] election campaign, cries of husbanding all strength for the later Prussian election. . . . Our Fuehrer . . . never worried, but stated with satisfaction the immense advance of the National Socialist party fighting a lone battle against the foe's eleven united parties. . . . At this moment, when the will of his followers threatened to waver beneath the prodigious burden of the struggle, Adolf Hitler proved an absolute leader.

It was midnight, and no time was to be lost. The extra editions [of the *Völkischer Beobachter*] lay there before going to press. At this very moment, with the publication of the figures of election results, the public and our movement must be told that Adolf Hitler was not beaten. . . .

Our Fuehrer rapidly dictated: "We must resume attack immediately and most ruthlessly. The National Socialist, recognizing his foe, does not relent till his victory is complete. I command you to begin this instant, the fight for the second election! I know that you, my comrades, have accomplished superhuman tasks during the past weeks. Only today, there can be no pause for reflection. Previous sacrifices only serve to prove further necessity for battle. The work shall and must be increased, if necessary, redoubled. Already this evening, orders are being issued to our organizations for the continuation and reinforcement of the struggle. The first election campaign is over, the second has begun today. I shall lead it!"[27]

The runoff election would be an uphill fight for the Nazis. It was now obvious that Hitler couldn't beat Hindenburg, so there was a danger that some of his supporters would not bother to vote. On March 19, Goebbels wrote in his diary: "We shall only be able to reenlist the interest of the masses by some striking efforts."[28] Hitler would make his campaign tour by plane, and the theme would be "Hitler Over Germany."

On April 3, the new campaign began with four mass meetings in Saxony. In a rented plane, Hitler flew from Dresden to Leipzig to Chemnitz to Plauen, speaking to a total of over a quarter of a million people. The airplane was just the tool Hitler needed. It made possible a new kind of campaign that corresponded to his own indefatigable energy and offered the possibility of utilizing his supreme power of personality in a way never previously anticipated. His campaign flights captured the imagination of Germany and the world. Never before had a politician conducted a speaking tour by plane. "It was," said Otto Dietrich, "political propaganda which eclipsed even American methods."[29]

The pace of campaign by air imposed extreme hardships on Hitler and his staff. Their day began in the early morning when one of the Fuehrer's adjutants, Julius Schaub, awakened the group. Hitler was usually the first out of bed and ready. The others had difficulty getting dressed and shaved as quickly, but if they were late it was at the expense of their breakfast. Coffee was strictly forbidden in the morning because of its bad effects during flight. Their usual diet consisted of milk, porridge, and toast. During breakfast, Hitler discussed the program of the day with his other adjutant, Captain Bruckner, who had already made up a preliminary schedule. After Hitler approved the map and timetables, last-minute coordinating arrangements were made by phone with the party headquarters in the cities where the mass meetings were to be held.

Everything was timed to the last minute. The cars were waiting at the hotel to race the group to the airport where the plane had already warmed up its engine and was prepared for takeoff. On landing at their first destination, the group would hurriedly get into waiting cars that would speed them to the meeting. As soon as Hitler was finished speaking to the multitudes, it was back to the plane and the routine began again. The furious speed of the campaign tour allowed no time for relaxation, and no one got to bed before midnight. Hitler made up for lost sleep by napping during the flight, but even this was not easy, as flying in the early passenger planes was anything but comfortable.

Who paid the bills for Hitler's presidential campaign? The expenses were enormous. Not everything used in the campaign was as expensive at Hitler's rented airplane, but the rented plane was a good illustration of the fact that no cost was too great if the Nazis thought it would bring them victory. The price of the paper and printing for the pamphlets, posters, and newspapers alone was a staggering sum. The rented cars, trucks, meeting halls, the travel expenses for the party propagandists, all had to be paid for by someone.

Although a vast majority of industrialists and big businessmen supported Hindenberg, there were a few exceptions who contributed to Hitler. Of those who gave to the Nazis, most tried to keep the fact of their donations secret. Publicly, they only admitted a "sympathy" for some of Hitler's ideas. For business and social reasons they remained members of their conservative parties. A typical example was Fritz Thyssen, who was still a member of Hugenberg's Nationalist party long after he had been contributing heavily to the National Socialists. In truth, many of these men did not agree with everything Hitler said and were using their donations to seek some kind of leverage over Hitler. Nevertheless, they supplied a significant portion of the money for the Nazi election campaigns.

A few weeks after the first presidential election, wealthy men who were members of the Kepler Circle, which was ostensibly formed to give Hitler advice on economic matters, came to the Kaiserhof in Berlin to meet Hitler.[30] The meeting lasted several hours, but unfortunately there is not a complete record of everything that was said. Yet, it is known that Hitler spoke at length, giving an account of the party's performance in the election and of the expenditures incurred.

From the first presidential election to the second there was a fundamental change in Hitler's campaign strategy. In the first campaign, Hitler had attacked his enemies, in the second he spoke of himself. In the first, he had spoken of the miseries in Germany—"the people in debt; the children going hungry; the unemployed young men; literally millions of them standing in line for the dole without any possible hope of a job." Now he described a brilliant future awaiting Germany when he was in power. Sometimes at his fourth mass meeting of the day, he was so hoarse that he could hardly speak, but he continued to depict a future of boundless happiness for Germany. On one occasion he went as far as to say: "In the Third Reich, every German girl will find a husband."

The climax of Hitler's second campaign for the presidency came on April 8, when a violent storm raged over Germany and all air traffic was grounded. Undoubtedly, Hitler guessed the propaganda value of keeping his engagement under such conditions. He ordered the plane to be prepared for takeoff as planned; "the masses were waiting for him in Düsseldorf." As Hitler and his staff flew through the tempest, thousands waited patiently at the racetrack in Düsseldorf. A local party speaker kept the crowd from leaving by giving them progress reports from time to time, saying that the Fuerher's plane had just been reported passing over such and such a place and was still struggling on its way. The Fuehrer was risking life and limb, flying through a terrible storm just to speak to them. When Hitler finally arrived, the thousands were still waiting and Nazi propaganda blared away that here at last was the man with the courage needed to save Germany.

The German people went to the polls to cast their votes in the second presidential election on April 10, 1932. The day was dark, cold, and rainy. A million fewer citizens took the trouble to vote in this runoff election. Late that night, the final results were announced:

Hindenburg	19,359,983	53.0%
Hitler	13,418,547	36.8
Thaelmann	3,706,759	10.2

By this brilliant campaign performance Hitler had increased his total vote by more than two million and Hindenburg had gained less than one million, but the old president was in by a clear majority. Hitler was able to capture most of the former Nationalist voters, since Duesterberg was no longer in the running. The Kaiser's eldest son, Crown Prince Friedrich Wilhelm, who had quietly voted for Düesterburg in the first election, then broke with Hindenburg publicly by making a statement to the press: "Since I regard it as absolutely necessary for the national front to close its ranks, I shall vote for Adolf Hitler."

However, it was not only the Nationalists who were going over to the Nazi camp, for Thaelmann's vote fell by over a million since the first election. Those had had voted Communist in the first election out of desperation were perfectly willing to shift their support to anyone who might provide a change. In his diary, Goebbels wrote: "To our great satisfaction, we can affirm that our numbers have everywhere increased. We come far short of defeating the enemy, but have managed to rope in nearly all the votes of the conservative parties. Thaelmann had failed miserably. His defeat is our greatest success." Then, thinking of the Prussian state elections, which were little more than a week away, he said:

"The Prussian campaign is prepared. We go on without breathing space."[31]

While the party was once again launching itself on a furious election campaign, Hitler and the other leaders of the movement had much to ponder. In spite of its impressiveness, how was Hitler's electoral success to be turned to political advantage when a majority still eluded him? Strasser thought that the party should make a deal with the government. He argued that Hitler's refusal to compromise was destroying the very success of the "policy of legality." Although Hitler distrusted Strasser and was not yet ready to enter a coalition government, he did not dismiss the idea completely. Still, there were others who felt that the whole policy of legality should be scrapped.

After talking with the commanders of the S.A., the Brownshirt storm troopers, and the S.S., the elite black uniformed bodyguard units, Goebbels noted in his diary: "Deep uneasiness is rife everywhere. The notion of an uprising haunts the air." Again, on April 2, he wrote: "The S.A. getting impatient. It is understandable enough that the soldiers begin to lose morale through these long-drawn-out political contests. It has to be stopped, though, at all costs. A premature putsch . . . would nullify the whole of our future."[32] But before Hitler could make up his mind how to respond to Strasser's criticisms or the impatience of the S.A., the government struck.

When the government of Prussia declared that police raids on the homes of various important Nazis furnished evidence that they were preparing for a putsch, Chancellor Bruening thought that his moment for a decisive move against Hitler had come. Three days after the second election, under pressure from the Social Democrats and trade unions, General Groener, as minister of interior, declared that the S.A., S.S., and Hitler Youth were banned throughout Germany. There was some difficulty in getting Hindenburg to sign the decree because General von Schleicher, chief of the army's political office, who had approved of it at first, began to whisper objections to the old man. But President von Hindenburg yielded and signed the decree, which officially dissolved the uniformed Nazi units because they "formed a private army whose very existence constitutes a state within the State."[33]

At last the government had taken a decisive measure against the Nazis. This was a stunning blow to Roehm and the S.A. leaders. They urged resistance to the order; after all, the S.A. had 400,000 men under its command, four times the size of the German Army, which the Versailles Treaty had limited to 100,000 soldiers. But Hitler, sensing that this was no time for a rebellion, demanded the ban be obeyed. Overnight the Brownshirts disappeared from the streets, but the organization of the S.A. remained intact. The S.A. went underground; its men now appeared as ordinary party members. Roehm had little to fear, for only weak organizations are destroyed by attempted suppression. Fully confident, Hitler declared Bruening and Groener would get their answer in the coming Prussian elections. He had received information there was a growing division within the government itself. On April 14, the day the ban was enacted, Goebbels noted in his diary: "We are informed that Schleicher does not agree with his [Groener's] action." And a few hours later that day: "Phone call from a well-known lady friend of General Schleicher's; [She says] the General wants to resign."[34]

In addition to winning elections, Hitler would have to concentrate on intrigues with other parties and be willing to make compromises and alliances, for his principal objective now was to bring about the dismissal of Bruening and Groener at any cost before they took further action against him.

10

BIG BUSINESS ATTEMPTS TO STOP HITLER

It took the German government a long time to take any decisive measures against the Nazis. Finally in April of 1932, things got so bad that Chancellor Bruening banned the S.A. and the S.S. In the meantime, however, a few of the more courageous industrialists had taken steps on their own to break the strength of the Nazi party. Since their weapon was money, their strategy would necessarily have to be covert.

Once a large segment of the people begin to look upon a revolutionary political movement as the source of their deliverance, it is very difficult to stop that movement by direct suppression; its momentum is simply too great. However, this does not mean that the established order is simply to give up. Any rapidly growing revolutionary party is subject to schism. In the case of the Nazis, with the monolithic leadership of Hitler, they were less vulnerable to this weakness but not completely immune. Between 1930 and 1932, there was a certain amount of internal friction with the Nazi party.

A prominent industrialist, Paul Silverberg, decided to disrupt the Nazi party by financing Hitler's rival, Gregor Strasser. Silverberg was born on May 6, 1876, in Bedburg, a small town in the Rhineland. On both sides of his family, Silverberg's ancestors were Jewish businessmen. His father, Adolf, founded a wool factory and the linoleum industry in Bedburg. Later, he also became head of the Fortuna lignite mining and briquet manufacturing company.

Paul and his two sisters were raised as Protestants. He attended school in Bedburg and Koblenz, after which he went to the University of Munich and Bonn to study law. In a short time, he graduated with a doctorate of law and in 1903 set up a law practice in Cologne. In September of that year, his father died. Following the previously expressed wishes of Adolf Silverberg, the board of directors of the Fortuna Company selected his twenty-seven-year-old son as the new president of the company. Within a few years, he became head of the Rheinish Coal Mining and Briquet Manufacturing Company, which grew to be one of the largest coal companies in the world.[1]

Because Paul Silverberg was concerned about the prosperity of the German industrial community, he naturally took a great interest in the nation's political activities and problems. During the inflation, he came to the realization that the multiparty system of the Weimar Republic was not working in the difficult conditions that existed in Germany after World War I. He decided that other ways would have to be found to overcome the economic problems, the class hostility, and the restrictions of the Versailles Treaty. One possible approach to strengthening the government would be a chancellor ruling by presidential decree. But Silverberg saw no easy solutions to the problems facing German industry and Germany as a whole.

After the victory of the Nazis in the July 1932 Reichstag elections, Silverberg began an attempt of his own to subvert the Nazi party. Because of his Jewish background, he thought it wise to use a go-between, Werner von Alvensleben, the secretary of the Berlin Herrenklub, an exclusive conservative gentleman's club. Through Alvensleben, he had established contact with Gregor Strasser, who was then known to be Hitler's principal rival for leadership within the party. In 1932, Silverberg secretly gave financial assistance to Strasser through several intermediaries.[2]

Whether Strasser was actually cooperating with Silverberg or simply taking the industrialist's money and deceiving him, it is difficult to say.[3] Nor is it certain whether Silverberg hoped to split the Nazi party by financing Gregor Strasser, or if he actually thought Strasser was a reasonable man with whom it would be possible to compromise.

More of an idealist and socialist than Hitler, Strasser was regarded as the leader of the Nazi left wing. To the Nazis in northern Germany, he was almost more popular than Hitler between 1925 and 1929. Strasser wanted to attract the industrial workers with policies advocating the eight-hour day, nationalization of corporate property, and the breakup of the large agricultural estates. Without this sort of socialist program, he was afraid that the workers would turn to communism instead of nazism. At the Bamberg Conference on February 14, 1926, Hitler had severely reprimanded the Nazi left-wingers for their pro-Russian attitude and their advocacy of the expropriation of the German princes. Even though they were disappointed, Strasser and the "socialist" Nazis acquiesced to Hitler.

By the spring of 1926, the ideological split in the party had healed over, and the Nazis seemed strongly united. After recovering from injuries incurred in a serious automobile accident, Strasser was given a more powerful position to bring about organizational reform in the party. In 1928, Hitler made him the head of the party's administration. Utilizing his organizational abilities, Strasser set to work tightening the administrative structure of the party through centralization, standardization, and bureaucratic efficiency. At the end of 1932, Strasser headed a staff of ninety-five managerial and clerical employees, spread over fifty-four separate rooms in the Brown House.[4]

Strasser hoped that with his administrative reforms, the Nazis would be able to enter into a governmental coalition and gradually neutralize any opposition groups by taking them over from within. This strategy of sneaking to power through the back door had good chances of succeeding. But its main disadvantage was the length of time that it required. The S.A. were restless and would be difficult to keep under control if Hitler did not come to power soon. By the time Strasser's plan would have been achieved, Hitler was afraid the S.A. would be disillusioned and lose their morale.

Of course, Silverberg did not want to see Strasser realize his plan, but he thought there would be more opportunity to compromise with someone willing to enter a coalition government than with someone like Hitler, who was demanding the chancellorship for himself. This opinion was shared by other business interests who subsidized the National Socialists in order to exercise an influence over the party and strengthen the "sensible" and "moderate" elements within its leadership.

According to August Heinrichsbauer, a well-known public relations man for German heavy industry and an intermediary between the National Socialists and some leading executives of the coal industry, a monthly subsidy of 10,000 marks (about $2,400) was entrusted to Gregor Strasser in the spring of 1931 for the use of the Nazi party. This money was collected from some of the directors of individual coal mining firms and some mine owners. "In making these payments," Heinrichsbauer explained, "[it was] reasoned that contact must be established and maintained continuously with the [Nazi] Party and that steady subsidies seemed to be the best way to accomplish this. . . . After it became evident that there was little possibility of limiting the influence of National Socialism from the outside, there remained no other course than continuing the effort to contain the movement within the proper bounds by influencing it from within."[5]

Some coal mine owners also contributed about 3,000

marks monthly to Walther Funk for his National Socialist economic news service. For the 1931 Reichstag election Hitler was given 100,000 marks (about $24,000) by several coal companies, but this amount, Heinrichsbauer insisted, was considerably lower than what was contributed to the other nonsocialist parties. Some money went to the local Nazi headquarters in Essen. But such donations were made only by local mine operators and probably did not exceed 5,000 marks for the two years 1931 and 1932. "The money given by individuals in the coal industry about which I have knowledge," Heinrichsbauer concluded, "for the years 1930 to 1932, was not in excess of—I estimate—a total of 600,000 marks (about $144,000). This included the payments made to Strasser and Funk."*

Many mine owners saw the National Socialist movement as a powerful counterbalance to communism, which they considered to be "an acute danger" during the depression. In Gregor Strasser they believed they had found a man who would be willing to work in cooperation with other parties and, if necessary, able to split the Nazi party itself. The coal industry, Heinrichsbauer insisted, never wanted a one-party dictatorship. Like some coal men, said Heinrichsbauer, the industrialist Otto Wolff also subsidized Strasser in 1932 at the request of Wolff's friend, General Kurt von Schleicher, who hoped to make Strasser more independent of Hitler.

Considering the backing Strasser was receiving from moderate industrialists like Silverberg, would he be able to oust Hitler from his position as party leader? The amounts stated in the existing evidence of contributions to Strasser are not that substantial, but only a faction of the donations may have been uncovered so far. Yet even if Strasser was receiving ten times the amount now known and bringing in as

---

* It seems that this money was not given by any official organization of the coal industry, but was gathered as voluntary contributions of individuals in the coal business. Certainly there were many mine owners who did not participate.

much from big business as Hitler, the party treasury would still not have been dependent on him because the primary source of party revenue was not big business.

The increasing indebtedness of the National Socialist party, which must have risen to around ninety million marks by 1933, could not possibly have been met by the contributions from big business alone. Even the highest figures mentioned for donations and subsidies from major German industrial interests remain far behind the party's expenditures. However, it should be emphasized again that the term "big business" does not describe the German business community as a whole. In the early 1930s there were thousands of small industrial concerns operating in Germany. Their importance can quickly be seen from the fact that they employed over half of the nation's industrial workers.

There is evidence that Hitler received considerable support from small and medium-size companies.[6] Many of these smaller firms were in serious financial difficulties as a result of the depression. Unlike the big companies and cartels, such as the steel interests, which repeatedly received financial assistance from the Reich government, the owners of small factories and businesses knew they could hope for no such government aid when they faced bankruptcy. Feeling that the Weimar government was insensitive to their plight, and that they were being squeezed by giant competitors from above and organized Marxist labor from below, many desperate small industrialists and businessmen turned to Hitler as their savior.[7]

One talent of Hitler's that has rarely been discussed was his unusual ability to raise money in small amounts from the general public, much like discount stores that profit from a large volume of small sales.[8] He was a clever money-maker who lost no opportunity to convert the enthusiasm he had whipped up into a flow of cash. Hitler believed that the true test of his followers' political convictions was their willingness to pay their own way.[9] In the Nazi party there was a price tag on everything—admission fees to meetings, membership dues, pamphlets, books, newspapers, flags, uniforms, and insignias of rank. By the early 1930s, the quartermaster department of the S.A. had itself become a big business, selling clothing, equipment, and even insurance to thousands of men.[10]

The Nazi gauleiter of Hamburg, Dr. Albert Krebs, said the financial affairs of the National Socialist party were conducted on a completely different basis than those of the other nonsocialist parties, which were absolutely dependent on large subsidies from big business. "One must not use the experiences of the middle-class parties," said Krebs, "as a standard of comparison for a party with regularly collected dues and systematically gathered contributions, not to mention several sound businesses [the publishing houses, insurance firms, quartermaster's stores]. All this provided a financial understructure that would assure continued freedom of movement even if individual contributions from industrial and financial circles became more meager."[11]

The necessity of financing their own work meant a real sacrifice for many Nazi party members. The workers of the established bourgeois parties in contrast were always well paid and were really active only during elections. On the individual level, there was a tremendous amount of dedication and fervor as many ordinary Nazis sacrificed both their time and money day after day. One Nazi industrial worker later wrote: "Both as an S.A. man and a cell leader, I was constantly on the go. We all had several jobs to take care of. And everything cost money—books, newspapers, uniforms, propaganda trips, and propaganda material. So it happened that many of us frequently went hungry." The amount that party members paid for party activities was dependent on how sincere were their beliefs about National Socialism. The S.S., for example, were required to buy a much more expensive uniform than the S.A. In addition to all this, there were continual collections for every conceivable party cause from election contributions to aid for unemployed S.A. men.

For the Nazi party, money management became a very important basis for evaluating the success of particular GAUs and local groups. Each GAU was to adopt business-like accounting procedures and the finances of the GAU were put into the hands of a full-time salaried business manager who was accountable less to the gauleiter than to party treasurer Schwarz's offices in Munich. The fact that an admission fee was charged for all Nazi public meetings was an incentive to local leaders to insure that their meetings were organized efficiently and with adequate advance propaganda. Thus, by keeping strict watch on money matters, the financial situation of the party gradually improved as its strength increased.

Yet with the numerous election campaigns in the early 1930s, the Nazi party treasury remained continuously short of funds. In 1932, many new members of the party received the following sort of notice from their local branch: "Dear Comrade, you now belong to the NSDAP [Nationalist Socialist party] and realize that this membership brings with it duties. Since we wish to save the German people, we must demand from every individual member that he take on some job. You can choose one and send your declaration of agreement by return. You can be: (1) an S.A. man or S.A. reserve man; (2) an S.S. man; (3) in the women's department; (4) a political functionary; or (5) take on special duties." One of the special duties was "to donate ten marks a month to Party funds."[12] In other words, ten marks a month was the cost of maintaining one S.A. man.

Occasionally a local Nazi unit was lucky enough to have one or two generous benefactors in their area. "I was the big financier of the movement in our town," recalled a shop owner from central Germany who had been a thirty-year-old reserve officer during World War I.

Of course, during the depression my business wasn't doing very good either, but I had received a tidy little inheritance from an uncle who had gone to America.

When the Party was first founded here we had only sixteen members. I paid to have some leaflets printed about the Jewish Stock Exchange swindle and our men handed them out at the meetings of the conservative parties; we weren't yet strong enough to hold our own meetings. For the next few years, I personally paid for most of the expenses of our unit. Later on the burden became too great, but I continued to pay for more than my share.

Things were really bad for our local Party group in the 1930s. We were always short of money. Almost half of the S.A. men were unemployed or working only part-time. Whenever our S.A. troop needed transportation to meetings in nearby towns or to the Party rally in Nuremberg each year the group leader always came to me for help. . . .

I kept my membership in the Party secret until about 1931, because some of the men I had to do business with were Jews. The local Marxists always carried on with a lot of silly drivel about the Nazis being financed by Krupp and the big industrialists; little did they know that it was my money that paid the bills.[13]

Since party members with money to spare were usually few and far between and the majority of Nazis were either poor or unemployed, it is amazing that frequent collections yielded substantial sums. Nevertheless, passing the hat in the dingy back rooms of beer halls was the main source of income for the local group. The two key factors in producing donations seems to have been the ability of Nazi speakers to stir up a "revivalist" atmosphere and the patriotic dedication of the audience.

These two factors are well illustrated by the account a young man gave after attending his first party meeting:

At the end of his speech the leader made an appeal for contributions, since this movement, unlike the rest, did not have the support of Jewish moneylenders. To this end two tables were placed near the exit, where all who wished could leave their contributions. As I stepped up to the table to give my modest bit, I saw to my amazement that there were only bills on the plate. Somewhat taken aback, I lit a cigarette and stood aside, as I had no more than three marks in my possession. Thereupon a white-haired lady came up to me, saying, "Young man, if you smoked one less cigarette each day and gave five pfennigs to the cause, you would be doing a good deed." I never knew the exact amount of my contribution, I only know that I left the place with a sense of humility, and the knowledge that the woman was a true National Socialist.[14]

Aware that Hitler's ability to seduce the masses earned not only millions of votes for him, but also, when every pfennig was counted, great sums of money, the economist Peter Drucker observed as early as 1939: "The really decisive backing came from sections of the lower middle classes, the farmers, and working class, who were hardest hit. . . . As far as the Nazi Party is concerned there is good reason to believe that at least three-quarters of its funds, even after 1930, came from the weekly dues . . . and from the entrance fees to the mass meetings from which members of the upper classes were always conspicuously absent."[15]

Once the presidential elections were over, the Nazi propaganda machine immediately switched its focus to the state elections. On April 24, 1932, almost four-fifths of the total German population would go to the polls in Prussia, Bavaria, Hamburg, Wuerttemberg, and Anhalt. Hitler began a second series of highly publicized flights over Germany. Altogether, he spoke in twenty-six cities between April 15 and 23, but the main effort of his campaign was concentrated in Prussia. By far the largest of the German states, Prussia embraced almost two-thirds of the territory of the Reich and had a population of forty million, which was more than half the total German population of sixty-five million. Since 1918 the Prussian Diet and state government had been ruled by a coalition of Social Democrats and the

Center party. Thus, for the National Socialists a victory in the Prussian elections would be almost as important as winning a majority in the Reichstag.

Hitler's campaign throughout Prussia was well received but nowhere were the masses so enthusiastic as in East Prussia. Patriotism ran especially high in this region because it was cut off from the rest of Germany by the "Polish Corridor." The threat of a Russian or Polish invasion had been a daily fear here for hundreds of years. The soil of East Prussia was poor, and the depression was particularly harsh in this already impoverished land. On his campaign tour, Hitler flew to Koenigsberg, the largest city of East Prussia, and from there went by car to the land of the Masurian Lakes, where the famous battle of Tennenberg had been fought in World War I. Even Dr. Otto Dietrich, Hitler's press chief, was somewhat amazed at the overwhelming reception they received from the people. Dietrich said:

> On our journeys through the Reich, despite all the sympathy and devotion to our cause, we had always been conscious of the inner opposition of compatriots incited against us, we had seen clenched fists and scowling faces amongst the many cheering hands. But here, in the Masurian border-districts, Adolf Hitler had the vast majority behind him, already at the time of the first Reich presidential election. But on this journey it seemed as if the whole land of Masuria was faithful to the Hooked Cross [swastika].
>
> Here the nation's poorest children were the most true of all. Hitler flags lined all the roads, pictures of Hitler decorated all the houses, and garlands draped the entrance to every village; hope and loyalty were prevalent everywhere!
>
> Wherever our Fuehrer approached, every man and woman came out. Crowds lined all the streets. Aged grandmothers, on whose distressed faces the direst poverty was written, raised their arms in greeting. Wherever

we stopped, the women stretched out their children toward our Fuehrer. There were tears of joy and emotion.[16]

In summing up his comment on Hitler's East Prussian election tour, Dietrich admitted a fact of the utmost importance: "In Germany wherever economic and moral distress was greatest, wherever things seemed most intolerable, there, confidence in our Fuehrer was the strongest and gripped all the people."[17]

Election day in Prussia witnessed another Nazi landslide. The National Socialists became by far the strongest single party in the Prussian Diet, where their representatives leaped from 6 to 162 deputies. The long-dominating coalition of Social Democrats and Center party lost its majority, and governing the state without Nazi cooperation became an impossibility. Yet once again, the Nazis themselves were not able to make up a majority. They were furious, however, when Bruening allowed the socialist ministers Braun and Severing to remain in office without a majority. As one Nazi said: "Bruening's Center party thus cheated the Nazis of their legal reward for a legal fight. The bill would be presented to them later."[18]

April 24, the day of the National Socialist victory in Prussia, also saw their party become the largest in Wuerttemberg, Hamburg, and Anhalt. In Bavaria, the Nazis received 32.5 percent of the vote and were now as strong as the Bavarian People's party. But everywhere they were still short of a majority. For the moment, the deadlock continued, but a careful analysis of voting trends in the past three elections revealed that Hitler and his party had shattered all traditional voting patterns and were still on the rise. The once strong German Nationalist party had now lost over half of its supporters to the Nazis. The middle class was going over to Hitler in record numbers, and of course his support from the unemployed and impoverished continued to grow as this tragic group itself increased in size. The National Socialists were even beginning to make some headway among the workers, but by and large, Hitler's success in winning supporters from the ranks of the socialists and Communists remained minimal.

In June of 1932, after Hitler's victory in the Prussian elections, Hjalmar Schacht, the former president of the Reichsbank, began an attempt to establish a link between big business and the National Socialist party. Why was a prominent banker like Schacht interested in working with the Nazis? Schacht was known to have many Jewish friends in high banking circles and was generally thought of as an advocate of liberal democracy.[19] A study of his background, however, reveals that he was always an ambitious loner and something of a maverick.

Hjalmar Schacht came from a middle-class family of Schleswig-Holstein. His father had immigrated to America in the late 1870s and became an American citizen. Schacht's mother, who was a baroness by birth, soon followed. But Germany, after the victory over France in 1871, seemed more promising for a young businessman than America, so after six years, the Schachts returned to the Reich. They raised three sons, one of whom, born on January 22, 1877, was named Horace Greeley Hjalmar Schacht in honor of an American his father greatly admired.

The young Schacht had many talents and interests. After receiving his secondary education in Hamburg, he first studied medicine in Kiel, then German philology in Berlin and political science in Munich, before receiving his degree at the University of Berlin in economics. As he himself said, his interest was more practical than theoretical. With his formidable intellect and his quick grasp of the essence of monetary problems, he rose rapidly in the world of banking. At the age of thirty-nine, after a brilliant career at the Dresdener Bank, he was appointed a director of the National Bank.

During World War I, Schacht worked in the economic section of the German administration in Belgium. His job was to obtain as high a Belgian contribution to Germany's war production as possible. Germany's defeat in 1918 left him bewildered. The disorders in the streets, revolution and violence were an unpleasant shock to his orderly and logical mind. Schacht, however, always considered himself a "democrat," and after the war he helped found the German Democratic party, although he continued to think of himself as a monarchist at the same time.

Although not a fanatic, Schacht was a patriot and fervent German nationalist. He was incensed by the French attempts after World War I to divide Germany, their invasion of the Ruhr, and their demand for reparation payments that could not possibly be made. Schacht immediately pointed out that the amount demanded for reparations was twelve times the six billion gold francs Germany had obtained from France in 1871. With his self-confidence and intellectual vanity, Schacht did not easily tolerate the arrogance of the many Allied officials with whom he came in contact after World War I. On one occasion he abruptly left the office of the French foreign minister because he was kept waiting twenty minutes. He had to be brought back by a panting secretary who ran after him and promised an immediate audience.

Schacht became president of the Reichsbank in 1923 at the age of forty-six and was primarily responsible for devising the method of stopping the runaway inflation by a new currency backed with foreign loans. Schacht later became disillusioned with the Weimar government's acquiescence to the demands of the Allies and resigned his post at the Reichsbank. After the sudden success of the Nazis in the 1930 Reichstag elections, Schacht began to take an interest in Hitler.

On board a ship going to the United States for a speaking tour, Schacht read *Mein Kampf* and the Nazi party program.[20] In his first major speech in New York to the German American Commerce Association, Schacht said that if Germany were allowed to enter into world trade she could pay reparations, but that would demand international cooperation.

It was the realization by the lower classes that they had to bear the burden of the reparations that caused the rise of fascism. He concluded by claiming that the Nazi landslide in the September election had been an indictment of the Versailles Treaty. At another speech, in New York, before an audience of important businessmen, he said: "I am no National Socialist but the basic ideas of National Socialism contain a good deal of truth."

Schacht's first personal contact with the Nazis came shortly after his return from the United States. At the invitation of one of his old friends, bank director von Strauss, he attended a dinner where he met Hermann Goering. During the next few months Schacht carefully studied the political situation in Germany, conferring with various men in banking and industry. Then in February of 1931, he went to see Chancellor Bruening to explain that since the National Socialists had 107 seats in the Reichstag and were the second largest party, they should be taken into the coalition government. He argued that responsibility would tame the Nazis and that their mass following would be very useful if harnessed, but if they were left out of the government they would probably come to power on their own. Many other influential people agreed with Schacht's thinking. The British ambassador reported that Reichsbank president Luther said the Nazis would quit their nonsense if given real responsibility. The ambassador went on to say that this view was "shared by a number of people with whom I and my staff come into contact."[21] Bruening refused Schacht's appeal to take the National Socialists into the coalition. Schacht said it was a simple choice: either the Nazis or the Communists would ultimately enter the government.

Schacht was still formally a non-Nazi, but he was now ready to use his influence to raise money for the party. He traveled frequently in Germany and abroad to talk, as he said, to "leading circles" in Copenhagen, Bern, and Stockholm to explain the need for ending reparations and describe Hitler's nationalist movement. Although Bruening still called on him for financial advice during the deepening depression, Schacht's talents were increasingly placed at Hitler's disposal. He undoubtedly hoped to influence Hitler in the direction of conservative economic policies.

Like Walther Funk, another one of Hitler's economic advisers, Schacht wanted to save as much of a free market as was salvageable. He believed the government should take a variety of progressive but conservative economic measures: rearm within prudent economic limits but keep out of war at all costs, restore employment through useful public works, put an end to strikes, and crush the threat of communism. Schacht's endorsement of Hitler undoubtedly helped the party to tap sources of money that hitherto had been afraid of its economic "radicalism."[22] Schacht's most important fund-raising projects for Hitler, however, were yet to come.

As the year of 1932 progressed, the German economy showed no signs of improvement. In contrast, the financial situation of the Nazi party was good.[23] Since the beginning of the year, many small businesses that were dependent on Nazi customers were contributing to the party. In Hanover, for example, one of the largest cafés and several other businesses were all giving regularly to the S.A.[24]

With Hitler now commanding more popular support than all the moderate nonsocialist parties put together, Chancellor Bruening was in a desperate situation. The only possible way out for the government seemed to be to move to the left and nationalize the bankrupt East Prussian estates that were a continuous drain on the budget. This course of action was undoubtedly sanctioned by the spokesmen of light industry who, as early as the fall of 1930, had been shocked by the Hitler landslide and had urged Bruening to take some Social Democrats into his government.[25]

If tariff protection and subsidies continued to be given to Junker agricultural interests, it might mean the doom of German industry as a whole. Light industry in particular was suffering from the protection the government was extending to nonprofitable agrarian enterprises. It was now a life-and-death struggle between various sectors of the economy. Heavy industry, light industry, agriculture, banking, commerce, and labor were each thinking only of defending their own position and forcing the burden of the depression onto the others. But one thing was certain: all could not survive; someone would have to be sacrificed.

Bruening and his allies underestimated the strength of the agrarian reactionaries. Greatly perturbed by the government land reform program, the landowners struck back at once. They overwhelmed Hindenburg with furious protests. The old president had been briefly informed of the plan but had not grasped its significance until the complaints aroused his attention. On his visit to East Prussia he was shocked to hear the plan denounced as an attempt to socialize German agriculture and confiscate from some of Prussia's oldest families land that had been theirs for centuries. His old friend Baron von Gayl warned him that such expropriations might undermine the will of the East Prussian upper class to defend their country against foreign attack, and this, he added, was a serious worry to the high command of the Reichswehr.

These warnings were part of a renewed reactionary effort to convince Hindenburg that Bruening's dismissal must be delayed no longer. "The whole thing will lead to a dictatorship, which we shall claim of course for a man of the right," Hindenburg's ultrareactionary friend, Oldenburg-Januschau, predicted confidently. The protests also worried Oskar von Hindenburg, who had accompanied his father to the family estate of Neudeck in East Prussia. Oskar was especially disturbed by the accusation that the Bruening government was promoting socialism, because he feared that the charge might reflect on him and his father. In addition, General von Schleicher was in constant communication with him and kept him informed on the army's growing uneasiness and the insistence of the eastern front commanders that for purely military reasons a firm understanding should be reached with Hitler and the S.A. On visits to neighboring estates and nearby garrisons, Oskar von Hindenburg encountered nothing but bitter opposition against Bruening's handling of the country's political and economic problems.

In the beginning the heavy industrialists had no fundamental objection to Bruening insofar as his economic philosophy or program were concerned, for he was basically conservative.[26] Although heavy industry was generally opposed to any socialistic measures, they had no sympathy for Junker agricultural interests, which they had always seen as an expensive liability and an obstruction to sound tariff policies; so they were not about to oppose the chancellor over his plan to nationalize the bankrupt Prussian estates. However, being essentially a representative of light industry, Bruening refused to enact the harsh anti-union legislation and wage cuts heavy industry demanded. Chancellor Bruening was concerned with breaking the strength of the agrarian forces, primarily in order to minimize import quotas and tariff restrictions and thus increase international trade, which would benefit light industry.[27]

Meanwhile, the economic and political situation was becoming ever more critical, and other than the proposed nationalization of the bankrupt East Prussian estates, Bruening's policy was simply to wait until an improved international situation would bring with it a general economic upturn. The heavy industrialists themselves had no real policy other than this, with the exception of wage reductions in an attempt to minimize their losses.

During this waiting period it was absolutely necessary that the government should be in the hands of someone who could count upon the unquestioned support of the Reichswehr (army) to maintain public order. When the government's plan to nationalize the bankrupt Junker estates became known, Bruening incurred the hostility of a large percentage of the Junker-dominated Officer Corps. Schleicher informed the leading industrialists that the Reichswehr could not be counted upon to obey Bruening in case it was necessary to use armed force against the National Socialists. It was highly uncertain if the loyalty of the army officers to the civil government was still strong enough for them to oppose a putsch by a fanatically nationalist movement like the Nazis.

General von Schleicher, who was eyeing a better position for himself, decided that the time had come to move against General Groener, the minister of defense, who had been his patron for years, and Chancellor Bruening. Originally, Schleicher had been the one who had maneuvered to put Bruening in power, thinking that he would be able to gain the support of the people and unite the nation. But it was now clear that this had failed. Only Hitler had the popular support of the masses, so General von Schleicher began to lay his plans for cooperating with the Nazis.

Sometime before the presidential elections, Schleicher had renewed his contacts with Roehm, the commander of the S.A., and Count von Helldorf, the chief of the Berlin S.A. At this stage of the game, Schleicher was conspiring with Roehm behind Hitler's back to incorporate the S.A. into the army as a militia. Undoubtedly Schleicher wanted the S.A. attached to the army, where he could control it. However, after Hitler's show of strength in the presidential and state elections, he was also attracted by the idea of bringing Hitler, the only nationalist politician with any mass following, into the government, where he could control him as well.

Even before the ban against the S.A. had been enacted, General von Schleicher had voiced several objections to it. Next, he went behind the back of his commander, General Groener, to the president. He persuaded Hindenburg to write a sharp letter to Groener asking why the Reichsbanner, the paramilitary organization of the Social Democratic party, had not been suppressed along with the S.A. Schleicher stirred up more opposition in army circles against his commander by circulating rumors that General Groener was too ill to remain in office and even that he had become a convert to Marxism.

By the first week in May, Schleicher's intrigues were developing as planned. On May 4, Goebbels wrote in his diary: "Hitler's mines are beginning to explode. . . . The first to be blown up must be Groener and after him, Bruening." Four days later Goebbels reported: "The Fuehrer has an important interview with Schleicher in the presence of a few gentlemen of the president's immediate circle. All goes well . . . Bruening's fall is expected shortly. The president of the Reich will withdraw his confidence in him." He then outlines the scenario that Schleicher and the men around Hindenburg had planned with Hitler. "The Reichstag will be dissolved [and] a Presidential Cabinet constituted." The ban against the S.A. will be lifted and elections held in the near future. So that Bruening's suspicions would not be aroused to the plan, late that night Goebbels drove Hitler away to Mecklenburg. "The Fuehrer quits Berlin as secretly as he came."[28] The Nazis now knew that Bruening was on his way out. On May 18, Goebbels noted in his diary: "Bruening is being severely attacked by our Press and Propaganda. Fall he must. . . . His position is becoming untenable. And the amusing part of it is that he does not seem to notice the fact. . . . His cabinet shrinks visibly and he can find no substitutes for his losses. . . . The rats flee from the sinking ship."[29]

General von Schleicher finally approached Hindenburg, and claiming to speak with the authority of the army, announced that the army no longer had confidence in Chancellor Bruening. A stronger man was needed, he said, to deal with the situation in Germany, and he already had a suitable candidate in mind: Franz von Papen. Hindenburg was not sure. Schleicher then added his winning argument: the Nazis had agreed to support the new government. Also, with Papen, the president would be assured of a ministry that would be acceptable to his friends of the Right and the army. At the same time, the Papen government would command popular support from Hitler's following. This was the elusive combination that Bruening had never been able to provide. Hindenburg was convinced. On May 29, the president summoned Bruening and abruptly asked for his resignation. The following day, the chancellor resigned.

On May 29, 1932, Hitler was in Oldenburg just wrapping up his campaign in the state elections there, which provided the National Socialists with a timely success, 48 percent of the votes and a clear majority of seats in the Diet. He had just left for Mecklenburg to begin another campaign there, when the news came through that Bruening was out. Goebbels came from Berlin to meet Hitler and discuss the political situation with him as they drove back. There wasn't much time, for President von Hindenburg had requested to see Hitler at four o'clock. Once in Berlin, they met Goering, who then accompanied Hitler to see the president. Hindenburg confirmed the basic points of the agreement that he Nazis had worked out with General von Schleicher on May 8: a presidential cabinet of Hindenburg's choosing, the lifting of the ban against the S.A., and the dissolution of the Reichstag. The president then said that he understood that Hitler had agreed to support the new government. Was this correct? Hitler replied that it was.

On hearing that the Reichstag was to be dissolved and new elections held, Goebbels wrote in his diary: "The poll! The Poll! It's the people we want. We are entirely satisfied."[30] However, in reality political power no longer resided in the Reichstag, the voice of the people, but was now placed in the hands of eighty-five-year-old President Hindenburg and those "friends" who were able to influence him. Hitler realized this and was clever enough to adjust his methods accordingly. Schleicher, Papen, and the men around Hindenburg were all intriguing for power, but Hitler could play at this game too. After all, alliances and compromises could always be repudiated; besides, he had the one thing they needed—the support of the masses.

The new chancellor chosen by President von Hindenburg, at Schleicher's suggestion, was Franz von Papen. Everyone was amazed because Papen had no political backing whatso-

ever. He was not even a member of the Reichstag. He had
strong political ambitions, but so far had achieved nothing
more than a seat in the Prussian Diet. However, the fifty-
three-year-old Papen came from a family of the Westphalian
nobility and had important friends in the right places. He
was a former General Staff officer, a skillful horseman, and
a man of great charm. After a successful marriage to the
daughter of a wealthy Saar industrialist, he bought a large
block of shares in the Center party's newspaper, *Germania*.
Yet, he was hardly known by the public except as the former
military attaché at the German embassy in Washington who
had been expelled during the war for "complicity" in planning "sabotage" while the United States was still neutral.

Although Papen belonged to the Center party, he had
continually opposed the left-wing coalition government of
Social Democrats and Center party, which had ruled Prussia
up to the April elections of that year. Politically, von Papen
was an ultraconservative, at least on domestic policy. In contrast, his ideas on foreign policy were very progressive for
his day. He belonged to a committee for French-German
understanding and had friends among French as well as
German industrialists. Feeling that democracy was a pretentious sham, he thought a lasting peace in Europe could only
be brought about through an international leader class. He
was also one of the founders of the exclusive Herrenklub (a
Berlin gentlemen's club). It is easy to see why such a man
was not a very popular politician.

With his appointment as chancellor, the Center party expelled Papen, accusing him of treachery against Bruening,
the party's leader. But this made little difference, since President von Hindenburg had asked him to form a government
of "National Concentration" that would be above parties.
He was able to do so immediately because Schleicher had a
list of ministers for the new government ready and waiting.
Of the ten ministers, seven belonged to the nobility, two
were corporation directors, and the minister of justice, Franz
Guertner, had been Hitler's protector in Bavaria during the

1920s. At Hindenburg's insistence, General von Schleicher was forced to give up his position behind the scenes and become minister of defense.

Enjoying little support in the Reichstag, the power of Papen's "barons' cabinet" was openly based on the backing of the president and the army. Some said that Papen was a man taken seriously by neither his friends nor his enemies, and everyone knew that Schleicher had chosen him because he thought he would be a willing and easy tool. This proved to be a serious underestimation of the crafty new chancellor's ambition, tenacity, and unscrupulousness. One of the first people to take Papen seriously turned out to be President von Hindenburg, who was delighted with the background and charm of his aristocratic officer. Papen soon established a close relationship with the old field marshal such as no other chancellor ever had.

In an editorial attack against Papen's government, the Social Democratic newspaper *Vorwärts* wrote: "This little clique of feudal monarchists, come to power by backstairs methods with Hitler's support . . . now announces the class war from above."[31] Papen's first act as chancellor was to honor Schleicher's pact with Hitler. On June 4, he dissolved the Reichstag and called for new elections on July 31. All was not well, however, between the Nazis and their conservative "allies." When the lifting of the ban on the S.A. was postponed, the Nazis became suspicious, and relations between Hitler and the new government were quickly strained. Goebbels wrote in his diary on June 5: "We must disassociate ourselves at the earliest possible moment from the temporary bourgeois Cabinet."[32]

The small group of individuals who engineered the overthrow of Bruening and the formation of the Papen government could assure the industrialists that the control of the army was in their hands. When confronted by the possibility of a completely National Socialist government as an alternative to the Bruening cabinet, the Papen-Schleicher coup seemed to the industrialists as a heaven-sent means of escaping such a hard alternative. The industrialists were aware that von Papen was backed by reactionary agrarian forces, but his two redeeming assets, the loyalty of the Reichswehr and apparently the ability to gain some cooperation from the Nazis, more than made up for this. Still, the heavy industrialists had not been so enthusiastic about getting rid of Bruening that they became involved in the project. At the most, they remained neutral; their spokesmen in the political parties and the press were silent as reactionary pressures against Bruening mounted.

It is almost impossible to describe the tremendous momentum the National Socialist movement had at the time the Bruening government was toppled. Everyone seemed to be going over to the Nazis. Hitler was the most popular politician in the country and the leader of the largest political party.* By all tradition, if not by law, President von Hindenburg should have appointed Hitler chancellor. Instead, the German ruling class staked their hopes on Papen, a man supported only by the agrarian reactionaries and the army. The industrialists fully sanctioned this move to block Hitler's path to power, which would probably either materially weaken the Nazi movement or push it to the left. Up to this time the conservatives had avoided a decision that would definitely align them against the National Socialists, for if they did, the use of Hitler's movement as a counterbalance against the growth of communism would become uncertain.

If the downward movement in world economic conditions had continued at an uninterrupted pace, it is doubtful if the heavy industrialists would have agreed to the decisive measures that were taken in the summer of 1932 against Hitler's march to power. Instead, they probably would have tried to work out an agreement with the Nazis for some sort of coalition government. By June 1932, however, there could be seen the first faint signs of a temporary economic

---

* Although Hindenburg received more votes in the presidential election than Hitler, he was never a charismatic popular idol like Hitler.

upturn in the United States. The economic situation in England was also showing some indications of improvement. The German industrialists came to the conclusion that this was a sign of the turn of the cycle for Germany as well. If economic conditions improved sufficiently, the Communist danger would pass and big business would no longer have any use for the National Socialist party.

The dangers that the new Papen government faced were very real. When it refused to lift the ban against the S.A., the S.S., and the Hitler Youth, it had to prepare itself to fight on two fronts, against Hitler and against the Marxist parties.* But Papen felt certain that neither of his mutually antagonistic enemies would dare to attempt a putsch against him as long as he had the machine guns of the Reichswehr and the prestige of President von Hindenburg behind him.

Political moderates rallied in surprisingly large numbers to the Papen cabinet when they perceived that the government did not intend to turn the power over to Hitler. They concluded that the real mission of the Papen government all along had been simply to bridge over a difficult period and prevent Hitler from seizing power. Actually, this was just what the industrialists had in mind when they agreed to Bruening's dismissal.

The Papen cabinet, however, did not see itself as simply a temporary government and began to consolidate its power. Papen's refusal to lift the ban against the S.A. indicated that he had planned to double-cross Hitler all along and had simply used the Nazis to get himself to power. Whether or not the "baron's cabinet" would be able to stay in power remained to be seen, but for the moment, once again Hitler was stopped.

Afraid that the Nazis might become more belligerent, Papen finally lifted the ban against the S.A. on June 15. The Communist leader, Thaelmann, denounced the lifting of the

---

* If the ban was lifted, Hitler had agreed that the Nazis would come to Papen's aid in case of a Communist uprising.

ban as "an open provocation to murder." A state of virtual anarchy now prevailed in the streets of Germany. With the ban lifted, the Brownshirts were everywhere in evidence again and four private armies confronted each other. There were the Nazi S.A., the Communist Red Front, the Social Democratic Reichsbanner, and the Nationalist Stahlhelm. Their weapons were clubs, brass knuckles, knives, and revolvers. They ran shouting in the squares and rampaging through the towns.

The wave of political violence continued to mount. Between June 1 and July 20 there were 461 political riots in Prussia alone, in which eighty-two people were killed and over four hundred wounded. The worst fighting was between the Nazis and the Communists; of the eighty-six people killed in July 1932, thirty-eight were Nazis and thirty were Communists. The Communist Red Front was more aggressive than ever before. Dr. Goebbels's election campaign in the industrial cities of the Ruhr were given a rough reception, and Nazi speakers were frequently in need of S.A. protection. On Sunday, July 10, eighteen people were killed in street battles. The worst riot of the summer took place one week later on Sunday, July 17, at Altona, an industrial suburb of "Red" Hamburg. Under police escort the Nazis marched through the working-class neighborhoods of the town and were greeted by shots from rooftops and windows. They immediately returned fire. Nineteen people were killed and 285 wounded on that day alone.

All parties except the Nazis and the Communists demanded that the government take action to restore order. There was a good reason for this, even though the Nazis and Communists were suffering the greatest losses in men. Everywhere the people were swinging toward extremism, and the two most radical parties were reaping the political rewards. Thousands of Social Democrats flocked to the Communists and thousands of Nationalists joined the Nazis.

Papen responded to the popular demand for order by two

measures. He banned all political parades until after the July 31 elections. And he took a step that was intended not only to conciliate the Nazis but to greatly increase his own power. On July 20, he deposed the unconstitutional Prussian government and appointed himself Reich commissioner of Prussia. As an excuse Papen claimed that the Altona riot proved the Prussian government could not maintain law and order and could not be relied on to deal firmly with the Communists. Besides, the Social Democratic and Center party coalition government had remained in office without legal majority in the Diet. But the socialist Prussian ministers refused to give up without a fight, so Papen obligingly made a show of force. Martial law was proclaimed in Berlin, and the army moved in with a few armored cars and a handful of men to make the necessary arrests.

Once again, the Nazis mounted a major campaign in preparation for the July 31 Reichstag elections, the fourth election contest in Germany within five months. By this time the Nazis' propaganda machine was in top form. Hitler concentrated his propaganda on the bourgeois masses suffering from the economic crisis, on working men stricken by unemployment, farmers ruined by debt and unfavourable markets, countless intellectuals who could see no way out of their distress, and the old soldiers and adventurers whom the dissolution of the army had thrown into the streets. They had everything to gain, and nothing to lose. The promise that if the National Socialists came to power, things would change was a powerful attraction in the summer of 1932.

The German masses were driven almost to the limit of their endurance by two years of the worst economic depression in history. The unemployed, now numbering well over six million, almost a third of Germany's total labor force, swarmed the streets. And yet, the government had continually failed to make the slightest progress to relieve the nation's ills. All across the country, the young were rising in defiant protest against the wretchedness of a life that their fathers' generation seemed to have spoiled for them. Whether National Socialists or Communists, they were resolved for a change, for a new order.

The Nazis were having considerable success winning over young people of all classes and social backgrounds. Even the younger generation of the upper and upper middle class was far more favorable to National Socialism than their parents. The leader of the Hitler Youth, Baldur von Schirach, was himself from a wealthy upper-class background. Years later, when Hitler was discussing his rise to power with some associates, he said that the party had found it a very successful technique to approach industrialists through their children, who could easily be converted.[33]

The account of a conservative industrial executive seems to confirm Hitler's opinion:

> One day I discovered that my seventeen-year-old son was a Nazi. Being myself, a member of the conservative Deutschnationale Volkspartei [Nationalist party] I promptly forbade my son to associate with these revolutionaries. The boy, however, paid no attention to this prohibition, and even had the nerve—or the courage—to come home in his brown uniform. Thereupon I gave him such a beating that my wife thought I would kill him. The boy, however, reassured his mother with the words, "Even if father kills me, I shall remain true to Hitler." That was a crucial hour for me. For a long time I pondered how it was possible that my only son would be willing to let himself be killed for an idea. It struck me that there must be something about that idea, other than what I had heard about it. In all secrecy I bought myself a copy of *Mein Kampf*. Then I went to some National Socialist meetings, and I began to see the light.[34]

Completely ignoring the sentiments and demands of the youth and the lower classes, Papen behaved as if he were living in the past. The members of his cabinet believed that the only way to restore prosperity was to lower still further the costs of production. As a result, one of the basic points in the cabinet's program of "economic reconstruction" was to lower wages. Collective bargaining was abolished and employers were permitted to reduce wages unilaterally. The regular unions only protested against Papen's policy of lower wages, but the Communist and sometimes the Nazi union cells fought the wage reductions with a series of "wildcat" strikes. The leaders of the moderate Social Democratic trade unions, who had tolerated Papen's decrees, had reached the extreme limit of possible concessions. If they yielded more, they risked losing their following to the Communists.

From the Right and from the Left came the cry, "Things must be different!" In the air was a swelling spirit of revolt against the capitalist system. The Nazis were able to give expression to this spirit yet remain unhampered by the rigid doctrines and class exclusiveness of communism. In a speech before the Reichstag in May, Gregor Strasser voiced the demands of rebellious Germany seeking the right to work: "The anticapitalist yearnings which animate our people do not signify a repudiation of property acquired by personal labor and thrift. They have nothing in common with the senseless and destructive tendencies of the International. But, they are a protest against a degenerate economic system, and they demand from the State that it shall break with the demon GOLD, with the habit of thinking in export statistics and in bank discounts and shall, instead, restore a system that gives an honest reward for honest work."

The Reichstag elections were set for July 31, 1932. That summer the people saw little hope of economic recovery and increasingly turned to revolutionary solutions; the Communists might have been victorious in such a situation if they had had any strong leaders. Nevertheless, the Nazi election campaign encountered vicious hostility from the combined forces of the Communists and socialists in the industrial regions of Germany.

In his diary, Dr. Goebbels described his campaign trip through the Ruhr in mid-July, 1932, just two weeks before the nation went to the polls:

> July 12. We fight our way through the seething mob at Düsseldorf and Elberfeld. A wild trip! We had no idea that the situation would turn out to be so serious. Innocuous, we drive into Hagen quite openly, uniformed, and in an open car. The streets are swarming. Full of the mob and Communist rabble.
>
> July 13. Now we drive through the country in plain clothes only. We are continually passing groups of Communists lying in ambush. It is hardly possible to get into Dortmund. We have to travel by secondary roads so as not to fall into the hands of the "Reds" who have blocked all principal thoroughfares.
>
> July 14. A drive through the Ruhr involves mortal peril. . . . We take a strange car, as our Berlin number is already known and noted everywhere.
>
> July 15. In front of the hotel the "Red" mob is howling. The police refuse to intervene as they do not consider it their duty to protect politicians in opposition to the government . . . I have to clear out of my native town like a criminal. Sworn at and insulted, spat at and showered with stones[35]

Hitler again took to the skies for a third "Flight over Germany," during which he spoke in nearly fifty different cities and towns in the last two weeks of July. Typical of Hitler's many mass meetings during the election campaign was one that took place at a small village in Brandenburg. Several hours before Hitler arrived, all the roads within miles of the village became crowded with cars, wagons, and thousands of people on foot, all headed in the same direction. A large meadow outside the village had been marked off with banners, and a high platform at one end was draped with a huge, flaming swastika flag. Below the platform, in the bright summer sun, stood hundreds of uniformed storm troopers (S.A.) ranked in solid squares. Two bands played while the audience, with many women and children among them, filed into the rough wooden benches. Those who could not find seats stood up, row after row, around the field.

The first speaker, a Nazi Reichstag deputy, addressed the crowd. While he was speaking an airplane zoomed over the field; every head turned to follow its descent. As soon as it landed, Hitler emerged and hurried to the platform. He was greeted by what one witness called "the loudest cheer I had ever heard in my life." Sixty thousand arms were lifted in the Nazi salute and sixty thousand peasant faces bright with expectation looked toward the man in a simple brown shirt now standing alone on the platform. Though hoarse already, Hitler spoke "with furious power." The crowd roared its approval whenever he paused. At last, at the psychological moment, he concluded and stepped down, leaving the entire audience suspended on the oratorical heights to which he had lifted them. He had no time to wait for the applause to die away, for that same afternoon he was scheduled to speak in Potsdam, and that night in Berlin. As he walked quickly toward the plane, he stopped only long enough to pat the head of a small child who handed him flowers, and shake hands with an old party comrade he recognized. The cheers and applause did not cease until the plane had taken off and was out of sight.

Without even counting the spectacular mass meetings, the Nazi campaign was being conducted on an impressive scale. In the streets of Berlin swastika flags were in evidence everywhere. Huge posters and Nazi slogans screamed from windows and kiosks, blazoning forth messages about duty and honor, national solidarity, social justice, bread, liberty, and the virtue of sacrifice. Passers-by wore little swastika lapel pins and uniformed S.A. men elbowed their way through the crowds. On every newsstand, copies of the *Völkischer Beobachter* and *Der Angriff* (the Berlin Nazi newspaper) were piled high. Munich remained the organizational center of the party, as it had been from the beginning, but the heavy political barrage was now being directed from under the shadow of the Riechstag itself. In Berlin, Hitler was waging a hand-to-hand battle with the leaders of the "system." Everything was keyed to the highest pitch. The whole city bore evidence of the intensity of the struggle and showed how close Hitler was to victory.

A great evening rally at Grunewald Stadium in Berlin was to wind up the entire election campaign. Detailed preparations had been made by Dr. Goebbels, for unlike the Brandenburg rally, this was no rural fair for peasants and villagers, but an event that had to make sophisticated Berlin open its eyes in amazement. Several hours before the meeting began, the approaches to the stadium were jammed with throngs of people. As those inside took their seats, the light of the long July day still lingered above the open amphitheater. By the time night began to steal over the field, more than a hundred thousand people had paid to squeeze inside, while another hundred thousand people had packed a nearby racetrack where loudspeakers had been set up to carry Hitler's words. Meanwhile, at home, millions were waiting at the radio, open to the Nazis for the first time in this campaign. The stage setting inside the stadium was flawless. Around the entire perimeter of the vast stone arena, flags and giant banners were silhouetted against the darkening sky.

Here in this vast bowl, so carefully arranged for the occasion, the intensity of the long election campaign was brought to a focus. Yet not everyone in the audience was friendly to the Nazis. In the boxes one could see tight little groups of men, obviously political observers or industrialists and business leaders who had come here only to watch and corroborate the deep mistrust and fear that Hitler still inspired. It was interesting to observe, said a Nazi member of the audience, how the expressions of these hard-boiled individuals became softer as the rally progressed; some even showed undisguised emotion.

Suddenly a wave surged over the crowd; everyone leaned forward, the word was passed from man to man: "Hitler is coming! Hitler is here!" A blare of trumpets sounded through the air, and a hundred thousand people leaped to their feet in tense expectancy. All eyes were turned toward the platform, awaiting the approach of the Fuehrer. There was a low rumble of excitement, and then releasing its pent-up emotion, the audience burst into a tremendous ovation, the "Heils" swelling up until they were like the roar of a mighty cataract.

Hitler stepped through a passageway and walked to the speaker's stand. He stood there alone, bathed in light, in his brown shirt, briskly saluting. When the tumult, like a thunderstorm receding, had finally subsided, the firm sound of his voice came over the loudspeakers and microphones into the falling darkness of night. In this vibrant atmosphere, the crowd of a hundred thousand had but one mind. "I felt," said one witness, ". . . the invisible lines of force which radiated from Hitler. To be within the sound of his voice, as I was clearly aware . . . watching the response from the masses, was like being within the field of a powerful magnet. Whether one was repelled or attracted, one was electrified."[36]

When Hitler finished speaking there was a roar of cheers that continued and even grew louder until the dozen S.A. bands struck up "Deutschland über Alles."

This great rally was the Nazis' last effort before the voting. From the confident mood of the crowd pouring out of the stadium, it was obvious Hitler's followers were optimistic they would do well in the elections, indeed many were expecting a landslide. One man in the crowd reflected on how far Hitler and the party had come in the last ten years. "In the early days," he said, "the Nazis had to struggle to find the money for paste to put up a few posters, and now, they could afford to put on such a show."

Despite the successive election campaigns the party had been engaged in since the beginning of the year, the Nazis were not terribly short of funds at the time of the July Reichstag elections. Hitler credited this accomplishment principally to party treasurer Schwarz, who, he said, was "so skilled in the management of the revenues of the Party derived from subscriptions, collections, and the like, that our movement was able to launch the decisive campaign of 1932 from its own financial resources."[37]

The Nazis may have been able to "launch" the campaign from their own resources, but the enormous expenses soon far exceeded the party funds. Even the special election contributions did little to help meet campaign expenses.

The party's creditors, printers, suppliers of paper, agencies that rented cars and trucks, etc., were all threatening to discontinue their services in the middle of the election unless they were paid immediately. Various wealthy bankers and industrialists who were sympathetic to National Socialism were willing to help underwrite election costs, but they demanded some guarantee for the repayment of their money. Hitler met with the party's outstanding creditors, and the prospective financiers. Agreements were reached. Later Hitler said: "My most tragic moment was in 1932, when I had to sign all sorts of contracts in order to finance our electoral campaign. I signed these contracts in the name of the Party, but all the time with the feeling that, if we did not win, all would be forever lost."[38]

Late on the night of July 31, the results of the elections were announced. It was a resounding victory for the National Socialist party, winning 13,745,000 votes and 230 seats in the Reichstag, more than double the support they had won in the September elections of 1930. They were now by far the largest party in Germany. Their nearest rivals, the Social Democrats, received slightly less than eight million votes. The working class was obviously swinging over to the Communists, who won 5,250,000 votes and became the third largest party. The Catholic Center party increased its strength slightly, polling 4,500,000 votes. However, the other moderate parties and even the Nationalist party were completely overwhelmed. There were 608 deputies elected to the Reichstag:

National Socialists	230
Social Democrats	133
Communists	89
Catholic Center	76
Nationalists	37
Bavarian People's party	21
All other parties	22

In the four years since 1928, Hitler had gained about thirteen million votes, an impressive victory by any standards. He had won about six million votes from the moderate middle-class parties and gained the support of most of the six million new voters. The vast increase in the Nazi poll came primarily from the impoverished middle class. About half of those who voted National Socialist in 1932 had voted for the middle-class parties in 1928. The People's party, the Democrats, and the Economic party received a combined vote of over five and a half million in 1928; in 1932, they polled less than one million. Of the six million new voters who backed the Nazis, about half were young people, most of whom were unemployed and saw the future as hopeless; the other half were people who had never bothered to vote before because they had little faith in party politics.

11
NAZI SUPPORT
DECLINES

The National Socialist party was now the largest in the Reichstag. Hitler had won his greatest election triumph, but the question remained: would he be able to translate his votes into actual power? After the July Reichstag elections, intrigue dominated the political scene in Germany. All the major political groups—the Nazis, the Social Democrats, the moderate parties, and the Communists—had so paralyzed one another that a few men representing powerful economic interest groups would be able to make history. The only official power that remained for Hitler to reckon with was President von Hindenburg. Since his reelection, Hindenburg seemed more willing than ever to govern by emergency decree. Behind the old president stood a small group of important advisers. There were Hindenburg's son, Oskar, State Secretary Meissner, General von Schleicher, Chancellor von Papen, and his "barons' cabinet."

It is a mistake to view the political intrigues of this period as the personal rivalries among "unscrupulous, ambitious" men. Some historians place undue emphasis on the flaws in the characters of these individuals. On the one hand there was the vain ex-cavalry officer Papen, with his aristocratic manners, striped trousers, and finely tailored jackets, supposedly wanting to make himself a reactionary dictator simply because of his inordinate ambition. Papen's rival, the smooth General von Schleicher, who cut a dashing figure in Berlin high society and whose specialty was betraying his friends, was supposedly carrying out his behind-the-scenes wire pulling simply out of a love of Machiavellian manipulation and the sense of power it gave him. Recent evidence, however, reveals that Papen and Schleicher opposed each other because they were acting as the representatives for different economic and social interest groups. They intrigued with Hitler only because they found it impossible to maintain a stable government on their own.

Although it has never been properly emphasized, the major political question in Germany during this period was "Can Hitler be bought?" The upper-class economic interest groups such as heavy industry, light industry, and the Junkers were now competing against one another for their economic survival. But none of these groups was strong enough to maintain itself in power without the help of the Nazis.

Meanwhile, Hitler had problems of his own. In spite of the fact that the National Socialists had recently been victorious in the elections, they were in desperate shape financially. Hitler was faced with the tremendous day-to-day expenses of maintaining the largest party in the country, with thousands of employees in addition to the gigantic S.A. army. Debts exceeded contributions, and the party faced bankruptcy. Hitler had to get to power quickly or see his party collapse for lack of funds.

Many of Hitler's old benefactors like Fritz Thyssen, the steel tycoon, were having financial difficulties of their own and could no longer afford to contribute. But if the industrialists would not give willingly, there might be a way to compel them: blackmail. This was one of Hitler's trump cards. The Reichstag had called for an investigation of some of the corrupt deals of big business and the Junkers through which billions in public funds had been embezzled. As the largest party in the Reichstag, the Nazis could vote to silence such investigations—if certain contributions were forthcoming.

But before the conflict between Hitler and the upper class could be resolved, events took a startling turn. In the fall of 1932, economic conditions began to improve slightly. As a direct consequence, those factors that caused Hitler's rise started to lose their impact. For one last moment, as in classical drama, everything seemed to reverse itself. The size of the Nazi party began to decline immediately, and some disenchanted members changed their allegiance to the Communist party, whose membership thus multiplied almost overnight. The "Red threat" was suddenly as dangerous as the Nazi one. Now the industrialists and the Junkers were faced with a crucial decision: would they let the Nazi movement collapse and risk facing the impoverished half-starving masses alone or would they come to Hitler's aid with financial assistance and form a coalition government with him?

With the overwhelming but inconclusive National Socialist victory in the July Reichstag elections (they still lacked a majority), the last series of tactical maneuvers in the struggle for power began. Certainly by tradition, if not by law, the cabinet resigned after an election if its supporters had not attained a majority, and the president asked the leader of the strongest party in the new Reichstag to form a cabinet. The people's mandate had been given decisively to Hitler's party. With not even 10 percent of the new Reichstag in support of his government, von Papen should have presented the resignation of his cabinet.

The men behind Hindenburg, however, saw that by observing this tradition they would be forced to work with Hitler, whom they still held in suspicion and contempt. Moreover, another cabinet seemed impossible, since no party had a clear majority in the Reichstag and a parliamentary alliance between the Nazis and the Center party was most improbable. This provided the Hindenburg faction with a nominal excuse for continuing to govern by emergency decree under Article 48 of the Weimar Constitution. The fact that this measure required the approval of a two-thirds' majority in the Reichstag and that no such majority existed did not trouble the gentlemen of the Papen cabinet, but they must have realized that they could not continue for long against the constitution, against the Reichstag, and against an overwhelming majority of the people.

By the fall of 1932, an increasing number of wealthy aristocrats were supporting Hitler. The royal family, the princes of the small states, and the high nobility had lost more in the revolution of 1918 than anyone else. The precapitalist feudal order on which their power was based was largely destroyed. Nevertheless, by compromising and maintaining a low profile during the first years of the Republic, they were able to retain some of their wealth. With the coming of the depression and the obvious failure of the Weimar Republic, on which big business had staked its hopes, the reactionary monarchists became more aggressive. In order to recover their lost privileges and smash the Left once and for all, many members of the nobility began to contemplate an alliance with Hitler.[1]

The duke of Mecklenburg, former governor of German Togoland in Africa and brother-in-law to the queen of Holland, saw the Nazis as the only salvation against communism. He voted for Hitler in the presidential election and used his international connections to travel abroad, propagating Hitler's ideas. The duke was a special friend of Hjalmar Schacht, the pro-Nazi former president of the Reichsbank, and exercised a certain influence in economic affairs. Although he was not thought of as a political radical, even some of Hitler's more extreme ideas like anti-Semitism found favor with the duke.

Many nobles and aristocratic landowners probably would not have supported Hitler if he had not been favored by Kaiser Wilhelm. The kaiser had given one of his younger sons, Prince August Wilhelm, permission to join the National Socialist party and the S.A. The son-in-law of the kaiser, the duke of Brunswick, was also a "regular donor" to Hitler.[2]

The most unprincipled opportunist among the royal family was Crown Prince Wilhelm. Personally, he had nothing but utter contempt for most of the Nazi leaders. He had many Jewish friends and his political opinions were either moderate or nonexistent. Nevertheless, the Crown Prince supported the Harzburg Front (the temporary alliance of the Nazis and the conservative Nationalists in 1931) and openly endorsed Hitler in the second presidential election. Like the other members of his family, Crown Prince Wilhelm hoped for a restoration of the monarchy. But it was himself rather than his father, the kaiser, that he was plotting to put on the throne.

The Crown Prince had a foot in every political camp. For a time, he had been a strong supporter of Chancellor Bruening in the hope that he would sponsor his candidacy for the throne. By the early 1930s, however, the moderate parties were losing their strength. It was during this time that Crown Prince Wilhelm became a regular guest in the Berlin salon of the ambitious Frau Viktoria von Dirksen. Frau von Dirksen had become infatuated with Hitler in the late 1920s, and as an enthusiastic Nazi wore a large diamond swastika pin on her bosom, which earned for her the nickname the Mother of the Movement. It was widely known that Frau von Dirksen was a heavy financial contributor to the National Socialist party. The dream of this gossip-loving society lady was the restoration of the monarchy by Hitler, who—if things went as she wished—would designate the Crown Prince as the new kaiser.

The Crown Prince also kept in contact with the Nazis through Hermann Goering. On May 6, 1932, the prince celebrated his fiftieth birthday with a lavish party at his palace. The guest list was very selective; only the higher nobility, the very wealthy, and Hitler's representative, Hermann

Goering, were invited. One of the guests said: "Goering appeared after the dinner in civilian clothes . . . and retired into a corner with the noble host and hostess, where I saw hopes arise in the Crown Princess at the explanations which he was obviously making to her."[3]

Actually, Hitler had a very low opinion of the Crown Prince, whom he regarded as a lightweight, interested only in horses and women. Yet this did not stop him from making promises to get what he wanted. On one occasion, Crown Prince Wilhelm optimistically pointed to the chairs in his library where, a short time before, Hitler, Goering, Goebbels, and Roehm had sat, and credulously told his guests, "Hitler told me here: 'My goal is the restoration of the Empire under a Hohenzollern.' "[4]

While the Crown Prince was plotting behind his father's back to get the throne for himself, the ex-kaiser was not sitting idle. Although in exile himself, the kaiser had many representatives in Germany arguing the case for the restoration of the monarchy. One of the most effective of his agents was his young, attractive second wife, the "Empress" Hermine.

In 1922, while living in exile in Holland, Kaiser Wilhelm received in his mail a letter of respect and sympathy from a young boy. He answered by inviting his youthful admirer to visit Doorn. In escort came the mother, Princess Hermine, a widow of thirty-five who had been married to Prince Schönaich-Carolath. She and the kaiser became very fond of each other, and on November 3, 1922, they were married. By this time his youngest child, the duchess of Brunswick, was herself thirty, and the arrival of younger stepchildren added interest and gaiety to his life. The Empress Hermine, however, was a capable and clever woman who was determined that her husband would once again sit on the German throne.

Even before her marriage to the kaiser, Princess Hermine had owned vast estates in Silesia and consequently was very rightist in her political sympathies. Sometimes after 1930, she became a "passionate follower" of Hitler. A representative of the Crown Prince said: "The Princess [Empress] Hermine saw Germany's future in Hitler and trusted him completely. She seemed firmly convinced that when he held the power of Germany in his hands, it would be only a question of a short time until she would see her husband return to his hereditary place. In any event, it was clear to me that in the Princess I had a convinced disciple of National Socialism before me."[5]

The Empress Hermine frequently came to Berlin to socialize and advance her husband's cause. When attending an afternoon reception given by Countess von der Groeben, she was greeted by her eighty-five-year old hostess, who said in an impeccably courteous and grand manner: "Your Majesty, I have been told that your sympathies are with the National Socialists. Is it true that His Majesty has made a donation to the National Socialists?"[6] The empress, who wanted to keep her support for Hitler quiet, if not secret, stood in embarrassed silence, then turned and walked away.

Who supported the idea of the restoration of the monarchy besides the ex-kaiser and his ambitious wife? Surprisingly, a very large number of influential and wealthy people: a majority of the nobility and Officers Corps and even many industrialists. Aware of the financial power wielded by the monarchists, Hitler was very careful not to irritate them. In two pamphlets published in 1929 and in 1932, respectively, it stated that Hitler intended to establish a National Socialist dictatorship for "a transitory period" only. The Nazi party wanted to take over the state only until the German people had been freed from the threat of Marxism and could then reach a decision as to whether the final form of government would be a republic or a monarchy.

Fritz Thyssen was among those industrialists still loyal to the kaiser. "I thought at that time," related Thyssen, "that Hitler's taking office as chancellor was merely a transitional stage leading to the reintroduction of the German monarchy. In September 1932, I invited a number of gentlemen to my house in order to put their questions to Hitler. Hitler answered all questions put to him to the utmost satisfaction of all present. On that occasion he said in distinct and unambiguous tones, that he was merely the pacemaker of the monarchy."

Among the industrialists assembled at Thyssen's home were Hitler's old conservative sympathizer Emil Kirdorf and Albert Voegler, the director of United Steel. "In the fall of 1932," Thyssen further notes, "Goering paid a whole week's visit to ex-Kaiser Wilhelm II at Doorn."[7] Even the Crown Prince did much to confirm the wishful thinking of many ultraconservatives about the Nazis' ultimate aims. The contact between Hitler and certain monarchist circles appeared to be so close that it alarmed some of the more socialist-minded party leaders. Ernst Roehm, the commander of the S.A., repeatedly voiced his concern that Hitler might become, or perhaps already was, the captive of the monarchist clique.

Despite the many aristocrats who supported the Nazis, the leading political representative of the upper class, Papen, was no more willing to cooperate with them than ever. When Hitler failed to receive a summons from Papen to discuss the possibilities of a compromise after the Nazi election triumph in July, he became worried. He hurried to Berlin, not to see the chancellor, but for an interview with the man behind the government, General von Schleicher.

On August 5, at Fuerstenberg barracks, north of Berlin, Hitler saw Schleicher and made his demands: the chancellorship for himself, and other Nazis appointed heads of the state government of Prussia, the Reich and Prussian Ministries of Interior (which controlled the police), the Ministry of Justice and two new Ministries, Aviation and Popular Enlightenment and Propaganda. Naturally Schleicher himself would remain as defense minister and have control of the powerful Ministries of Foreign Affairs and Economy. Hitler said that this was a true compromise on his part and, in turn, demanded that the government allow him to seek an enabling act from the Reichstag authorizing him to rule by decree for a specified period. And if the enabling act was refused, the Reichstag would be "sent home."

Whatever Schleicher said, Hitler came away from the meeting with high hopes, under the impression that the general would cooperate with his plan. But Goebbels remained cynical, even after listening to Hitler's optimistic report of the meeting with Schleicher. "It is well to watch developments with reserve," he wrote in his diary. He was, however, certain of one thing: "Once we attain power we shall never relinquish it unless we are carried off dead."[8]

On August 9, Wilhelm Frick, the Nazi who was now minister of interior in Thuringia, and Gregor Strasser came to see Hitler in Bavaria with discouraging news. The violent behavior of the S.A. after the election, especially the continual street fighting with the Communists, was making conservative people ask if the Nazis were really fit for power. There were also rumors General von Schleicher had changed his mind and was now saying that if Hitler became chancellor he would have to rule with the consent of the Reichstag. Then Funk arrived with the report that his friends in big business were worried about a Nazi government taking power. He also carried a message from Schacht, the former president of the Reichsbank, saying established business interests were afraid the Nazis might begin "radical economic experiments."

On August 11, Hitler decided to bring matters to a climax one way or another. He arranged for appointments with the chancellor and the president before beginning the drive north to Berlin. On the way, he stopped for a conference with other Nazi leaders by the shore of Lake Chiemsee. Summing up the results of the conference, Goebbels said: "If they do not afford us an opportunity to square accounts with Marxism, our taking over power is absolutely useless."[9] After reaching Berlin late on the evening of the twelfth, Hitler had his interview with Papen and Schleicher the next day at noon. The discussion quickly became stormy.

Schleicher backed out of the agreement he had made the week before. He supported Papen in maintaining that the most Hitler could possibly have was the vice-chancellorship for himself and the Prussian ministry of interior for one of his lieutenants. They politely set aside Hitler's claim that the leader of the largest party in the Reichstag was entitled to be chancellor. Papen said Hindenburg was insistent that an extremist leader like Hitler could not head a presidential cabinet. Hitler was outraged. Losing his temper and beginning to shout, he said that he must be chancellor, nothing less. He talked wildly of mowing down the Marxists and of a coming St. Bartholomew's night."* Schleicher and Papen were both shocked by the raging figure who now confronted them. He assured them that he had no designs on the Ministries of Defense, Foreign Affairs, or Economics but was only asking for as much power as Mussolini had claimed in 1922. Stunned, Papen terminated the interview by saying the final decision would have to be left up to Hindenburg.

Hitler left in a rage of disappointment and went back to Goebbels's apartment. At about 3 P.M., a phone call came through from the president's office. Frick answered and said there was no point in Hitler's coming to see Hindenburg if a decision had already been reached. "The president will talk to Hitler first," was the reply. This revived a vague hope. Perhaps the "Old Bull" would bow to the voters' mandate and allow Hitler to become chancellor after all.

It is difficult to say just how involved the old president actually was in the decision-making process. He was eighty-six years old, and his mental powers were not what they had been. He did have periods of lucidity, especially in the mornings, but he liked to get business over quickly and then fall into reminiscences about his earlier military career. He frequently had difficulty recalling the details of World War I, but his memory was clear about the wars of 1860 and 1870.

---

*Hitler often referred to the historic St. Bartholomew's night massacre of the French Huguenots in 1572.

Often he would sit for hours, talking about the officers and men who had served under him more than fifty years ago. Sometimes his conscience troubled him. "How is history going to judge me?" he would say. "I lost the greatest war. I was unable to help my country, which honored me with its highest post."

Hindenburg might have been capable of acting as a purely ceremonial head of state, for he still made an imposing appearance on the parade grounds. But with no majority existing in the Reichstag, a role of almost unlimited power fell on his office. Being a monarchist, he felt uncomfortable as president of the Republic. He was further perplexed when he found it impossible to govern by the constitution he had sworn to uphold. Yet this tired old man was the only real power the German state had left, so he continued to govern by emergency decree, heavily dependent on his small circle of "advisers."

Accompanied by Roehm and Frick, Hitler went to the Presidential Palace. Hindenburg waived all formalities and courtesies. He did not even ask Hitler to sit down. Standing up, leaning on his cane, flanked by his son and his secretary Meissner, he asked the Nazi leader point blank whether he would accept the vice-chancellorship and support a "national" government as he had promised. Once again, Hitler refused; cooperation in a position subordinate to Papen was out of the question, he must be chancellor or nothing. Hindenburg wasted few words. He said that he could not in good conscience risk transferring power to a new party such as the National Socialists who were intolerant, noisy, and undisciplined. Then the three Nazi leaders were dismissed. The interview had lasted barely ten minutes.[10]

What Hitler could not obtain from the government by compromise, he now tried to win through a war of nerves. In the hands of a clever strategist like Hitler, a mass of fanatical followers such as the S.A. could become a weapon of flexibility and finesse. The storm troopers were the uprooted and disinherited and had absolutely nothing to lose and everything to gain by a civil war. Many of them even felt that if worse came to worst and they were defeated, they at least would have the satisfaction of taking their hated enemies down with them. Hitler could mobilize these belligerent legions and bring them to a halt just short of catastrophe, but the willingness of the Brownshirts was so obviously genuine that the Hindenburg clique could not know where they would stop—or even be sure that they would stop.

In spite of the temporary victory of Schleicher and Papen, Hitler realized that intrigue was a game that two could play. In late August, the Nazis approached the Center party. Together they could command a majority in the Reichstag, so Hitler proposed they pass a joint motion to depose the current president of the Reichstag, a Social Democrat, and elect a National Socialist in his place. In his diary Goebbels wrote: "We got in touch with the Center party . . . merely to bring pressure to bear upon our adversaries."

He saw three possible courses of action: (1) a presidential cabinet; (2) coalition with the Center party; or (3) remain in opposition. But he also noted: "It is quite impossible to see through all this intrigue. So many are pulling in different ways that one cannot tell who on the other side is the betrayer or who is the betrayed." Late that night, he returned to Berlin and discovered "Schleicher already knows of our feelers in the direction of the Center Party." He added: "That is a way of bringing pressure to bear upon him. I endorse and further it."[11]

The contacts between the National Socialists and the Center party, though never intended to be more than a means of pressuring the Papen government, paid off on August 30, at the reconvening of the Reichstag when the Nazis and the Center party joined in electing Goering as the president of the Reichstag. Paul Loebe, the bespectacled, shy little Social Democrat who had clung to the Reichstag presidency for twelve years, had to step down for the Brownshirt Nazi colossus—Captain Hermann Goering. Goering was well suited to the job, at least from the Nazi point of view. Through practice and sincere effort he had developed into an able speaker, and although he aped Hitler's style and phrases, he had the necessary volume and imposing physical bulk to make himself noticed. Goering was also a war hero with an upper-class social background that would serve him well in his dealings with the aristocrats around Hindenburg. After the election of its first National Socialist president, the Reichstag adjourned until September 12, when it would reconvene for its first working session.

Anticipating trouble, Chancellor von Papen had obtained in advance from President von Hindenburg a decree for the dissolution of the chamber. This was the first time that the death warrant of the Reichstag had been signed before it had even met to discuss business. Papen was confident he was in complete command of the situation. However, before he had a chance to present the decree of dissolution, the Nazis and Communists joined in a vote of censure against the Papen government.[12] Five hundred and thirteen Reichstag deputies voted against Papen and only twenty-one deputies supported him. It was a humiliating experience for the chancellor. Nevertheless, he claimed the vote was invalid, since the Reichstag was already dissolved when it was taken. After sitting for less than a day, the deputies yielded and went home when President von Hindenburg declared the Reichstag dissolved; however, the constitutionality of this action was clearly arguable. The chancellor set new elections for November 6, and the Nazis now faced their fifth major political campaign in less than a year.

Schleicher and Papen intended to wear Hitler down and bankrupt the Nazi party so that it would be ready for collapse at the decisive moment. Hitler was racing against time; but he had one trump card in his hand. Many industrialists and Junkers were reluctant to see the Nazis pushed to desperation at a time when a Reichstag investigation into certain deals that had taken place during the regimes of Bruening and Papen would prove dangerous.

On a sunny October afternoon just before the opening of the November election campaign, Hitler's caravan of three big Mercedes convertibles left Munich for Potsdam, where a Nazi Youth rally was to take place. Hitler rode in the first car, wearing a long leather coat, leather aviator's helmet, and motoring goggles. Even though he never took the wheel himself, Hitler had a passion for speed and always sat in front next to his chauffeur. The second car was filled with the Fuehrer's eight S.S. bodyguards who, with their black uniforms, leather aviator's helmets, goggles, revolvers, and sjambok whips, were described by one witness as looking like men from Mars.

After spending the night in a small Bavarian inn, they were on the road early the next morning and by 4 P.M., entered Brandenburg and began passing trucks full of Hitler Youth, who were overjoyed at the sight of their Fuehrer. About eight o'clock, they reached the outskirts of Potsdam, where they were met by Baldur von Schirach, the Nazi Youth leader, and his staff, in two big cars. The procession of five cars then continued into the city, which looked as though an army had occupied it. Tents and trucks were everywhere. Children from fourteen to eighteen wearing the Hitler Youth uniform were seen on all sides. Near the Potsdam stadium the human mass became so dense that both the police and the S.S. had all they could do just to get Hitler's convoy of cars through.

At dusk, the stadium was lit with thousands of torches. Massed units of boys and girls stood in formation on the field surrounded by a vast ring of humanity. Hitler mounted the platform and was saluted by Schirach, who made his official report to the Fuehrer—some sixty-four thousand boys and fifteen thousand girls present and accounted for. When Hitler then stood alone on the platform, still wiping the road dust from his eyes, a fantastic roar of jubilant cheers rose into the night. Then he raised his arms and dead silence fell over the stadium. He burst into a flaming speech that lasted only about fifteen minutes, but for that short time his oratory was "fiery, spontaneous, and full of appeal." Then, again, the roar of applause and cheers.

Immediately after the speech, Hitler and his staff went on into Berlin, where they were to have dinner with Prince August Wilhelm, the son of the kaiser. The prince, who had joined the Nazis several years before, had become a Reichstag deputy and a brigadier general in the S.A. Considering that Hitler used to be uneasy in the company of the upper class, it was interesting to observe his manner with the prince. He was courteous, addressed him as "Royal Highness," but was absolutely poised. The prince, who was wearing his S.A. uniform, was exceptionally respectful but equally at ease, even when his elbow knocked a wineglass to the floor.

Hitler was distressed when the prince, who had a villa in Potsdam, told him of the difficulties the rally had created. The Nazis had been prepared to take care of forty thousand children at the most, but twice that number had arrived and thousands of them had been on the road for days.

"What are we going to do?" asked Hitler, in a worried tone. "Those thousands of children mustn't sleep under the open sky."

"I've taken fifty-five into my house—impossible to take more," replied the prince, equally troubled. "Perhaps we could make a house-to-house canvas."[13]

Hitler was so concerned that after dinner he drove out to Potsdam again, at midnight, and did not return until he was sure that everything possible was being done for the comfort of the children. However, in spite of this, thousands of them had to sleep in the open, which was no joke in October. The Fuehrer didn't get to bed until well after four, but by seven, he was back again in Potsdam, walking around trying to inspire the cold and weary children.

Some consider it to be a revelation of the human side of Hitler's character, that he "fussed with anxiety" about the sleeping arrangements of the Nazi Youth, and that "his face glowed like that of a proud parent and tears came to his eyes as he looked at them."[14] However, even a demagogue must be genuinely concerned about the fate of his followers, just as the good mechanic takes care of his tools. This is not to say that Hitler had no human feeling for his men, because he certainly did consider them as his comrades, partners in his struggle. But this is a part of the function of any charismatic leader: he must have a true understanding of, and sympathy for, his adherents.

By eleven o'clock the next day, the morning mist with its chill was gone and a warm breeze was blowing at Potsdam. The great review, the climactic moment for which thousands of children had endured days of hardships, finally began. From out of the forest behind the stadium there came marching a steady column of brown-shirted Hitler Youth. For several hours they marched on, children from every part of Germany, even from Austria, Bohemia, Memel, and Danzig, with their thousands of banners fluttering in the light breeze.

When one strong teenager came marching at the head of his section, carrying his five-year-old brother on his shoulders, a storm of applause rang through the air. Hitler signaled the two brothers to approach the reviewing stand and shook hands with them. Finally, in the fading sunset, six thousand black-uniformed S.S. men drilled past in a parade march that the old Imperial Guard would have envied, and the rally was over. "Its propaganda value," said one Nazi, "would be incalculable. No spectator could escape its pull. There was no longer the slightest doubt in my mind that, whatever the political setbacks ahead, the Fuehrer would triumph."

The great enthusiasm shown at the Potsdam rally was an indication of Hitler's hold over the youth of the nation. It was also a sign that in spite of setbacks the party members would remain loyal to Hitler. But what about the masses of uncommitted voters who had cast their ballots for the Nazis in July? Would they do the same in the coming election on November 6? It was not likely, for the average German was tired of elections and the unending political disputes. Realizing that this campaign would be the most difficult of all, Dr. Goebbels wrote on September 16: "Now we are in for elections again! One sometimes feels this sort of thing is going on forever. . . . Our adversaries count on our losing morale, and getting fagged out."[15]

Underlying all the difficulties the Nazis were encountering was the fact that economic conditions were beginning to improve. The bottom of the depression had been hit in the summer and early fall of 1932; by late fall the recovery had begun. There was a growing number of optimistic predictions that were seen to have some basis in reality because industries were reporting more orders and more work to do. The number of unemployed, which had been well over 6 million during the winter of 1931 to 1932 had declined to 5.1 million in the autumn. Meanwhile, the burden of international political debts had practically vanished. It was now clear that France would not resort to force or other restrictive measures in an attempt to collect reparation payments. It was no coincidence that the first signs of confidence and recovery appeared just at the same time as the first signs of Hitler's decline.

In addition to the problem of maintaining its hold on the electorate, the party itself was in deep financial difficulties. Big business and banking interests were now backing Papen, who had given them certain concessions. As Schacht had warned, the upper classes were becoming increasingly distrustful of Hitler because of his refusal to cooperate with Hindenburg and his voting with the Communists to embarrass Papen. Instead of moderating their position, the Nazis replied to the conservatives' criticism by ever more violent attacks on the "Government of Reaction." The results could have been expected. In the middle of October, Goebbels complained in the privacy of his diary: "Money is extraordinarily difficult to obtain. All gentlemen of 'Property and Education" are standing by the Government."[16]

Chancellor von Papen, however, had problems of his own.

Throughout the summer and fall of 1932, difficulties for the Papen government had continually mounted. As long as no one had been quite sure what the government intended to do, the success of this small group of aristocratic conspirators had been phenomenal. Even the Social Democrats had felt a certain relief when the Papen cabinet had shown that it intended to oppose Hitler's advance to power. Consequently, for a time, the opposition of the Social Democrats against Papen had been more formal than real. But after the takeover of the Prussian government*, Social Democrats became seriously alarmed and in their press began a series of bitter attacks against the cabinet. Their anger increased as more and more government officials who were Social Democrats were dismissed and their places filled with conservative Nationalists. In addition to the popular opposition against the Papen cabinet that was now developing on every side, the industrialists withdrew their support of Papen and began to exert their influence against him.

Why did the industrialists choose this time to oppose the head of a conservative government? The fact that the small band of Papen's conspirators could halt Hitler's sweep to power had been considered almost impossible prior to the event. But, after it had actually been done without the Nazis offering any armed resistance, German businessmen breathed easily again and soon began to think that it had only been a nightmare after all. Consequently they felt that it was no longer necessary to support the Papen government

---

*The Social Democrats, who ruled the Prussian state government for years, were defeated in the April 1932 elections. But when the opposition parties could not form a coalition with a majority, the old Social Democratic administration remained in office. Chancellor von Papen, however, was eager to take over the Social Democratic–dominated Prussian police force. In a move of questionable legality, he made use of the chancellor's special "emergency" powers to dismiss the Social Democratic officials of the Prussian state government. When the Prussian administration refused to obey Papen's orders, he sent a handful of army troops to physically expel them from their offices.

unless it demonstrated its willingness to give proper consideration to the interests of industry.

The Papen cabinet, on the other hand, primarily had the interests of agriculture at heart. To a certain extent, this was because the principal party support for the government came from the Nationalists, who by now were largely a Junker, agrarian party. In addition, the Papen cabinet thought of itself as the government that would be controlling Germany's destiny for a long time, and in view of the desperate conditions of the depression, it was determined a policy that would have some permanent effect upon the economy should be taken. The Papen government decided a fundamental step in this direction would be to secure the home market almost exclusively for the produce of German agriculture. Therefore, a policy of quotas was introduced in order to restrict the importation of agricultural products. Almost immediately other countries began to retaliate against German manufactured goods. The industrialists reacted at once and began a strong opposition to the government's quota policy.

A few days before the election, the streetcars and subways in Berlin came to a stop when the transportation workers went out on strike. For once, the Nazis were forced to demonstrate the sincerity of their campaign against "reaction." The strike was caused by the Papen government's cutting the workers' wages as an "emergency measure" necessitated by the depression. The trade unions and the Social Democrats disavowed the strike because they had agreed to go along with the government's measures of "economizing." However, the strike was supported by the Communists, and to everyone's surprise, the Nazis joined them in backing the workers. This caused a further drying up of financial contributions from business interests just when the Nazis needed funds most, in order to bring the campaign to a whirlwind finish.

It looked as if many of the party's most reliable financial supporters were about to drop away. Some of them had gone back to the Nationalists, and others like Fritz Thyssen were having money problems of their own. In early November, Thyssen told Hitler that his ability to contribute to the party was almost at an end. He would buy one more carload of political pamphlets for the *Völkischer Beobachter,* but after that they could not longer count on him.

Even Adolf Mueller, the printer of the *Völkischer Beobachter,* threatened to stop his presses unless he was paid at least some of the money the Nazis owed him. Hitler tried to pacify Mueller and considered his good favor almost as important as Hindenburg's. Once in a while, he would lose his temper and shout, but the printer was partially deaf, so it made no difference. In his calm, good-natured way, Mueller would explain to Hitler that the *Völkischer Beobachter* was ruining him; he was able to make ends meet only because he was doing a good business printing literature for the Catholic Church. Even though Mueller himself was not a Nazi but a member of the Catholic Bavarian People's party, he always reluctantly agreed to go along with Hitler "until next month" because the Nazi orders were too big to lose, even if they weren't paid on time.

On November 2, Goebbels wrote: "Scarcity of money has become chronic in this campaign. We lack the amount necessary for carrying it through efficiently. The strike is grist for the mill of the bourgeois press. They are exploiting it against us freely. Many of our staunch partisans, even, are beginning to have their doubts. But in spite of that we must hold firm. . . . Middle class people are being scared away from us on account of our participating in it. But this is only temporary. They are easily to be regained; but once the worker is lost, he is lost for ever."[17]

Further explaining the reasons for the party's course of action Goebbels wrote: "The entire press is furious with us and calls it bolshevism; but as a matter of fact we had no option. If we had held ourselves aloof from this strike . . . our position among the working classes would have been shaken. Here a great occasion offers once again for demonstrating to the public . . . that the line of action we have taken up in politics is dictated by a true sympathy with the people, and for this reason the National Socialist Party purposely eschews the old bourgeois methods."[18]

In an effort to publicize the Nazis' support of the strike, Goebbels pulled some tricks that certainly went beyond "the old bourgeois methods." He ordered some of his Brown-shirts to dress as workers and put them to "work" on the streetcar tracks. Other Nazis also disguised as workers stood along the sidewalk threatening and cursing them as "scabs." Soon the police appeared and drove the hecklers away. Order then prevailed as the "scabs" ripped up the rails under the protection of the police, who were convinced that the work was done under the direction of the transit company. In the Nazi press the next day, Goebbels then triumphantly admitted to the sabotage in the hopes of winning the support of the workers.

Although the conservatives accused the Nazis of "bolshevism," Hitler's economic proposals remained ambiguous as usual. The people must begin to think in terms of "German labor" rather than "the working class," said the Nazi speakers. As they described it, the true idea of socialism was represented by the principle of achievement of the self-sacrificing German civil servant. Slogans such as "an honest living for honest work" had a more persuasive ring than all of Marx's theories put together. In fact, it was the vagueness of the Nazi language that made it so popular and enabled it to find supporters among all classes of the population.

The Nazi leaders were not overly optimistic about the outcome of the election. In this fifth campaign of the year, their propaganda encountered a mood of stubborn apathy and indifference on the part of the people. Hitler campaigned hard, waging an uphill fight. Once again, he used an airplane and spoke in forty-nine cities in a period of less than four weeks. November 5 was the last day of the election campaign; that evening, Goebbels wrote in his diary: "Last attack. Desperate-drive of the Party against defeat. . . .

We succeed in obtaining ten thousand marks at the very last moment. These are to be thrown into the campaign on Saturday afternoon. We have done all possible. Now, let fate decide!"[19]

The German people went to the polls on November 6; that night the results were announced. It was a severe setback for the Nazis, who lost two million of the 13,745,000 votes they had received in July. Their deputies in the Reichstag were reduced from 230 out of 608, to 196 out of 584, though they remained the largest party in the country. The Communists gained almost a million votes and the Social Democrats lost about the same number; thus the Communists increased their seats from 89 to 100, while the Social Democrates fell from 133 to 121. The only party in the election that supported the Papen government, the Nationalists, had their first success in years and increased their seats from 37 to 52.

The reasons for the Nazis' defeat were twofold and seemingly contradictory. On the one hand, those who recognized the signs of economic improvement left the National Socialists and went back to the Nationalist party. These individuals, mostly members of the middle and upper classes, saw Papen as the first chancellor who was unafraid to come to grips with the depression by cutting wages and instituting a voluntary labor service. But on the other hand, many of the unemployed and impoverished had not yet noticed even the slightest improvement in their living conditions. What did it matter to them if factories were reporting a *few* more orders? True, industries were beginning to hire a few more workers, but this was little consolation to those who were still unemployed. Many of the most desperate felt they had gotten nowhere by supporting the Nazis, so they were willing to give the Communists a try.

It was the corresponding success of the Communists that made the defeat of the Nazis particularly significant. It indicated that Hitler was beginning to lose his hold on the wave of discontent and revolt that had so far carried him forward. Looking for a truly revolutionary party, the disillusioned supporters of the Nazis and Social Democrats were turning to the Communists in large numbers. Although Papen was jubilant with what he considered to be "his" victory over the National Socialists, many other upper-class Germans were asking themselves, How long can Hitler hold the allegiance of the masses? How long would it be before more of the unemployed and destitute turned to the Communists?

For the first time the legend of Nazi invincibility had been shattered; its spell was broken. Papen was convinced that their fall would be as rapid as their rise. He thought Hitler was in a much weaker position to bargain for power than he had been in July. In fact, if the Nazis wanted any consideration from his government at all, they had better come to terms before their votes dwindled still further. Feeling that he could at last force Hitler to accept his conditions, Papen put aside his "personal distaste" for the Nazi leader and on November 13 wrote him a letter inviting him to bury their differences and renew negotiations. However, the chancellor was a bit shocked when on November 16 he received a reply from Hitler that could only be considered an open rebuff. This time the Nazis were sitting tight. Hitler demanded several conditions for the renewal of negotiations, the first of which was that all agreements would be put down in writing, so that there could be no "misunderstanding" this time about what was said. With this Papen rashly abandoned all further efforts of reaching a compromise with "the Nazi upstart."

Papen, who was perfectly willing to plunge Germany into another election in order to bring the Nazis to their knees, encountered unexpected opposition in his own cabinet, from his friend and sponsor General von Schleicher. The clever general was irritated by Papen's attitude of increasing independence and the close relationship he had established with the old president. In addition, he was alarmed by the chancellor's personal quarrel with Hitler, especially since he seemed determined to force it to the limit. This was becoming an obstacle to obtaining a coalition of "patriotic" forces which, in Schleicher's view, had been the only reason for making Papen chancellor in the first place. Meanwhile, Papen had some new ideas of his own and was beginning to talk about governing by authoritarian methods if Hitler refused to come to his senses.

Reflecting on the ominous increase in the Communist vote and the willingness of most Nazis to support such a radical cause as the Berlin transportation workers' strike, General von Schleicher was worried. He was more afraid than ever of the possibility of a simultaneous uprising of the Nazis and the Communists. Papen, like Bruening before him, was becoming more of a hindrance than an asset to the general's plan of bringing the Nazis into the government.

The industrialists were not at all impressed by the small degree of support that the Papen cabinet had attracted among the voters. Heavy industry consequently withdrew its backing from Papen and once again began to oppose the government's foreign trade policies. Light industry, on the other hand, which had never supported the Papen government in the first place, changed from merely attacking the cabinet's tariff and quota policy to mounting a full-scale campaign to force Papen out of office.[20]

Soon after Papen's failure to bring Hitler into the cabinet, it became obvious that light industry, led by the big chemical, electrical, and exporting firms, was supporting the candidacy of Schleicher for the chancellorship, while the Junker agrarian interests continued to back Papen. The heavy industrialists were in a predicament; liking neither Schleicher nor Papen and having no alternative candidate of their own, they, for the most part, remained neutral.

Why had Schleicher suddenly emerged as a candidate? Certainly the general had had his own ideas for a long time about solving Germany's political and economic problems, but in the past he had preferred to remain as the éminence grise manipulating from the background. Now, however, he saw in the weakened position of the Nazis an opportunity to destroy them by a strategy of divide and conquer. It seemed to him that the effect of the election setback upon the Nazi leaders would be to strengthen the position of those who supported Gregor Strasser and would be willing to enter a coalition cabinet.

The light industrialists were so adamantly against Papen's policy of quotas, which were destroying the German export business, that they began to look for a possible candidate for chancellor. General von Schleicher seemed to be the right man; he was in a powerful position and his plans for coping with the political and economic crisis seemed to be compatible with their ideas. As the intrigue behind the scenes developed, it became apparent that the backers of Schleicher desired a compromise cabinet that would rule with dictatorial powers but that would also attempt to work out an accord with the trade unions and even the Social Democrats. It was hoped that Schleicher's military background would guarantee the unquestioned loyalty of the Reichswehr and rally to his support all who were interested in protecting public order.

Schleicher let it be known that he favored a foreign trade policy very similar to that desired by the light industrialists, and that as soon as he was in office the policy of import quotas would be abandoned. In contrast, those who favored a cabinet led by Papen wanted an authoritarian government that would not compromise with the trade unions, Social Democrats, or export industries. A Papen cabinet would mean an agrarian, Junker, no-compromise cabinet.

Papen was urged to resign, in order to break the political deadlock. Confident that Hindenburg could not reach a compromise with Hitler, Papen cleverly swallowed his anger and resigned on November 17, feeling sure that his friend, the old president, would soon reappoint him. President von Hindenburg immediately sent for Hitler, who had not expected to be called to Berlin so quickly. He wanted Goering to accompany him when he saw the president, but Goering and Rosenberg, the Nazi philosopher, had gone to

Italy to attend a European congress of the Roman Academy of Sciences. As soon as Goering received the news, he rushed back to Berlin by plane in less than six hours.

On the morning of the nineteenth, Goering went to see State Secretary Meissner to negotiate a proper reception for his Fuehrer. When Hitler arrived for his appointment with President von Hindenburg, he found the old field marshal much more cordial than he had been on August 13.

The president received Hitler in his study. The room, which reflected a somber Prussian atmosphere, usually awed most visitors. War pictures hung along the walls: *Schwering's Death at Prague*, a portrait of the Iron Chancellor, and one of Frederick the Great. There were heavy dark tapestries, and heavy dark furniture. By the window was a bulky, carved writing desk. Across the room in a corner were deep leather armchairs and a low round table. In his deep voice, Hindenburg told Hitler to sit down and motioned to a chair. The two men sat down and talked for over an hour. This time, Hitler succeeded in arousing the president's interest.

Later, Hitler described the meeting to some of his close associates:

> Hindenberg said to me: "Herr Hitler, I wish to hear from your own mouth a summary of your ideas." It is almost impossible, across such a gap, to communicate to others one's own conception of the world. I tried to establish contact with the field marshal by having recourse to comparisons of a military nature. Connection was fairly rapidly made with the soldier, but the difficulty began the instant there was a question of extending our understanding to politics. When I'd finished my summary, I felt that I'd moved Hindenburg and that he was yielding. At once, he made this a pretext for reproaching me with an incident that had occurred in East Prussia: "But your young people have no right to behave as they do. Not long ago, at Tannenberg, they shouted out, so that I could hear: Wake up,

wake up! And yet, I'm not asleep." Certain uncharitable souls had given the old gentleman to suppose that the shout was meant for him personally, whereas in reality our supporters were shouting "Wake up, Germany."[21]

After a long general conversation, Hindenburg got down to business and offered Hitler the chancellorship if he could obtain a working majority in the Reichstag. On the surface this seemed like a fair offer, but it was impossible for Hitler to accomplish. The Center party had agreed to support him, on the condition he not attempt to establish a dictatorship, but Hitler still could not obtain a workable majority because the Nationalists refused to cooperate.* Besides, Hitler really did not want to be a parliamentary chancellor anyway, limited by shifting coalitions; so he renewed his demands for the same powers Hindenburg had given to Papen. The old president, however, refused to appoint the leader of a "radical" party as a presidential chancellor. If Germany had to be governed by decree, there would be no point in replacing his friend, Papen. Once again, Hitler's policy of legality had led him to a cul-de-sac.

Hitler's interview with the president went exactly as Papen thought it would. He fully expected to be reappointed chancellor when he and Schleicher would officially call on Hindenberg on December 1. Meanwhile, Schleicher was maneuvering behind Papen's back. The general had been in contact with Strasser, proposing that the Nazis join a coalition cabinet. In this cabinet, Schleicher rather than Papen would be the chancellor.

Some historians have thought that Papen was unaware of Schleicher's "betrayal."[22] If the intrigues had been based merely on personal rivalry, this might have been so, but actually Papen was well aware that he and Schleicher repre-

---

*Papen had known in advance that the Nationalist party would refuse to cooperate with Hitler, so he had made no effort to disuade Hindenburg from offering Hitler the chancellorship.

sented different social and economic interest groups and was expecting competition from the general. However, he was still not able to determine exactly what Schleicher was planning.

Although Papen officially resigned on November 17, in order to facilitate President von Hindenburg's negotiations with Hitler, in fact he continued as acting chancellor. During this interim period of "cabinet crisis," which lasted from November 18 to December 2, the wildest rumors circulated in the press. The morning newspapers would report that a Schleicher cabinet had been decided upon, while the midday papers would state that Papen was certain to resume office, only to be followed by a report in the evening papers that Schleicher was bound to be the next chancellor. Naturally the newspapers owned or controlled by interests affiliated with light industry were instrumental in circulating reports that undermined Papen and pointed to Schleicher as the better alternative. Of course, Papen was not without his advocates too, especially among the conservative and reactionary sections of the press.

In Berlin, on the evening of December 1, Papen and Schleicher went together to make their official call on President von Hindenburg. Papen confidently proposed his program for the future: he would resume office as chancellor, adjourn the Reichstag indefinitely, and "amend" the constitution to reestablish the rule of the conservative classes, as in the days of the empire. While his "reforms" were being carried out he would declare a state of emergency, govern by decree, and if necessary use force to suppress any opposition. He assured Hindenburg in the most solemn tone that he was justified in considering the welfare of the nation before his oath to the constitution as Bismarck had once done, "for the sake of the Fatherland."

Schleicher then interrupted with objections. The general, who was well aware of Hindenburg's reluctance to violate his oath to the constitution, stressed that the actions proposed by Papen were unconstitutional. And since Papen was unpopular with the vast majority of the people, as had been seen in the past two elections, such "reforms" would place the government in a difficult position in case of civil war. There was no excuse for such drastic action, Schleicher argued, if it could be avoided—and he was sure it could be. He was convinced that if he himself were to head a cabinet it could secure a majority in the Reichstag. Briefly, the general outlined his plan: he would win over Strasser and at least fifty Nazi deputies from Hitler, he could count on the moderate bourgeois parties and, with a little persuasion, on the Social Democrats.

Schleicher thought the old president would have no choice but to accept his plan because in the last few days many prominent industrialists and trade-union leaders had called on Hindenburg urging him not to reappoint Papen. But the influence of big business meant nothing to the old field marshal. The fact that the business community had such little power was one of the crucial imbalances in the Weimar government. Hindenburg, who now had the only real power left in the state, had absolutely no realization of the importance of economic issues.[23]

The aged president sat in silent amazement for a few seconds and then, as if nothing the general said had registered with him, he turned to von Papen, asking him to go ahead and form a new government. Schleicher was dumbfounded; for the first time the old man had disregarded his "advice." A heated argument developed between Schleicher and Papen and continued after they had left the president. On parting, the general looked at Papen, then in the famous words addressed to Luther as he left for the Diet of Worms, said: "Little Monk, you have chosen a difficult path."[24]

Papen thought he had been victorious until the cabinet met the next morning. Then General von Schleicher in his capacity as defense minister declared that the army no longer had confidence in Papen. The army, he said, was not prepared to take the risk of a civil war, against both the Nazis and the Communists at the same time, which Papen's policy might cause. To support his case, the general called in Colonel Ott, who had made a strategic study for the General Staff on the possible outcome of a civil war. Ott assured the cabinet that the army and the police were not strong enough to suppress a simultaneous Nazi and Communist uprising, and at the same time protect the nation from a foreign invader. Therefore, it was the "recommendation" of the army that the government not declare a state of emergency.

Papen was finished; there was nothing he could say. As a last chance, he hurried to Hindenburg with the news, hoping that he might convince him to dismiss Schleicher. The old president was deeply stirred by Papen's report. He asked "his" chancellor not to think ill of him, but went on: "I am an old man, and I cannot face a civil war. . . . If General von Schleicher is of this opinion, then I must—much as I regret it—withdraw the task with which I charged you last night."[25]

12

BRIBES AND
BLACKMAIL

On December 3, 1932, the press and stock exchange received the news of the formation of the Schleicher government with great satisfaction. In his maiden speech, which he delivered over the radio, the new chancellor said that he was neither a capitalist nor a socialist and repudiated the rumors that he intended to set up a dictatorship. The general made it clear that he had no intention of carrying out any plan of constitutional reform but instead intended to devote all his energies to the pressing problem of unemployment. The speech had a most favorable reception after the severe lectures from Papen.[1] For a moment Germany breathed easier. The long awaited "strong man" had stepped from behind the scenes to take up the reins of power.

Schleicher's intrigues and maneuvers, which had brought about the dismissals of Mueller, Groener, Bruening, and most recently Papen, had finally brought him to the chancellorship. Although he preferred to conceal his manipulations, he was now forced to come out in the open and assume personal responsibility for his plans, even if they failed. The "general chancellor" was immediately confronted with two problems: he could not get Papen out of the way completely and he had lost the trust of the president. Schleicher offered to make the ex-chancellor ambassador in Paris, but Papen declined. President von Hindenburg, said Papen, had asked that he stay in Berlin "within reach." Berlin was the best place to plot intrigues against the new chancellor whose influence over the president, which he had used heavily in the past, was destroyed. The old field marshal had tolerated the maneuvers that led to the dismissal of Groener and Bruening, but he could neither forget nor forgive the "shameful" way Schleicher got rid of Papen.

All his intrigues notwithstanding, Schleicher was a very intelligent man. Of the men around the president, he was the only one who had any idea of the real seriousness of the economic and social crisis that had plagued Germany since 1929. Unlike Papen, he was not foolish enough to believe that a "strong" government in itself would remedy the crisis. From 1930 on, Schleicher had correctly estimated the strength of the extremist appeals made by the Nazis and Communists. His objective, which he consistently pursued for three years, was to harness the dynamic energy of the National Socialists by bringing them into the service of the state.

Two factors were in the chancellor's favor: the series of reverses from which the Nazis had been suffering, and the strong desire of all political parties to avoid another repetition of the general elections that had already convulsed the country five times in less than a year and from which, it was generally realized, the Communists alone stood to gain. In his political armory Schleicher had but one weapon, that of attempting to divide the parties from within by intrigue. He now employed this weapon on the Nazis and concentrated his energies more than ever on the negotiations with Gregor Strasser.

For some time, General von Schleicher had been working on an agreement with Gregor Strasser, the most popular

Nazi leader next to Hitler. In these years of poverty and economic uncertainty, it was Strasser's anticapitalist radicalism that won millions of working-class votes for the Nazis. As head of the party organizations, he was in direct contact with the local branches and thus realized more than anyone else the feeling of disillusionment spreading through the movement. He was particularly worried because the more radical Nazis were going over to the Communists.

In addition, the party was practically bankrupt.[2] There simply was no money to pay the salaries of thousands of party officials or to maintain the S.A. Even Goebbels had admitted as much in his diary on November 11: "Received a report on the financial situation of the Berlin organization. It is hopeless. Nothing but debts and obligations, together with the complete impossibility of obtaining any reasonable sum of money after this defeat [November 6 elections]."[3] Strasser was convinced that the only way to save the party from immediate collapse was to make a compromise and get into power, even if as part of a coalition. He believed Hitler's "all or nothing" demand for the chancellorship was destroying any possible benefits of the policy of legality.

The day after he was appointed chancellor, Schleicher met with Strasser, asking him to enter his cabinet as vice-chancellor and president of Prussia. If Strasser wished, he could administer Schleicher's great reemployment project, the "voluntary labor service." He could put the S.A. in charge of the labor service and burden the government treasury with its debts and expenses. To be sure, he would have to cooperate with the Social Democratic unions, but Strasser was already respected by many socialist leaders, so an understanding was not inconceivable.

Offering the vice-chancellorship to an important National Socialist was a clever move on Schleicher's part. Not only was the idea attractive to Strasser as a way out of the party's difficulties, but it would almost certainly cause a split between the Nazi leaders. If Hitler persisted in his refusal to cooperate with the government, Strasser might enter the cabinet, bringing about one-third of the party with him. On the evening of December 3, several hours after Schleicher's conference with Strasser, the results of the Thuringian state elections came in, showing nearly a 40 percent decline in the Nazi vote since July. This added a new sense of urgency to Schleicher's offer, in order to avoid more elections at all costs.

Although there is no existing record of Paul Silverberg, the Jewish coal tycoon, having played any direct part in Schleicher's negotiations with Strasser, it looked as if his plan of splitting the Nazi party from within was about to be accomplished. The liberal-minded industrialist Otto Wolff of Cologne, who was a friend and business associate of Silverberg, was known to be in almost daily contact with Schleicher at this time. Like Silverberg, Wolff had contributed heavily to Strasser because he too saw him as the one Nazi leader with whom it might be possible to compromise. Just how much Strasser's great power in the Nazi party was due to the subsidies of the moderate industrialists is difficult to say. Certainly Strasser was an able leader in his own right, and it was only natural that his socialistic economic philosophy would have great appeal during the depression, but extra money could only have helped, not hurt.

On December 5, the party leaders and Nazi Reichstag deputies met at the Kaiserhof in Berlin. Strasser demanded that the Nazis at least "tolerate" the Schleicher government, and he was supported by Frick, the head of the Nazi block in the Reichstag. More and more of the unexpressed sentiment in the party was gathering behind Strasser. Goering and Goebbels argued against compromise, and Hitler stated that their point of view was correct. He would not "tolerate" the Schleicher cabinet; however, he was ready to "negotiate" with it. But for this task he appointed Goering, not Strasser, whom he felt had already gone behind his back. Then, in an attempt to inspire his Reichstag deputies with courage, Hitler delivered a short speech in which he tried to minimize the defeat in the Thuringian elections. But everyone realized how serious the situation really was. Continuing, Hitler insisted that no great movement had ever achieved victory by taking the road of compromise. As the showdown drew near, the sacrifices must become greater. "Only one thing is decisive," he said: "Who in this struggle is capable of the last effort, who can put the last battalion in the field." However, for Reichstag deputies afraid that they themselves would be the first sacrificed in the next election, this was little consolation.

Did the thousands of party officials possess the courage to struggle on in desperate opposition if Strasser's plan offered them the opportunity of becoming ministers, mayors, provincial officials, police sergeants, or even civilian employees in army arsenals? Many Nazi leaders thought it would be better to have a share of government posts, some access to the state treasury, and some relief from the tremendous debts the party had accumulated rather than nothing at all. Would it not be more reasonable to accept Schleicher's bribe? they asked.

Hitler and Strasser had another discussion on December 7, at the Kaiserhof, but without the restraints of a large audience this time. In the course of the conversation Hitler bitterly accused Strasser of betrayal, of going behind his back, and of trying to oust him from the leadership of the party. Strasser angrily replied that he had been loyal and was only trying to save the party from almost certain collapse. The argument ended with mutual threats, reproaches, and accusations of betrayal.

Overflowing with rage, Strasser returned to his room at the Hotel Excelsior and wrote Hitler a long letter in which he gave vent to the anger and resentment that had been swelling within him since 1925. He accused Hitler of betraying the ideals of the movement, of irresponsibility, personal ambition, and inconsistency in tactics. He ended the letter with his resignation from his position in the party.

The letter reached Hitler at noon on December 8, with the impact of a bombshell. This was the most serious threat to the party's survival since the putsch in 1923. Strasser's revolt threatened to undercut the very base of Hitler's own authority within the party and left him more deeply shaken than any election setback ever had. That evening, Goebbels invited the Fuehrer to his apartment, where several of the Nazi leaders sat around brooding.

In his diary, Goebbels described the mood that night: "It is difficult to be cheerful. We are all rather downcast, especially in view of the danger of the whole party's falling to pieces, and of all our work being in vain. We are confronted with the great test. Every movement which desires power must prove itself, and this proving generally comes shortly before the victory, which decides everything. . . . Phone call from Dr. Ley [the gauleiter of Cologne]: The situation in the party is getting worse from hour to hour. The Fuehrer must immediately return to the Kaiserhof."[4]

At two o'clock in the morning, Goebbels was called to join Hitler at the Kaiserhof. It seemed that Strasser had given his story to the morning newspapers, which were just beginning to appear on the streets. Roehm and Himmler, the chief of the black uniformed S.S., were also summoned to join the group at the Kaiserhof where everyone was "dumbfounded" that Strasser had actually given his story to the papers, although they had been aware that the split was brewing for some time. "Treachery! Treachery!" noted Goebbels. "For hours, the Fuehrer paces up and down the room in the hotel. It is obvious that he is thinking very hard. He is embittered and deeply wounded by this unfaithfulness. Suddenly he stops and says: 'If the Party once falls to pieces, I shall shoot myself without more ado.' "[5].

However, Strasser lacked the necessary determination to carry through with the challenge to Hitler's leadership. He was never thorough or Machiavellian enough to plan a mutiny such as Hitler suspected. Just when he might have rallied the prosocialist wing of the party against Hitler, and perhaps changed the course of history, Strasser gave up. In vain, Frick was driving around Berlin searching for him, in the hope that he might be able to convince him to patch up the dispute with Hitler to save the party from disaster. But Strasser was nowhere to be found; fed up with it all, he had taken the train south for a vacation in sunny Italy.

With the news of Strasser's disappearance, Hitler recovered his confidence and acted decisively, striking the opposition swift and hard. The powerful office of party organization, which Strasser had formed, was broken up, part of the duties being taken over by Dr. Ley, under the Fuehrer's supervision, the rest being transferred to Goebbels and Hess, Hitler's personal secretary. Several of Strasser's friends were purged from their positions of authority in the party, while all the gauleiters, deputies, and party leaders were summoned to Berlin to sign a new declaration of loyalty to Adolf Hitler. When Gottfried Feder, one of the coauthors of the original party program, who sympathized with Strasser's socialist ideas, questioned the purpose of a "declaration of loyalty," he was told to sign or get out. He quickly signed.

Using his usual combination of threats and persuasion, Hitler then made a short speech in which he appealed to the loyalty of his old comrades, bringing tears to their eyes. With a sob in his voice, he said that he never could have believed Strasser guilty of such treachery. Julius Streicher, the rabid anti-Semitic gauleiter of Nuremberg, stood up and stammered: "Maddening that Strasser could do this to our Fuehrer!" At the end of the meeting, said Goebbels, "The district leaders and deputies burst into spontaneous ovations for the Fuehrer. All shake hands with him, promising to carry on until the very end. . . . Strasser now is completely isolated, a dead man."[6]

Meanwhile, Chancellor von Schleicher continued his efforts to establish a stable government. Even though his plan to attract Strasser had failed for the time being, he was optimistic; the Reichstag had given him a free hand and at last the economy seemed to be improving. On December 15, Schleicher made a "fireside" broadcast to the nation outlining the policy of his government. Asking his listeners to forget that he was a general, he said: "My heretical view is that I am a supporter neither of capitalism nor socialism. For me, concepts like private economy or planned economy have lost their terrors."

His principal objective, he told them, was to provide work for the unemployed and get the economy going again. There would be no tax increases or further wage cuts. In addition, he would end the agricultural quotas that Papen had established for the benefit of the large landowners; instead, he was beginning a program to take over 800,000 acres from the bankrupt Junker estates in the east and give them to 25,000 peasant families. The chancellor concluded with the promise that the government would keep down the prices of such essentials as coal and meat by rigid controls if necessary.

Schleicher's attempt to win the support of the masses was unsuccessful. Even after his promises, the Social Democrats and union leaders still mistrusted him and declined to cooperate. The broadcast not only failed to convince the Left, but worse, it also stirred up violent opposition among reactionary circles of the Right. Many industrialists were frightened by Schleicher's overtures to the trade unions; however, the chancellor was to find his most dangerous foe in the East Prussian landowners, who denounced his program of land settlement as "agrarian bolshevism." Though many of their estates were bankrupt, the Junkers were still a powerful force in the German power elite. Their opposition had brought down Bruening; how they would deal with Schleicher remained to be seen. The leading figures in the German chemical and electrical industry seemed to be standing firm behind Schleicher and opposing the Nazis. Hermann Buecher of the German General Electric Company (A.E.G.), and Robert Bosch, the famous producer of the spark plug and other electrical goods, were both opponents of Hitler. Even earlier, Carl Friedrich von Siemens, head of the Siemens electrical firm, became aware of the Nazi danger. In 1931, speaking to a group of General Electric executives in New York, he pointed out that Hitler was a threat because he appealed to the patriotism and unselfishness of the Germans. "Too few people realize that Hitler is drawing idealists from all sections of the population to his banner." He left no doubt that industrialists like himself were opposed to Hitler, but that this circumstance should not blind one to the fact of his popularity among the masses.

The chemical industry had a strong liberal tradition. Carl Duisberg, the founder of the giant I.G. Farben chemical trust, and his successor, Carl Bosch, were both determined anti-Nazis. But even under these two men there were a few directors on the board of I.G. Farben who believed the company should establish some contact with the Nazis. From its formation in 1925, the firm gave financial assistance to all political parties with the exception of the Communists and the Nazis.[7]

However, two top Farben executives began to give contributions to Walther Funk, one of Hitler's economic advisers, sometime in 1932.[8] I.G. Farben had a vested interest in keeping on good terms with all political parties. The company had invested heavily in a process to manufacture high-grade synthetic gasoline. The initial production costs were so high that I.G. Farben could hope to enter the domestic market only if there were a protective tariff against imported oil. The Bruening government, which Farben had heavily subsidized, had passed such a tariff, and it was later approved by the Papen cabinet, but because of the country's continued political instability the directors of the firm remained anxious about the tariff question.

When attacks against I.G. Farben began to appear in the Nazi press in 1932, the company suddenly became concerned about the attitude of the nation's largest political party. Two representatives of the firm were sent to Munich in the fall of 1932 to see Hitler and "to clarify the position of the National Socialist Party regarding the question of German synthetic gasoline production.[9] Hitler told his visitors that when a Nazi government came to power, he would actively support the production of synthetic gasoline.

The Farben men found Hitler reasonable and left somewhat reassured. Hitler, for his part, was very pleased with himself. The attacks against Farben in the Nazi press had served their purpose. Hitler's plan was to manipulate Farben into contributing to him in order to silence Nazi criticism and in effect pay protection money to the largest party in the Reichstag. No request for money had been made on this occasion, he simply wanted to present the immage of a man open to persuasion and allow the situation more time to ripen.

In spite of his difficulties, Chancellor von Schleicher continued to be confident. In mid-December, one of the nation's leading industrialists made a statement that led investors to think the depression was almost over. "The world economic situation," said Gustav Krupp, "in the money market, shows signs of an improvement; the low point seems definitely past." The improvement of the economy was sufficient reason for optimism, but Schleicher's confidence was also based on a fatal underestimation of his opponents' strength. When Kurt von Schuschnigg, the Austrian minister of justice, visited him a few weeks after his broadcast, Schleicher assured his guest that "Herr Hitler was no longer a problem, his movement had ceased to be a political danger, and the whole problem had been solved, it was a thing of the past."[10]

Undoubtedly there were some indications that the strength of the Nazis was declining. The party was seriously short of the funds needed to keep the "state within a State" running. On December 10, Goebbels noted in his diary: "The financial situation of the Berlin district is hopeless. We must institute strict measures of economy." And again, on December 22: "We must cut down the salaries of our district Leaders, as otherwise we cannot manage with our finances."[11]

The biggest expense on the budget was maintaining the S.A., whose hard core was made up of unemployed men living free in S.A. barracks. The costs were immense. As a last desperate measure to keep the party going, Hitler sent his storm troopers into the streets to beg for money. The S.A. men, many of whom were clad only in their thin brown shirts, stood on street corners shivering in the December wind, rattling their metal cups as an appeal for a few pfennigs from patriotic passers-by. Hitler, Goebbels, Ley, and Goering were speaking several times a day to party members throughout Germany in a desperate effort to keep up morale, but the future looked dim. At the end of 1932, Goebbels brooded in the privacy of his diary: "The year 1932 has brought us eternal ill luck . . . the future looks dark and gloomy; all chances and hopes have quite disappeared."[12]

Hitler and Goebbels were not the only ones disturbed by the declining fortunes of the National Socialist party. Many members of Germany's established power elite, including ex-chancellor Papen, were worried to see Hitler's followers deserting to the Communists. Although no longer chancellor, Papen remained as Hindenburg's unofficial advisor. The old president had requested that he stay near him; so even though Papen was now only a private citizen, he still retained his apartment in the chancellery. By coincidence, the adjacent presidential palace was being remodeled that winter, and as result, Hindenburg had to move into the chancellery for a while. Thus, during the crucial months of December and January 1932 to 1933, Hindenburg and Papen lived down the hall from each other, and together with the president's son, Oskar, and State Secretary Meissner they made up a kind of family. It is easy to imagine what the main topic of their conversation on those cold winter evenings must have been: what will we do about the National Socialists? After all, we wanted to use them, not destroy them. Aren't we missing our chance?

However, during the month of December, Papen kept in contact with the Nazis through men like his old army friend Joachim von Ribbentrop and Wilhelm Keppler, who was known as the Nazi "contact man" in industry. The reason Papen sought an understanding with Hitler is not what some sensationalists have tried to make it out to be. His primary motives were not envy of Schleicher, or a desire for revenge against the man who ousted him. With each passing day, communism was becoming more appealing to the unemployed and impoverished; Papen wanted to make use of Hitler, soon, while he could still bring the masses into the Nationalist camp.

Both Schleicher and Papen were reasonably intelligent men trying to accomplish definite programs for the best interests of Germany, as they saw them. By the dark winter of 1932, few German politicians sought high office for reasons of personal glory. In fact, everyone shunned responsibility; no one wanted to be held accountable by the hungry masses in the streets. That is why the leaders of the Social Democratic administration in Prussia, weary with failure, had allowed themselves to be ousted from power with an indifference that would have been unthinkable five years before. That was also why Groener and Bruening abandoned their posts in disgust almost without a word.

After a speech at the exclusive Herrenklub on the evening of December 10, Papen had a private chat with a fellow member, Baron Kurt von Schroeder, a Cologne banker who was known to be sympathetic to the Nazis. Papen hinted that the financier might try to arrange a secret meeting for him with Hitler.[13] A few days later, Wilhelm Keppler got in touch with Schroeder with a similar proposal from Hitler. The date of the meeting was set for January 4, when Papen would be staying in the Saarland and Hitler would be opening an election campaign in nearby Lippe. Every possible precaution was taken to keep the meeting secret. Accompanied by his staff, Hitler took the night train to Bonn, where he was met by his car the next morning, and proceeded on to Godesberg. After a short stop for breakfast, Hitler, Keppler, Himmler, and Hess changed into an inconspicuous car in which they departed for an unknown destination. The rest of the staff was instructed to drive on to Cologne in

Hitler's Mercedes, where they were to wait for him three kilometers on the other side of the city on the road to Düsseldorf.

When Papen arrived at the meeting place, the home of Baron von Schroeder in Cologne, he was surprised to see a photographer as he went in the gate but gave it little thought until the next day. After a light lunch, Hitler and Papen left their aides in the parlor and retired to Schroeder's study, where they continued their discussion behind closed doors, witnessed only by their host, the baron.

Papen came quickly to the point: he was interested in the prospects of replacing Schleicher's government with a Nationalist and Nazi coalition in which he and Hitler would be joint chancellors. But, Hitler replied that "if he were made chancellor it would be necessary for him to be head of the government, but that supporters of Papen could go into his government as ministers if they were willing to go along with him in his policy of changing many things. These changes included elimination of Social Democrats, Communists, and Jews from leading positions in Germany and the restoration of order in public life."[14] Hitler and Papen reached an agreement in principle but decided that further details would have to be worked out later.

To the great embarrassment of both participants, their "secret" meeting was reported in the headlines of the Berlin newspapers the next morning. Chancellor von Schleicher's agents had followed Papen; one of them was the photographer who had snapped his picture as he entered Schroeder's home. Harsh editorials accused Papen of trying to undermine the Schleicher government, but the ex-chancellor denied that the meeting was in any way directed against Schleicher; his main purpose, he claimed, had been to persuade Hitler to enter the Schleicher cabinet. General von Schleicher, of course, was well aware of what was afoot, for as Bismarck would have said: "No story is worth believing until it has been officially denied."

It would be wrong to suppose that a Hitler–Papen govern-

ment was agreed upon at the Cologne meeting; further negotiations would certainly be needed before Papen would
submit to serving as Hitler's subordinate. However, the first
contact had been made; both parties were now desperate
and willing to deal with each other. Moreover, Hitler got
one thing of the greatest value from the Cologne meeting.
Papen, who had been intervening in business circles to cut
off financial support from the Nazis, made it clear that he
no longer disapproved of large contributions to the National
Socialists. But this was not enough for Hitler; the Nazi party
was overburdened with debts, and creditors were threatening to foreclose.

Now it was Schroeder's turn to enter the discussion. The
meeting had not been held at his house simply by chance,
as if a wayside café would have done just as well. Schroeder
was an internationally known financier well connected with
industry, and known to be a supporter of Hitler.[15] According
to Otto Strasser, the brother of the Nazi leader Gregor Strasser, Schroeder then agreed to "foot the bill" for the National
Socialist Party.[16]

However, it is not likely the deal was so simple, for that
is not the way bankers operate. The evidence seems to indicate that instead of paying the Nazi party's bills himself,
Schoeder formed a syndicate of investors who agreed to
underwrite the party's debts.[17] Schroeder later said: "When
on November 6 the National Socialist Party suffered its first
setback and appeared to have passed its peak, the support
of German heavy industry became a matter of particular
urgency."[18] Most of those whom Schroeder got to "invest"
their money to cover the debts of the Nazi party came from
heavy industry and big banking circles. The exact identities
of all those involved are not known.[19]

As far as their participation in the Schroeder deal to cover
the Nazi party's debt was concerned, the "investors" could
later claim that technically they had not contributed to the
Nazi party. Once it was known that Baron von Schroeder
and his syndicate of investors were standing behind the par-

ty's debts, none of the creditors tried to foreclose on Hitler but, on the contrary, were willing to extend further credit. And once Hitler became chancellor, the party had no difficulty paying off its debts from the government treasury. So Schroeder and his associates were never actually required to give any of their money to the Nazis.[20] The financial arrangement Baron von Schroeder worked out for Hitler's party soon accomplished its primary purpose. Eleven days later, on January 17, Goebbels noted in his diary that "the financial situation has improved all of a sudden."[21]

By meeting with Hitler, Papen was also thwarting Schleicher's renewed attempts to break up the Nazi party. The chancellor's efforts were just then entering a critical phase. Although Hitler had dismissed him from his party posts, Strasser had reentered the political arena. He returned to Berlin on January 3, and Schleicher once again offered him the vice-chancellorship. On January 4, the day when Papen and Hitler met in Cologne, Strasser had been taken to see the president. Hindenburg was impressed with Strasser's disciplined calm, so different from the tense awkwardness of Hitler.

President von Hindenburg indicated that he would welcome Strasser as a vice-chancellor in Schleicher's cabinet. In fact, he now thought he had a choice of National Socialist vice-chancellors: Strasser under Schleicher or Hitler under Papen. Papen, in reporting his meeting with Hitler, gave the aged president the impression that he, Papen, would head a Papen-Hitler cabinet.[22] But even after the news of the Hitler-Papen meeting broke, Schleicher remained greatly encouraged. The old field marshal seemed to be coming over to his side again.

Walther Funk's trip through the Ruhr late in 1932 to collect money for the Nazi party from heavy industry was a dismal failure. A few months earlier, after the November elections, Wilhelm Keppler, Baron von Schroeder, and Dr. Hjalmar Schacht, the former president of the Reichsbank, decided, with the approval of Hitler, to approach the leading heavy industrialists with the request to sign a petition in which President von Hindenburg was urged to make Hitler chancellor. Hitler's appointment, the letter asserted, would help stabilize conditions, for "we recognize in the National Movement . . . the promise of a new era. By ending the class struggle it will create the indispensable foundation for a new rise of the German economy."

The response was not encouraging. The only major heavy industrialist who signed the petition was Fritz Thyssen. Other signers were either politically minded small industrialists like Keppler or right-wing bankers like Schacht, Schroeder, and Reinhardt, plus a few aristocrats and wealthy extremists.[23] Dr. Schacht's report to Hitler on the progress of the campaign was worded very carefully: "I have no doubt that the present development of things can only lead to your becoming chancellor. It seems as if our attempt to collect a number of signatures from business for this purpose was not altogether in vain, although I believe that heavy industry will hardly participate, for it rightfully bears its name 'heavy industry' on account of its indecisiveness."[24]

With heavy industry unwilling to openly oppose his government, Schleicher felt safe for the time being. In addition, there was another factor that boosted the chancellor's confidence; for the moment Hitler did not want a showdown with him. The National Socialists did not want an immediate vote in the Reichstag, nor were they willing to have the Reichstag adjourned for a considerable period. A vote of no-confidence against the Schleicher cabinet would have meant another national election. For this, the Nazis had neither the desire nor the financial resources. On the other hand, Hitler was not willing to wait quietly and allow Schleicher to benefit from an improvement in the economic situation. He did not believe that an improvement was going to occur, but he did not want to take any chances. What Hitler needed was a period of a few weeks in which to maneuver.

To counter Schleicher's threat to dissolve the Reichstag, ostensibly because there was no working majority, Hitler began making the initial moves in a clever project he had been planning ever since his cold rejection by Hindenburg on August 13. The objective of the plan was no less than the impeachment and removal from office of President von Hindenburg himself on a charge of unconstitutional use of Article 48 of the Weimar Constitution.

In launching this project, Hitler showed himself to be an unscrupulous master of parliamentary maneuvering; again he was using the weapons of democracy to destroy democracy itself. A motion of impeachment of the president of the Reich under Article 59 of the constitution required the support of at least 100 deputies of the Reichstag, and the National Socialists held 196 seats. To remove the president from office, however, the approval of a two-thirds' majority was needed. Yet Hitler was confident of obtaining the required 290 votes, for in addition to the 196 Nazi deputies he could safely count on the cooperation of the 100 Communists on an issue such as this, which would be a disaster for the established order. It was even possible that the motion would receive the support of a few left-wing Social Democrats who were anxious to avenge Papen's humiliating takeover of the Prussian government.[25]

Before Hitler's plan would become operational, however, there was one important obstacle to be remedied. In the event of the president's death or a vacancy of his office for "other causes," under Article 51 of the constitution the functions of the head of state were to be temporarily exercised by the chancellor until a successor had been elected. Naturally, Hitler was not about to see Hindenburg replaced by Schleicher, so to rule out such an eventuality he ordered his men in the Reichstag to introduce legislation substituting the president of the Supreme Court for the chancellor. On December 9, the bill was passed by 404 votes to 127 and became law.

By finding one "revolutionary" issue that the Nazis and Communists could support in common, Hitler had shrewdly taken advantage of the principal weakness of the current situation—the two "revolutionary" parties held the majority in the Reichstag. It was after the legislation necessary to activate his plan was passed, however, that he showed the malevolent subtlety of his intellect. Instead of immediately using his advantage to embarrass the old order and bring about a chaotic situation in which anything might have happened, he restrained himself, setting aside his personal dislike of Hindenburg. He used the threat of impeachment as a weapon of blackmail in the crucial moment for "negotiation" with the president or government.

As the days of early January 1933 passed, Hitler experienced a growing feeling of desperation. The economic situation might improve drastically overnight. The Nazis had to get power before that happened. Time was running out. Hitler knew he would have to make his bid for power before the end of February, while the impoverished masses were still in the gloom and misery of a harsh winter. Impatiently, the Nazis looked for a sign of weakness in their adversaries. The forces of the old order would have to be divided before they could be conquered. Clever maneuvering had given Hitler several trump cards, but the crucial thing was to play them at the right time before it was too late. The most agonizing thing for Hitler was that he had to sit and wait for his opponents to act; he could not take the initiative until they moved first.

There were about six million "officially registered" unemployed in mid-January 1933, which was approximately the same number as that date the previous year. The masses of the population were not interested in statistics about the "rate of increase in industrial production" or stock prices. They only knew that things had not improved for them. In fact, among the masses there was little hope of improvement; the people had waited too long and had been disappointed too often.

Economic conditions favored Chancellor von Schleicher's chances of imposing a dictatorship. By the end of 1932, a consensus was developing among the German upper class that an authoritarian government was needed, at least until the economic situation improved.

Late in 1932, President von Hindenburg met with the leaders of the four principal nonsocialist parties (with the exception of the Nazis) to ask their advice on solving the crisis. The talks, however, produced no solutions. Hugenberg (Nationalist party), Kaas (Catholic Center party), Dingeldey (German People's party), and Schaeffer (Bavarian People's party) all agreed on the need for a "strong government" and that the Nazis should be taken into the cabinet if possible, but with the exception of Kaas they had reservations about Hitler's appointment as chancellor. Although he had once been Hitler's ally, Hugenberg had the strongest misgivings, perhaps because of the several difficult experiences he had had with him. "I have not found much willingness on Hitler's part to honor commitments," he warned; "his way of handling political matters would make it very difficult to entrust him with the chancellorship. I would have the most serious objections."

Monsignor Kaas's reluctant willingness to accept Hitler as chancellor stemmed from his fear that a dictatorship without popular backing might plunge the country into civil war.* "We are facing a terrible winter," he warned the president; "twelve million Germans oppose the government on the Right and thirteen and a half million on the Left. The goal of a 'national concentration' including the National Socialists is thus a necessity."

Behind Kaas's urgency lay the haunting fear that the decline of the Nazis would benefit the Communists. If Hitler's desperate lower-class followers became dissatisfied, where would they turn for an even more radical alternative? Millions of hungry, unemployed workers might also desert their traditional moderate Social Democratic leaders and suddenly bolt into the Communist camp. With one hundred

---

*Monsignor Kaas was both a priest and the leader of the Catholic Center party.

seats in the Reichstag the Communists presented less of a threat than the Nazis, but their sweeping challenge to the existing order aroused apprehensions that made the Nazis seem the lesser evil. Moreover, Hitler and his propagandists skillfully nursed such fears and warned that their electoral setbacks were not a victory for their bourgeois opponents.

In *Der Angriff* Dr. Goebbels wrote: "We are entering a winter which lets us expect the worst. . . . Overnight the one hundred Bolsheviks in the Reichstag may double in number as a result of the economic depression and the limitless misery in which the majority of the German people finds itself. The hopeless desperation in which the masses are vegetating allows for even the most absurd possibility to come true. As a rule, the 'responsible circles' do not take our warnings very seriously; but if words carry no conviction, the facts are speaking an unmistakable language."[26] A few industrialists thought these warnings were well founded.[27] "Should we let the Nazis break their back," one businessman asked, "and have the whole tide of masses come flowing back upon us?"

If Hitler hoped to get the best possible terms in his deal with Papen, it was necessary to remove the impression that the strength of National Socialism was declining. In order to do so, he decided to concentrate the total resources of the party on winning the election in the little state of Lippe. The best Nazi orators were thrown into this campaign, even though the total vote at stake was only ninety thousand. Hitler himself, who for years had been addressing thousands, traveled around the small state for ten days, speaking in villages to audiences of a few hundred peasants at the most. The idea that a famous national figure would make the effort to come and talk to them greatly flattered the peasants of Lippe. People of all political persuasions came in record numbers to the Nazi meetings, which were usually held in big tents, since there were no meeting halls large enough in the villages, and even the most devoted listeners could not be expected to stand outdoors in January.

On January 15, the National Socialists were rewarded for their efforts in Lippe by a victory at the polls in which they obtained 40 percent of the votes, an increase of almost 17 percent over the last election. Immediately the party propaganda machine began to beat the drums of success: "The tide is turning"; "The party is on the march again"; "The signal from Lippe" became the slogan of a postelection propaganda campaign by Goebbels to impress the nation with the scale of the victory. The Nazis succeeded in making so much noise over their "renewed offensive" that even the Hindenburg clique was impressed.

A strenuous propaganda campaign helped to swell the number of Nazi votes in the Lippe election, but there was another factor, with broader national implications, that gave the peasants reason to take a renewed interest in Hitler. In the winter of 1932 to 1933, German agriculture was "cursed" with a record harvest. There was a surplus of grain, potatoes, and even meat, which unemployed people without money could not buy. The result was insufficient demand and crashing prices. Germany's military leaders had always insisted that the country should be able to feed itself "like a besieged fortress," without imports. Now that the German peasants and landowners had finally achieved this historic feat, it was destroying them. In a country with more than its share of starvation, the minister of food supply, Baron von Braun, said that emergency measures had to be taken to limit grain production in order to obtain "healthy prices."

In December of 1932, British tariffs destroyed the market for Danish butter in England. The desperate Danish producers responded by dumping their butter on the German market at prices that undercut the already overproduced German butter. The small dairy farmers in western and northern Germany loudly demanded that Chancellor von Schleicher bar Danish butter from Germany as Papen had planned to do. When Schleicher refused, the leading German farm organization, the Landbund, declared the chancellor was "hostile" to the interests of German agriculture. The

Junker landowners could now become more aggressive, since the enraged peasants and small farmers had joined them in demanding Schleicher's dismissal.

This issue of proposed tariff increases on food products brought the Junkers into direct conflict with the interests of the industrialists, for they feared that if the demands of the peasants were not met, a wedge would be driven between them and the peasants and their influential positions in the powerful agricultural associations would be undermined. In their desperation, the small farmers turned to Hitler as their savior. As early as the fall of 1932, the Nazi takeover of agricultural interest groups was so obvious that the Papen government had attempted countermeasures "to drive the peasants away from the National Socialists."[28] The Junkers, however, were forced to take increasingly extreme measures in order to maintain their alliance with the small farmers. Thus peasants and landlords, although their interests were by no means identical, became united in their opposition to the Weimar system.

When the leaders of the Social Democratic party refused to back General von Schleicher because of his reputation as an intriguer and his prior dealings with Papen and the Nazis, he turned elsewhere for support. He thought he could build up a popular following among the landless farm laborers, who made up about 28 percent of the rural population,[29] and the unemployed by beginning to enact his land settlement program for the impoverished. This program was very similar to Bruening's, which promised the impoverished farm workers, 800,000 acres from the bankrupt estates of East Prussia. On January 12, the Landbund, the most powerful agricultural association, launched its counterattack against the chancellor. Its president, Count von Kalkreuth, called in person upon Hindenburg to protest against the planned confiscation of the bankrupt estates.

Taking agrarian matters most seriously, President von Hindenburg immediately summoned Schleicher and several key cabinet ministers for a meeting with the spokesman of the Landbund. The old president chaired the meeting himself as the representatives of the agrarians told grim stories of the plight of farmers in all parts of the country. There were warnings that the farmers were turning to communism because their problems were being neglected. One of the Landbund officials looked in the president's direction and hinted that the latter's wishes were being ignored. Schleicher's resettlement plan was sharply attacked; if the Junkers as well as the small farmers were being abandoned, the defense of the nation would be seriously endangered. The argument fell on receptive ground; as a military man, Hindenburg was familiar with the theory that the grain-producing estates of the east would be needed to make the country self-sufficient in food in wartime. The representatives of the Landbund concluded by asking for a suspension of all foreclosures for three to six months as an emergency measure to save German agriculture.

Chancellor von Schleicher replied by pointing out that the farmers did not exist in a vacuum. He cautioned that other sectors of the economy (i.e., industry and commerce) also had rights that he could not ignore. A suspension of all foreclosures would ruin tradesmen, rural businesses, and even some banks—therefore, it was out of the question.[30]

A few days later, the chancellor counterattacked the Junkers with a threat to publish the report of the Reichstag investigation into the government-sponsored Osthilfe loans. These loans had been given to the East Prussian agricultural districts to modernize the farms so they would be more efficient. As it turned out, most of the money went to the great estates rather than the smaller farms. The Reichstag investigation turned up more than a few unsavory scandals. There was, for example, a landowner, bankrupt through his own ineptitude, whose estates had been given subsidies three times; after a fourth financial breakdown, his estates had been ceded under the Osthilfe to a daughter who was still a minor. There were absentee landlords who splurged the government-loaned money on automobiles, women, and trips to the Riviera, leaving banks and tradesmen who had given them credit to sing for their money. Implicated in the scandals were the aristocratic leaders of the Landbund itself, and some of the oldest families of Prussia.

The Osthilfe matter even touched—though indirectly—President von Hindenburg himself. In 1927, when the family estate of Neudeck had been presented to the old field marshal on his eightieth birthday, the deeds had been made out in the name of his son, Oskar, in order to evade the payment of inheritance taxes. This illegality was customary among Junker families at the time, and though it had no direct connection with the Osthilfe scandal, the president's friend Oldenburg-Januschau immediately warned Oskar that Schleicher would certainly publish the story of the tax evasion along with the Osthilfe Report.

With the threatened disclosure of the Osthilfe Report, Schleicher hoped to force the Junkers into submission. Once again, he was using his favorite weapon of "divide and conquer;" he planned to pit the Nazis against the Nationalists, since he was certain of National Socialist support on an issue that would be popular with the masses. However, the chancellor failed to recognize that he was cutting himself off from his base of support. For over two hundred years, the Junkers and the Officer Corps had been inseparably bound by common interest. Although a member of the exalted caste himself, Schleicher was threatening to divide these interests. In embarking upon his struggle against the Landbund, he underestimated the strength of the political and economic interests he was attacking.

The role of the Junker class in the German political struggle of 1933 is an interesting case of differentiation and interaction between political and economic power. Big business had increased its economic status as a result of the depression, which provided it with an opportunity to consolidate its position against the trade unions. In contrast, the Junkers experienced a decline in their economic status during the depression, which brought many estates to the brink of bankruptcy. The Junkers, however, maintained their hold on the principal institution of the state's power, the army, whereas big business had seen their political influence, which rested on the democratic and moderate parties, steadily eroded.

So great was the military and social prestige of the Prussian Junkers that they were able to resist almost all attempts by democratic forces after 1918 to weaken their privileged position. In the mist-laden region east of the Elbe, a feudal atmosphere lingered into the twentieth century. On the great East Prussian estates, the Junker landlords, preserving a medieval idea of their authority, were accustomed to treating their farm laborers like serfs. Most of these agricultural laborers were deprived of basic political rights. They had to vote alongside their master for the conservative candidate or else "pack their bundles."

The coming of the depression, however, undercut the economic basis of the Junker aristocracy. Because of poor soil, great efforts were needed to make the Prussian estates profitable even in prosperous times. During the economic crisis, state subsidies became an absolute necessity. But Junker agricultural undertakings were not the only sector of the economy that was in difficulty. By the winter of 1932 to 1933, every interest group was clamoring for state assistance, and there was no longer enough money to go around. Big business came to the conclusion that all unprofitable sectors of the economy would have to be cut if the German economy as a whole was to survive. It was obvious that the country could no longer afford the luxury of a subsidized aristocracy. The battle lines were drawn between the progressive big business interests and the Junkers, with the latter fighting for their very survival.

Angered by Schleicher's threat to their subsidies, the Junker-dominated Nationalist party withdrew its support from the government on January 20. This was an open declaration of war between the Junkers and the chancellor. Two days later Hitler, who fully realized the implications of the Nationalist move, asked Oskar von Hindenburg to meet with him. Aware of some of the pressures that might be used on him, the president's son asked State Secretary Meissner to accompany him and remain present during any conversation he might have with Hitler.

On the evening of January 22, young Hindenburg and Meissner left the presidential palace on foot to avoid being noticed. They walked a few blocks, hailed a taxi, then proceeded directly to the suburban home of Joachim von Ribbentrop, Papen's friend and supporter of Hitler. They were met there by Papen, Hitler, Frick, and Goering. Up to this time, Oskar von Hindenburg had been opposed to any dealings with the Nazis. However, after about half an hour of general conversation, Hitler insisted on having a talk with the president's son, alone; to Meissner's astonishment, Hindenburg agreed and withdrew with Hitler to another room. In about an hour the two emerged

There is no record of what was said between Hitler and Oskar while they were alone. However, it is not difficult to imagine the arguments Hitler used: if he was not appointed chancellor soon, the National Socialists would proceed with their threat to impeach the president and would disclose Oskar's tax evasion on the Neudeck estate.* On the other hand, if Oskar would use his influence with his father in Hitler's interests, the Nazis would loyally support the field marshal as chief of state and Oskar would receive a military promotion.† "In the taxi on the way back," said Meissner,

---

*The tax evasion issue was more dangerous to Hindenburg than Schleicher's threat to publish the Osthilfe Report, since Hindenburg had not taken or squandered any Osthilfe money illegally.

†In August 1933, seven months after Hitler had taken office as chancellor, five thousand acres were added, tax free, to Neudeck estate, and a year later, when Hitler became supreme commander of the army on the death of President von Hindenburg, Oskar was promoted to the rank of major general.

"Oskar von Hindenburg was extremely silent, and the only remark he made was that it could not be helped—the Nazis had to be taken into the government."[31]

Sunday, January 22, had been a good day for Hitler; not only did he gain the support of Oskar von Hindenburg, who probably exercised more influence on his father than anyone else, but earlier in the day, the S.A. had won a significant victory over the Communists. While Hitler spoke of order and legality to the Papen-Hindenburg group, he spoke to his storm troopers of violence and terror in the streets. In the last months of his struggle for power, Hitler practiced a cunning strategy of duplicity. He methodically shattered what was left of the political order in Germany by fighting with the Communists in the streets and collaborating with them in the Reichstag. After their electoral victory in Lippe, the Nazis used every trick they knew to prove they were capable of smashing communism. They sent the S.A. more boldly than ever into working-class neighborhoods, the centers of Communist power. Meanwhile, in the Reichstag, the National Socialist-Communist majority stood together in opposition to the feeble moves of the government.

In support of Hitler's strategy, Goebbels began a new propaganda effort designed to prove that a decline of the National Socialist party would be the greatest possible misfortune for middle-class Germans. It was not difficult to convince people of the truth of this argument, especially when Chancellor von Schleicher privately admitted the National Socialist party must not be allowed to disintegrate, for if it did, there would be ten million Communists in Germany the next day. In order to convince the people that only the Nazis could stand up to the Communist danger, it was announced that some ten thousand men of the Berlin S.A. would demonstrate on Sunday, January 22, in the Bülowplatz, facing the broad facade of the Karl Liebknecht House, Communist party headquarters. Two days before the demonstration, Goebbels wrote in his diary: "The S.A. is to parade in front of the Karl Liebknecht House. . . . We shall stake everything on one throw to win back the streets of Berlin for the German nation."[32]

When the Communists ordered a counterdemonstration at the same hour, the most violent street battle since 1923 seemed inevitable. Attempting to appease the larger party, Schleicher's government banned only the Communist demonstration and offered the Nazis all possible police protection. This was quite a change from the days when only the socialists enjoyed the protection of the law in Berlin and the Nazis faced a new ban at every turn; this in itself was a sign of the times. Escorted by police, the S.A. marched to conquer "Red Berlin," as the Marxists so proudly called it.

Goebbels, the man who organized this dress rehearsal for the coming Nazi revolution, described the scene:

> Our marching in the Bülowplatz has caused great commotion. The police are patrolling the slums with machine guns and armored cars. In spite of the prohibition, the Communists have proclaimed a huge demonstration. If it fails, they will suffer an irreparable loss of prestige. . . . Meanwhile, we assemble on the Bülowplatz. One really risks one's life to get through. But everything goes well. The square looks like a military camp. The Communists are making an uproar in the side streets. Armored cars and machine guns are everywhere to be seen. The police have posted themselves on the roofs and at the windows facing the Platz, waiting the course of events. Punctually at two o'clock the Fuehrer arrives. The S.A. marches to the Karl Liebknecht House. . . . Outside the Karl Liebknecht House the S.A. is posted, and in the side streets the Communists are shouting with impotent rage. The S.A. is on the march and overawes the Reds on their own ground, Berlin. The Bülowplatz is ours. The Communists have suffered a great defeat.[33]

Although heavy industry apparently played no direct role in the fateful political events at the end of January 1933, their attitude toward the Schleicher cabinet indirectly determined the course of events. On the one hand, they refused to support the Schleicher government because it favored the interests of light industry and commerce, and on the other, they declined to join the agrarian reactionaries in their attempts to overthrow it. Thus Schleicher was too weak to stay in power and Papen was too weak to take power—too weak to take power without Hitler's help, that is. Having no suitable candidate of their own to support, the heavy industrialists decided to do nothing for a while in the hopes that economic conditions would soon improve and provide a better climate for positive action.

From January 22 on, the Nazis continued to negotiate with Papen. As the end of the month approached, Schleicher's position was becoming desperate. He had failed to win over the National Socialists or divide them by his offer to Strasser. The Social Democrats and Center party, whom he had counted on, never gave him their full support. Amazingly, the Social Democratic party, the second largest party in the country, exercised little or no influence on the course of events during the winter of 1932 to 1933. There were several reasons for this. The leaders of the Social Democrats were middle-aged bureaucrats whose first concern was to protect their own jobs and the status quo. Moreover, they had a general feeling of apathy and impotence from their years of failure while in power and had lost faith in their own socialist solutions for the depression. Schleicher was the only man who still would have been capable of welding them into an effective political force against Hitler, but they did not trust him.

At last, Schleicher recognized the impossibility of assembling a majority in the Reichstag, so he called on the president, demanding its dissolution and the emergency powers to rule by decree under Article 48 of the constitution. Schleicher finally found himself in the same position Papen had been in when Papen in early December had wanted to rule by decree and Schleicher had wanted to form a government with the support of the Nazis. Now the roles were reversed. The general was asking for a dictatorship while Papen assured the president that he could form a coalition government with Hitler that would secure a majority in the Reichstag. The old President received Schleicher and refused him the decree of dissolution. Why?

Hindenburg undoubtedly understood little of the economic conflict between heavy industry, light industry, and agrarian interests; however, Schleicher's threatened investigation of the Osthilfe scandal was a definite indication that he intended to destroy the privileged economic and political position of the East Prussian landlords and the Junker class; this the old president understood. The large East Prussian estates were seen by Hindenburg as the indispensable producers of foodstuffs in wartime. This was one of the few economic convictions the old field marshal had, and since it was related to the military sphere, he was not about to let his advisers change his mind on it. But above all, he saw these estates as the homes of the old Prussian families that to him were the country's backbone. If they lost their properties, they would be destroyed as a class, and the nation would be deprived of that social elite which alone could recapture its greatness.

Faced with Hindenburg's opposition, Schleicher had no choice but to offer his resignation. However, the general was not yet ready to give in completely and remarked to his friend General von Hammerstein, "I shall not allow myself to be plucked to pieces."[34] At noon, on January 28, when the Schleicher cabinet officially resigned, Papen was still hesitant. He was torn between the desire to establish a "great" Hitler-Papen-Hugenberg coalition and the desire to double-cross Hitler at the last moment and become chancellor himself in a Papen-Hugenberg cabinet. In doubt, Papen sounded out his former colleagues who were still ministers ad interim in the Schleicher cabinet. Confronted with a choice of either compromising with Hitler or facing the masses during a harsh winter with another government supported only by the Nationalist party, the majority reluctantly preferred the former.

Old President von Hindenburg was bewildered, tired, and able to concentrate on the complex situation for no more than half an hour at a time. He was still thinking of a Papen cabinet with Hitler as vice-chancellor. But now, Papen himself was suggesting that Hitler be appointed chancellor.[35] In his confusion, Hindenburg consulted the leaders of the moderate parties. All of them had finally turned against General von Schleicher. They, too, suggested that the time had come to give Hitler the chancellorship, with all the appropriate guarantees of course. They believed that once the Nazis were in the government, they could be tamed and exhausted. The grueling day-to-day work would dull their glamour; they would be forced to pass unpopular laws signed by Hitler and Goebbels instead of by Bruening or Papen. From their own years of experience, the moderate party leaders were certain Hitler would be unable to fulfill all his vague promises. These professional politicians knew what a thankless role it was to be in power during a depression. They hoped that Hitler, like all the chancellors before him, would be broken by the responsibilities of office.

Sunday, January 29, was an important day for the various intriguers making their last desperate attempts to secure power. Hitler later said, "The twenty-ninth, naturally, was buzzing with conferences, in the course of which I succeeded in obtaining Hugenberg's agreement to the dissolution of the Reichstag."[36]

Meanwhile, General von Schleicher had been seeking advice from his influential friends and business leaders throughout the country. Among those whom he telephoned was Otto Wolff, "the steel king" of Cologne, who told him some shocking news. Without the knowledge or consent of Schleicher, who was the minister of defense, General von Blomberg, the chief German military delegate at the Geneva Disarmament Conference, who was known to be pro-Nazi, had been ordered to report immediately to President von

Hindenburg.* He was to leave Geneva at once. Although Blomberg was not yet aware of the fact that Hindenburg intended to appoint him minister of defense, Wolff had somehow learned of it. Wolff advised Schleicher to make use of the powers still left to him as interim chancellor and minister of defense to proclaim a state of emergency, declare martial law, and establish a military dictatorship for a limited period. Once this was accomplished, the general should move old Hindenburg and his son under "protective detention" to Neudeck and have Blomberg arrested as soon as his train crossed the Swiss border.[37]

Both Schleicher and General von Hammerstein, the commanding general of the army, were furious with the president's recalling Blomberg behind their backs. But Schleicher hesitated to take the forceful measures advised by Otto Wolff. In the moment of crisis, a general was not willing to act as decisively as an industrialist.

Schleicher decided to try to divide his opponents by sending General von Hammerstein to negotiate with Hitler. Their meeting took place at Charlottenburg, in the home of Hitler's patron Carl Bechstein. Hammerstein warned Hitler that Papen still might leave him out in the cold and they would wake up the next morning to find a Papen-Hugenberg cabinet a fait accompli. Still believing that certain compromises would have to be worked out with the Nazis, Schleicher had instructed Hammerstein to suggest a Hitler-Schleicher coalition to rule with the united support of the army and the National Socialists. As instructed, General von Hammerstein exerted all his influence in this direction.

It was then four o'clock in the afternoon, and Hitler still did not know whether or not Goering's negotiations with

---

*The Geneva Disarmament Conference took place intermittently between 1932 and 1934. Representatives of sixty nations attended and tried to reach an agreement on the reduction of national armaments. One of the major problems in the early stages of the conference was the refusal of France to reduce the size of its army.

Papen were being used as a screen for a double cross by the latter. The Nazi Fuehrer found himself confronted with a difficult decision: both Schleicher and Papen were now offering him the chancellorship. But could he trust them? With whom would he align himself: Schleicher, whose offer was more direct, or the Papen-Hugenberg interests, with whom the negotiations were more complicated? Here Hitler showed himself to be more than just an ambitious seeker of power. He was not concerned so much with becoming chancellor as with becoming chancellor in a way that would permit him to carry out the revolution he had planned. He declined the easy path, to unite with Schleicher, who really had more force behind him. Hitler chose his partners for their weaknesses, and chose them well. Already he was thinking ahead to the day when he could dispense with them.

For the moment, however, Hitler promised to let the general know as soon as he had any definite news and added an assurance of his willingness to retain Schleicher as minister of defense when he should become chancellor.

A few hours later that afternoon, Hitler was having coffee and cakes with his lieutenants when Goering burst in with the news: "Tomorrow, the Fuehrer is to be appointed chancellor!"[38] A deal had finally been agreed upon with Papen and his allies. None of this information was conveyed to General von Hammerstein as promised.

As he waited at Goebbels's apartment on the long night of January 29 to 30, Hitler was well aware of the possible complications that could still arise on the part of the Papen-Hugenberg group. He was still adamant in his demand for an immediate dissolution of the Reichstag, and it was not yet certain that President von Hindenburg would yield on this matter. But also disturbing Hitler was the possibility that the army under Generals von Schleicher and von Hammerstein might try at the last moment to prevent the formation of a Hitler-Papen cabinet. Schleicher, as interim minister of defense, was the only man among Hitler's rivals who actually had any force behind him, but that force, the army, could be decisive.

Suddenly, Werner von Alvensleben, a leading figure in the Herrenklub and formerly one of Schleicher's chief liaison men with the Nazis, arrived at Goebbels's apartment with a startling piece of news. According to von Alvensleben, Generals von Schleicher and von Hammerstein were planning to call out the Potsdam garrison and settle things by force.

This was what Hitler had been afraid might happen. Goering left immediately to warn Papen and Hindenburg. Hitler quickly summoned the commander of the Berlin S.A., Count von Helldorf, ordering him to put his men in a state of alert. Then he called Major Wecke of the police, who was a known Nazi sympathizer, and advised him to prepare six police battalions to close off the area around the chancellery and Presidential Palace if the army should attempt to move in. The wildest panic spread through the government quarter of Berlin. Meissner was awakened at two o'clock on the morning of the thirtieth by a telephone call and was informed that Schleicher was preparing to transport the president and his son to Neudeck "in a lead-lined truck" and that he, Papen, and Hugenberg were to be arrested.

Was Schleicher really planning a coup? The army had always regarded itself as the ultimate source of power and security within the Reich. Both Schleicher and Hammerstein were convinced, after their recent interviews with the elderly field marshal, that he was no longer in possession of his mental powers. He might embark upon any folly with the intriguing Papen as his trusted confidant. To the generals, it seemed that now, if ever, it was the duty of the army to protect Germany.

The night of January 29 passed slowly for the Nazi leaders assembled at the Kaiserhof. "We sit up till five o'clock in the morning," wrote Goebbels in his diary, "we are ready for everything, and have considered the thing from all angles. The Fuehrer paces up and down the room."[39]

That night in Geneva, General Werner von Blomberg was boarding the express train for Berlin in response to the summons that he had received from Hindenburg and Papen, ordering him to return to Germany at once, to become the minister of defense in a Hitler-Papen government. Blomberg had first been introduced to Hitler's ideas by Ludwig Mueller, the Protestant chaplain of the East Prussian Army, who was himself an enthusiastic National Socialist. At the Geneva Disarmament Conference this aristocratic general had shocked the other German representatives when he advised them to read *Mein Kampf* and even quoted passages to them.

When the night train from Geneva brought Blomberg into the Berlin Station, shortly after dawn on the morning of January 30, he was met at the boarding platform by two officers who had conflicting orders for him. One was Major von Kuntzen, General von Hammerstein's adjutant, who ordered him to report to the commander in chief of the army; the other was Colonel Oskar von Hindenburg, his father's adjutant, who commanded Blomberg to report to the president. Blomberg went to President von Hindenburg, who immediately swore him in as minister of defense, thus giving him the authority to suppress any putsch. But the general was warned not to go to this new ministry without an armed escort lest he be arrested.

The fear of a possible putsch by Schleicher forced Papen and Hugenberg to carry through with the agreement they had made with the Nazis. On the cold wintery morning of January 30, Hitler received the long-awaited summons from the president. In spite of a sleepless night, he was fresh with excitement as he got into the car that would take him the short distance to the chancellery.

In his memoirs Papen described the last-minute difficulties and disputes before the new government took office.

At about half-past ten, the members of the proposed cabinet met in my office and walked across the garden to the

Presidential Palace, where we waited in Meissner's office. Hitler immediately renewed his complaints about not being appointed commissioner for Prussia. He felt that this severely restricted his power. I told him . . . the Prussian appointment could be left until later. To this, Hitler replied that if his powers were to be this limited, he must insist on new Reichstag elections. . . .

This produced a completely new situation and the debate became heated. Hugenberg, in particular, objected to the idea, and Hitler tried to pacify him. . . . By this time it was long past eleven o'clock, the time that had been appointed for our interview with the President, and Meissner asked me to end our discussion, as Hindenburg was not prepared to wait any longer.

We had had such a sudden clash of opinions that I was afraid our new coalition would break up before it was born. . . . At last we were shown into the President and I made the necessary formal introductions. Hindenburg made a short speech about the necessity of full cooperation in the interests of the nation, and we were then sworn in. The Hitler cabinet had been formed.[40]

Papen was quite satisfied with his own cleverness, for the National Socialists made up a small minority of the new government, which he was sure he could dominate. Only three of the eleven cabinet posts were held by Nazis, and with the exception of the chancellorship these were positions of lesser importance. Frick was the minister of interior, but he did not control the police, as that office did in many European countries; in Germany the police were under the authority of the individual states. Goering was made minister without portfolio, with the understanding he would become minister of aviation as soon as Germany had an air force. However, Goering was also named as minister of interior of Prussia, an office that received little notice but controlled the Prussian police.

The important posts in the cabinet went to the gentlemen

of the Right. Baron von Neurath, a career diplomat, continued as minister of foreign affairs, while the aristocratic General von Blomberg became minister of defense. Count Lutz
Schwerin von Krosigk was minister of finance. The Ministry
of Labor was given to Seldte, the leader of the monarchist
Stahlhelm. True, Hitler had the chancellorship, but the real
power, as Papen had planned it, rested in the hands of the
vice-chancellor, Papen himself. It was the vice-chancellor,
not the chancellor, who enjoyed the special confidence of
the president. In fact, Hindenburg had promised never to
receive the chancellor unless he was accompanied by the
vice-chancellor. It was also the vice-chancellor who held the
key post of minister-president of Prussia, and who could
command the loyalty of all but two of the other ministers.

The German press devoted several leading articles to
pointing out that Hugenberg was really the new dictator
of Germany. By his stubborn negotiations with Hitler, the
Nationalist leader had achieved his goal: he had become
both minister of economics and minister of agriculture. He
issued a public statement saying that he was sure the Reichstag would give the new government one year in which to
work undisturbed. During that time, he would "remold"
the economy along "sounder" lines. The implication was
clear. Hugenberg and his party of Junkers intended to enact
a reactionary economic policy for the benefit of the big agricultural interests and let industry and labor be damned.

So far, things had worked out just as Papen had planned
them: Hitler would play his role of "drummer"; his name
would be first, but the real decisions would be made by
those who outnumbered him eight to three in the cabinet
and held most of the key posts. After countless detailed
explanations of his plan, Papen had overcome President von
Hindenburg's reluctance to appoint Hitler chancellor. Thus,
Papen had finally succeeded in winning the mass support
of the Nazis for the government, something Schleicher had
been trying in vain to do for several years. Little did the
new vice-chancellor know how badly he was underestimat-

ing Hitler and the forces he controlled. Yet, as dusk began to fall over Berlin that night, a spectacle began to unfold that should have been a warning to Papen and Hugenberg.

From about seven o'clock until far past midnight, Nazi storm troopers in brown shirts marched past the chancellery in a massive torchlight parade to celebrate Hitler's triumph. Out of the Tiergarten they came by the tens of thousands in disciplined columns. From a window in the Presidential Palace, old Hindenburg looked down on them, beating time to the military marches with his cane, pleased that at last he had picked a chancellor who could arouse the people in a traditional patriotic way.

Goebbels had organized this massive demonstration in just six hours. Papen and Hugenberg could not have assembled as many men in six days or even six weeks. Hitler would not be so easily controlled as the Nationalists thought. For the Nazis this was just the beginning of their revolution.

ENDNOTES

CHAPTER 1

A Mysterious Beginning

1. Hjalmar Schacht, *Confessions of the "Old Wizard"* (Boston: 1956), 257.

2. Ibid.

3. Ibid.

4. Leonard Mosley, *The Reich Marshal: A Biography of Hermann Goering* (New York: 1974), 123.

5. Alan Bullock, *Hitler, A Study in Tyranny* (New York: 1964), 372.

6. Hermann Rauschning, *The Voice of Destruction* (New York: 1940), 60.

7. Bullock, *Hitler,* 372.

8. William L. Shirer, *The Rise and Fall of the Third Reich* (New York: 1960), 125.

9. Adolf Hitler, *Mein Kampf* (New York: 1940), 50–63.

10. See: H. R. Trevor-Roper's introductory essay, "The Mind of Adolf Hitler," in *Hitler's Secret Conversations* (New York: 1953).

11. Hitler, *Mein Kampf,* 291–93.

12. Ibid., 294.

13. Ibid., 296–97.

14. Ibid., 300.

15. For a history of the Thule Society, I am indebted to Reginal H. Phelps, "Before Hitler Came: Thule Society and Germanen Orden," *Journal of Modern History*, 35 (September 1963). Also, see: Rudolf von Sebottendorff, *Bevor Hitler Kam: Urkundiches aus der Fruhzeit der national-socialistischen Bewegung von Rudolf von Sebottendorff* (Munich: 1934).

16. Robert Cecil, *Nyth of the Master Race* (New York: 1972), 22.

17. Sebottendorff, *Bevor Hitler Kam*, 57–60.

18. Sebottendorff tried to give the impression that Harrer acted on his own. See: Sebottendorff, *Bevor Hitler Kam*, 81.

19. For Drexler's account of the event, see: Anton Drexler, "Der beginn meines politischen Denkens," typescript of speech, NSDAP Hauptarchive (HA), no. 78.

20. The London *Times*, May 5, 1919.

21. Hitler, *Mein Kampf*, 297–98.

22. Ibid., 492.

23. Konrad Heiden, *Der Fuehrer* (Boston: 1944), 89.

24. Bullock, *Hitler*, 67.

25. Kurt Lüdecke, *I Knew Hitler* (New York: 1938), 245.

26. Heiden, *Der Fuehrer* 26–33.

27. *Hitler's Secret Conversations*, 267.

28. Ibid., 268.

29. Ibid., 180.

30. Lüdecke, *I Knew Hitler*, 92.

31. All other German parties were funded by big business or organized labor. See: Louis P. Lochner, *Tycoons and Tyrants* (Chicago: 1954), 91.

32. Hitler, *Mein Kampf*, 59–62.

33. Norman H. Baynes, ed., *The Speeches of Adolf Hitler, April 1922–August 1939*, 2 vols (London: 1942), 1–87.

34. Ernst Hanfstaengl, *Unheard Witness* (Philadelphia: 1957) *op. cit.*, 71.

35. See: Dietrich Eckart's letter to Max Amann, May 10, 1923, HA roll 54, folder 1317.

36. Cecil, *Master Race*, 23.

37. Konrad Heiden, *Hitler, A Biography* (New York: 1936), 45.

38. Joachim Fest, *Hitler* (New York: 1974), 24.

39. Hanfstaengl, *Unheard Witness*, 57.

40. Cecil, *Master Race*, 24.

41. Ibid., 30.

42. *The Protocols of the Learned Elders of Zion*, trans. Victor Marsden, privately printed. For the historical background of the *Protocols*, see: Norman Cohn, *Warrant for Genocide* (New York: 1966).

43. Heiden, *Der Fuhrer*, 19.

44. Hitler, *Mein Kampf*, 506–14.

45. John W. Wheeler-Bennett, *The Nemesis of Power* (New York: 1954), 46.

46. Alan Bullock, for example, mentions Frau Hofmann in the same category as Frau Bechstein and Frau Wagner, who were both socially prominent and wealthy. Bullock, *Hitler*, 392.

47. Lüdecke, *I Knew Hitler*, 74–75.

48. Wheeler-Bennett, *The Nemesis of Power*, 79.

49. Hans Hofmann, *Der Hitler putsch* (Munich: 1961), 55.

50. Oron J. Hale, ed., "Gottfried Feder Calls Hitler to Order: An Unpublished Letter on Nazi Party Affairs," *Journal of Modern History* 30 (1958), 360.

51. Hanfstaengl, *Unheard Witness*, 45.

52. *Hitler's Secret Conversations*, 179–80.

53. Hanfstaengel, *Unheard Witness*, 46.

54. Hitler, *Mein Kampf* 736.

55. *Hitler's Secret Conversations*, 376.

56. Jean Michel Angebert, *Hitler et la Tradition Cathare.* Published in English as *The Occult and the Third Reich* (New York: 1974).

57. *Hitler's Secret Conversations*, 179.

58. Ibid., 509.

59. Ibid.

1. *Hitler's Secret Conversations,* 223.

2. Ibid.

3. Ibid.

4. Fritz Sternberg, *Capitalism and Socialism on Trial* (New York: 1968), 191–94.

5. For example, see: Bullock, *Hitler,* 68.

6. Hanfstaengl, *Unheard Witness,* 54.

7. Ibid., 55.

8. Ibid.

9. Ibid.

10. Ibid.

11. Ibid.

12. Ibid., 57.

13. Ibid., 56.

14. Quoted in Konrad Heiden, *Hitler: A Biography,* 96.

15. Sternberg, *Capitalism and Socialism,* 258–60.

16. Fritz K. Ringer, ed., *The German Inflation of 1923* (New York: 1969), 82–83.

17. Konrad Heiden called him an actor by profession. (Heiden, *Hitler,* 95) H. H. Hoffmann said he was an elderly East Prussian (H. H. Hoffmann, *Der Hitler Putsch* [Munich: 1961].)

18. Aktenvermerk, State Ministry of Exterior, date cir. Nov. 15, 1923.

19. William H. Chamberlain, *The Russian Revolution* (New York: 1935), vol. 2.

20. HA, reel 53, folder 1263.

21. Walter Laqueur, *Russia and Germany: A Century of Conflict,* 108.

22. Hanfstaengl, *Unheard Witness,* 44.

23. *Hitler's Secret Conversations,* 291.

24. Friedeland Wagner and Page Cooper, *Heritage of Fire: The Story of Richard Wagner's Granddaughter* (New York: 1945), 30.

25. Quoted in Werner Maser, *Hitler: Legend, Myth and Reality*, 199.

26. Ibid., 200.

27. Lüdecke, *I Knew Hitler*, 96.

28. Ibid., 56.

29. Ibid.

30. Quoted in Konrad Heiden, *Der Fuehrer*, 127.

31. Ibid., 131.

32. Hanfstaengl, *Unheard Witness*, 57–58.

33. Ibid.

34. Quoted in Heiden, *Hitler*, 122.

35. *Hitler's' Secret Conversations*, 498.

36. Ibid.

37. Ibid.

38. Mosley, *The Reich Marshal*, 90.

39. Lüdecke, *I Knew Hitler*, 131.

40. Mosley, *The Reich Marshal*, 67–71.

41. Ibid., 70–71.

42. Fritz Thyssen, *I Paid Hitler* (New York: 1941), 82.

43. Ibid., 80.

44. Ibid., 54.

45. Ibid., 80–82.

46. Ibid., 82–83.

47. Hanser, *Putsch* (New York: 1970), 361.

48. Hanfstaengl, *Unheard Witness*, 108.

49. For example, see: Arthur Schweitzer, *Big Business in the Third Reich* (Bloomington, Indiana: 1964); and Franz Neumann, *Behemoth: The Structure and Practice of National Socialism* (New York: 1941).

CHAPTER 3

Ford and Hitler

1. Heiden, *Hitler*, 221.

2. William C. Richards, *The Last Billionaire* (New York: 1948), 89.

3. Ibid., 95. One of the "two very prominent Jews" later revealed himself by filing a $200,000 damage suit against Ford because of the nasty accusations; he was the well-known journalist Herman Bernstein, who wrote a book in 1921 about the *Protocols* entitled *History of a Lie.*

4. Ibid., 5.

5. David L. Lewis, *The Public Image of Henry Ford: An American Folk Hero and His Company* (Detroit: 1976), 135.

6. Ibid., 136.

7. Raymond L. Stebbins, *Henry Ford and Edwin Pipp: A Suppressed Chapter in the Story of the Auto Magnate,* ed. C. L. Hold (typed manuscript, Hebrew Union Library, xy1/S81, Cincinnati, n.d.), 4.

8. Richards, *The Last Billionaire,* 90.

9. Lewis, *Public Image,* 139.

10. Ibid., 140.

11. Allen Nevins and Frank Ernest Hill, *Ford: The Times, The Man, the Company* (New York: 1954–63), 3 vols., vol. 2: *Expansion and Challenge,* 311).

12. Keith Sward, *The Legend of Henry Ford* (New York: 1948), 159. Also Norman Cohn, *Warrent for Genocide: The Myth of the Jewish World-Conspiracy and the Protocols of the Elders of Zion* (New York: 1966), 162.

13. Lewis, *Public Image,* 148.

14. Ibid., 143

15. Ibid.

16. Ibid.

17. Quoted in John Roy Carlson, *Under Cover: My Four Years in the Nazi Underworld of America* (New York: 1943), 210.

18. Cohn, *Warrant for Genocide,* 138.

19. Lewis, *Public Image,* 148.

20. Ibid., 143; Hitler, *Mein Kampf,* editors' fn., 929.

21. *Hitler's Secret Conversations,* 228.

22. Cohn, *Warrant for Genocide,* 183.

23. Hitler, *Mein Kampf,* 155.

24. *The International Jew: World's Foremost Problem,*

abridged from the original as published by Henry Ford, in the *Dearborn Independent*, ed. Gerald L. K. Smith (Los Angeles: 1964), 40. All following quotations from *The International Jew* are cited from this edition, which is more available than earlier editions.

25. Hitler, *Mein Kampf*, 413.

26. *The International Jew*, 191–92.

27. Ibid, introduction by Gerald Smith, 9.

28. Hermann Rauschning, *The Voice of Destruction* (New York: 1940), 328.

29. Hitler, *Mein Kampf*, 424.

30. *The International Jew*, 63.

31. Richards, *The Last Billionaire*, 88.

32. Henry Ford, *My Life and Work*, in collaboration with Samuel Crowther (Garden City, NY: 1922; reprint ed., New York: 1973), 250–52. Also: Ford, *Today and Tomorrow*, 27.

33. *Hitler's Secret Conversations*, 304.

34. *The International Jew*, 157.

35. Richards, *The Last Billionaire*, 90–91.

36. Ibid., 93.

37. *The International Jew*, 157.

38. Ibid., 167.

39. *The International Jew*, 126, 159.

40. Hitler, *Mein Kampf*, 960.

41. *The International Jew*, 128, 206–07.

42. Joseph Nedava, *Trotsky and the Jews* (Philadelphia: 1971), 147.

43. *The International Jew*, 22–31.

44. *Dearborn Independent*, May 29, 1920.

45. Ibid.

46. Hitler, *Mein Kampf*, 251.

47. *Dearborn Independent*, May 29, 1920.

48. Historians who have investigated Ford's anti-Semitism agree that *The International Jew* was written under his specific direction. One of his biographers, William C. Richards, wrote, "He caused to have published a series of articles in which he set up the major postulate that there was a Jewish

plot to rule the world by control of the machinery of commerce and exchange—by a super-capitalism based wholly on the fiction that gold was wealth." (Richards, *The Last Billionaire*, 87). In his book *Warrant for Genocide*, Professor Norman Cohn came to a similar conclusion. "There is no real doubt that Ford knew perfectly well what he was sponsoring. He founded the *Dearborn Independent* in 1919 as a vehicle for his own 'philosophy' and he took a keen and constant interest in it; much of the contents consisted simply of edited versions of his talk." (Cohn, *Warrant for Genocide*, 162.)

49. Lewis, *Public Image*, 144.

50. Georg Seldes, *Facts and Facism* (New York: 1943), 122.

51. Konrad Heiden, *A History of National Socialism* (New York: 1935), p. 109.

52. *The New York Times*, December 20, 1992.

53. Cohn, *Warrant for Genocide*, 161.

54. Norman Hapgood, "The Inside Story of Henry Ford's Jew-Mania," *Hearst's International*, July issue.

55. Lüdecke, *I Knew Hitler*, 217.

56. Ibid.

57. Robert Williams, *Culture in Exile* (London, 1972), 350.

58. Lüdecke, *I Knew Hitler*, 191.

59. Ibid., 192.

60. Geoffrey Skelton, *Wagner at Bayreuth: Experiment and Tradition*, foreword by Wieland Wagner (London: 1965), 140.

61. Author's interview with Frau Wagner, October 1977.

62. Ibid.

63. Ibid.

64. Lüdecke, *I Knew Hitler*, 194.

65. Ibid., 195.

66. Ibid., 200.

67. See Chapter 7, "Hitler's Agents in Highand Low Places."

68. *Detroit News*, July 31, 1938.

69. Lewis, *Public Image*, 150.

70. Ibid.

71. Ibid., 151. Although Ford kept the medal, he was urged by his family and friends to give the public and especially the American Jews a statement explaining his actions. His excuse appeared in *The New York Times* on December 1, 1938: "My acceptance of a medal from the German people does not, as some people seem to think, involve any sympathy on my part with Nazism. Those who have known me for many years realize that anything that breeds hate is repulsive to me."

CHAPTER 4

Thyssen Gives a Big Contribution

1. Lüdecke, *I Knew Hitler*, 182.

2. Lochner, *Tycoons and Tyrants*, 18.

3. Walter H. Kaufmann, *Monarchism in the Weimar Republic*, 160.

4. Albert Krebs, *The Infancy of Nazism: The Memoirs of Ex-Gauleiter Albert Krebs*, 1923–1933, ed. and trans., William Sheridan Allen (New York: 1976), pp. 225–26.

5. Max H. Kele, *Nazi and Workers: National Socialist Appeals to German Labor*, 1919–1933 (Chapel Hill, NC: 1972), 75.

6. Strasser, *Hitler and I* (Boston: 1940), 92.

7. Dietrich Orlow, *The History of the Nazi Party*, 1919–1933 (Pittsburgh: 1969), 68–70.

8. Joseph Goebbels, *The Early Goebbels Diaries*, 1925–1926, ed. Helmut Heiber (London: 1962), 67.

9. For a description of the financial problems of GAU Hanover-South Brunswick in 1928, see: Jeremy Noakes, *The Nazi Party in Lower Saxony*, 1921–1933 (London: Oxford University Press, 1971), 143–44.

10. Other sources say that 9,473 copies were sold during the first year. Sales dropped to 6,913 in 1926 and to 3,015 in 1928. The second volume was published at the end of 1926.

For more about the number of copies of *Mein Kampf* sold, see Bullock, *Hitler*, 133, and Shirer, *Rise and Fall*, 121.

11. O. J. Hale, "Adolf Hitler, Taxpayer," *American Historical Review* (July 1955), 830–42.

12. Ibid., 834.

13. Author's interview with a German steel executive.

14. Thyssen, *I Paid Hitler*, 50–51.

15. Ibid., 52.

16. Ibid.

17. Ibid., 53.

18. For a brief description of the Stinnes-Legien Agreement, see: Lochner, *Tycoons and Tyrants*, 126–27.

19. Thyssen, *I Paid Hitler*, 55.

20. Ibid., 57.

21. For a detailed economic analysis of why it was impossible for Germany to make the payments demanded by the Versailles Treaty, see: John Maynard Keynes, *The Economic Consequences of the Peace* (London: 1919).

22. Theodore Abel, *Why Hitler Came into Power* (New York: 1938) 72.

23. Thyssen, *I Paid Hitler*, 68.

24. See Chapter 2, "Billions."

25. U.S. Group Control Council (Germany, Office of the Director of Intelligence. Field Information Agency, Technical). Intelligence Report no. EF/ME/1, 4 September 1945. "Examination of Dr. Fritz Thyssen," 13.

26. Thyssen, *I Paid Hitler*, 98.

27. Lüdecke, *I Knew Hitler*, 434.

28. Ibid.

29. Thyssen, *I Paid Hitler*, 100.

30. Ibid.

31. R. G. Waldeck, *Meet Mr. Blank* (New York: 1943), 49.

CHAPTER 5

What Did Big Business Want?

1. William Manchester, *The Arms of Krupp*, 1587–1968 (Boston: 1964), 249.

2. Lochner, *Tycoons and Tyrants*, 32.

3. Herbert Hoover, *The Ordeal of Woodrow Wilson* (New York: 1958), 234, 241–42.

4. Abel, *Why Hitler Came into Power*, 30–31.

5. For the best analysis of the Versailles Treaty, see: Keynes, *The Economic Consequences of the Peace.*

6. Ludwell Denny, *America Conquers Britain* (New York: 1930), 351.

7. Ibid., 363.

8. Paul Douglass, *The Economic Dilemma of Politics: A Study of the Consequences of the Strangulation of Germany* (New York: 1932), 26.

9. See: Sir Josiah Stamp, *The Financial Aftermath of War* (London: 1932), 102.

10. International Military Tribunal Document, D-64.

11. The National Association of German Industry, of which Gustav Krupp was one of the leading members, repudiated the Kapp putsch.

12. Carl Duisberg to Dr. E. A. Merck, October 17, 1918, *Autographen-Sammlung von Dr. Carl Duisberg, Werksarchiv*, Farbenfabrik Bayer, Leverkusen.

13. Wheeler-Bennett, *The Nemesis of Power*, 25.

14. In Germany, political parties had traditionally been based on economic interests and social class. See Kaufmann, *Monarchism*, 13–29.

15. General Hans von Seeckt, *Die Reichswehr* (Leipzig: 1933), 16.

16. Friedrich von Rabenau, *Seeckt, aus seinem Legen* (Leipzig: 1940), "vol 2". 347–48.

17. Manchester, *The Arms of Krupp*, 324.

18. Ibid., 354.

19. Ibid., 352.

20. Gustav Krupp, "Objectives of German Policy," *Review of Reviews*, November 1932.

21. Fest, *Hitler*, (New York: 1974), 253–54.

22. Adolf Hitler, *Mein Kampf* (Boston: 1971), 610.

23. Norman H. Baynes, *The Speeches of Adolf Hitler, April 1922–August 1939*, (New York: 1942) vol. 1, 43–44.

24. Manchester, *The Arms of Krupp*, 358.

25. Rudolf Olden, *Hitler* (New York: 1936), 227.

26. Wyndham Lewis, *Hitler* (New York: 1931), 6.

27. Thyssen, *I Paid Hitler*, 90.

28. Ibid., 88.

29. Ibid., 89.

30. *Der Angriff*, September 23 and October 13, 1929.

31. See: Hible, Ortsgruppe Schwabing, December 31, 1929, HA, roll 2A, folder 224.

32. George W. F. Hallgarten, *Hitler, Reichswehr und Industrie* (Frankfurt: 1962), 96.

CHAPTER 6

Depression

1. Bullock, *Hitler*, 136.

2. *Hitler's Official Programme and Its Fundamental Ideas* (London: 1938), 29–37.

3. See: Fritz Dickmann, "Die Regierungsbildung in Thuringen als Modell der Machtergreifung," Vierteljahrschefte fur Zeitgeschichte, XIV (October, 1966), 461–62.

4. Quoted from Rudolf Heberle, *From Democracy to Nazism: A Regional Case Study on Political Parties in Germany* (new York: 1970), 86.

5. Abel, *Why Hitler Came into Power*, 159–60.

6. Sternberg, *Capitalism and Socialism*, 277–13.

7. Thyssen, *I Paid Hitler*, 87.

8. At Thyssen's request, Hitler met several times with Duesterberg for negotiations, HA, roll. 69, folder, 1509.

9. Wheeler-Bennett, *The Nemesis of Power*, 182–84, 198–99.

10. Strasser, *Hitler and I*, 109–17.

11. Orlow, *The History of the Nazi Party, 1919–1933*, 210–11.

12. Henry A. Turner, "The Ruhrlade, Secret Cabinet of Heavy Industry in the Weimar Republic. *Centeral European History* (September 1970)" 209–10.

13. Told to the author by Otto Lang, September, 1976.

14. For more information on Schwarz's able administration of Nazi funds, see Orlow, *The History of the Nazi Party*, 59–60, 137. Also see *Hitler's Secret Conversations*, 376.

15. Orlow, *The History of the Nazi Party*, 186.

16. Gordon W. Prange, ed., *Hitler's Words* (Washington: 1944), 42.

17. *Hitler's Secret Conversations*, 388.

18. Ibid., 145.

19. Ibid., 113–14.

20. Ibid., 267.

21. Ibid., 267–68.

CHAPTER 7
Hitler's Agents in High and Low Places

1. Thyssen, *I Paid Hitler*, 91.

2. Ibid., 92.

3. Heiden, *Der Fuehrer*, 403–04.

4. Hitler's complete statement is not recorded in the transcript of the trial. The quotations given here are taken from several press reports. See Peter Buchter, *Der Reichswehrprozess: Der Hochverrat der Ulmer Reichswehroffiziere* 1929/30, Boppard, 237. Also: *Frankfurter Zeitung*, September 26, 1930.

5. After the trial Hitler's speech was given extensive coverage in the press. A European correspondent for the Hearst newspapers, Karl von Wiegand, asked Hitler to write two or three articles for the Hearst chain. Hitler was given three

or four thousand marks for each article. See Hanfstaengl, *Unheard Witness,* 160.

6. Mosley, *The Reich Marshal,* 110.

7. Ibid., 111.

8. Ibid., 112.

9. Ibid., 113.

10. Wheeler-Bennett, *The Nemesis of Power,* 342.

11. Mosley, *The Reich Marshal,* 114.

12. Curt Riess, *Joseph Goebbels* (New York: 1948), 38.

13. Abel, *Why Hitler Came into Power,* 88.

14. Bella Fromm, *Blood and Banquets: A Berlin Social Diary* (New York, London: 1942), 63–65.

15. Mosley, *The Reich Marshal,* 117.

16. Ibid., 122.

17. Fromm, *Blood and Banquets,* 163.

18. Mosley, *The Reich Marshal,* 124.

19. Unfortunately, the Reichsbank did not show sufficient understanding of the situation. A central bank can cope at any time with a run by its creditors by issuing more notes, thus tiding the banks over the difficulty and enabling them to meet all payments. However, in the case of a run on foreign currency payments, the central bank is entirely dependent on its reserves in foreign exchange. The Reichsbank curiously took the view that all foreign demands must be met as promptly as possible, and then the run would cease. The exact opposite happened. The more other countries realized the dwindling of the Reichsbank's foreign reserves, the more they hastened to get their money back before the reserves were completely exhausted—and the devil take the hindmost!

20. Bullock, *Hitler,* 160–61.

21. *Nazi Conspiracy and Aggression,* supplement A, 1194, (Nuremberg Document), EC-440.

22. Heiden, *Der Fuehrer,* 420.

23. A description of the Harzburg Rally was given to the author by Friedrich Christian Furst zu Schaumburg-Lippe.

24. Otto Dietrich, *With Hitler on the Road to Power* (London: 1934), 12. (Hereafter referred to as *With Hitler.*)
25. Flick Trial, Exhibit no. 679.
26. Emil Helfferich, *Ein Leben*, vol. 4 (Jever: 1964), 15.

CHAPTER 8
Hitler's Foreign Financiers

1. Kurt Lüdecke, *I Knew Hitler*, p. 68.
2. Ibid., 70.
3. Ibid., 135. Although Italy had been an enemy of Germany in World War I, there was no feeling of bitterness between the two countries that would have precluded the Italian Fascist government from giving to a German political party. Italy saw Austria as her primary enemy during the war, and after the war the Italians, especially the Fascists, felt that Italy had been betrayed at Versailles. Hence, Mussolini and other Fascist leaders considered Italy along with Germany to be a have-not power.
4. Lüdecke, *I Knew Hitler*, 138.
5. Ibid., 139.
6. See the section on Hungary in this chapter.
7. Most of the leaders of the Fascist party, with the exception of those close to the Foreign Office, did not have extensive knowledge of the Nazi party. They regarded it simply as a German copy of the Fascist party, a nationalist, anti-Communist movement with a strong paramilitary organization. Interview with Senator Giovanni Lanfre.
8. Adrian Lyttelton, *The Seizure of Power: Fascism in Italy, 1919–1929* (New York: 1973), 428.
9. Ibid.
10. Alan Cassels, *Mussolini's Early Diplomacy* (Princeton, New Jersey: 1970), 161–62, 261.
11. Lyttelton, *Seizure of Power*, 428.
12. Colin Cross, *The Fascists in Britain* (London: 1961),

90–93. Also see: Robert Skidelsky, *Oswald Mosley* (New York: 1975), 463, and Sir Oswald Mosley, *My Life* (London: 1968), 350–51.

13. André François-Poncet, *The Fateful Years: Memoirs of a French Ambassador in Berlin, 1931–1938*, trans. Jacques LeClercq (New York: 1949), 238.

14. According to Braun, the cost of the Nazis' first electoral success was about twenty million marks, of which eighteen million had come from Italy. He stated that "Hitler is receiving enormous sums from Italy. They come to Munich through a Swiss bank." *Saturday Evening Post*, July 31, 1941.

15. Cassels, *Mussolini's Early Diplomacy*, 161; and Gaetano Salvemini, *Prelude to World War II* (New York: 1954), 44.

16. Lüdecke, *I Knew Hitler*, 190.

17. Ibid., 202.

18. Glyn Roberts, *The Most Powerful Man in the World: The Life of Sir Henri Deterding* (New York: 1938), 312.

19. Brian Johnson, *The Politics of Money* (New York: 1970), 59.

20. Andrew Boyle, *Montagu Norman: A Biography* (London: 1967), 174.

21. Ibid., 194.

22. Ibid., 198.

23. Ibid.

24. Ibid.

25. Schacht, *Confessions*, 185.

26. John Hargrave, *Montagu Norman* (New York: 1942), 220.

27. Quoted in A.J.P. Taylor, *Beaverbrook* (London: 1972), 322.

28. Lochner, *Tycoons and Tyrants*, 111.

29. After the September 14, 1930, election, Rothermere's article appeared in the *Daily Mail* and the *Völkischer Beobachter*. For excerpts of the article, see: Konrad Heiden, *Der Fuehrer*, 354–55; Lüdecke, *I Knew Hitler*, 344–45.

30. Franklin R. Gannon, *The British Press and Germany, 1935–1939* (Oxford: 1971), 25.

31. *Sunday Times*, March 26, 1939, 7.

32. *Hitler's Secret Conversations*, 557.

33. Frances Donaldson, *Edward VIII: A Biography of the Duke of Windsor* (Philadelphia and New York: 1974), 207.

34. Sir Henry Channon, *Chips, The Diaries of Sir Henry Channon* (London: 1967), 35.

35. Ibid., 84.

36. Donaldson, *Edward VIII*, 217.

37. Mosley, *The Reich Marshal*, 265–66.

38. *Hitler's Secret Conversations*, 551.

39. Brian Inglis, *Abdication* (New York: 1966), 122.

40. Donaldson, *Edward VIII*, 219.

41. Ralph G. Martin, *The Woman He Loved* (New York: 1973), 390.

42. Donaldson, *Edward VIII*, 215.

43. Roberts, *Henri Deterding*, 319.

44. Ibid., 266. Also see: Willi Muenzenberg, *Brown Book of the Hitler Terror*.

45. *Wall Street Journal*, March 27, 1928.

46. Denny, *America Conquers Britain*, 230.

47. Roberts, *Henri Deterding*, 317.

48. Ibid., 305.

49. Edgar A. Mowrer, *Germany Puts the Clock Back* (New York: 1933), 145.

50. Roberts, *Henri Deterding*, 322.

51. Lochner, *Tycoons and Tyrants*, 111.

52. Hitler, *Mein Kampf* (Boston: 1971), 660.

53. Kaufmann, *Monarchism*, 82.

54. Richard M. Watt, *The Kings Depart: The Tragedy of Germany* (New York: 1969), 492.

55. Ibid., 170.

56. Kaufmann, *Monarchism*, 82.

57. Harold J. Gordon, *Hitler and the Beer Hall Putsch* (Princeton: 1972), 34–35.

58. For more on the activities of the separatists, see: Lüdecke, *I Knew Hitler*, 114–15.
59. Gordon, *Beer Hall Putsch*, 234.
60. Heiden, *Hitler*, 222.
61. Lüdecke, *I Knew Hitler*, 114–15.
62. Heiden, *Hitler*, 223.
63. Lüdecke, *I Knew Hitler*, 401.
64. See Chapter 11, "Nazi Support Declines."

Hitler Runs for President

1. Otto Dietrich, *Hitler* (Chicago: 1955), 171.
2. Ibid.
3. Dietrich, *With Hitler*, 12.
4. Ibid.
5. Ibid., 13
6. Ibid., 36.
7. Dietrich, *Hitler*, 17.
8. Ibid., 111.
9. Heiden, *Der Fuehrer*, 431.
10. Ibid., 433.
11. Dr. Joseph Goebbels, *My Part in Germany's Fight*, trans. Dr. Kurt Feilder (London: 1935), 16–17.
12. Dietrich, *Hitler*, 4.
13. Goebbels, 15.
14. Ibid., 39.
15. For an English translation of the speech, see Norman H. Baynes, ed., *The Speeches of Adolf Hitler, April 1922–August 1939* (New York: 1942), vol. 1, 777–829. The German text of the speech appeared in pamphlet form under the title: Vortrag Adolf Hitlers vor westdeutschen Wirtschaftlern im Industrie-Klub zu Dusseldorf am 27. Januar 1932. (Munich, 1932).
16. Manchester, *The Arms of Krupp*, 360.

17. Thyssen, *I Paid Hitler*, 101.

18. Dietrich, *Hitler*, 230.

19. Goebbels, 46.

20. *Frankfurter Zeitung*, January 19, 1932.

21. August Heinrichsbauer, privately printed manuscript, *Heavy Industry and Politics* (Essen-Kettwig, 1948), 56.

22. Hallgarten, *Hitler, Reichswehr und Industrie* (Frankfurt a. M., 1962), 106.

23. H. R. Knickerbocker, *Germany: Fascist or Soviet?* (London: 1932), 20.

24. Ibid., p. 75.

25. Ibid., 164–65.

26. Goebbels, 58.

27. Dietrich, *With Hitler*, 18–19.

28. Goebbels, 63.

29. Dietrich, *With Hitler*, 21.

30. Lochner, *Tycoons and Tyrants*, 106.

31. Goebbels, *My Part*, 73–74.

32. Ibid., 57, 70.

33. Bullock, *Hitler*, 184.

34. Goebbels, 76.

CHAPTER 10

Big Business Attempts to Stop Hitler

1. Paul Silverberg, *Reden und Schriften*, with an introduction by Franz Mariaux.

2. Otto Meynen, "Dr. Paul Silverberg," *Der Volkswirt*, (1951), 9–11. Also see: Turner, "The Ruhrlade, Secret Cabinet of Heavy Industry in the Weimar Republic." *Central European History*, Sept. 1970, 221–2.

3. Gregor Strasser was certainly a sincere Nazi, and it is even doubtful if he was ever attempting to usurp Hitler's position. See Orlow, *The History of the Nazi Party, 1910–1933*, 269.

4. Orlow, *History of the Nazi Party*, 264.

5. August Heinrichsbauer, *Heavy Industry and Politics*, 39–52.

6. Werner Maser, *Die Fruhgechicte der NSDAP: Hitlers Wegge bis 1924* (Frankfurt a. M., 1965), 396–412. Also, see: Ernst Lange, "Die politische Ideologie der deutschen industriellen Unternehmerschaft," unpublished doctoral dissertation, University of Griefswald, 1933, 36, 80.

7. These small and medium-size businessmen cannot possibly be included in the ranks of "big business" or "monopoly capital" as Marxist historians contend. For the Marxist point of view, see: Eberhard Czichon, *Wer Verhalf Hitler zur Macht? Aum Anteil doer deutschen Industrie an der Zerstorung der Weimarer Republic* (Cologne: 1967).

8. Orlow, *History of the Nazi Party*, 177.

9. Ibid., 81–82.

10. *Völkischer Beobachter*, November 27, 1928; Walter Oehme and Kurt Caro, *Kommt "Das Dritte Reich"* (Berlin, 1930), 92.

11. Krebs, *The Infancy of Nazism*, 225.

12. Quoted in Noakes, *Nazi Party*, 158.

13. Author's interview with Peter Muller, October 1977.

14. Abel, *Why Hitler Came Into Power*, 91.

15. Peter Drucker, *The End of Economic Man* (London: 1939), 105.

16. Dietrich, *With Hitler*, 29.

17. Ibid., 29.

18. Lüdecke, *I Knew Hitler*, 363.

19. Fromm, *Blood and Banquets*, 323.

20. Nuremberg document XII, 419.

21. Quoted in Amos E. Simpson, *Hjalmar Schacht in Perspective* (The Hague: 1969), 68.

22. *Nazi Conspiracy and Aggression*, vol. II, 741.

23. Goebbels, *My Part*, 124.

24. Noakes, *Nazi Party*, 186., fn.

25. *Punder, Reichskanzlei*, entries of September 14, 16, 1930, 59–60.

26. Many of the executives of heavy industry thought Bruening was not a strong enough chancellor and had an unrealistic approach to economic problems.

27. The chemical industry regarded Bruening as the only hope to escape the radicalism of both the Left and Right.

28. Goebbels, 88–89.

29. Ibid., 93.

30. Ibid., 99.

31. Bullock, *Hitler*, 191.

32. Goebbels, *My Part*, 102.

33. *Hitler's Secret Conversations*, 84.

34. Abel, *Why Hitler Came into Power*, 116–17.

35. Goebbels, 121–23.

36. Lüdecke, *I Knew Hitler*, 377.

37. *Hitler's Secret Conversations*, 376.

38. Ibid, 377.

CHAPTER 11

Nazi Support Declines

1. For a personal account of one aristocrat's view of Hitler, see: Friedrich Christian Furst zu Schaumburg-Lippe, *War Hitler Ein Diktator?* (1976).

2. Riess, 43.

3. Klaus Jonas, *The Life of Crown Prince William* (Pittsburg: 1961), 178.

4. Ibid., 182.

5. Ibid., 176.

6. Fromm, *Blood and Banquets*, 56.

7. Thyssen, *I Paid Hitler*, 110.

8. Goebbels, *My Part*, 133.

9. Ibid., 136.

10. Dietrich, *With Hitler*, 40.

11. Goebbels, 142–43.

12. Shirer, *Rise and Fall*, 239.

13. Lüdecke, *I Knew Hitler*, 534.
14. Collin Cross, *Adolf Hitler* (New York: 1973), 190–91.
15. Goebbels, *My Part*, 157.
16. Ibid., 172.
17. Ibid., 182.
18. Ibid., 181.
19. Ibid., 184.
20. Daniel Guerin, *Fascism & Big Business*, (New York: 1939), 24. fn.
21. *Hitler's Secret Conversations*, 182.
22. Shirer, *Rise and Fall*, 243.
23. The executives of the chemical industry generally considered Hindenburg to be unfit for the office of the presidency due to his age and his lack of experience in political and economic matters.
24. Shirer, *Rise and Fall*, 174.
25. Nuremberg Trial, Part XVI, p. 272.

CHAPTER 12

Bribes and Blackmail

1. The speech aroused hostility only among the heavy industrialists and Junkers. See: Speech of Gustav Krupp to the *Hauptausschuss* of the Reichsverband der Deutschen Industrie, December 14, 1932.
2. Lochner, *Tycoons and Tyrant*, 90.
3. Goebbels, 189.
4. Ibid., 206.
5. Ibid., 207.
6. Ibid., 209.
7. The financing of political parties was not seen as incompatible with democracy by the executives of the chemical industry; in fact, the financing of the moderate parties was seen as the only alternative to dictatorship.
8. See statement of Max Ilgner, Microcopy T-301 (Records

of Office of U.S. Chief Counsel for War Crimes, Nuremberg), roll 13/NI-1293.

9. I.G. Farben Case, vol. 1, Nuremberg, NI-8788.

10. Kurt von Schuschnigg, *Farewell Austria* (London: 1938), 165–66.

11. Goebbels, *My Part*, 209, 214.

12. Ibid., 215.

13. Papen claimed that von Schroeder suggested the idea. See: Franz von Papen, *Memoirs* (London: 1952), 226.

14. *Nazi Conspiracy and Aggression*, vol. 2, 512–13, (Nuremberg Document), EC-456.

15. Schroeder was a member of the Keppler Circle. See: Lochner, *Tycoons and Tyrants*, 106.

16. Strasser, *Hitler and I*, 139.

17. In mid-December, a "financial council" was reported to have been held at Papen's request to investigate the possibilities of arresting the decline of the Nazi party. See: Oswald Dutch, *The Errant Diplomat: The Life of Franz von Papen* (London: 1940), 167. This meeting was undoubtedly held in preparation for the agreement with Hitler. Participants included Thyssen, Vogler, Krupp, and other Ruhr industrialists. See *Ibid.*, 167.

18. IMT case no. 10, The U.S.A. Against Alfred Krupp et al. (Nuremberg, 1947), testimony of Kurt von Schroeder, 690.

19. For Funk's testimony, see: Nuremberg Document EC-400. Also see: Bullock, *Hitler*, 173–74. Although there is no concrete evidence that all these firms participated in the Schroeder deal, it is logical to assume that many of them did because they had not contributed to the Nazi party up to this time and Funk's list was only of those who had supported Hitler *before* he was in power.

20. Baron von Schroeder himself was rewarded for his efforts by being made one of the most powerful bankers in the Third Reich. See the listing of Schroeder's business affiliations by 1940 in United States Congress, Senate Hearings before a Subcommittee of the Committee of Military

Affairs. *Elimination of German Resources for War*. Washington Government Printing Office, 1945, 871.

21. Goebbels, *My Part*, 228.

22. Meissner, *Staatssekretar*, 251–62.

23. Trial of Major War Criminals, IMT Nuremberg, November 14, 1945, to October 1, 1946, XXXIII, 531–33.

24. Schacht to Hitler, November 12, 1932, exhibit no. 773, IMT.

25. Heinrich Bruening, "Ein Brief," *Deutsche Rundschau* (July 1947): 13–14.

26. *Der Angriff*, November 17, 1932.

27. IMT case No. 10, The U.S.A. Against Alfred Krupp et al. (Nuremberg, 1947), testimony of Kurt von Schroeder, 690.

28. *Reichskanzlei-Aufzeichnungen aus den Jahren* (1929–1932m ed, Tgilo Vogelsang (Stuttgart, 1961), 149.

29. About 55 percent of the rural population consisted of small peasants owning about five hectares of ground. See: Guerin, *Fascism & Big Business*, 42.

30. For minutes of the Hindenburg-Landbund conference of January 11, 1933, see: Graf Henning von Borcke-Stargordt, *Der ostdeutsche Landbau zwischen Fortschritt, Krise und Politik: Ein eitrag zur Agrar and Zeitgeschichte* (Wurzburg: 1957), 176–80.

31. Meissner Affidavit, November 28, 1945 (3309-PS) Nuremberg.

32. Goebbels, 229.

33. Ibid., 230–31.

34. Hammerstein Memorandum.

35. Wheeler-Bennett, *The Nemesis of Power*, 279–83.

36. *Hitler's Secret Conversations*, 404.

37. Hammerstein Memorandum.

38. Goebbels, *My Part*, 234.

39. Ibid., 235.

40. Papen, *Memoirs*, 243–44.

BIBLIOGRAPHY

The following bibliography comprises only works in English which are available to the public. Documents and German sources are cited in the footnotes.

Abel, Theodore. *Why Hitler Came Into Power*. New York, 1938.

Absagen, K. H. *Canaris*. London, 1956.

Allen, William Sheridan. *The Nazi Seizure of Power: The Experience of a Single German Town, 1930–1935*. Chicago, 1965.

Angebert, Jean-Michel. *The Occult and the Third Reich*, trans. Lewis Sumberg. New York, 1974.

Angress, Werner T. *Stillborn Revolution: The Communist Bid for Power in Germany, 1921–1923*. Princeton, 1963.

Bewley, Charles. *Hermann Göring and the Third Reich*. New York, 1962.

Boyle, Andrew. *Montague Norman: A Biography*. London 1967.

Bracher, Karl. *The German Dictatorship*. New York and Washington, 1970.

Bramsted, Ernest K. *Goebbels and National Socialist Propaganda, 1925–1945*. East Lansing, 1965.

Brasol, Boris. *The World at the Cross Roads*. Boston, 1921.

Bullock, Alan. *Hitler, A Study in Tyranny*, rev. Ed. New York, 1962.

Burdick, Charles B., and Ralph H. Lutz, eds. *The Political Institutions of the German Revolution 1918–1919*. New York and Washington, 1966.

Carlson, John Roy. *Under Cover: My Four Years in the Nazi Underworld of America*. New York, 1943.

Carsten, Francis L. *The Reichswehr and Politics: 1918 to 1933*. Oxford, 1966, and Berkeley, 1973.

Cassels, Alan. *Mussolini's Early Diplomacy*. Princeton, 1970.

Cecil, Robert. *The Myth of the Master Race*. New York, 1972.

Chamberlain, William H. *The Russian Revolution*. 2 vols. New York, 1935.

Channon, Sir Henry. *Chips, The Diaries of Sir Henry Channon*. London, 1967.

Cohn, Norman. *Warrant for Genocide: The myth of the Jewish World-Conspiracy and the Protocols of the Elders of Zion*. New York, 1966.

Craig, Gordon A. *The Politics of the Prussian Army, 1650–1945*. New York, 1968.

Cross, Colin. *Adolf Hitler*. New York, 1973.

———. *The Fascists in Britain*. London, 1961.

Dahrendorf, Ralf. *Society and Democracy in Germany*. New York, 1969.

Davidson, Eugene. *The Trial of the Germans: An Account of the Twenty-two Defendants Before the International Military Tribunal at Nuremberg*. New York, 1966.

Denny, Ludwell. *American Conquers Britain*. New York, 1930.

Diamond, Sander A. *The Nazi Movement in the United States, 1924–1941*. Ithaca, 1974.

Dietrich, Otto. *Hitler*. Chicago, 1955.

———. *With Hitler on the Road to Power*. London, 1934.

Dodd, William. *Ambassador Dodd's Diary, 1933–1938.* London, 1941.

Donaldson, Frances. *Edward VIII: A Biography of the Duke of Windsor.* Philadelphia and New York, 1974.

Dorpalen, Andreas. *Hindenburg and the Weimar Republic.* Princeton, 1964.

Douglass, Paul. *The Economic Dilemma of Politics: A Study of the Consequences of the Strangulation of Germany.* New York, 1932.

Dreisziger, Nandor A. F. *Hungary's Way to World War II.* Toronto, 1968.

Drucker, Peter. *The End of Economic Man.* London, 1939.

Dutch, Oswald. *The Errant Diplomat: The Life of Franz von Papen.* London, 1940.

Eschenburg, Theodore, et al. *The Path to Dictatorship, 1918–1933,* trans. John S. Conway. New York, 1963.

Eyck, Erich. *A History of the Weimar Republic.* 2 vols. New York, 1970.

Feder, Gottfried. *Hitler's Official Program.* New York, 1971.

Fest, Joachim C. *The Face of the Third Reich: Portraits of the Nazi Leadership.* New York, 1970.

Fischer, Fritz. *Germany's Arms in the First World War.* New York, 1967.

Ford, Henry. *The International Jew: The World's Foremost Problem,* ed. Gerald L. K. Smith. (Abridged from the original publication in the *Dearborn Independent.*) Los Angeles, 1964.

——. *Today and Tomorrow.* Garden City, 1926.

——, with Samuel Crowther. *My Life and Work.* Garden City, 1922. (Reprint edition, New York, 1973.)

Francois-Poncet, Andre. *The Fateful Years: Memoirs of a French Ambassador in Berlin, 1931–1938,* trans. Jacques LeClercq. New York, 1949.

Fromm, Bella. *Blood and Banquets: A Berlin Social Diary.* New York and London, 1942.

Gannon, Franklin R. *The British Press and Germany, 1936–1939*. Oxford, 1971.

Goebbels, Dr. Joseph. *The Early Goebbels Diaries*. London, 1962.

————. *My Part in Germany's Fight.*, trans. Kurt Fiedler. London, 1935.

Godspeed, D. J. *Ludendorff*. London, 1966.

Gordon, Harold J. *Hitler and the Beerhall Putsch*. Princeton, 1972.

Granzow, Brigitte. *A Mirror of Nazism: British Opinion and the Emergence of Hitler, 1929–1933*. London, 1964.

Grunberger, Richard. *Germany 1918–1945*. London, 1964, and New York, 1967.

Grunfeld, Frederic B. *The Hitler File: A Social History of Germany and the Nazis, 1918–45*. New York, 1974.

Guerin, Daniel. *Fascism & Big Business*, trans. Frances and Mason Merrill. Introduction by Dwight Macdonald. New York, 1939.

Gun, Nerin. *Eva Braun*. New York, 1969.

Gutman, Robert W. *Richard Wagner: The Man, His Mind, and His Music*. New York, 1968.

Hale, Oron J. *The Captive Press in the Third Reich*. Princeton, 1964.

Halperin, S. William. *Germany Tried Democracy: A Political History of the Reich from 1918 to 1933*. New York, 1946.

Hanfstaengl, Ernst. *Unheard Witness*. Philadelphia, 1957.

Hanser, Richard. *Putsch!* New York, 1970.

Hargrave, John. *Montagu Norman*. New York, 1942.

Heberle, Rudolf. *From Democracy to Nazism: A Regional Case Study on Political Parties in Germany*. Baton Rouge, 1945. (Revised edition, New York, 1970).

Hedin, Sven. *Germany and World Peace*. London, 1937.

Heiber, Helmut. *Goebbels*, trans. John K. Dickinson. New York, 1972.

Heiden, Konrad. *Der Fuehrer*. Boston, 1944.

————. *A History of National Socialism*. New York, 1935.

————. *Hitler, A Biography.* New York, 1936.

Heinz, Heinz A. *Germany's Hitler.* London, 1934.

Hitler, Adolf. *Hitler's Secret Book.* Introduction by Telford Taylor. New York, 1961.

————. *Hitler's Secret Conversations, 1941–1944.* Introduction by H. R. Trevor-Roper. New York, 1953.

————. *Mein Kampf.* New York, 1940.

————. *Mein Kampf.* Boston, 1943.

————. *The Speeches of Adolf Hitler, 1922–1939,* ed. Norman H. Baynes. 2 vols. New York, 1942.

Hoffmann, Heinrich. *Hitler Was My Friend.* London, 1955.

Hohne, Heinz. *The Order of the Death's Head.* New York, 1970.

Hoover, Calvin B. *Germany Enters the Third Reich.* New York, 1933.

Inglis, Brian. *Abdication* New York, 1966.

Jenks, William A. *Vienna and the Young Hitler.* New York, 1960.

Johnson, Brian. *The Politics of Money.* New York, 1970.

Jonas, Klaus. *The Life of Crown Prince William.* Pittsburg, 1961.

Kaufmann, Walter H. *Monarchism in the Weimar Republic.* New York, 1973.

Kele, Max H. *Nazis and Workers: National Socialist Appeals to German Labor, 1919–1933.* Chapel Hill, 1972.

Keynes, John Maynard. *The Economic Consequences of the Peace.* London, 1919.

Kirkpatrick, Clifford. *Nazi Germany, Its Women and Family Life.* Indianapolis and New York, 1938.

Kirkpatrick, Sir Ivone. *Mussolini, A Study in Power.* New York, 1964.

Klemperer, Klemens Von. *Germany's New Conservatism: Its History and Dilemma in the Twentieth Century.* Princeton, 1957.

Knickerbocker, H. R. *Germany: Fascist or Soviet?* London, 1932.

Krebs, Albert. *The Infancy of Nazism: The Memoirs of Ex-Gauleiter*

Albert Krebs, 1923–1933, ed. and trans. William Sheridan Allen. New York, 1976.

Kulski, Wladyslaw (Knight-Patterson, William). *Germany from Defeat to Conquest.* London, 1945.

Lebovics, Herman. *Social Conservatism and the Middle Classes in Germany, 1914–1933.* Princeton, 1969.

Leonard, Jonathan N. *The Tragedy of Henry Ford.* New York, 1932.

Lewis, David L. *The Public Image of Henry Ford: An American Folk Hero and His Company.* Detroit, 1976.

Lewis, Wyndham. *Hitler,* New York, 1931.

Lochner, Louis P. *Tycoons and Tyrants: German Industry from Hitler to Adenauer.* Chicago, 1954.

Louis, Ferdinand, Prince. *The Rebel Prince.* Chicago, 1952.

Lüdecke, Kurt. *I Knew Hitler.* New York, 1938.

Lyttelton, Adrian. *The Seizure of Power: Fascism in Italy, 1919–1929.* New York, 1973.

Macartney, C. A. *October Fifteenth: A History of Modern Hungary, 1929–1945.* Edinburgh, 1957.

Magee, Bryan. *Aspects of Wagner.* New York, 1968.

Manchester, William. *The Arms of Krupp, 1587–1968.* Boston, 1964.

Manvell, Roger, and Heinrich Fraenkel. *Dr. Goebbels: His Life and Death.* New York. 1960.

———. *Hess: A Biography.* London, 1971.

Marie, Queen of Roumania. *The Story of My Life.* New York, 1934.

Martin, James S. *All Honorable Men.* Boston, 1950.

Martin, Ralph G. *The Woman He Loved.* New York, 1973.

Marx, Karl. *A World Without Jews.* New York, 1959.

Maser, Werner. *Hitler: Legend, Myth & Reality,* trans. Peter and Betty Ross. New York, 1973.

———, ed. *Hitler's Letters and Notes.* New York, 1974.

Merkl, Peter H. *Political Violence Under the Swastika: 581 Early Nazis.* Princeton, 1975.

Mitchell, Allen. *Revolution in Bavaria.* Princeton, 1975.

Montgomery, John F. *Hungary: The Unwilling Satellite.* New York, 1947.

Mosley, Leonard. *The Reich Marshal: A Biography of Hermann Goering.* New York, 1974.

Mosley, Sir Oswald. *My Life.* London, 1968.

Mosse, George L. *The Crisis of German Ideology: Intellectual Origins of the Third Reich.* New York, 1964.

Mowrer, Edgar A. *Germany Puts the Clock Back.* New York, 1933.

Nagy-Talavera, Nicholas M. *The Green Shirts and the Others: A History of Fascism in Hungary and Rumania.* Stanford., 1970.

Nedava, Joseph. *Trotsky and the Jews.* Philadelphia, 1971.

Neumann, Franz. *Behemoth: The Structure and Practice of National Socialism.* New York, 1941.

Nevins, Allan, and Frank Ernest Hill. *Ford: The Times, The Man, The Company.* 3 vols. New York, 1954. (See Vol. 2: *Expansion and Challenge, 1915–1933.*)

Nicholls, Anthony J. *Weimar and the Rise of Hitler.* New York, 1968.

Noakes, Jeremy. *The Nazi Party in Lower Saxony, 1921–1933.* Oxford, 1971.

Nolte, Ernst. *Three Faces of Faxcism.* New York, 1966.

Nyomarkay, Joseph. *Charisma and Factionalism in the Nazi Party.* Minneapolis, 1967.

Olden, Rudolf. *Hitler.* New York, 1936.

Orlow, Dietrich. *The History of the Nazi Party, 1919–1933.* Pittsburgh, 1969.

Papen, Franz von. *Memoirs.* London, 1952.

Pauwels, Louis, and Jacques Bergier. *The Morning of the Magicians.* New York, 1991.

Payne, Robert. *The Life and Death of Adolf Hitler.* New York, 1973.

Prang, Gordon Ward. *Hitler's Words*. Washington, 1944.

Price, G. Ward. *I Know These Dictators*. London, 1937.

Pridham, Geoffrey. *Hitler's Rise to Power*. New York, 1973.

Pulzer, P. *The Rise of Political Anti-Semitism in Germany and Austria*. New York, 1964.

Rauschning, Hermann. *The Conservative Revolution*. New York, 1940.

———. *The Revolution of Nihilism*. New York, 1937.

———. *The Voice of Destruction*. New York, 1940.

Ribbontrop, Joachim von. *Ribbontrop Memoirs*. London, 1962.

Richards, William C. *The Last Billionaire*. New York, 1948.

Ringer, Fritz K., ed. *The German Inflation of 1923*. New York, 1969.

Rivkin, Ellis. *The Shaping of Jewish History*. New York, 1971.

Roberts, Glyn. *The Most Powerful Man in the World: The Life of Sir Henri Deterding*. New York, 1938.

Rosenberg, Alfred. *Memoirs*, eds. S. Lang and E. von Schenck. New York, 1949.

Ryder. A. J. *The German Revolution of 1918*. Cambridge, 1967.

Salvemini, Gaetano. *Prelude to World War II*. New York, 1954.

Sayers, Michael and Albert E. Kahn. *The Great Conspiracy: The Secret War Against Soviet Russia*. Boston, 1946.

Schacht, Hjalmar. *Account Settled*. London, 1948.

———. *Confessions of the "Old Wizzard."* Cambridge, 1956.

Schoenbaum, David. *Hitler's Social Revolution*. London, 1969.

Schuschnigg, Kurt von. *Farewell Austria*. London, 1938.

Schweitzer, Arthur. *Big Business in the Third Reich*. Bloomington, 1964.

Seldes, George. *Facts and Fascism*. New York, 1943.

Shirer, William L. *The Rise and Fall of the Third Reich*. New York, 1960.

Simpson, Amos E. *Hjalmar Schacht in Perspective*. The Hague, 1969.

Sinclair, Upton. *The Flivver King: The Story of Ford America.* Pasadena, 1937.

Skelton, Geoffrey. *Wagner at Bayreuth: Experiments and Tradition.* Foreword by Wieland Wagner. London, 1965.

Skidelsky, Robert. *Oswald Mosley.* New York, 1975.

Sombart, Werner. *The Jews and Modern Capitalism.* new York, 1913.

Stamp, Sir Josiah. *The Financial Aftermath of War.* London, 1932.

Stebbins, Raymond L. "Henry Ford and Edwin Pipp: A Suppressed Chapter in the Story of the Auto Magnate." Ed. G. L. Holt. Typewritten manuscript, Hebrew Union College Library, Cincinnati, n.d.

Steel, Johannes. *Escape to the Present.* New York, 1937.

Stern, Fritz. *The Politics of Cultural Despair: A Study in the Rise of the Germanic Ideology.* Berkeley, 1961.

Stern, J. P. *Hitler: The Fuhrer and the People.* Berkeley, 1975.

Sternberg, Fritz. *Capitalism and Socialism on Trial.* New York, 1968.

Strasser, Otto. *Flight from Terror.* New York, 1943.

————. *Hitler and I.* Boston, 1940.

Struve, Walker. *Elites Against Democracy: Leadership Ideals in Bourgeois Political Thought in Germany, 1890–1933.* Princeton, 1973.

Sutton, Antony C. *Wall Street and the Rise of Hitler.* Seal Beach, 1976.

Sward, Keith. *The Legend of Henry Ford.* New York, 1948.

Taylor, A.J.P. *Beaverbrook.* London, 1972.

Thyssen, Fritz. *I Paid Hitler.* New York, 1941.

Toland, John. *Adolf Hitler.* New York, 1976.

Turner, Henry A., ed. *Stresemann and the Politics of the Weimar Republic.* Princeton, 1965.

Wagner, Friedelind, and Page Cooper. *Heritage of Fire: The Story of Richard Wagner's Granddaughter.* New York, 1945.

Waite, Robert G. I. *Vanguard of Nazism.* New York, 1952.

Watt, Richard M. *The Kings Depart: The Tragedy of Germany.* New York, 1969.

Weber, Max. *The Theory of Social and Economic Organization* New York, 1947.

Wheeler-Bennett, John W. *The Nemesis of Power: The German Army in Politics. 1918–1945.* New York, 1954.

Wilkins, Mira, and Frank E. Hill. *American Business Abroad: Ford on Six Continents.* Detroit, 1964.

Williams, Robert C. *Culture in Exile: Russian Emigres in Germany, 1881–1941.* Ithaca and London, 1972.

Winterbotham, Frederick W. *Secret and Personal.* London, 1969.

Zeman, Zbynek. *Nazi Propaganda.* London, 1964.

INDEX